CU00555718

ENGLAND, SPAIN
AND THE
GRAN ARMADA

1585–1604

ENGLAND, SPAIN AND THE *GRAN ARMADA*

1585–1604

Essays from the Anglo-Spanish Conferences
London and Madrid 1988

Edited by

M. J. RODRIGUEZ-SALGADO

Department of International History
London School of Economics

and

SIMON ADAMS

Department of History
University of Strathclyde

JOHN DONALD PUBLISHERS LTD
EDINBURGH

ISBN 0 85976 300 5

British Library Cataloguing in Publication Data

England, Spain and the Gran Armada, 1585–1604 : essays from
  the Anglo-Spanish conferences, London and Madrid 1988.
  1. Spain. Armada
  I. Rodriguez-Salgado, M. J.   II. Adams, Simon
  942.055

Typeset by Pioneer Associates, Perthshire
Printed and bound in Great Britain by
Billing and Sons Ltd., Worcester

PREFACE

The *Gran Armada* of 1588 marked in a most spectacular fashion the beginning of open war between Philip II and Elizabeth I. The campaign, which was expected to change the balance of political and religious forces within Europe, achieved little. But it rapidly became enshrouded in myths, many of which still survive after four centuries. The fourth centenary of the event yielded, as expected, a veritable flood of publications, most of which were more popular than scholarly. There were, however, exceptions. The international exhibition at the National Maritime Museum, Greenwich took a strictly non-partisan view. Equally balanced — even revisionist — was the treatment of the subject by Colin Martin and Geoffrey Parker. The Armada was also the topic chosen for the fourth Anglo-Spanish conference held in May 1988 at the Institute of Historical Research under the auspices of the British National Committee of the International Commission of Historical Sciences. Among the participants were the editors of this volume and members of the Instituto de Historia y Cultura Naval, led by their Director, the enthusiastic and energetic Admiral Fernando Bordejé y Morencos. In 1980 the Instituto had established a commission of historians to investigate all aspects of this troubled war. Their visit to London coincided with the publication of the first volumes of their extensive research. To date (1990), seven technical monographs and the first volume of a vast documentary series covering the whole of the Anglo-Spanish war from 1585 to 1604 have appeared.[1] The exchange of papers, information and views in London proved so productive that it was decided to hold a second conference. Funds from the Ministerio de Defensa made possible a seminar in Madrid in November 1988.

This collection combines papers given at those conferences with related essays by either the participants or other members of the *Gran Armada* commission.[2] It is not our intention to provide a comprehensive account or another narrative of the Armada campaign. Our aim has been to bring the important work undertaken in Spain to the attention of a wider audience and to address some of the major issues arising from recent research on the Armada. The essays are thus a composite of naval, military, diplomatic and economic history.

The central questions addressed by the collection are Philip II's motives in launching the enterprise of England and the nature of the Spanish naval and military effort. In dealing with the apparently minor issue of Philip's claim to the English throne, Rodríguez-Salgado shows how complex his motivation was. Adams suggests that the circumstances under which hostilities broke out in 1585 owed as much to accident as design and Croft demonstrates that whatever the economic pressures leading to war, there were equally strong, if not greater, commercial forces against. Thompson and Gómez-Centurión analyse the way in which the war with England produced a major shift in the orientation of the Spanish monarchy that led to powerful internal tensions. Casado Soto, Gracia Rivas and O'Donnell produce exciting new evidence on Spanish naval and military preparations and organisation, while Rodríguez-Salgado and Adams reveal the manner in which basic problems of navigation determined the way the naval campaign was fought.

In completing the volume in 1990 we are fully conscious of the way in which we have benefited from earlier research on the Armada, particularly that published in 1988 and 1989. If we have made criticisms of points of detail, our debt to those historians whose work we have employed is in no way diminished. We do not claim that these essays are necessarily definitive, but we are confident that anyone seeking an understanding of the *Gran Armada* and its place in the history of the sixteenth century will find them of value.

September, 1990   M. J. R-S
                                                         S. A.

NOTES

1. Details of the monograph and documentary series will be found in the notes.
2. Earlier versions of Essays 2 and 4 have appeared in Spanish in *La Gran Armada. Cuadernos Monográficos del Instituto de Historia y Cultura Naval,* III (1989) and Essays 5 and 6 in the *Revista de Historia Naval,* XXIII (1988).

ACKNOWLEDGEMENTS

We should like to thank the organisers of the Anglo-Spanish Armada Conference at the Institute of Historical Research, particularly Professor F. M. L. Thompson and Professor T. J. Barker. The generosity of the Ministerio de Defensa, the Museo de Historia y Cultura Naval and the Instituto de Historia y Cultura Naval made possible the second conference in Madrid.

Simon Adams would like to thank the British Academy and the Carnegie Trust for the Universities of Scotland and M. J. Rodríguez-Salgado the London School of Economics for grants in support of their research. The illustrations have been reproduced by kind permission of the Archivo General de Simancas, the National Maritime Museum (Greenwich), the Nederlands Historisch Scheepvart Museum, and the Instituto de Historia y Cultura Naval.

This volume is published with the help of a grant from the late Miss Isobel Thornley's Bequest to the University of London.

CONTRIBUTORS

Simon Adams
Senior Lecturer in History, University of Strathclyde

José Luis Casado Soto
Director of the Museo Marítimo del Cantábrico (Santander)

Pauline Croft
Senior Lecturer in History, Royal Holloway and Bedford New College

Manuel Gracia Rivas
Director of the Laboratory of Clinical Analysis in the Policlínica Naval (Madrid)

Carlos Gómez-Centurión Jiménez
Lecturer in Modern History, Universidad Complutense, Madrid

Hugo O'Donnell y Duque de Estrada
Secretary-General of the Comisión Española de Historia Marítima

M. J. Rodríguez-Salgado
Lecturer in International History, London School of Economics

I. A. A. Thompson
Senior Lecturer in History, University of Keele

CONTENTS

ABBREVIATIONS AND CONVENTIONS

ACC
  Las Actas de las Cortes de Castilla (60 vols., Madrid, 1877–1974)

AGI
  Archivo General de Indias
  IG   Indiferente General
  RP   Real Patronato

AGS
  Archivo General de Simancas
  CJH   Consejo y Juntas de Hacienda
  CMC 2e   Contaduría mayor de Cuentas 2ª época
  CMC 3e   Contaduría mayor de Cuentas 3ª época
  CS 1e   Contaduría del Sueldo 1ª época
  CS 2e   Contaduría del Sueldo 2ª época
  E   Estado
  GA   Guerra Antigua
  MPyD   Mapas, Planos y Dibujos

ARA
  Algemeen Rijksarchief, The Hague

BL
  British Library, London

BMO I
  J. Calvar Gross, J. I. González-Aller Hierro, M de Dueñas Fontán, Mª del Campo Mérida Valverde (edd.), *La Batalla del Mar Océano*, Vol. I (*Génesis de la empresa de Inglaterra de 1588 (28 Junio 1568 – 30 Enero 1586)*) (Madrid, 1988)

BNM
  Biblioteca Nacional, Madrid

CSPFor
  J. Stevenson *et al.* (edd.), *Calendar of State Papers, Foreign Series, Elizabeth I* (23 vols., London, 1863–1950)

CSPSp

M. A. S. Hume (ed.), *Calendar of Letters and State Papers . . . in the Archives of Simancas* (4 vols., London, 1892–99)

CSPVen

R. Brown *et al.* (edd.), *Calendar of State Papers . . . in the Archives . . . of Venice* (38 vols., London, 1864–1940)

Casado Soto, *Barcos*

J. L. Casado Soto. *Los barcos españoles del siglo xvi y la Gran Armada de 1588* (Instituto de Historia y Cultura Naval, Serie Gran Armada, IV: Madrid, 1988)

Chaunu

H. and P. Chaunu, *Séville et l'Atlantique (1504–1650)* (8 vols., Paris, 1955–9)

Codoin

Colección de documentos inéditos para la historia de España (113 vols., Madrid, 1842–95)

Corbett, *Spanish War*

J. S. Corbett (ed.), *Papers relating to the Navy during the Spanish War, 1585–1587* (Navy Records Soc., XI: 1898)

Corbett, *Drake*

J. S. Corbett, *Drake and the Tudor Navy* (2 vols., London, 1912)

FD

C. Fernández Duro, *La Armada Invencible* (2 vols., Madrid, 1884–5)

Fernández Duro, *Disquisiciones*

C. Fernández Duro, *Disquisiciones Náuticas* (6 vols., Madrid, 1880)

Gómez-Centurión, *Comercio*

C. Gómez-Centurión Jiménez, *Felipe II, la empresa de Inglaterra y el comercio septentrional (1566–1609)* (Instituto de Historia y Cultura Naval, Serie Gran Armada, I: Madrid, 1988)

Hakluyt

R. Hakluyt, *The Principal Navigations* (12 vols., Glasgow, 1903–5)

Herrera Oria, *Armada*

E. Herrera Oria (ed.), *La Armada Invencible. Documentos procedentes del Archivo de Simancas (1587–9)* (Archivo Histórico Español, II: Valladolid, 1929/Madrid, 1930)

HMC
Historical Manuscripts Commission

Laughton
J. K. Laughton (ed.), *State Papers relating to the defeat of the Spanish Armada Anno 1588* (Navy Records Society, I–II: 1894–5, repr. 1987)

MM
The Mariner's Mirror

MNM
Museo Naval, Madrid
CN Collección Navarrete

Martin and Parker
C. J. M. Martin and G. Parker, *The Spanish Armada* (London, 1988)

Maura
G. Maura y Gamazo, duque de Maura, *EL designio de Felipe II y el episodio de la Armada Invencible* (Madrid, 1957)

Monson, *Tracts*
M. Oppenheim (ed.), *The Naval Tracts of Sir William Monson* (Navy Records Soc., XXII–III, XLIII, XLV, XLVII: 1902–14)

PRO
Public Record Office, London
E   Exchequer
HCA High Court of Admiralty
SP   State Papers

Rodríguez-Salgado, *Catalogue*
M. J. Rodríguez-Salgado *et al.*, *Armada. The Official Catalogue of the National Maritime Museum's Exhibition* (London, 1988)

Thompson, *War*
I. A. A. Thompson, *War and Government in Habsburg Spain* (London, 1976)

Unless otherwise noted the dates employed are those of the Gregorian (N.S.) calendar. Where events in England or English documents have required the Julian (O.S.) calendar, the conventional double date (e.g. 10/20 July) is used.

1

THE ANGLO-SPANISH WAR:
THE FINAL EPISODE IN 'THE WARS OF THE ROSES'?

M. J. Rodríguez-Salgado

On 23 March 1587 the count of Olivares, Philip II's ambassador to Rome, reported his discussions on the proposed invasion of England with two prominent English exiles, William Allen and Robert Persons. Persons had advocated military action in the past so his support had been expected. There had been some doubt about Allen, but Olivares assured Philip that he had now accepted that this was the only way to restore catholicism in England; 'what reassures me above all' the ambassador added, 'is his generosity and fervour in religious matters . . . and the fact that his family have always supported the house of Lancaster'.[1] Modern readers would expect to find a religious justification for the activities of the exiles, but the allusion to the protracted and confused civil wars in England quaintly known as the 'Wars of the Roses' may seem anachronistic and surprising. The concern of recent historiography with ideological conflict has led to a neglect of dynasticism in the second half of the sixteenth century: its powerful influence has been underestimated. The accession of Elizabeth I, an unmarried woman with dubious rights to the throne, had inevitably reawakened interest in the tortuous and confusing history of English royal dynasties throughout Europe.[2] Each plot to depose her prompted further talk on the succession and the *Gran Armada* campaign was no exception. Historians have largely ignored this important dimension of the struggle which, I will argue, illuminates certain aspects of Philip II's strategy, his periodic hesitation over the campaign, and the reluctance of catholic powers to participate actively in a war widely presented as a conflict between protestants and catholics. Moreover, by analysing the role of dynasticism in the *Gran Armada* campaign the historian is confronted with fundamental questions about Philip II's foreign policy during the last two decades of the sixteenth century.

1

1. Background

Philip II did not want a war with England. He was well aware of the value of England's alliance and neutrality. His primary strategic concerns within Europe were the defence of his lands, and to maintain communications between the two principal states in his sprawling empire, Spain and the Netherlands. Although Philip had agreed to peace with France in 1559 and seen this most powerful state in Europe intermittently abandon itself to civil strife in the following decades, he continued to fear France and with reason. Indeed he would regard France and the Islamic powers in the Mediterranean as his chief enemies throughout the reign, and the Netherlands as his most exposed European possession, threatened by both German and French ambitions. Only England could guarantee the safety of the Channel route, which was the best, at times the only, artery between Spain and the Netherlands. England could offer a safe haven for shipping and an excellent base from which to threaten France. Moreover, close commercial links bound the island both to Spain and the Netherlands.[3] To court her alliance or maintain her benevolent neutrality Philip was willing to ignore countless incidents that proved Elizabeth's growing hostility towards him. His tolerant attitude would have earned him less condemnation but for the intensification of ideological passions in Europe during the second half of the sixteenth century. While censorious voices had been heard over alliances between catholic and protestant leaders before 1559, after the peace of Cateau-Cambrésis led to a cessation of hostilities between the inveterate enemies France and the Habsburg lands, there were great expectations that the christian powers would realign into opposing ideological camps. As the councils of the Church had failed to bring peace to a divided Christendom, the only option left was war. The seemingly simple dictate to annihilate God's enemies had great power, but in a world in which the combatants were convinced that catholic and protestant were roughly equal in force, initiating a struggle to the death inevitably aroused images of Armageddon. During the second half of the sixteenth century the formation of hostile international religious leagues was as expected as it was feared. While there was much talk of 'religious' wars, and exploitation of religious minorities to justify foreign intervention, there was also much fear of a final struggle that could only end in the destruction of most of Christendom. Moreover, traditional alliances as well as commercial and political links cut across the religious divisions.

European states lurched uneasily from conflict to compromise with the opposing creed.

When Elizabeth Tudor made it clear in 1559 that she intended to follow an independent foreign policy and establish a protestant church in England, Philip II's advisers felt threatened on both counts. Convinced that they could contain France only with England's support, and opposed to dismantling the catholic church they had helped to restore in England, some of them suggested an immediate invasion and her deposition.[4] The plan was strongly supported by Pope Paul IV who was desperate to retain the first protestant state to have returned to the catholic fold. He offered to excommunicate Elizabeth and to invest Philip with the title. There was strong competition, namely from France. Mary Stuart, queen of Scotland and France, was the legitimate granddaughter of Henry VII. Although passed over in Henry VIII's will, to some her claim to the English throne was stronger than that of Elizabeth, whose illegitimacy and heresy should have prevented her succession. Her relations, led by the duke of Guise, kept up relentless pressure for the catholic world to accept her claim. While there were other internal candidates, the dynastic dispute was projected at an international level in stark terms as a battle between Mary and Elizabeth. Philip II's respect for dynastic right was never in doubt and he acknowledged that Mary Stuart had the best claim. As she had been raised in the French court and married a Frenchman, he was also never in doubt that she would bring England within the French camp. Her succession, however desirable for catholicism, represented a grave danger to Philip's empire.

Indeed Philip and his advisers believed it threatened Christendom because if either he or the French king attempted to conquer England, the other would challenge the conquest and so unleash a major war. If either succeeded in controlling England, it might tip the balance of power in his favour and enable him to establish hegemony over Europe.[5] Even advocates of an invasion in 1588 acknowledged that fear of a Franco-Spanish war was a major deterrent: 'the usual objection people raise . . . is that if the Catholic King makes a move against England it would reawaken the ancient emulation between the king and the royal house of France'.[6] The Habsburg-Valois wars had devastated Christendom for over half a century, and the spectre of this conflict still haunted the European powers. Yet this was not the only reason Philip preferred to leave Elizabeth alone. An attack on the island required a delicate balance of internal as well as international conditions. Above all it was essential to secure the cooperation of Castile (for funds) and the

Netherlands (from which an invasion would have to be launched). After the outbreak of the revolt in 1566, and as late as 1584, Philip's officials argued that it would be impossible to divert forces from the Netherlands to England without grave risks to his position there. Nevertheless Philip never lost a sense of commitment to the English catholics; this and his claim to be the secular head of Christendom inevitably brought pressure to bear on him to act against Elizabeth. On occasion, as in 1571, he seemed poised to abandon his policy of prevarication and friendship and support a plot.[7] Each time he drew back from a direct confrontation. While the hostile acts of the English, particularly in the New World and the Netherlands could not fail to affect relations, they were not very serious threats, certainly not of the magnitude of the Ottomans and North African powers in the Mediterranean, nor of France. Philip devoted the bulk of his resources and attention before 1585 to these and to internal conflicts. Given his commitments and the fear of creating a powerful French block across both sides of the Channel, Philip's policy was to maintain Elizabeth in power rather than to encourage further unrest or to depose her.

2. Precipitants of the War

The acquisition of Portugal (1580–3) so increased Philip's power that it revived the spectre of Habsburg hegemony. It was also the most striking instance of Philip's pursuit of dynastic rights, patiently prepared over a number of years. He negotiated with Portuguese nobles and disseminated genealogies and propaganda to prove his claim, but it did not prevent a war as he had hoped. While the dukes of Braganza and Ranuccio Farnese, eldest son of Alexander Farnese, duke of Parma, set aside their claims in deference to Philip, Dom António, illegitimate son of the infante Dom Luis, sought foreign aid and was supported by some Portuguese.[8] Philip threatened war against his supporters, but France and England intervened in an attempt to weaken him. On his return from the successful expedition to clear the Azores of Dom António and his Franco-English forces in 1583, the marquis of Santa Cruz urged an attack on England to avenge Elizabeth's persecution of English catholics, and her hostile acts against Philip in the New World, the Portuguese empire and the Netherlands. Santa Cruz assured the king that the French had lost a great deal of reputation — thus implying that they were not in a position to go to war with Philip over England, particularly as they were angry with Elizabeth who had not fulfilled her promises of substantial aid for the Azores expedition. The time thus appeared propitious, and Santa Cruz dismissed the usual talk of financial difficulties by asserting that God would give Philip the means to execute such a godly task.[9] But the king was anxious to consolidate his new lands and did not want war. Nevertheless expectations of a conflict were fanned by proposals put forward by the duke of Guise and the pope.

In 1583 the duke of Guise appealed for catholic support in a plot to overthrow Elizabeth. To pave the way for her deposition, Guise asked the pope to renew Pius V's excommunication of Elizabeth, to declare the campaign a crusade, and to appoint William Allen bishop of Durham and papal nuncio — preparatory moves which Philip was to follow later.[10] The king was sceptical of the plan from the start but he could not afford to offend the Guise, his principal allies in France, nor did he want to undermine his credentials as the leading catholic monarch. He offered a small sum — 50,000 ducats — towards the campaign, and after further pressure 4,000 men, but he refused to send a fleet.[11] It was for this invasion plan and not, as is often assumed, because he had conceived his own or been influenced by Santa Cruz, that Philip requested Parma's opinion and ordered a thorough enquiry of the ports and coasts of England. His cautious response was interpreted negatively in Rome and Paris and laid him open to charges of obstruction.[12] His ambassador in England, Bernardino de Mendoza, was more enthusiastic and his participation in the Throckmorton conspiracy — which was at the heart of the Guise proposal — provoked the final breach in Anglo-Spanish diplomatic relations. Ejected from England, Mendoza went on to encourage plots against Elizabeth from his new post as ambassador in France.[13] It may not have escaped the notice of Philip's allies that despite his bland assurances, he was reducing his military establishment during these years — a clear sign of his lack of desire for war.[14]

The situation changed in 1585 when Elizabeth agreed to a number of initiatives which, viewed together, were easily interpreted as a coherent and aggressive campaign against the Spanish Monarchy. In response to the perceived threat from the catholic powers — especially the recent alliance between Philip and the Catholic League in France (31 December 1584) and Guise's involvement in Scottish and English plots[15] — and under the impression that war was inevitable, Elizabeth and her advisers decided on a preemptive strike. She sent ships against the Newfoundland fisheries, gave her blessing to colonising ventures in Virginia that would challenge Philip's sovereignty and the safety of his New World possessions, and licenced a major expedition by Drake. Contacts were made with the Ottoman sultan and the North African states, who were encouraged to attack Philip's Mediterranean possessions. France was the key to European politics and therefore to her strategy. In order to neutralise the catholics there, she encouraged a new Huguenot offensive which was to be supported by an invasion from her allies in the Palatinate. Later, fear of alienating Henry III made the queen hesitate, then go back on her promises of substantial support, thus delaying it and greatly contributing to the failure of this protestant initiative.[16] The Netherlands was the other key area in Anglo-Spanish strategy. By now it was widely believed that England's survival depended on the survival of the rebellion there. Once Philip was free of that war, he would have the additional resources, as well as the ideal base, for an attack against England. When the rebellion looked set to collapse under the dual strain of the duke of Parma's inspired leadership of loyalist troops and the death of the two principal rebel leaders — William of Orange and the duke of Anjou — Elizabeth was convinced that only open intervention on behalf of the rebels would ensure their survival. Although Elizabeth denied any intention to invade Philip's lands and refused an outright offer of sovereignty, her action was widely acknowledged as a direct challenge to his sovereignty both because she demanded direct control of certain Dutch towns and lands as pledges for the repayment of her expenditure, and because her commander, the earl of Leicester, exercised powers which usurped sovereign functions.[17]

In response to news of a major English offensive Philip decided to form a large fleet in Lisbon for which he embargoed foreign vessels, the normal practice in this period. An incident between an English ship and royal officials in Portugalete led to the rapid escalation of hostilities: the seizure of English ships and goods matched by the issue of letters of marque against Spanish shipping.[18] However unwelcome, war with England was increasingly likely, particularly as the Portugalete incident coincided with news of Drake's attack on Portuguese and Spanish lands and confirmation of Elizabeth's formal alliance with the Dutch (August 1585).[19] Philip was also under increasing pressure from the pope and, somewhat surprisingly, from Henry III to take action against Elizabeth. Henry sent secretary Villeroy to propose a joint invasion of England as soon as Mendoza arrived, and the ambassador — evidently a believer in miracles — thought it was a genuine offer and urged Philip to embrace the alliance. He admitted that in the past the French would rather have died than allow Philip to set foot in England, but he thought 'the fact that they have made this proposal with such warmth is God's particular will and desire. He has heard the cries of the English catholics who are so grievously afflicted'.[20] Philip's response in July 1585 was suitably sceptical. He suspected the French of plotting to weaken him by embroiling him in a major war. As he predicted, when he demanded specific details of the French contribution, Henry III was suddenly unavailable and unable to comment and the initiative rapidly evaporated, giving Philip the chance to lecture the French on the necessity of eliminating 'the heretics in their own realm' before meddling in the affairs of others; 'it is far more important to eliminate those near us', he commented sourly, 'than those who are far away'.[21]

Philip was busy deflecting plans for an invasion of England from the grand duke of Tuscany,[22] and the Guise,[23] when he was faced with ardent injunctions from Sixtus V to execute some glorious deed ('alguna empresa famosa', literally some famous expedition). In vain he tried to persuade Sixtus that the war in the Netherlands fitted the category of 'fama' when measured in terms of human and financial cost, time, and above all, its cause — the defence of God's church and therefore of papal authority. Sixtus dismissed such arguments and proposed campaigns against England, Geneva and Algiers.[24] As late as August 1585 therefore, Philip was eschewing alliances and plans for an invasion of England. His main concern was the safe arrival of the fleets from New World: the *flota* from New Spain docked in mid September, the *Tierra Firme* ships in mid October.

Elizabeth made sure there would be a war by sending a powerful fleet under Drake which attacked the Galician coast in October, and continued its voyage of plunder and destruction to the Canary Islands and the Caribbean. These raids were deeply offensive to Philip and seriously dented his reputation, but did they force him to war? Martin and Parker argue that the attack on Vigo was 'the last straw — the final proof that the English problem could no longer be deferred' and that it prompted Philip's letters of 24 October 1585 expressing his acceptance of an invasion of England and asking for papal support.[25] The problem with this date, as they appreciate, is that Philip did nothing else. In fact these letters relate to the negotiations between the king and the pope over the 'famous expedition'. Sixtus had proposed a crusade against Algiers, which would have been welcome to many Spaniards and Italians.[26] Philip could not participate in a major war in the north if the conflict in the Mediterranean revived, however, so he ordered Olivares to find out which of the two campaigns the pope preferred. If pushed, the king would declare in favour of the English plan. The October letters were a statement of choice between two evils rather than a positive proposal.[27] The *Gran Armada* commission maintain that the letters of 29 December 1585, in which Philip again speaks of an invasion, mark the definitive moment when he decided on the war; this time he also issued orders for the formation of an army and fleet. The reasons they give for Philip's decision are first, Drake's attacks on the Canary Islands and Caribbean; second, a change in the situation in France which was now quiet.[28] This date is more convincing, but the explanation is not. In one of these letters, Philip commented rather dismissively on the English attack against Galicia 'where their daring was more impressive than the harm they did',[29] but even on 2 January 1586 he did not know what Drake had done in the New World, although he was extremely apprehensive. He also mentioned Elizabeth's subsidies to German troops whom he believed were poised to invade France.[30] The situation in France was propitious, but not because it was peaceful; a new civil war was imminent which would firmly tie down Henry III and prevent him from coming to Elizabeth's rescue.[31] Moreover, we should not underestimate the impact of events in the Netherlands: Elizabeth's treaty with the rebels was justified publicly in October, and Leicester took control in December. As the year ended Philip was seriously considering war and had began the usually lengthy preparations, but that is not the same as saying he was irrevocably committed to a major campaign against England. While Elizabeth's aggression gave him sufficient cause, no firm policy decision could be made until internal and international conditions permitted.

Much has been made of the additional facilities Philip could draw on in the 1580s, particularly the shipping, sailors and ports of Portugal, and the increased revenues from the Indies.[32] While these eased the almost herculean task of organising a fleet in Iberia, they did not prompt Philip's bellicosity. There were few Portuguese ships and Lisbon was so far from the ideal centre for the fleet that subsequent campaigns and the permanent Atlantic squadrons were based in Spanish ports. As for the Indies revenues, they amounted to a million or a million and a half ducats annually, roughly an eighth of Philip's Spanish revenues, and about a tenth of the total cost of the campaign. Philip did not launch an invasion because of a marked improvement in his financial or naval circumstances — the fundamental factors were political and strategic. One of the crucial missives sent in December 1585 was addressed to the duke of Parma. The king reminded Parma that he had argued against the invasion of England in 1583 on the grounds that it could not be tackled until 'the islands' and Antwerp had been taken. Although the islands were still in rebel hands, and no deep water port was available, Antwerp had fallen. Philip wished to know if the new circumstances allowed them to plan an invasion of England. Parma's answer was positive.[33]

3. The Succession: Lancaster v. York

Before a final decision could be made Philip also had to be sure of papal support. In January 1586 he instructed Olivares to ask for confirmation of Elizabeth's excommunication, and the rights to the English crown. The ambassador was to say that Philip had decided to mount the campaign because he had been deeply moved by the pope's zeal, and was convinced that Sixtus would make a substantial contribution. The aims of the war were simply put: 'to subdue that kingdom to the authority of the church of Rome and to give it to the queen of Scots'.[34] She deserved it because of her firm adherence to catholicism in the face of persecution, and because she had the support of English and Scottish catholics. Interestingly, there was little reference to her dynastic rights. Philip intended to exert some influence on English affairs by choosing a suitable husband for her — this was tantamount to deciding who would rule England during her lifetime.[35] More importantly, since she was too old to bear children, Philip wanted to make arrangements for the succession *before* she took power, because

> after the queen of Scotland dies it would be a grave impediment if she were succeeded by the king of Scotland, her son, who is a confirmed heretic. If this occurs all we will have achieved is to make the situation worse, and increased the power of the heretics at the expense of catholic money and lives; because England, Ireland and Scotland will then be united and controlled by a vigorous male, whereas now they are divided and in the hands of a woman.

James might feign conversion to get the inheritance, and Mary, 'misguided by motherly love', would accept it or, worse still, a protestant successor. Philip made it a condition of the campaign that Sixtus should exclude James.[36] He had expressed similar concerns and demands two years earlier.[37] Sixtus V agreed that they must prevent a protestant succession but he was convinced James would convert to get the English throne. In case he did not, Sixtus thought Mary should be married to an English noble who would remain king after her death. Negotiating on Philip's behalf, the count of Olivares argued that they could not guarantee James's conversion, and that Mary's marriage to an English noble would almost certainly lead to a civil war in England — her past experiences in Scotland bore this out. Moreover, the prospect of the succession would surely tempt Mary's husband to get rid of her. Sixtus was perplexed by these arguments: his failure to refute them proved their validity. Olivares seized the initiative in late February 1586 and proposed a compromise: a decision on the succession would be deferred until Mary was on the throne; then the pope must accept Philip's choice of a successor. Both the pope and the king assented.[38]

The pope was afraid of Philip, but he may not have suspected how far the plans for the succession had evolved. In private the king stated that the most suitable successor to the English throne was the person who brought the kingdom back to the faith. In his case it was doubly appropriate since he had an excellent dynastic claim. Yet Philip did not think it wise to add England to his already unmanageable empire. Instead he wished to transfer his rights to his eldest daughter, the infanta Isabel, who would rule England with her future husband — one of her Austrian cousins. Philip realised the danger of making such a bid public, particularly in the curia. The pope was a miser and the king feared that instead of making a substantial contribution 'he will try to buy me off with expectations and to persuade me that given my interest in the matter, I must settle for much less'. Olivares was therefore instructed to secure a papal grant first, after which they would press hard on the succession. The ambassador agreed wholeheartedly: the slightest hint that Philip had a direct personal interest in the war, he warned, would result in the withdrawal of papal support.[39] He was already finding it extremely difficult to persuade Sixtus that 'the aim and justification of the enterprise is to reduce that kingdom to the obedience of the Roman church and to place the queen of Scotland on the throne'. The Pope insisted that Philip was taking the offensive to avenge Elizabeth's attacks, to clear the oceans of English pirates, to guarantee the safety of the Indies, and because until the English troops were ejected from the Netherlands, he would not defeat the rebels.[40] In vain Philip argued that if these were his sole or primary motives he need only organize a punitive expedition — for which he already had sufficient forces — and to improve defence. Only a massive campaign could restore catholicism in England, however, and this is what he was proposing.[41] If the catholic powers admitted that the campaign was primarily aimed to restore the faith, they had as much duty to participate in and finance it as Philip, consequently they refused to acknowledge that this was Philip's motivation. Nevertheless, Sixtus did not want Philip to abandon the campaign. Conscious that this war would so seriously dent and divert Philip's resources that unless aided he might direct his forces elsewhere. Sixtus agreed in December 1586 to contribute one million ducats to the enterprise — half what Philip had requested.[42]

In the course of 1586 Philip was made aware that notwithstanding earlier pressures, the catholic powers were fundamentally opposed to his campaign against Elizabeth. In July he wrote with some pessimism to Olivares: 'I appreciate that many will be sorry to see it change hands, because among the French and others the zeal for Christendom and desire to see that realm return to the catholic fold is not so powerful that it can outweigh other interests'.[43] He might have admitted that these were legitimate interests. Catholic powers feared that if he succeeded in England he would establish the much-feared Habsburg *monarchia* in Europe. To avoid the creation of such a great power, they would unite with protestants against him. As one of Philip's closest advisers stated bluntly:

> even if God gives us good fortune, it would not be wise for Your Majesty to appropriate that kingdom, because it would cost so much to maintain that the rest of the empire would be ruined. Besides, it would create great difficulties for the campaign if it were understood that this was your intention.[44]

Victory might prove more dangerous than failure. Philip's hesitant and seemingly inconclusive attitude towards the campaign during these months is surely related to these intractable difficulties.

It was plainly unrealistic to expect Philip to conquer England and then give it away unless he was repaid and had guarantees of long-term support from the new ruler. There were many other campaigns that would advance the faith and benefit his empire; it was foolish therefore to take such grave risks and drain his resources for an entirely altruistic motive. Kings had a duty to serve their subjects as well as their faith. When Sebastian of Portugal was killed fighting in North Africa his ministers were condemned for treason, not praised for purity of motives.

Despite the warnings from his ministers, therefore, Philip reopened the succession question in Rome as soon as the pope had agreed to the grant. It would have happened anyway: on 23 November Mary Stuart wrote to Sixtus announcing her decision to leave her kingdoms and rights to Philip if James VI remained a protestant. Mary had informed Philip of this in May 1586 when requesting his support for the Babington plot; his response was to praise her religious zeal, now more potent than her motherly affection.[45] All agreed it must be kept secret but Mary's disclosure — intended perhaps as a way to warn the world that her death would bring greater dangers — shook the courts of Christendom.[46] Philip himself wondered in January 1587 if Mary could be helped or saved if it were made public that Philip was next in line to the English throne.[47] Olivares was now under the impression that Philip intended to stake his claim openly and that this was to be a central issue in the justification of the campaign. He was still convinced that this was extremely risky because he expected opposition to be so powerful that it would endanger the invasion. Nevertheless he did his best to secure information and support for his master. In February he sent documents about the competing claims to England, including a book by the bishop of Ross and a family tree.[48] With some trepidation he broached the succession with William Allen and Robert Persons in mid March and for the first time he revealed Philip's direct interest.[49] This was the occasion when the Lancastrian colours of the Allen family served their turn. Allen assured Olivares of his attachment to the house of Lancaster and his conviction that Philip had legitimate claims to the English throne, but he was adamant that it must not be made public until after the invasion: 'when God has given victory to your Majesty's arms, your Majesty's relationship to the royal house of Lancaster may be justly and seasonably pleaded in the assembly of the estates . . . where the matter can be most easily managed by the archbishop of Canterbury . . .'[50] Somewhat disconcertingly for a man seemingly persuaded of Philip's superior dynastic claim, Allen also stated that 'kingdoms are no less justly won by legitimate warfare than they are inherited through propinquity of blood', and that this war was just because it aimed 'to avenge the wrong done to religion and to obtain reparation for injuries received'.

Persons also favoured the house of Lancaster but he argued that according to strict hereditary succession after Mary Stuart's death the English throne should pass to Ranuccio Farnese, eldest son of the duke of Parma, and his siblings thereafter. Since the best Lancastrian rights

Table 1 Tree of the English succession.

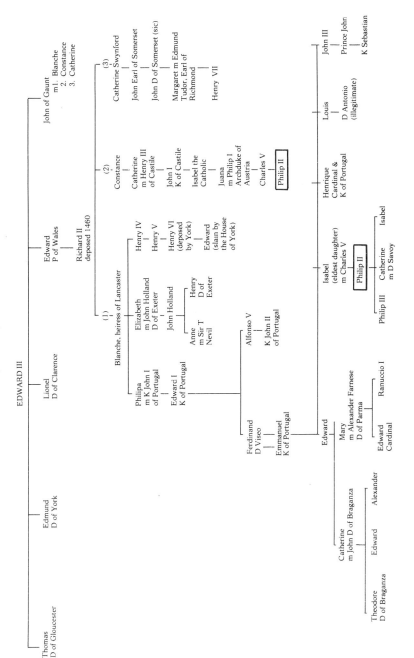

R. Doleman, *A conference about the next succession to the crowne of Ingland* (1594)
Note that Philip inherited claims from both his father and his mother to the English
throne. Compare with the genealogical information given by Stow.

Table 2 *The Tudor succession. Frontispiece from Stow's* Annales *(1592)*

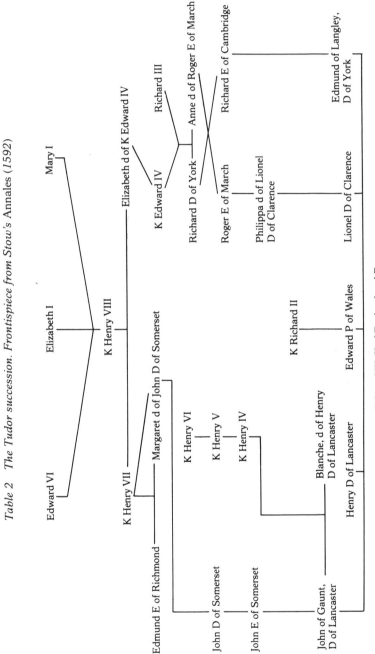

STOW'S ANNALES (1592)

descended through the Portuguese royal family, Allen and others argued that as king of Portugal Philip had the better claim. Persons, Charles Paget and other exiles thought this was irrelevant.[51] They were not the only Parma supporters. Don Juan de Zúñiga, one of Philip's closest councillors, suggested a match between Mary Stuart and the widowed duke of Parma, because of his personal qualities and because he would fight with even greater valour if he knew he would get the throne. As king of England he would also help Philip recover the rebel provinces in the Netherlands. Zúñiga did not dwell on Ranuccio's claim to the English throne, but it is clear by his impassioned defence of Parma that the matter was being openly debated. To counter the 'malicious talk' at court he assured Philip that Parma would not abuse his position as king consort and seize England for his family, nor would he use English forces to impose his son on the throne of Portugal.[52] Whatever Philip thought of Parma's loyalty at this point, it was natural that Parma would seek to advance his son and his dynasty. One of Philip's basic rules of statesmanship was that a relatively weak enemy should not be supplanted by a potentially powerful one. The situation was complicated by the fact that Philip had designated Parma as commander of the invasion for three reasons that made it imperative to retain him: first, he had powerful connections at the curia that made him acceptable to the pope and would counter the influence of the Guise. The duke of Guise wanted to lead the campaign and Philip wanted to prevent this both in order to eliminate all French influence, and to ensure that catholicism in France was not further weakened by the absence of its leader.[53] The second reason to favour Parma's command was his unquestionable military prowess and popularity with the troops. Finally, he could be more easily controlled. With competing claims to England and Portugal at stake it was folly, as the popular saying goes, to leave the rabbit in charge of the lettuce. Philip's choice of a strategy that entailed a dual attack on England and sharing power between two commanders, was surely affected by his need to constrain Parma in England.

Olivares was vexed by the contradictory evidence on the succession and ordered Persons and Allen to write to Philip directly. He was concerned by what he rightly perceived as dangerous and inconsistent aspects of Philip's policy. If he claimed England by dynastic right rather than by right of conquest, and then a majority opinion declared in favour of the Farnese, Olivares argued, he would then lose everything. Moreover, if Philip justified his claim on strict hereditary succession he could not give the kingdom to Isabel as he intended, because this contravened the very principle of hereditary succession. Prince Philip might become involved in civil war with his sister to make good his claim to the realm.[54] Persons was worried by the external dangers: 'this campaign is odious to all the other princes, both heretical and catholic, who would argue that it was done not for religion but for reasons of state, because Spain wants to lord it over all Europe'. He feared the Guise and Parma factions in Rome would use their power in the curia to prevent this saintly war because of Philip's demands.[55] Persons and Allen also feared that Scottish and English catholics would be alienated by Philip's claim, especially the Scots who naturally hoped for James's succession.[56] Ultimately, however, they were so anxious to encourage Philip to invade, that they hastened to reassure Philip of their unstinting support for his claim, and offered to write a book to prove it — on condition that the matter was kept secret until Philip had successfully invaded England.

Although no one said so at the time, the book would not be easy to write for the simple reason that the dynastic claims of Mary Stuart and Philip II were incompatible. To establish Mary's claim it was necessary to prove the legitimacy of the Tudor monarchy. As can be seen by the outline of the family tree Allen and Persons produced (p.18) they begin from the premise that Henry VII was the legitimate heir to the house of Lancaster and simply dismiss all his other successors on the grounds of bastardy and heresy. Mary was 'legitimate heir by virtue of blood and succession'.[57] Without dwelling on a confused history spanning over two centuries they concluded that 'once the successors of this union [between Henry and Elizabeth of York] fail, by virtue of death, bastardy or heresy, the ancient rivalry between the houses of Lancaster and York will be revived: the Catholic King is the heir to the house of Lancaster, and the count (sic) of Huntington heir to that of York'.[58] Mary's death was a blessing for the genealogists, as Persons and Allen admitted. It was no longer necessary to insist on Tudor legitimacy, so Philip's Lancastrian claim could be made more explicit. Indeed they guaranteed to prove that Henry VII's sole claim to the throne was by force of arms as his Lancastrian rights were inferior to those of the Spanish and Portuguese royal houses. Persons (whose conversion to Philip's cause was complete) further undertook to prove that the Spanish line alone could succeed, all others being barred from the succession through bastardy and heresy.[59] Allen and Persons also reminded the king of the many reasons and justification for the campaign. They started with his hereditary rights, and rather inconsistently (as they had just denied the Tudor-Stuart claim) said it was reinforced by Mary Stuart's will. The war was further justified in their view by Elizabeth's provocation and aggression, the damage England had done to catholicism and to Philip's empire, and the right of all catholic princes to annex the lands of excommunicated monarchs.[60]

This was most gratifying and Philip naturally wanted it made public at once. Furthermore he believed that Mary's death allowed him to act on the papal agreement of the previous year and that he could now nominate a successor.[61] The leading exiles, his ambassadors and advisers were adamant, however, that he must not make his intentions public or the invasion would be stopped by all those who were jealous and fearful of his power. Philip finally accepted the advice at the end of June 1587 and ordered the negotiations to cease. He insisted that once in England he would force the pope to adhere to the February 1586 agreement: Sixtus must confirm the exclusion of James and accept Philip's choice of a successor, that is the Infanta Isabel.[62] Olivares tried to persuade him that Sixtus would never support Isabel's claim because of his fear that she would one day inherit the whole of the Spanish Monarchy. The young prince Philip (born 1578) and Isabel were the last of Philip's eight children; even if the prince survived, the high death rate among the Spanish Habsburgs made it likely that the empire would one day pass to Isabel or her progeny. Consequently it was wiser to put forward a candidate who stood a chance of investiture: perhaps the archduke who was chosen as Isabel's husband. Philip disagreed and simply adopted rougher tactics: the ambassador was told to insist on Philip's own rights to the throne so that Sixtus would be so frightened he would himself suggest Isabel as a compromise candidate.[63]

Evidently there could be no formal declaration of war on Philip's part until the dynastic issue had been resolved. If it was to be used at all, it must play a major part in the public justification of the invasion. The formal reasons for declaring war were always a matter of the gravest consequence. Philip could allege rightful retaliation for Elizabeth's aggression, but this was not a very impressive reason for war and gave him no claim on the moral and material support of other catholic powers. Religion would, and was the best justification for war along with defence and dynastic rights. The danger was that it might trigger off a panic reaction and lead to the creation of a protestant league, thereby unleashing a general war in Europe. An open declaration of war was also undesirable at this stage as it would commit Philip irrevocably

Table 3 Genealogical chart by Persons & Allen to prove Philip II's title to the English throne.

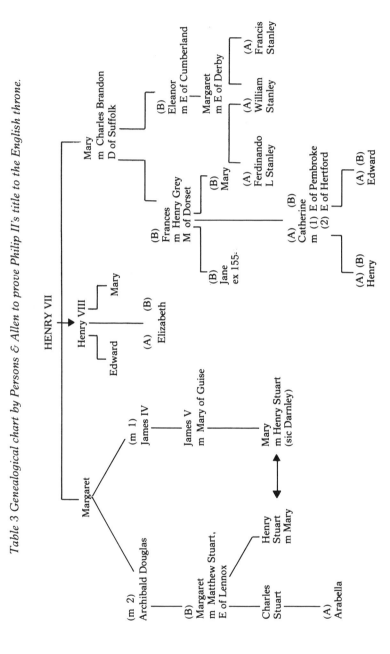

Source: A.G.S. E.949 f.57, A=alive; B=illegitimate.

to the conflict, and he was now uncertain as to whether this invasion was worth the attempt. For her part Elizabeth could not formally declare war since she had no cause other than the largely provoked embargo of English ships and goods in the spring of 1585. She could not play the religious card either as she was appealing for support from Islamic powers, protestants, and she would ultimately need the help of the (catholic) French king. Without open discussion of Philip's claim to the throne there was nothing to unite the protestants behind Elizabeth, and she made little effort during 1586–7 (unlike her energetic and wide-ranging activity in 1585) to purchase the support of those who could be bought, such as James, the Danes and some German princes. Indeed she alienated her allies — the Huguenots and John Casimir of the Palatinate, let down over the invasion of France in 1586–7; and the Dutch who rightly feared her independent peace negotiations with the duke of Parma. There was thus no declaration of war on either side, although the campaigns of 1588–9 left no doubt that a state of war existed. Without the formation of a protestant league the catholic princes felt no need to join Philip; they remained aloof and hostile to his aggrandisement. Foreign princes may have missed the subtleties of the arguments in favour of Lancaster and York, but they certainly understood the implications of a vacant throne. And no one was convinced that this conflict was solely or primarily motivated by ideological concerns.

Free from the need to promote Philip's succession openly, Allen and Persons steered clear of the dynastic debate, which was also omitted in contemporary Spanish writings. Allen's *Admonition to the nobility and people of England* (1588) was to be disseminated at the time of the invasion and was the closest thing to a war manifesto. It built the case against Elizabeth on the papal excommunications, her heresy and illegitimacy, her 'manifold wickedness', her heinous crimes and impiety, the execution of catholics and other anti-catholic acts in England. Parliamentary acceptance of Elizabeth's rights was discounted because all parliaments since the exclusion of catholic bishops were illegal. Following tradition Allen condemned Elizabeth of having destroyed the ancient nobility and put new base men in power, as well as of oppressing the people and other despotic acts. He assured the English nobles that Philip had decided to attack England only after repeated requests from several popes, and because he felt a special love for the kingdom he had once ruled. His action was also explained in the context of the traditional alliance and mutual support of the ruling houses of Burgundy and

England. Allen added that Mary Stuart's death affected Philip deeply, as had his 'owne vnspeakable zeale and pietie', and the humble and continuous supplication of English catholics. For good measure it was denied that Philip intended to annex England or dispossess the English.[64] Spanish writers echoed most of these arguments, but they naturally tended to emphasise religious factors and the need to respond to English aggression. Philip's actions were promoted as a major step for catholicism, but the Spaniards were also promised direct benefits as the war would eliminate English hostilities and thus allow a reduction of defence expenditure, as well as facilitate the recovery of the Netherlands.[65]

4. The War, 1588–9

The preparations for a campaign had continued while the debate over the succession underwent its tortuous course. Although no plan had been formally adopted, the marquis of Santa Cruz and the duke of Parma certainly thought they were intended for war against England. Protestants in Germany and the Netherlands believed this was a ruse and that the blow would fall against them. It was Elizabeth herself who ensured that the might of Philip's empire was directed against her by sending a large fleet to attack his lands in 1587. News of its imminent departure caused intense alarm in Iberia where it was rumoured that the Dutch and North African powers would actively participate in a campaign intended to establish Dom António on the Portuguese throne. It was imperative to act quickly: to expedite the preparations, Philip ordered the embargo of the best ships from the Indies trade in March 1587 despite the disruption and opposition it would cause.[66] A few days later news of Mary Stuart's execution arrived at court. This merely confirmed the need to act against Elizabeth. The fleet was far from ready when Drake arrived in Spain in April, however, and the destruction of some twenty ships and provisions in the spectacular raid on Cadiz caused further delays. Philip was not much concerned by the physical damage caused, but by the blow to his reputation: 'their audacity is intolerable', he fumed.[67] In the weeks that followed king and councillors met repeatedly, often in a state of confusion and despair, to debate where Drake would strike next: would it be Portugal, Spain, or the New World? Opinions also varied as to the best method of retaliation: some urged Philip to send his fleet against Drake, others an immediate attack on England; the council of war and the duke of Parma wanted both simultaneously, although they must have known this was beyond Philip's resources.[68] The king decided that the defence of the New World must take priority. Every effort was made to prepare the fleet, but it was July before Santa Cruz could sail after Drake. Insurmountable problems of distance, transport, victualling — the basic drawbacks of an under-developed economy and bureaucratic infrastructure — delayed both the fleet and the reinforcements for Parma.[69]

Santa Cruz spoiled for a fight, but the two fleets did not meet. In his absence the king decided that he would retaliate against Elizabeth as soon as his forces returned by sending a punitive expedition to Ireland. Anticipating opposition he justified his decision by arguing that he did not have sufficient resources for the 'negocio principal', that is the invasion of England, which would have to be deferred. Few, if any, were persuaded. Parma and Santa Cruz protested; both were eager to win reputation and (in the words of a contemporary) 'eternal renown' by participating in the invasion of England. While we should not dismiss Philip's explanations entirely — there were severe financial and logistical problems which made a smaller expedition more attractive — his decision has to be seen in the context of the failed negotiations over the succession, and the perception that a major success against Elizabeth would bring greater dangers than dividends.

In the ensuing debate supporters of a major invasion were able to back their strategic and ideological arguments by reference to the favourable international situation — which had been one of the chief reasons Philip had speeded up preparations in the spring of 1587. At that time the catholics had gained the upper hand in France, the Germans (princes and emperor) were preoccupied with Poland, the Ottomans were fighting the Persians, the Moroccans were not ready to strike, and Elizabeth was isolated. Philip's lands were quiet, and in the Netherlands Parma had captured Sluys, which he assured Philip greatly facilitated the task of gathering an invasion force against England.[70] Aware that such a favourable conjuncture would not last, Philip was under pressure to act while it held. There was an additional advantage to launching an invasion before the end of 1587: the prospect of anticipating the papal subsidy through loans promised by Italian bankers.[71] Partly for these reasons those in favour of a major invasion prevailed. In September 1587 the king issued the first detailed instructions to his commanders for a dual invasion of England using a fleet from Spain and the army of the Netherlands. The joint forces were to head straight for London. Having made his choice, Philip wanted action immediately. In the succeeding months he urged his commanders to set sail at once to keep the all-important advantage of surprise. But his conversion was not complete. On several occasions he proposed sending a smaller expedition to Ireland or the south of England, either as an alternative to, or as the initial step of, an assault on England. The chief commanders opposed him consistently and insisted that this would not suffice: faith and honour required a major invasion of England.[72] It was not perhaps until January 1588 that Philip abandoned hopes of substituting a punitive raid for the invasion, and that was due once again to Elizabeth's preemptive actions. On hearing that she would send another fleet against his empire that spring, Philip declared his intention to avoid such 'an intolerable shame and disaster'. Whereas until then his primary concern was the speedy departure of the fleet even if it meant taking fewer ships, he now ordered that the maximum number of vessels should go: a massive show of force was required. Honour and reputation could not be satisfied unless his fleeet exceeded, or at least matched, the English fleet.[73]

But what was he now hoping to gain? The deterrent and punitive aspects of the campaign were paramount; the recovery of reputation a primary concern. Yet more than ever Philip was convinced that the war was over religion: 'my primary aim in this campaign . . . is to reduce that realm to our Holy Catholic faith', he instructed Parma in late March–early April 1588.[74] In order to avoid alienating the protestants, however, this was not to be made public. The king's conviction that he was executing God's work left little room to doubt its ultimate success: 'I trust in God, whose cause this is, and to whom I have dedicated this action, that He will not allow any misfortune.' Consequently he was anxious to put the issue to the test and rejected in advance any peace overtures Elizabeth might make before his troops landed. If successful he intended to dictate his own terms — these were not specified in the instructions but would clearly have entailed setting Isabel on the throne. Even in his most exalted moments, however, Philip never lost his pragmatism: Parma was also instructed that if the victory was not complete he was to negotiate for the toleration of catholics in England and the rebel provinces in the Netherlands, the full withdrawal of English forces from the Netherlands and a sizeable compensation for the English attacks and the war. If the victory was less impressive, Philip accepted that he might secure only the toleration of catholics in the Netherlands, and the withdrawal of the English from one of their fortified positions — he preferred the deep-water port of Flushing — and perhaps some compensation. If English resistance was great, Philip realised he would have to alter his order of priorities; he knew he could not easily obtain toleration, so he advised Parma to broach this subject only after he had secured the return of Flushing and compensation.

As death, disease, storms and a plethora of lesser problems delayed the departure of the fleet from Spain and therefore the invasion, the king and his subjects placed quite unrealistic hopes in the campaign which became a panacea. The *cortes* noted among the expected benefits that it 'would ensure peace for us and the security of the seas and of the Indies'.[75] Philip observed that 'If God grants our fleet success, I put my trust in Him that all will be well.'[76] Despite the delays the international situation remained favourable: it even improved in the spring of 1588 with the death of Frederick of Denmark, the rebellion of the earl of Huntly and catholic lords in Scotland, and the successful coup of the catholics in Paris (Day of the Barricades) which neutralised Elizabeth's potential supporters. But it changed adversely during that summer — precisely when the *Gran Armada* sailed. The Ottomans were at peace, as were the French, and James crushed the rebellion. By then, Philip was too deeply committed to an attack to pull back but the tension was dramatically increased and there were serious fears for the safety of Iberia, the Indies and the Netherlands. The council of war was particularly concerned by the threat from North Africa. Despite Philip's decision to leave the Mediterranean fleet almost untouched, they feared (as Spaniards always did in times of weakness) that there would be a muslim invasion coinciding with a morisco revolt.[77]

The story of the *Gran Armada* is well known and needs no retelling here. The excessive expectations of the campaign in Iberia made it extremely difficult to accept, let alone account for, the failure of the invasion. As the count of Fuentes commented, 'merely to think about it confounds all understanding'.[78] Speculation regarding the purity of the king's motives for the war, as well as the morals of the court and kingdom led to mutual recriminations and repentance: God was clearly punishing Philip and his subjects and his wrath must be assuaged.[79] Prayers were not the only answer, however, practical measures were needed. The council of war at once informed Philip that it did not matter whether the enterprise had been a complete or a partial disaster, 'what matters is that we should show great courage and continue what we have started'.[80] By mid October half the *Gran Armada* ships and over a third of the men had reached Santander and its environs; a few more were scattered in Galician ports,[81] but their condition was such it would take months before they were fit to serve. By late November the councillors were in despair. They calculated that the English would be able to destroy Santander and the damaged ships in a matter of hours.[82] Philip's nerves too were shaken. He despaired of organising his forces in time to counteract an English attack: 'If God does not grant us a miracle, as I hope He will before such a thing happens, I hope and pray He will take me to Him so that I will not see such misfortune and misery'.[83] This was a far cry from the confident monarch who expected to establish his daughter on the throne of England. Indeed the fortunes of war had turned the tables on the two antagonists. It was now Philip who braced himself for an invasion.

Despite the bleak situation, the king and councils decided in December that as 'there are many drawbacks to defence, not least that it would encourage those who are watching the outcome of this war if they saw us slacken our grip', the offensive must continue. Predictably the councillors went on to say that God would surely help them since this was His affair too. Orders for the embargo of ships 'to join the relics of the armada' were dispatched. An ambitious ship-building programme was speedily implemented and every effort was made to hasten the repairs to the damaged ships, which were hampered by the lack of naval stores as English ships prevented supplies from the Baltic reaching Iberia. New levies were sent to the coast, and artillery brought from Milan.[84] The frenzied activity of Philip's government was impressive but it did not suffice. As the year drew to a close Antonio de Guevara had the temerity to say openly what many must have thought privately: it was impossible to launch a major offensive before 1590. The best they could hope for in 1589 was to organise a couple of defensive squadrons. Philip snapped: 'offense is the best defence'. Guevara should stick to financial advice, which is why the king had summoned him to court.[85]

The financial situation was critical. Spanish revenues were roughly eight million ducats per annum; the war had been financed by loans anticipating these revenues. Between 1585 and 1588 Philip borrowed some eleven million ducats; in 1589 another six million — a figure matched in the following year.[86] To pay back the loans and finance the new war Philip would have to increase taxation in his lands, and that meant primarily Castile. Stricken by the Armada's plight the Castilians were willing to offer a generous one-off payment but not a new tax. By dint of reasoned arguments, bribery, imprisonment and other pressures, the king succeeded in obtaining a new tax (the *millones*) but not until May 1589. It was October before the cities confirmed it and not until January 1590 were conditions finalised.[87] Philip's appeal to the pope to realise his contribution was unsuccessful. Sixtus insisted on keeping to the letter of the agreement which stipulated that he would only pay when Philip's troops landed in England.[88] The shortage of funds thus hampered preparations and led to a serious confrontation between the king and his Castilian subjects.

Lack of money also affected Elizabeth's plans, although her problems were of an entirely different magnitude, perhaps even of a different kind, since we are dealing here with perceptions of poverty despite the existence of reserves. Elizabeth had begun the war with £300,000 treasure and still had £55,000 to draw on; she was granted further taxation in September 1588 and requested a forced loan. Despite alarmist talk of financial ruin, she did not sell crown assets — always a sign of crisis financing — until November 1589, and even then she still had reserves of £29,000 and could have borrowed more if she had been willing to pay more than 10% interest.[89] Burghley was not alone, however, in fearing that any further fiscal pressures would lead to 'a general murmur of the people and malcontented people will increase to the comfort of the enemy'.[90] Uncertainty as to when the war would end also played its part. To keep costs to a minimum, the English queen agreed to mount a counter-offensive that was neither an official expedition nor a corsair raid but had elements of both. Offering only six of her second rate ships and £20,000, she expected the Dutch to provide all the transports plus supplies valued at some £10,000 and private investors, especially the leaders of the expedition, Sir Francis Drake and Sir John Norris, to supply more than half the ships and expenditure. Their brief was to destroy the remnants of the *Gran Armada* — which were expected to take shelter in Lisbon and Seville — take the Azores — a useful base to attack the treasure fleets — and later help to establish Dom António on the throne of Portugal.[91] Dom António's lavish promises persuaded Drake and Norris to invert these priorities when they sailed on 18/28 April 1589: with some 143 ships and 19,000 men they headed for Portugal, stopping briefly in La Coruña where they expected to capture some merchant ships. As investors they had no interest in destroying the Armada ships and prompted Elizabeth's sour comment: 'they went to places more for profit than for service'.[92] The English campaign, as Philip appreciated, could have eliminated his forces in the short term, and weakened him irreparably if even a foothold was seized in the Azores or Portugal. By March 1589 he knew that Elizabeth would send a fleet as powerful as the *Gran Armada* and what her instructions were.[93] His troops and ships were still not ready. Near panic he tried to avert the blow against Iberia by ordering a diversionary campaign in the Netherlands. Parma refused to risk his forces in a major campaign unless Philip made additional funds available at once. Predicting that no money was available, he left for Spa to recover his health and blithely told the king that as God had not given them the money, he clearly did not intend Parma to organise a northern diversion.[94] Nor was there hope of a diversion in France. On the contrary, the situation there deteriorated alarmingly in December 1588 when Henry III, heartened by Philip's temporary weakness, ordered the assassination of the duke and cardinal of Guise.[95] Shortly afterwards he allied with the Huguenots to fight the Catholic League.

Parma immediately warned Philip that unless he increased support for the League Henry III would destroy it and unite France by launching a campaign against the Netherlands: help must be sent immediately despite the fact that the French catholics would not give Philip anything in exchange, certainly not a Channel port or Cambrai.[96] Philip agreed; he even asked the pope to give the League half of the million ducats Sixtus had promised to contribute to the invasion of England.[97] But Philip had to concentrate on the English invasion first. Similarly, while Elizabeth was drawn into the French war, thinking it was the best opportunity to secure a French alliance as well as to advance the protestant cause, she could not finance two major campaigns simultaneously. The English expedition, however, ended in failure. The Portuguese did not rebel as expected, the sultan of Fez did not send aid, the English could fight untrained militias but could not prevail against regular troops and fortifications in Galicia or Lisbon. Even the attempt against the Azores was thwarted by severe weather. By early July almost all the ships had returned to England in poor condition and with little to show for their efforts. Half the men had died. The queen made another attempt against the Indies fleet — this time it fell to Sir Martin Frobisher to chase the chimera — without success. At the end of that month the refitted *Gran Armada* vessels sailed from Santander and San Sebastian and regrouped at La Coruña. Philip requested confirmation of Elizabeth's excommunication, indulgences, the status of crusade for the war, and the appointment of Allen as archbishop of Canterbury, as well as a dozen blank episcopal appointments for the king to fill. He demanded two million ducats from the pope — one million for each invasion attempt. Sixtus refused: he was concerned about the situation in France and convinced that Philip would now turn his attention there.[98] Just as the world waited for the next round of the Anglo-Spanish war, the two sides temporarily disengaged and concentrated on France.

5. The French Succession

The death of Henry III on 1 August 1589 and proclamation of the Huguenot leader, Henry of Navarre, as king of France made Spanish intervention inevitable. The new English campaign was suspended indefinitely. On 30 August 1589 Philip instructed Olivares to discuss the French situation with the pope. He was to stress that the catholic faith would collapse unless the League was generously supported, and to make it clear that Philip would not shoulder the burden of opposing Henry alone.[99] Naturally the question of the succession would be raised. Most catholics believed that Henry of Navarre was a usurper — despite Henry III's belated recognition of him as heir — because he was a protestant and excommunicate.[100] Cardinal Bourbon was recognised by the catholics (including Philip) as Charles X in his absence — he was a captive of Henry IV. His advanced age and ill-health prompted intense speculation over the succession. There was talk of the dukes of Savoy and Lorraine as the most likely 'foreign' successors. Philip would have none of this. In a letter which strongly echoed the initial steps to the English campaign, Philip ordered Olivares to press the pope for financial aid, to renew Henry's excommunication, and to make sure that his hereditary rights to the French throne, but especially those of the Infanta Isabel, were upheld. Isabel was the closest Valois successor if the salic law was ignored — and Philip dismissed the salic law as a mere invention.[101]

The king had learnt from his earlier experiences. He knew better now than to raise the issue of the succession immediately. These instructions were intended to provide Olivares with the necessary information and were not to be used unless the king's rights were threatened. Philip was also sensitive to the fears of catholic powers: he was willing to make her renounce her rights to the Spanish Monarchy so as to ensure that neither she nor her successors could inherit both Spain and France.[102]

More striking still was his decision to demand compensation if the catholic powers forced him to set aside his dynastic claims and wanted his support for their candidate: the pope must then agree to let him have Burgundy and other lands that the French had seized from his Burgundian and Spanish predecessors. It was just and right, Philip insisted, that he should benefit directly and substantially from participating in a war to recover the neighbouring kingdom for the catholic faith. His resources were scarce; his dynastic rights unquestionable.[103] Mendoza had already been instructed on Isabel's rights and warned that Philip expected repayment of his contributions to the Catholic League once Charles X was in power. In the meantime he demanded a Channel port.[104]

This was a radical departure in Philip's foreign policy: until now League propaganda had made much of the disinterested nature of Spanish support, as opposed to Elizabeth's demands for cautionary towns, repayment of loans, and England's traditional claims to the crown of France.[105] The French crisis provides further evidence of Philip's firm belief in his dynastic rights and of his new determination to secure direct returns from military intervention, best explained perhaps by reference to the resistance and adverse reaction he was encountering in Castile.[106] As predicted, his involvement in France forced him to withdraw resources from other fronts: apart from withdrawing from the English conflict, he was forced to draw his best troops away from the Netherlands, particularly for the relief of Paris (1590, 1592).[107]

Olivares was taken aback by Philip's instructions and Mendoza's letters. Given Sixtus' vehement opposition to the least increase in Philip's power Olivares thought it best to support the claims of a French catholic, the duke of Montpensier.[108] He was frightened by Sixtus' ambivalent attitude towards Henry IV and wisely made much of his master's decision to accept Cardinal Bourbon as king, restricting himself to a rather obscure and oblique reference to the infanta's rights. He was adamant that the slightest hint of Philip's direct interest would give Sixtus the excuse he wanted not to help the French catholics.[109] Nevertheless, when Cardinal Bourbon died in May 1590 Philip announced that his daughter had the best claim to the throne. He dismissed the arguments of the lawyer sent by the parlement of Paris to convince him of the validity of the salic law. Heartened by the formal acceptance of her candidacy by Parisian radicals in September 1591 he demanded a meeting of the estates general to settle the succession and sent a special envoy, the duke of Feria, to plead Isabel's case after the estates met in January 1593. By the time Feria arrived in early April the League estates, terrified at the prospect of a 'Spanish' succession, were already negotiating with Henry IV. Along with the Paris parlement, they rejected Isabel's candidacy.[110] Bitter hostility towards the traditional Habsburg enemy and fears of a future union of Spain and France had prevailed.[111] But Henry had learnt that he must embrace catholicism if he wanted to be accepted as king by the majority of his subjects: his conversion and Isabel's rejection were two sides of the same coin.[112]

6. 'A most pestilent book': The English Succession Reopened[113]

The troubled example of neighbouring France convinced many Englishmen of the wisdom of having an officially declared successor. Mary Stuart's death in 1587 had lessened the immediate danger for Elizabeth, deprived the catholics of a candidate they could all agree on, and significantly helped the protestants because they could now support James VI's claim on dynastic as well as religious grounds. Catholic English exiles were dismayed by Philip's diversion of resources to France. It is not unlikely that some may have thought the promise of the succession might encourage him to mount another invasion, and Isabel's rejection in France left her still as a viable candidate for the English throne. The timing would bear this out: Robert Persons (helped perhaps by fellow exiles William Allen and Richard Englefield) published *A Conference about the next succession to the crowne of Ingland* in 1594.[114] The author makes a spurious claim to impartiality which merely complicates an already confused argument. After a detailed review of the competing claims of Lancaster and York, the author adjudicates the title to Lancaster, and the best dynastic claim to Philip II and, failing that, the Farnese and Braganza. Dynasticism is not, however, the most important factor to determine the succession: just as the French radicals, Persons argued that religion was the most significant aspect of sovereignty, followed by justice and the ability to defend the realm. He argued that being ruled by a powerful, foreign prince was advantageous, allowing greater freedom for the native aristocracy. As for Isabel, she was unmarried and could be given a suitable husband; she was also 'a princesse of rare partes both for bewty, wisdome and pietie'.[115] Moreover, he concludes realistically that 'of any one forrayne prince that pretendeth, the Infanta of Spayne is likest to beare it away' because her father has the best dynastic title and the will to impose himself.[116] Two men were considered suitable husbands for her: the second son of the earl of Hertford and the youngest son of the countess of Derby. Both had reasonably good dynastic claims, but, more importantly, they were unmarried and young enough to be converted. Either match was good 'for making of compositions of peace and vnion with the opposite parties'.[117]

The book caused a great stir but Elizabeth's opposition to open discussion of the succession ensured that the response was muted. Several publications refuted its claims; one by the inveterate campaigner, Peter Wentworth. The primary objection to Persons' book was his challenge to dynastic rights which was seen as a threat to the hereditary principle and therefore a general danger to the fabric of society. The primary objective of these texts was to advance James VI's claim.[118] 'Doleman's book' became almost legendary. A popular publication declared that it had corrupted the nation and seduced it from its allegiance to the crown, thereby causing Charles I to be beheaded![119] What the book failed to do was to persuade the English catholics to unite behind one candidate. In an attempt to turn Philip's attention back to England, Persons suggested not long after its publication that a permanent English council should be created in the Netherlands to advise the king, coordinate the actions of the exiles, issue privateering licences against England, and work to make Isabel's candidacy open and acceptable to English catholics. But Philip must first openly declare his intention to claim the throne for his daughter.[120] The king remained silent. Although he made two other attempts against Elizabeth, in 1596 and 1597 — both dispersed by violent storms — he did not openly declare Isabel's rights. Indeed by 1596 he had made preparations for her to be sovereign of the Netherlands, although the process was not completed until after his death two years later. Her skilful rule in the Netherlands did not suffice to win back the rebel provinces, but it alarmed hispanophobes such as Sir Walter Ralegh who warned his countrymen after her arrival that she might attempt to seize the English crown for herself or for a male relative now that she 'hath the best army in all Europe in her hands, and may be past over into England in a night'.[121] Ralegh knew Doleman's book well, and his vehement rejection of a match between James VI/I's children and the Spanish and Savoyard princes was justified by references to it. In brief his argument was that these marriages were merely intended to place these contenders for the throne in a position to seize the realm.

7. Conclusion

During the last two decades of the sixteenth century, Philip was involved in three major dynastic disputes. The first, over Portugal, was his only success. It was also the only war he launched primarily to pursue dynastic goals. In the case of England and France his intervention was dictated by strategic and religious considerations. His hereditary claims were more tenuous, and the succession was gravely complicated by the bitter ideological conflicts dividing both countries. Lynch has argued that the ambitious foreign policy of the last two decades of the century proves that Philip had grown 'blind to rational argument' partly through the advice of 'fanatics who fed his ambitions'.[122] Pierson is equally harsh: prompted initially by 'moral imperatives', Philip fought England and France; but later he attempted 'to bring France into the Habsburg system' and this, 'Philip's grandest design . . . [was] doomed from the beginning, and in retrospect seems the costly folly of an old man'.[123] Philip's pursuit of dynastic claims certainly displayed ambition, the sort of ambition that coloured the policies of all contemporary princes. They had a duty and a right to take the lands and titles belonging to the dynasties they embodied. Philip's new palace at El Escorial amply demonstrated his powerful dynastic sentiments, with its grand mausoleum where members of the family were reinterred. At the Pardo palace he created a portrait gallery that was a visual manifestation of dynastic unity and hierarchy.[124] In other words, Philip's patronage of the arts as well as his policies reinforce his underrated sense of dynasty, which may have been more strident because of the need to assert the superiority of his line not only over foreign princes, but also the Austrian Habsburgs who had been given the superior title of Holy Roman Emperor. But he was neither a fanatic nor a fool; his persistent advocacy of Isabel had a political as well as a dynastic rationale. Philip wanted definitive solutions to problems which had haunted him throughout his life, perhaps because he was conscious of death: in 1587 he reviewed arrangements for the regency, and bouts of severe illness characterised his life thereafter.[125] After decades of inconclusive 'religious' wars which showed no sign of abating, and which had inextricably linked the affairs of England, France, the Netherlands and the Spanish Monarchy, Philip was ready to embrace radical solutions. As Persons put it in the case of England, it 'must be either a most dangerous enemy to his majesty, as it has been until now . . . or a friend and dependent, from which we would secure the opposite results; that is peace, security and wealth for your majesty's lands'.[126] What better way to secure 'a friend and dependent', than to establish a member of the family on the throne? History and experience proved that the way to change England's religion, was to change its ruler — and the same could be said of France. These wars are a testimony to the exhaustion of traditional methods of diplomacy and indirect intervention, and mark the move to a more radical but eminently rational policy.

Philip's decision to continue fighting against Henry IV after he had embraced catholicism has to be seen in this context. He rightly suspected that irrespective of his declared religion, Henry would use his position to guarantee the toleration of protestantism in France. But Henry's conversion gave the catholic powers the ideal excuse to unite in a coalition which included England and German protestants, aimed to prevent Philip's aggrandisement. The strength of the opposition, and his inability to isolate the conflicts in Western Europe ensured Philip's failure. The wars in France arguably saved Elizabeth: the new round in the Habsburg-Valois/Bourbon conflict overshadowed the renewal of the Wars of the Roses. Once his forces were divided Philip's enemies had more to gain by continuing the war. It was soon clear that the Spanish Monarchy could not prevail, but it was nevertheless too powerful to be destroyed. Peace, like war, had to involve all the powers whose destinies had been so closely bound for half a century. Philip begun the process of disengaging from the north by separating the Netherlands from the Spanish Monarchy; this facilitated the process of peace with France (1598), which in turn paved the way to peace with England (1604) and the Dutch rebels (1609).

NOTES

1. AGS E 949 f. 28.
2. M. Levine, *Tudor dynastic problems 1460–1571* (London, New York, 1973), provides a good general introduction; for Elizabeth's rights see in particular pp. 66–7, 71, 74. Elizabeth had been included in the third succession act (1544) and Henry VIII's will two years later, but was declared illegitimate in 1536 and never repealed the act. In 1559 parliament simply declared her (p. 98) 'rightly, lineally, and lawfully descended and come of the blood royal'. This and the 1544 act formed the basis of her claim (p. 98). Further details in Ibid., *The early Elizabethan succession question, 1558–1568* (Stamford, 1966).
3. Cf. Croft, below pp. 236–43, Gómez-Centurión, *Comercio*.

4. The proposals of 1559 and Philip's response in M. J. Rodríguez-Salgado, *The changing face of empire: Charles V, Philip II and Habsburg authority, 1551–1559* (Cambridge, 1988) esp. pp. 318–337.

5. A joint campaign was suggested by Henry II in 1559 and periodically thereafter, but both sides were convinced that partition was not viable and would eventually lead to war. However, this did not stop Elizabeth and her subjects from being haunted by the prospect of cooperation between France and Spain. R. B. Wernham, *Before the Armada. The growth of English foreign policy 1485–1588* (London, 1966) gives examples of this obsession pp. 298–300, 324. They were particularly apprehensive during Alba's regime, cf. W. S. Maltby, *Alba. A biography of Fernando Alvarez de Toledo, third duke of Alba, 1507–1582* (Berkeley-London, 1983) pp. 191, 193.

6. BNM mss 1750 ff. 217–227 'Discurso hecho el año de 1588 sobre la Armada'.

7. Relations in the earlier part of the reign, M. Fernández Alvarez, *Tres embajadores de Felipe II en Inglaterra* (Madrid, 1951); Maltby rather suggestively entitles his chapter on Alba's policy towards England 'England's protector', and shows his reluctance to participate in plots against Elizabeth, particularly Ridolfi's plot — *Alba*, pp. 195–203; Wernham, *Before the Armada* pp. 312–14, W. MacCaffrey, *The Shaping of the Elizabethan Regime* (Princeton, 1968) ch. XV for a more detailed internal analysis of Ridolfi's schemes.

8. The various claimants produced a flood of genealogical literature which in the best humanist tradition used biblical, classical and literary sources. A. Danvila, *Felipe II y la sucesión de Portugal* (Madrid, 1956) esp. pp. 44–52. Danvila denounced these writers for creating a 'confused labyrinth' with their 'uncontrolled discussion' and sterile, indigestible arguments (p. 46). The conquest was not welcome to many Spaniards, cf. Gómez-Centurión below, p. 296 m.70 and A. I. Watson, 'Attitudes in Spain towards Philip II's imperialism', in P. Gallagher & D. W. Cruickshank (edd.), *God's obvious design* (London, 1990) pp. 1–18.

9. AGS E 590 f. 125.

10. AGS EK 1561 f. 100 printed in *BMO* I pp. 397–8, except that Allen was to be given the see of Canterbury.

11. AGS E 944 f. 90 the count of Olivares to Philip II, 13 July 1583, printed in *BMO* I p. 302. Guise was convinced the Scots would invade England if Philip sent a fleet and soldiers from Spain.

12. *BMO* I esp. pp. 406–9, 411–12, 416, 420–1.

13. The failure of Throckmorton's plot made Philip even more reluctant to get involved in Guise's plan to intervene in Scotland some months later. As before, he did not give an outright refusal, but played for time and requested details of papal support before committing himself. AGS E 945

f. 42 in *BMO* I pp. 438-9, 441-4, 448-9; also *The letters and memorials of William Cardinal Allen (1532-1594)* ed. by the Fathers of the Congregation of the London Oratory (2 vols., London, 1882) hereafter *Letters . . . Allen*, II pp. lxiv–lxxi.

14. See Thompson below, pp. 73-5.
15. D. L. Jensen, *Diplomacy and dogmatism. Bernardino de Mendoza and the French Catholic League* (Cambridge, Mass., 1964) pp. 53-5; Guise continued to plot with Scottish nobles in 1585-6, pp. 79-82.
16. Jensen, *Diplomacy and dogmatism*, pp. 89-91. Elizabeth was widely blamed by the Huguenots and German protestants for its failure, and they paid her back in like kind by refusing to support her when Philip finally attempted to invade England.
17. Wernham, *Before the Armada* pp. 368-72; Adams below pp. 51-3, 55. Elizabeth's actions should not be seen merely in defensive terms: after so many years of hostile acts against Philip which had gone unpunished, Elizabeth and her councillors were overconfident. Even if Philip did retaliate, which was not certain, he would not be very effective while divided between so many enemies.
18. See Adams below, pp. 45-6 and references therein; also Croft pp. 241-2. *BMO* I prints a number of documents relating to this incident, esp. pp. 476-7, 487-91, 525-6.
19. By July Philip knew she would conclude this and send soldiers to the Netherlands. The news and rumours can be followed through the correspondence printed in *BMO* I; for the Netherlands AGS EK 1563 f. 99 (*BMO* I pp. 492-3) Mendoza to Philip, 16 July 1585.
20. AGS EK 1563 f. 78 to Philip, 7 June 1585 (*BMO* I pp. 478-80 quote p. 480).
21. AGS EK 1448 f. 29a, 17 Aug 1585 (*BMO* I pp. 497-8, quote p. 497).
22. From documentation in the Florentine archives, Martin and Parker, (p. 282 note 10) show that a Tuscan envoy arrived in late June 1585 to discuss plans for an invasion of England.
23. See notes 11 and 12.
24. AGS E 946 f. 224, 2 Aug 1585 (*BMO* I p. 496); Some weeks earlier he had commented with bitterness 'They evidently do not consider the [war] in Flanders "famous", nor can they have thought how much we are spending on it' AGS E 946 f. 43, in *BMO* I p. 478, Olivares to Philip, 4 June 1585, with Philip's annotations.
25. p. 111; note that these letters were sent to the pope and grand duke of Tuscany.
26. The king suspected that the grand duke of Tuscany had put him up to this, but he was sufficiently interested to respond positively: he offered to cover one third of the cost, at most a half, the rest was to be provided by the Italians. He warned the pope that his heavy commitments would hamper a greater participation in this war, and he must have been

ambivalent about a campaign that threatened the peace established with the Ottoman sultan since 1577.

27. AGS E 946 f. 245, and f. 248 Philip to Olivares, 6 Nov (*BMO* I pp. 535–6).
28. Talk given at the London May 1988 conference.
29. AGS EK 1448 f. 36, to Mendoza 29 Dec (*BMO* I pp. 500–1).
30. AGS E 947 f. 102 (*BMO* I pp. 553–4).
31. The drawback was that it required him to increase substantially the sums paid to the Catholic League.
32. J. H. Elliott, *Imperial Spain* (Harmondsworth, 1970 edn) pp. 269–70, 276. J. Lynch, *Spain under the Habsburgs* (2 vols, Oxford, 2nd edn., 1981) p. 318.
33. AGS E 589 f. 15 printed in *BMO* I p. 550. Parma to Philip, 20 April 1586, AGS E 590 f. 125.
34. AGS E 947 f. 102 printed *BMO* I pp. 553–4. Ideally Philip would have waited until William Allen persuaded Sixtus to request openly and formally that Philip should invade the kingdom. But the king realised that this would delay the issue as the pope would be most reluctant to shoulder the burden of having initiated the war, which is what it would have amounted to.
35. Mary's abysmal record in Scotland, tactfully passed over in these letters, was hardly a good recommendation. See J. Wormald, *Mary Queen of Scots. A study in failure* (London, 1988) esp. chs. 5–6.
36. AGS E 947 f. 102 Philip to Olivares, 2 Jan 1586 (printed in *BMO* I pp. 553–4); also E 947 f. 16 Olivares' account of the negotiations 24 Feb 1586. Philip had witnessed the rapid conversions of Elizabeth and Henry of Navarre when expedient, and their return to protestantism as soon as it was safe to do so.
37. AGS E 944 f. 147 and f. 186, Philip to Olivares 24 Sept 1583, published in *BMO* I pp. 406–7, 407–9. At this time, however, there were lingering hopes that Mary might produce another heir, so Philip thought her marriage and the prospect of being disinherited by a step-brother could be used to persuade James to embrace the catholic faith.
38. AGS E 947 f. 16. Olivares had pressed him hard on this point, and in his written account of the negotiations — which was seen and approved by the pope before it was sent to the king as an accurate summary of their discussion — Olivares included an unequivocal statement that the pope 'must accept Your Majesty's opinion on this' ('hauer de passar en esto por el parescer de V. M.d.'). Sixtus benefited because it meant that Philip could not use the excuse of an uncertain succession to pull out of the enterprise, and together with Mary, he could reasonably expect to prevail against Philip at a later date. On the other hand, Philip consoled himself with the thought that he had secured the right to nominate a successor.
39. AGS E 947 f. 102 Philip to Olivares, and response E 947 f. 16.

40. AGS E 947 f. 102.
41. Some examples of these exchanges AGS E 947 f. 110, E 947 f. 115 July and November 1586 respectively.
42. AGS E 949 f. 4 Olivares to Philip 22 Dec; E 949 f. 6 ibid., 30 Dec 1586 details of the agreement.
43. AGS E 947 f. 110 Philip to Olivares 22 July 1586.
44. AGS E 590 f. 127.
45. Mary must have known of Philip's objections to James's succession in 1583. Details of the letter, cited extensively, and Philip's reaction in Jensen, *Diplomacy and dogmatism* pp. 83–5. I cannot agree with Jensen, however, who concludes (p. 84) that the letter led Philip 'for the first time to take steps in her behalf against the Tudor queen'. His decision predates her promise, although Jensen is right to point out that Philip now sent her money directly and formally accepted to protect her. Guise was also negotiating with the Scottish catholics for a rising there, Ibid., pp. 79–82.
46. *Letters . . . Allen* II pp. 279–80, note 3 mentions the letter to Sixtus; AGS E 949 f. 6 Olivares to Philip 30 Dec 1586. The ambassador was so desperate to keep the succession issue quiet, he pretended it was a forgery done by Elizabeth!
47. AGS EK 1448 f. 91, Philip to Mendoza 28 Jan 1587 asking his opinion. Was it genuine concern or opportunism? Either way it shows his awareness that such a prospect would prove terrifying to many in England and abroad, and similar ideas may have prompted Mary's publication after she had enjoined silence. Mary's servants assured Mendoza that she had confirmed her concession to Philip before her death, AGS EK 1565 f. 85 Mendoza to Philip, 24 Oct 1587.
48. AGS E 949 f. 16.
49. In past discussions they had touched on the succession but Olivares had never mentioned Philip's personal interest.
50. He adds that the archbishop's 'lead will be followed by all the bishops and the Catholic nobles, who alone in consequence of the previous death or dismissal of the heretics, will have votes in that assembly'. *Letters . . . Allen* II p. xc, 19 march 87 — Latin orig AGS E 949 f. 23, printed ibid., pp. 272–5. The prominence given to the archbishop is understandable since Allen demanded the post. In the meantime Allen was closely instructed by Olivares on what he should and should not say to Sixtus on the matter, AGS E 949 f. 41 also printed in Ibid., pp. 289–90.
51. AGS E 949 f. 28 Olivares to Philip 23 March 1587. The ambassador did not help matters by pointing out that under Castilian law of noble entail, when two *encomiendas* were united, each followed its strict line of succession when no common male heir was available.
52. AGS E 590 f. 127 Some contemporaries were aware of Parma's claims;

in several seventeenth century accounts of the *Gran Armada* campaign his eagerness to participate is linked to his prospects and expectations of taking the crown, see e.g. *Certaine Miscellany Works of the Right Honovrable, Francis Lo. Verulan, Viscount St. Alban* (London, 1629) p. 46; *Pvrchas His Pilgrimes* (London, 1625) p. 1097.

53. AGS E 947 f. 102 Philip's instructions to Olivares Dec 1585; Guise claim AGS E 947 f. 15 Olivares to Philip, 24 Feb 1586. Relations between Philip and the Guise were always tense.
54. AGS E 949 f. 28.
55. AGS E 949 f. 25.
56. This is clear even in AGS E 949 f. 26.
57. AGS E 949 f. 57. Elizabeth was accused of having engineered Mary's downfall in Scotland and then lured her to England in order to prevent her from making good her claim to the throne.
58. AGS E 949 f. 57. Philip's claim is described as equal to those of the reigning monarchs Henry IV, V, VI and VII; by contrast Huntington is said to descend from the female and non-royal line of York.
59. AGS E 949 f. 26; Levine, *Tudor dynastic problems* pp. 33–4 details of Henry VII's rights: by strict hereditary order, Henry should not have succeeded. Philip received genealogies from others besides Persons and Allen, e.g. Mendoza ordered a book to be translated and sent — 27 November 1587, AGS E K 1656 f. 124, probably by Robert Heighington (sic) cf. AGS EK 1656 f. 120; cardinal Carrafa gave his opinion too (AGS E 949 f. 56).
60. AGS E 949 f. 40 sent by Olivares probably on 31 March 1587.
61. AGS E 949 f. 46 Olivares to Philip 23 April 1587.
62. AGS E 949 f. 65 to Olivares 24 June. In his letter to Mendoza, 4 April 1587 (AGS EK 1448 f. 114) Philip confirmed Mendoza's statement that he had the best claim to the throne after Mary Stuart, but bound him to secrecy for the time being.
63. AGS E 949 f. 65; E 949 f. 83. Olivares to Idiáquez 16 July 87.
64. Much the same arguments are rehearsed more succinctly in a publication to be distributed on landing, the *Declaration of the Sentence and Deposition of Elizabeth the usurper and pretended quene of England* (1588).
65. The jesuit Pedro Ribadeneyra was the most important polemicist on this occasion. His *Historia Ecclesiastica del Scisma del Reyno de Inglaterra* was published simultaneously (probably with official support) in Antwerp, Madrid, Zaragoza, Lisbon etc. in 1588. He had been in England in 1558 and was well informed. He also wrote another piece to promote the campaign, *Exhortación para los soldados y capitanes que van a esta jornada de Inglaterra* in *Historias de la Contrarreforma* ed. E. Ruíz, Biblioteca de Autores Españoles (Madrid, 1945), also in F. Díaz-Plaja

(ed.) *La historia de España en sus documentos. El siglo XVI* (Madrid, 1958) p. 747ff. Cf. Gómez-Centurión below pp. 272–8 for further details of Spanish propaganda.

66. AGS EK 1565 f. 26; FD I p. 199.
67. AGS GA 208 f. 366; further discussion of the raid in Rodríguez-Salgado, *Catalogue* p. 22 and references therein.
68. AGS GA 208 f. 343; GA 209 f. 66, E 592 f. 20.
69. See O'Donnell below pp. 225–31, also his *La fueza de desembarco de la Gran Armada contra Inglaterra (1588). Su origen, organización y vicisitudes* (Madrid, 1989).
70. A more detailed discussion of this and the following points in Rodríguez-Salgado's Introduction, *Catalogue* pp. 22–8.
71. AGS E 949 f. 14, E 949 f. 54; E 949 ff. 86, 87 and E 954 f. 242.
72. AGS E 594 f. 5 and E 165 ff. 6–7 instructions; Rodríguez-Salgado Introduction, *Catalogue* pp. 22–8, details of the changes in strategy. Thompson, below pp. 83–4, for a logistical explanation.
73. AGS E 594 f. 8; see also Rodríguez-Salgado below pp. 147–8 for some of the implications of this decision.
74. The corrected drafts of the instructions cited here in AGS E 165 f. 175 and 176–7. Further discussion of the religious fervour surrounding the campaign in Gómez-Centurión below, pp. 272ff.
75. AGS PR 80 f. 116. The document goes on to say they ordered 'many prayers, religious services and almsgiving to request that Our Lord should give us a great victory'. This draft may have been drawn up by royal officials for the representatives to send to their cities.
76. BL mss Add 28,263 San Lorenzo 25 May 1588; it continues: 'If he does not, it will affect all our affairs so gravely that truly I do not wish to think about it, but to place my trust in Him, who will surely have mercy on His people'.
77. AGS GA 235 f. 87 consulta 18 Sept 1588; GA 235 ff. 90–1 id 27 Sept; also E 165 f. 206. Such fears should not be underestimated simply because they were frequently expressed and ultimately proved unfounded. Thompson, below p. 80 note 50 points out that Iberian defences had been seriously depleted to fit out the Armada.
78. He fervently wished that 'Our Lord will provide the remedy we need and bring back safely those who are missing, give eternal glory to the dead and health to the living'. AGS E 431 f. 160, 8 Sept 1588.
79. Some thought God might be angry with Philip for interfering constantly in the running of the church, and particularly for meddling in the affairs the jesuits, or that he was testing the king to make him a saint — BL Add mss 28.263 ff. 463–6 letter from Luis de Santander, SJ 8 Feb 89; Ribadeneyra's *Tratado de la tribulación* and other reactions are discussed in Gómez-Centurión below pp. 280–3. More than one person reminded

Philip that God had also punished St. Louis with failure and even imprisonment in his failed crusades, Martin and Parker p. 256, BL Add mss 28,263 ff. 463–6. Most preferred to think that God had delayed the liberation of English catholics until a better occasion arose, AGS PR 80 f. 116, while some continued to explain England's adherence to protestantism as divine punishment for England's sins.

80. AGS GA 235 f. 71.
81. On 9 October there were 59 vessels, with just over 7,000 soldiers and nearly 3,000 sailors in Santander, AGS GA 221 f. 191; for Galicia see E 165 f. 329, GA 228 f. 104, GA 228 f. 110.
82. AGS GA 235 f. 154.
83. An extract from this letter to Mateo Vazquez in A. W. Lovett 'The vote of the millones (1590)' *Historical Journal* XXX (1987) pp. 1–20, p. 3 note 8; a more extensive quotation in English translation in Martin and Parker p. 258. Initially I was too sanguine in my assessment of the reaction in Spain.
84. AGS GA 235 f. 213 consulta Madrid 17 Dec 1588; new ships GA 228 f. 134 and GA 245 f. 11; repairs: AGS GA 236 ff. 186–8, 192 (Galicia); GA 228 f. 164 (Santander); artillery GA 228 f. 46.
85. BL Add mss 28,263 ff. 487–8 Billete of 25 Dec 1588.
86. Modesto Ulloa, *La Hacienda Real de Castilla en el Reinado de Felipe II* (2nd ed., Madrid, 1977) pp. 805ff, esp table p. 810. Ostensibly interest rates were 12% basic with extra for any delayed payments. In fact, the real rate was probably between 20–40%, and the net gain for the financiers was even greater, H. Lapeyre, *Simon Ruiz et les asientos de Philippe II* (Paris, 1953) suggests (p. 60) interest was 12% but on p. 66 he cites a loan for which Ruiz received 19.4%. The crown was paying for the transport of specie, as well as invariably failing to meet its payment deadlines, so the higher figure is probably nearer the mark.
87. The struggle can be followed through the documents in AGS PR 79; Lovett offers a clear and detailed account in 'The vote of the millones (1590)'. See also Gómez-Centurión below, pp. 283–6.
88. AGS E 950 f. 272, 26 Sept 1588; the ambivalent reaction of the Venetians, who wanted to extend the faith but to see Philip weakened, BNM mss 979 ff. 77–82 Giulio Sauorgnano to Filippo Pigafetta, 23 Sept 1588.
89. Wernham is sympathetic to the queen and claims that this was probably the only way 'whereby an enterprise of such magnitude could have been launched in time to take proper advantage of Spain's moment of weakness' — R. B. Wernham, 'Queen Elizabeth and the Portugal expedition of 1589', *English Historical Review* vol LXVI no. CCLVIII (1951) pp. 1–26 & 194–218, at p. 8; discussion on funding pp. 1–8. On the forced loan see also HMC *Calendar of the Manuscripts of the . . . marquis of Salisbury*, III (London, 1889) p. 366 and p. 413. Conyers Read was not

far from the truth when he coined the colourful phrase — 'to the end of her days she never spent a penny cheerfully and her wars were waged in the same cheese-paring spirit that characterized her days of peace'. Conyers Read, *Mr Secretary Walsingham and the policy of Queen Elizabeth* (3 vols, Oxford, 1925) III p. 334.

90. cit. Wernham, 'Portugal expedition', p. 4.

91. There is still debate and some confusion as to the order in which these three tasks should have been carried out; this is fully discussed by R. B. Wernham: *The expedition of Sir John Norris and Sir Francis Drake to Spain and Portugal, 1589* (Navy Records Society, 1988); *After the Armada. Elizabethan England and the struggle for Western Europe, 1588–1595* (Oxford, 1984) and in the 'Portugal expedition'. Contemporary accounts of the expedition to Portugal: Hakluyt IV pp. 306–354. Cumberland's voyage to Azores 1589 *ibid.*, pp. 355ff; Elizabeth had wanted to send her ships to intercept the Indies fleet even before she had confirmation that the *Gran Armada* was out of home waters. Howard thought 'that blow, after this he hath would make him safe' (Wernham, *After the Armada*, pp. 1–2), but the need to repair and refit the fleet and to watch for Parma's possible invasion kept the queen's forces in the Channel.

92. See note 91 above; quote Wernham, 'Portugal expedition' 207. M. C. Saavedra Vázquez, *María Pita y la defensa de la Coruña* (La Coruña, 1989) for a recent general account of the siege.

93. AGS E 596 f. 18 reports of Jan–Feb; ibid., f. 73 March 1589. By then he thought some 120–150 ships would come with a complement of 15–18,000 men. Philip had spies in the household of Dom António with whom all these plans were being discussed.

94. AGS E 596 f. 62 Parma to Philip, 6 May 1589 (received 7 June), replying to Philip's letter of 17 March. Parma had delayed his response initially hoping to conclude his negotiations with the mutinous Anglo-German garrison at Geertruidenberg. He took possession of the place on 9 April. Cf. Léon van der Essen, *Alexandre Farnèse, prince de Parme, gouverneur general des pays bas (1545–1592)* (5 vols, Brussels, 1933–1937) V esp. chapter 7 pp. 240ff., also Wernham, *After the Armada*. Philip had hoped that with the additional troops Parma would have successfully taken one of the deep-water ports in the Netherlands; he preferred Flushing or the island of Walcheren, but in the event Parma unsuccessfully attempted to take the island of Tholen and later Bergen-op-Zoom. The army secured victories in Bonn (28 Sept) and Wachtendonck (20 December), but these were followed by a period of relative inactivity which allowed the English and Dutch to consider a major expedition in Iberia. At the end of March 1589 Parma sent even more troops to Rheinberg.

95. For a brief moment it had appeared as if 'God has miraculously opened

their eyes .. to console Your Majesty', when Henry III offered an alliance against England. It was soon evident this had been to cover up his hostile moves against Philip's allies. AGS E 950 f. 268 Olivares to Philip II 12 Dec 1588, commenting on Mendoza's correspondence from Paris. J-M. Constant, *Les Guise* (Paris, 1984) a detailed study of the family and events leading to the murders (vividly described pp. 9–19).

96. The alternative was more costly and dangerous — to declare war on Henry III. Parma anticipated Philip's orders and sent money to the catholics, promising further subsidies and troops from Spain. Cf. his letters to Philip: AGS E 596 f. 3 (4 Jan 1589) E 596 f. 4 (14 Jan); E 596 f. 5 (21 Jan) also E 596 f. 6.

97. AGS E 954 f. 199–200 Philip to Olivares, 19 Aug 1589. He did not know Henry III had died.

98. Olivares was shocked by the financial demands: 'it is as easy to get 10,000 ducats out of him as to touch the sky'. AGS E 952 ff. 10–11 Olivares to Philip 9 Jan 1589; E 954 ff. 183–4 Philip to Olivares 22 June; E 952 f. 63 Olivares to Philip 23 July.

99. AGS 954 ff. 202–204 Philip to Olivares 30 Aug 1589. He expected Sixtus and the dukes of Lorraine and Savoy to contribute amply.

100. Discussion of the succession had begun on the death of the heir-apparent, the duke of Anjou, in 1584, cf. Constant, *Les Guise*, esp. ch VIII; ch X examines Guise's royal ambitions.

101. AGS E 594 ff. 202–4 Philip to Olivares, 30 Aug 1589; E 954 ff. 208–9 ibid., 18 Sept. Isabel was the eldest daughter of Isabel de Valois, herself the eldest daughter of Henry II and Catherine de Medici, and sister of the last three Valois monarchs.

102. Louis XIV was to find himself in a similar predicament a century later.

103. AGS E 954 ff. 224–6 Philip to Olivares, 8 Nov 1589.

104. Instructions AGS K 1449 f. 51 discussed at length in Jensen, *Diplomacy and Dogmatism* pp. 193–6.

105. M. Yardeni, *La conscience nationale en France pendant les guerres de religion (1559–1598)* (Louvain & Paris, 1971): examples contrasting the motives of Elizabeth and Philip, pp. 236–8. Anti-Spanish propaganda pp. 263–81; pamphlets related to the succession are discussed in pp. 224–41, the salic law 225–8, and the estates of 1593 pp. 299–308.

106. In fact neither Philip nor Elizabeth succeeded in gaining concessions, but their own interests were so closely enmeshed in the struggle in France they intervened nevertheless, even when Henry IV changed sides.

107. A clear outline of the campaigns in D. Buisseret, *Henry IV King of France* (London etc., 1984); M. Greengrass, *France in the age of Henry IV* (London, 1984); Jensen, *Diplomacy and dogmatism* pp. 208–10; H. A. Lloyd, *The Rouen campaign 1590–92* (Oxford, 1973), esp. pp. 169ss.

Van der Essen, *Alexander Farnese* V; English participation in Wernham, *After the Armada.*

108. AGS E 952 f. 133, 5 Dec 89, received 5 Jan 1590. Olivares had realised the danger of the Savoy claim and had taken steps to counter it. The duke of Savoy had been a close ally of Philip, marrying his youngest daughter, Catalina Micaela, in 1585. It would be her children, Philip's grandchildren therefore, who would inherit France. But the fusion of France and Savoy would prove extremely dangerous for Spain as it would undoubtedly threaten her possessions in Italy. Moreover Philip would be unhappy to see the dynastic order perverted by the succession of his youngest daughter's progeny rather than of his eldest.

109. AGS E 952 f. 141 Olivares to Philip 16 Dec 1589.

110. Jensen *Diplomacy and Dogmatism*, pp. 209–17. Philip was eager to marry Isabel to the archduke Ernest, then heir to the ailing emperor Rudolf II and this may account for the ambivalent attitude towards a French marriage.

111. Lloyd has argued (*Rouen campaign* esp. pp. 194–5) that Philip failed to impose Isabel because he appeared militarily weak. In my view greater force would have prolonged the issue, but nothing short of a massive invasion of France — impossible to sustain militarily — could have prevailed, even briefly. Such action would then have united catholics and protestants firmly against Philip and led to his expulsion from France, as indeed happened after 1595.

112. He announced that he would take instruction in May when Feria was openly demanding the abrogation of salic law and selection of the Infanta, and his conversion (the mass in St. Denis took place 25 July 1593) coincided with the decision of the estates to reject the infanta's claim. The close connection between Isabel's rejection and Henry's acceptance led some Spaniards to claim Henry's conversion as a Spanish victory.

113. This is how Sir Walter Ralegh described 'Doleman's' book in *A politique Discourse, by way of Dispute, about the happiest Marriage for the noble Prince Henry* (published 1611; reprinted J. Somers *A collection of scarce and valuable tracts* (16 vols, London 1748–1752); II pp. 199–207.

114. A pseudonym was used, R. Doleman, and it was dedicated to the earl of Essex. The BL catalogue attributes authorship to the three men, but it is more frequently associated solely with Persons. Note, however, that Persons refers to 'Doleman's book' in a later memorandum to Philip without admitting authorship, AGS E 839 ff. 125–9. Some parts of the book echo the documents produced by both men in the 1580s, but Persons had moved much further down the path of ideology as opposed to dynasticism. The death of other contenders, such as Ferdinando, earl of Derby (1593–4), may have helped to persuade another leading exile, William Stanley, of the infanta's claim. He was certainly considered

among her supporters later, AGS E 838 ff. 125-9 — see below for further discussion of this document; for Stanley, S. Adams 'A patriot for whom?' *History Today* XXXVII (July 1987) pp. 46-9.

115. *A conference about the next succession to the crowne of Ingland,* p. 256. Persons was not entirely cured of his earlier commitment to the Farnese cause, since he adds here that both the duke and cardinal of Parma 'are ympes in like manner of great expectation'.

116. *A conference about the next succession to the crowne of Ingland* p. 256 and p. 263 respectively. James VI's rights to the succession were dismissed because of his tenuous Lancastrian pedigree, because he was a foreigner and had been omitted from the succession in Henry VIII's will, and because his mother had been condemned of conspiracy — children of convicted traitors were excluded from the succession. Finally because it was against the public good chiefly as he would bring an influx of strangers into the kingdom. *Ibid.*, pp. 110-12, 242-4. Of course most of these points could be made against Philip and Isabel, but the author does not prize consistency.

117. *Ibid.*, p. 265.

118. P. Wentworth, *A Discourse containing the Authors opinion of the true and lawful successor to her Maiestie,* — the first time he came out openly on James's side; J. E. Neale, 'Peter Wentworth', *English Historical Review* XXXIX part I no. 153 (1924) pp. 36-54; part II no. 154 pp. 175-205, esp. 198-200. His pamphlet *Pithie Exhortation to her Maiestie for Establishing her Succession to the Crown* was published posthumously in 1598: *A Treatise Containing M. Wentworths Ivdgement Concerning the Person of the True and Iawfull successor to these Realmes of England and Ireland.* Other examples: Sir John Hayward, *The Right of Succession Asserted Against False Reasonings and Seditious insinuations of R. Dolman alias Parsons* (1603); Henry Constable (attd), *A Discoverye of a counterfecte conference* (1600); C. R. Markham (ed) *Sir John Harrington. A Tract on the Succession to the Crown (AD 1602)* (Roxburgh Club, 1880). I am grateful to Dr. Simon Adams for these references. James himself was spurred into action and promoted various publications to prove his hereditary claim, see J. R. R. Lyell, 'A tract on James VI's succession to the English throne', *English Historical Review* LI (1936); Sir Thomas Craig, *The Right of Succession of the Kingdom of England* (Edinburgh, 1603).

119. *The Plots of Jesuits* published by Michael Spark in 1653 also much reprinted; edition in *The Harleian Miscellany* (7 vols, London, 1744-6) I, p. 28. Similarly, unspecified Jesuit books were condemned by George Carlton for drawing catholics 'cleane from obedience of their Prince' and inspiring assassination attempts against Elizabeth. *A Thankfull Remembrance of Gods Mercie* by GC (1624 with many subsequent reprints).

Even Mary Stuart benefitted from the obsession with Jesuit plots and the succession. They were accused of manufacturing 'a feigned Title for the King of Spain . . . to draw off the Gentry from Her to the Spaniard' and drawing her into plots which finally ended her life. See *A Discourse concerning the Original of the Powder-Plot Together with a Relation of the Conspiracies against Queen Elizabeth and the Persecution of Protestants in France to the Death of Henry the Fourth* (London, 1674), p. 39.

120. AGS E 839 ff. 125–9.
121. He thought Isabel might pass her rights to Savoy because he was her nephew. The dukes of Savoy had a claim via the Portuguese royal family and Ralegh concluded that Savoy wanted to 'send a daughter into England, who might practice a party, either for her brother or for her uncle (Philip III)', *A politique discourse* p. 201, and to marry his son to princess Elizabeth to make doubly sure of seizing the crown. Although Savoy was then opposed to Philip III, Ralegh saw them as two sides of the same coin, and advanced the French marriage for prince Henry 'seeing there is none but a catholick lady for us'. p. 206.
122. J. Lynch, *Spain under the Habsburgs* I p. 333.
123. P. Pierson, *Philip II of Spain* (London, 1975) quote p. 196. He also notes: 'Philip's conduct at this period seems increasingly governed by moral imperatives rather than by prudence. Aged sixty in 1587, he seems to have been in a hurry to force things his way, confident in his growing resources and in the recent successes of his arms' (p. 181). Pierson also believes Philip was attempting to restore the empire of Charlemagne by the marriage between Isabel — who was to get France — and archduke Ernest, heir to the Emperor Rudolf, p. 193. But note that Isabel, from an early stage, had been designated to marry Rudolf, and as he would not marry, she was naturally promised to the cousin most likely to succeed him. The choice was dictated by family strategy and her status not by megalomania.
124. J. Woodall from the Courtauld Institute, London has included a very interesting reconstruction of the Prado portrait gallery in her unpublished London Ph.D. thesis (2 vols., 1989) 'The portraiture of Antonis Mor' vol. I.
125. AGS E 165 ff. 334–5.
126. AGS E 839 f. 129 point one.

2

THE OUTBREAK OF THE ELIZABETHAN NAVAL WAR AGAINST THE SPANISH EMPIRE: THE EMBARGO OF MAY 1585 AND SIR FRANCIS DRAKE'S WEST INDIES VOYAGE

Simon Adams

On 26 May/5 June 1585 the London merchant vessel *Primrose*, owned by Alderman William Bond, was boarded by a party of Spanish officials while anchored in the roadstead of Portugalete off Bilbao. The suspicious activities of the boats that accompanied the party alarmed the *Primrose*'s master. Although both the merchants travelling on his ship and their cargo had been landed, he decided to fight his way out. In doing so he carried away with him Francisco de Guevara, lieutenant-general to the *corregidor* of Vizcaya, and three companions. In Guevara's possession was a royal *cédula* to the *corregidor* dated 19/29 May, which ordered him to embargo all Dutch, German and English ships in the province, so that the best could be chosen for a fleet then being assembled at Lisbon and Seville. Only French vessels were to be exempted, for they were too small to be of use.

The *Primrose* reached London on 8/18 June.[1] Several days later the Privy Council deputed two men to interrogate the four Spaniards: the experienced diplomat Henry Killigrew and Arthur Atye, chief secretary to Robert Dudley, earl of Leicester. Atye, who had accompanied John Man on his unfortunate embassy to Philip II in the 1560s, had some fluency in Spanish and appears to have conducted the questioning. It was, understandably enough, concerned mainly with what lay behind the embargo: what was Philip II's purpose, had he issued any further instructions, why was he preparing a fleet, how strong was his navy, what were his intentions in France? Equally understandably, the four Spaniards had no idea, though one had heard a rumour that an English captain (not Sir Francis Drake) was planning to intercept the American *flotas* and that the king was assembling a fleet to protect them. He also reported speculation in Bilbao that an alliance had been formed between Philip II, the pope, the Holy Roman Emperor and the duke of Guise to safeguard catholicism in France, and that the king of France was a secret member of it. Otherwise the embargo was a mystery.[2]

Following the *Primrose* came further reports of seizures of English shipping and merchandise in Spain.[3] The major ports later claimed to have suffered considerable financial losses: London the largest (£39,000), followed by Ipswich and Bristol (both £29,000), while a further six towns reported smaller sums.[4] The English reaction was swift. A counter-embargo was imposed on Spanish shipping in England and four of the queen's ships sent to patrol the Narrow Seas. A further eight major warships were rigged and partially manned. On 20/30 June a commission was drafted — initially to Carew Ralegh, but in the event to Bernard Drake — to sail to the Newfoundland banks to warn English fishermen there not to take their cargoes to Spain. Then, 'by virtue of this our commission', Drake was to seize such Spanish fishing vessels as he could find and bring them to England.[5] Early in July the Privy Council drew up instructions for the issuing of letters of reprisal to merchants who claimed to have had ships or goods embargoed.[6] The first, according the file of recognizances entered into by the recipients, was issued on 12/22 July. With the exception of eight (two to Dutch shipowners) authorising the blockade of Dunkirk and the Flemish coast in October and November 1585, these letters of reprisal remained the sole type of privateering licence granted by the English government between July 1585 and March 1586.[7]

I

The most dramatic response, however, was the setting out of a fleet under the command of Sir Francis Drake — an expedition that later became celebrated as the West Indies Voyage. With these measures the nineteen-year long undeclared war at sea between England and Spain began. However, no little controversy has arisen over the purpose of the embargo and its relationship to the West Indies Voyage. The earliest connection was made by Drake himself, who announced to the local Spanish officials after his landing at Bayona on the coast of Galicia on 27 September/7 October 1585 that he had come to free the English merchants held there.[8] The same point was made more formally by Sir Christopher Hatton in a speech to the House of Commons on 22 February/6 March 1587 blaming Philip II for the outbreak of hostilities:

Concerning Mr. Drake's last voyage it was to meet with the restraints and seizures in Spain and there purpose was thereupon discovered; for there was found by the Master of Mr. Bonds Ship who took the Corrigedore, and others, a Commission from the King of Spain, whereby he termed us his Rebels, as he termed the Low Countries.[9]

None of the surviving contemporary accounts of the West Indies Voyage supply any information as to its aim, but Sir William Monson's early seventeenth-century commentary claimed it was to revenge wrongs (including the embargo) and to interrupt Spanish preparations.[10]

Modern scholarship has produced more varied explanations. In his introduction to *Papers relating to the Navy during the Spanish War 1585–1587*, Sir Julian Corbett claimed that the embargo was intended 'for the purposes of the expedition which Philip was preparing against England'. It produced a violent reaction among the merchants in the Iberian trade, and in response to popular pressure the queen released Drake.

Drake's orders were to proceed to the ports where the English prizes were detained and to procure their release. What further instructions he had is not known. Even what his intentions were has hitherto been very doubtful . . . [but] we can now see it as a thoroughly well conceived, if ambitious, design to destroy the source of Spanish transatlantic commerce and ruin her colonial empire.[11]

This argument was repeated in his later *Drake and the Tudor Navy*, but certain points were amplified. Corbett had since discovered that Drake had been planning a major voyage in 1584, apparently to attack Spanish possessions under the flag of the Portuguese pretender Dom António. Drake had received a commission for this voyage from Elizabeth on Christmas Eve 1584, but during the following spring the queen had drawn back. The embargo forced her hand: Drake received a new commission on 1/11 July, 'ostensibly for the release of the embargoed ships, but . . . Drake's real objective was the Plate Fleet and the West Indies'.[12]

K. R. Andrews' *Elizabethan Privateering* begins with the 1585 embargo, but does not go further into its causes and effects other than to note its decisive impact on the English Iberian merchants, hitherto a strong lobby against the provoking of Spain, and to suggest that the West Indies Voyage and Sir Walter Ralegh's Virginia expedition of the spring of 1585 were 'complementary' aspects of a major privateering campaign in which Drake's aim was to capture Cartagena and then to control the Isthmus of Panama.[13] However, in his more detailed study of the expedition in *Drake's Voyages*, Andrews raised some important caveats. He was less convinced of the degree of 'co-ordination' in the English maritime campaign, and he queried whether the embargo had anything to do with the Enterprise of England. He also noted that the proposed 1584 voyage had intended to go to the Moluccas, while for that of 1585: '[Drake] was authorised merely to make a demonstration on the Spanish coast to secure the release of the arrested merchantmen. For the rest he may have had secret instructions, but these have never come to light. . . . It would appear therefore that much was left to Drake's discretion.'[14]

In the introduction to her edition of the journals of the West Indies Voyage M. F. Keeler follows Corbett and Andrews. Drake's Moluccas Voyage was suspended in the spring of 1585, and then revived after the embargo with the commission of 1/11 July: 'The ostensible purpose, as his stop in Bayona shows, was to secure the release of the embargoed ships, but he also wanted to meet the treasure fleets and then to ransack various Spanish ports in the Caribbean area. . . .'[15]

The recent accounts of the Armada have advanced several further interpretations. According to Colin Martin and Geoffrey Parker, the embargo was intended to 'frighten Elizabeth into breaking off her negotiations with the Dutch and ending her support for privateering at Iberian expense'. Drake had been preparing a voyage to the Pacific in 1584, but was now redeployed and his attack on Bayona and Vigo 'seems to have been, for Philip II, the last straw — the final proof that the English problem could no longer be deferred'.[16] Peter Pierson reaches a similar conclusion about the purpose of the embargo, but discovered Drake outfitting at Plymouth for a voyage to the Caribbean when 'he received a new commission to sail for Spain and attempt to force the release of embargoed English merchantmen'.[17] Carlos Gómez-Centurión has proposed a novel explanation for the embargo. Its author was Cardinal Granvelle, always a believer in the effectiveness of economic warfare, and its target was Dutch trade with Spain. The English and the Germans were included largely because it was believed that they were carrying contraband Dutch cargoes.[18]

The debate over Drake's plans, intentions and commissions is not unique to the West Indies Voyage; similar controversy surrounds all his major expeditions. Not the least of the difficulties is that created by the fragmentary nature of the surviving archives of the Elizabethan navy.[19]

For Drake's 'commissions' of Christmas Eve 1584 and 1/11 July 1585 Corbett relied on versions recited in a commission Drake himself issued which was preserved among the Drake papers at Nutwell Court.[20] His intentions he deduced from a document dated 25 April/5 May 1586, which will be discussed below. The two 'commissions', together with a further warrant of 29 July/8 August 1584, were first published by Keeler from the texts recited, following the established practice, at the head of the account for the money the queen had supplied submitted by Drake's heirs to the Exchequer in 1596.[21] She appears to have been unaware, however, that the originals of these warrants, and a number of related documents, also survive. They had probably been attached to the account, but were later separated and then filed in a minor class of the State Papers in the Public Record Office.[22]

Examination of these warrants (the first two under the privy seal, the third under the sign manual) reveals immediately that none of them can be considered a commission. Nor does that of 1/11 July 1585 make any reference to freeing English shipping in Spain. It is clear, therefore, that the intentions of both the 1584 and the 1585 voyages, as well as the embargo, demand re-consideration. There are three central questions to be answered: what is known of the planning of the Voyage prior to the receipt of the news of the embargo in England in June 1585; the motive for the embargo; and, lastly, the impact of the embargo on the Voyage. These will be addressed in turn.

II

Two technical points deserve attention first. Hatton's claim (echoed by Richard Hackluyt) that the *cédula* brought to England by the *Primrose* deliberately included England among Philip II's rebels is based on a mis-reading (wilful or not) of an admittedly clumsy Spanish text. The text refers to ships of 'Olanda, Zelanda, Osterlanda, Aleman[i]a, Yngalaterra, y delos otros estados y señorios mios que estan rebelados de mi servicio excepto los de Francia'.[23] The other *cédulas* distinguish clearly between the shipping of the rebel Dutch and that of other nations.[24]

The second point is the role of Spanish intelligence reports, both as sources for English preparations and as the inspiration for the embargo. They deserve some comment. By the 1580s, Philip II, as his frequent letters on the subject make clear, gave the highest priority to information on English maritime activities, and particularly those of Drake.[25] His ambassador in England, Don Bernardino de Mendoza, was an enthusiastic gatherer of intelligence, but in January 1584 he was expelled and neither Elizabeth nor Philip were prepared to make the concessions necessary to re-establish diplomatic relations.[26] From Paris, where he was re-posted, Mendoza continued his efforts. His best agent in England was Pedro de Zubiaur, who had been sent to London by the consuls of Seville in 1580 to negotiate the restitution of Drake's plunder from the Circumnavigation Voyage.[27] In May 1585, however, following the interception of letters to the duke of Parma, Zubiaur was arrested, and throughout the crucial summer months Mendoza's intelligence was limited.[28] Moreover, even Zubiaur was unable to provide much information about the Anglo-Dutch negotiations. Ironically, the position improved in the autumn of 1585, when the Portuguese pretender Dom António arrived in England, for there were long-established Spanish agents in his household.[29]

The background to the '1584 Voyage' is the most diffuse, owing not only to the fragmentary evidence, but also to the need to take the evolution of Elizabethan foreign policy and strategic thinking into account.[30] The immediate origins of the Voyage can be traced back to the summer and autumn of 1583. In September 1583 the London merchant William Bird sent the earl of Leicester a globe and a map:

> understanding that your lordship hath lately been minding to make a great venture by sea from hence unto the South Sea and by that way to open a trade to the countries of Cathay and the Moluccas.[31]

This confirms slightly earlier Spanish reports that Leicester was planning a voyage to the Moluccas under Martin Frobisher.[32] This was Leicester's second attempt. The first, the 'Fenton Voyage', had tried to reach the Moluccas via the Cape of Good Hope, and, failing to do so, had returned to England in June 1583.[33] The new voyage was to follow Drake's old route to the Pacific; in the early months of 1584 Drake himself was reported as preparing a voyage to the Pacific via the Straits of Magellan.[34]

The English interest in the Moluccas was of comparatively recent date (1580), but it had two quite distinct inspirations. Drake's report of his negotiations with the sultan of Ternate on his return from the Circumnavigation Voyage had opened a prospect of direct English commercial contact with the East Indies.[35] However, the simultaneous Spanish annexation of Portugal provided an alternative means of access to the Spice Islands through the encouragement of the defection of the Portuguese colonies to the pretender Dom António. The importance of Dom António and Portugal to Elizabethan policy has not received the attention it deserves. The argument that Portuguese naval resources enabled Philip II for the first time to pose a serious maritime threat to England was less important than the opportunity Portugal offered (in combination with the Netherlands) for an alliance with France against the 'ambitions' of Philip II.[36] This was the central issue in the major debate provoked by the growing tension between England and Spain: was Philip II's hostility motivated by religion (as leader of a 'Catholic League' which the king of France might well join), or was he pursuing the Imperial designs of the house of Austria (in which case the king of France would be an ally of England)?

If Spain was confronted by an alliance of England and France, then much of the burden of the war would be shouldered by the French. If, on the other hand, there was a Catholic League in existence, England would be faced with a war against the kings of both France and Spain, with only the German Protestant states, the Dutch rebels and the Huguenots as allies. The imbalance of resources in such a conflict was a powerful incentive to a cautious and even isolationist foreign policy. An open challenge to Spain was foolhardy, as Sir Francis Walsingham himself had observed in 1571.[37] An answer to the dilemma emerged in the 1570s and soon became one of the clichés of Elizabethan strategy. This was the argument that the might of Philip II depended in the main on his American treasure and thus on sea-communications that were highly vulnerable to attack. As early as 1570 John Hawkins had advocated lying in wait for the American *flotas* off the Azores.[38] By the end of the decade a maritime offensive against Spain's communications with the Americas had become an essential corollary to a policy of opposition to Spain over the Netherlands. For those who, like Walsingham, argued that the Catholic League made it impossible for Elizabeth I to avoid supporting the Dutch rebels, a maritime war was the only means of redressing the balance of resources. In 1586 Lord Burghley recalled that 'sending some ships to impeach the Spanish king towards his Indyes . . . is a matter that many yers past I did project to the prince of Oranges ministers to have been attempted'.[39] The Circumnavigation Voyage exercised a decisive influence on the evolution of this offensive naval strategy, for, by revealing the weak defences of the Spanish Americas, it proved, apparently conclusively, that it would work.[40]

The years 1580 to 1584 form a phase of particular complexity in

Elizabethan foreign policy. The central issue was whether a viable alliance against Spain in both the Netherlands and Portugal could be made with France; on failing to obtain such an alliance Elizabeth refused to assist Dom António any further than by allowing her subjects to accept his letters of marque.[41] In 1584, however, the course of events forced the pace. The discovery of the Throckmorton Plot in 1583, with its plan for a Catholic rising backed by a Spanish landing, led to a brief invasion panic early in February 1584. Lord Burghley, in bed with gout, drew up a plan for a defensive naval mobilisation to counter a possible invasion during the summer, and in the following month an existing arrangement with William of Orange for the supply of Dutch warships in an emergency was confirmed.[42] More dramatic still were the deaths of the duke of Anjou and William of Orange in June and July of 1584: a decision over policy towards the Netherlands was now unavoidable.

During the twelve months from August 1584 until the making of the treaties of Nonsuch in August and September 1585 the question of military intervention in the Netherlands to prevent a total collapse of the shaken States-General was the central issue of English foreign policy. The stages of the evolution of the policy of intervention are of importance. The Privy Council assumed from the outset that Philip II would regard military intervention as a *casus belli*, and that a full-scale war would result if Elizabeth responded to Dutch appeals for aid. The queen's own preference was for intervention in alliance with France. When it became clear that Henry III was not interested in combining forces, the Privy Council held a major conference on Netherlands policy on 10/20 October 1584. The Council weighed carefully the arguments for and against a war with Spain and reached the apparently unanimous conclusion that one was inevitable, and that it was better to fight it with the Dutch as allies, rather than after they had been reconquered.[43] The queen was therefore advised that if the French did not assist the Netherlands independently, she would have no alternative but to do so herself. It was not until the beginning of March 1585, however, that Henry III made it clear that he would neither accept the sovereignty of the Netherlands nor intervene in any other form. Immediately thereafter an informal offer of English assistance was made to the Dutch, but it took another month before they responded. There then ensued, to mounting English impatience, a further delay while the individual provinces were consulted. English military preparation began in May, but it was not until the end of the month that the envoys for the States-

General received their commissions.[44] Their passage to England was further delayed by bad weather and they did not land in London until 24 June/4 July, several weeks after the return of the *Primrose*. Serious negotiations over the treaties did not begin until early July.

The summer of 1584 also initiated a new phase in the planning of Drake's voyage. On 20/30 July John Hawkins wrote to Burghley to propose a major privateering campaign against the Spanish empire under Dom António's flag.[45] His letter begins with the now standard premiss 'that the greatest traffic of all King Phillip's dominions must pass to and fro by sea, which will hardly escape intercepting'. He then proceeds to describe how a large-scale privateering war in Europe and the Americas would cripple Spain economically, and suggests that: 'The voyage offered by Sir Francis Drake might best be made lawful to go under that licence also, which would be secret till the time draw near of their readiness'. It is difficult to tell from the letter itself whether it was solicited, or, if not, what inspired it. Hawkins makes no reference to the death of the prince of Orange, and specifically (if optimistically) states that this campaign 'shall not by any means draw the King of Spain to offer a war', so it is doubtful that it was associated with intervention in the Netherlands. It may, however, have been a contribution to a debate over naval strategy initiated by the defensive mobilisation Burghley had proposed earlier in the year.

The involvement of Dom António, then resident in France, deserves comment. Since the loss of Terceira in 1583 Dom António had become steadily more attracted by the idea of a general privateering war against Spain and had discussed it with Richard Hakluyt, the maritime publicist, then chaplain to the English ambassador in Paris. In the autumn of 1584 Dom António's agent in the Netherlands began issuing letters of marque in quantity.[46] Nor was Hakluyt his only contact with England at this point; there was also the Portuguese physician at the English court, Ruy Lopez, and the shadowy Captain Edward Prynne, a servant of Leicester's.[47] Precisely what Hawkins meant by making Drake's voyage 'lawful to go under that licence' is not entirely clear; but the despatch of the voyage to the Straits of Magellan under Dom António's flag had been proposed earlier in the year.[48] It may be assumed, therefore, that by this stage the voyage had abandoned any initial commercial purpose, and may now have been intended to regain the Portuguese East Indies for Dom António.

Nine days later the queen became involved. On 29 July/8 August 1584 a privy seal warrant was directed to the Exchequer to pay out

£10,000 on the instructions of a commission consisting of Burghley, Walsingham and Lord Howard of Effingham 'to be issued from time to time in our causes and affairs as by them . . . shall be further ordered and assigned'.[49] This money, it is clear from other evidence, was the queen's investment in the voyage. It was fairly rapidly distributed: £6,600 to Drake, £2,400 to Hawkins, £550 to Carew Ralegh and £450 to William Hawkins.[50] The scale of the enterprise and extent of the preparations by the end of the year are outlined in a paper endorsed by Burghley 'The charge of the voyage to the Moluccas', and dated 24 November/4 December 1584.[51] It was to involve a substantial fleet (eleven ships, four barks and twenty pinnaces), carrying 1600 men, 500 of whom were to be soldiers. The total cost was estimated at £40,000. The queen was to provide both the £10,000 in cash and (now) ships worth £7,000, while the adventurers were to raise the remaining £23,000. By this date, however, they had only obtained £14,900, Drake himself contributing the largest share (£7,000), followed by Leicester (£3,000), Hawkins (£2,500), Sir Christopher Hatton and William Hawkins (both £1,000) and Walter Ralegh (£400).

The immediate context of this document is no clearer than that of Hawkins' earlier letter, but it may have been inspired by a request from Drake for a further subsidy from the crown to make up the remaining £8,100. K. R. Andrews has seen in the substantial number of soldiers and the absence of any reference to an investment in merchandise evidence that it was now definitely a voyage of war and no longer one of commerce.[52] Burghley's reference to a voyage to the Moluccas would appear to confirm the earlier suggestion that it was aimed at the Portuguese East Indies.

This phase of the preparations was brought to an end by a second privy seal warrant, dated 23 December 1584/2 January 1585.[53] It consists of three main clauses: an acknowledgement that a fleet of eleven ships, four barks and twenty pinnaces had been prepared 'to go under the conduction of Sir Francis Drake'; a confirmation that the adventurers would receive shares of the profit proportional to their investment; and, thirdly, a guarantee that should Elizabeth halt the voyage 'upon any consideration', the adventurers would suffer no financial loss, 'so as, the whole provision and things prepared be at our disposition to use and convert the same at our pleasure'. It is impossible to accept this warrant as a commission; essentially it was a guarantee of compensation should Elizabeth suspend the voyage, which may have been inspired by Drake's memory of Elizabeth's cancellation of the previous plans to aid Dom António in 1581.[54] But in exchange for such compensation, Elizabeth was now empowered to employ the expedition as she chose; henceforth it was to some degree under her control.

At the beginning of 1585 the voyage was indeed suspended and Drake took the opportunity to marry his second wife.[55] The reasons for the suspension probably lie in the diplomatic situation. It is possible that Elizabeth wished to avoid an unnecessary provocation to Philip II at this difficult juncture. It is more likely that the departure of Drake and his fleet on a voyage that would have lasted at least a year was now regarded as unwise. During the debate on the Netherlands in the previous October Burghley had noted one of England's assets to be 'the facility to offend the king of Spain by a power of the seas that may consist both of her majesty and of her people that will adventure'.[56] Should hostilities break out Drake and his fleet would be better employed directly against the Spanish empire than in the East Indies.

Between January and June 1585 little information about the expedition or the state of its preparations can be found in English sources. It was not, however, the only maritime project then under discussion. An undated memorandum in Walsingham's hand, entitled 'A plot for the annoying of the king of Spain', proposed an attack on the Spanish Newfoundland fishing fleet, which, he claimed, would cause Spain major losses of ships and mariners as well as foodstuffs.[57] A reference to 'the end of April' as being the best time to put the plan into operation suggests it originated during the winter of 1584–85. Walsingham had no doubt that Philip II would 'repute it an open act of hostility'; therefore he also proposed that it be followed by 'the enterprise for the Indias [sic]'. This scheme was in fact put into effect immediately after the embargo in the form of Bernard Drake's voyage.

The expedition to Virginia organised by Ralegh and commanded by Sir Richard Grenville has attracted more attention. Grenville left Plymouth on 9/19 April 1585 and took the usual route to the West Indies via the Canaries, reaching Dominica a month later. During May and June, in order to obtain supplies (especially cattle) for his settlement, he undertook wary negotiations with the Spanish authorities on Puerto Rico and Hispaniola, at one stage seizing a Spanish ship and holding its crew and passengers as hostages. After causing great concern in Havana (where the annual *flotas* would assemble), he departed in June for Virginia, which he reached in July. Only on his return to England in August did he capture a Spanish vessel, a straggler from the *flota* of New Spain. On sighting him it had fired a signal gun; this, Grenville later claimed, was aimed at his ship and led him to retaliate. However spurious his justification may have been, this was the first openly hostile act of the voyage.[58] Although Drake was clearly aware of this voyage and its destination, it cannot be considered part of a coordinated naval campaign, but only a private colonising venture by Ralegh. Even the letter that Ralph Lane (the commander left in Virginia) wrote to Sir Philip Sidney in August, describing the potential of the settlement as a base to attack the West Indies, refers to hostilities with Spain as potential rather than actual.[59]

News of Grenville's activities in the West Indies did not reach Spain until July.[60] However Zubiaur had followed his and Drake's preparations closely. From his information, Mendoza reported the suspension of Drake's voyage on 22 February, but also that its target was now the West Indies where it was intended to intercept the ships of the *flotas* before they assembled at Havana and possibly to capture Nombre de Dios. At the beginning of April Mendoza informed the king of Grenville's imminent departure and the continued suspension of Drake. Only on 24 April did he write that the queen's ship *Red Lion* [*sic*], Leicester's *Galleon Leicester* and the London ship *Primrose* were being fitted out for an expedition Drake was to lead against the *flotas*.[61]

Mendoza's reports were, however, overtaken by one that Zubiaur sent directly to the Casa de Contratación to the effect that Drake was preparing to depart for the West Indies in May to intercept the *flotas*.[62] It was received in Seville in the middle of March and counter measures were quickly put in hand; in April the marquis of Santa Cruz began assembling a fleet of thirty ships at Lisbon to meet the *flotas* at Havana and escort them home.[63] It was his failure to obtain adequate shipping that inspired the initial embargo — as the reference to the assembling of a fleet at Lisbon in the *cédula* makes clear. This type of embargo was simply the established right of the king to take ships and crews into his service. The resistance of the *Primrose* to what Philip regarded as the exercise of a legitimate prerogative and the 'kidnapping' of Guevara provoked him to retaliate with a further restraint specifically of English ships and goods in June.[64] The embargo itself had nothing to do with either the Enterprise of England or the Anglo-Dutch negotiations (about which Mendoza was able to discover very little); it was simply a response to sudden fears of an English attack on the *flotas*.[65]

In the event, even with the embargo Santa Cruz was unable to assemble his fleet. His failure and the reduction in intelligence from

England following Zubiaur's arrest caused Philip much anxiety over the safety of the *flotas* during the summer of 1585.[66] He was saved by the long delay in Drake's departure. The state of Drake's preparations when the *Primrose* returned to London is unknown, but there is some important evidence about the fitting out of the *Elizabeth Bonaventure* and the *Aid*, the two warships the queen contributed to the voyage. The earliest surviving reference to their assignment to Drake is a warrant of 12/22 June for supplying them with ordnance. However, between 11/21 May and 22 May/2 June they had been brought from Chatham to the dockyard at Woolwich for repair in the course of a routine refitting of seven of the queen's ships that took place between April and June. This dockyard activity may have inspired Mendoza's report of 24 April, but it may also have been the case that these two ships were not given to Drake until after the *Primrose*'s return, and that he then had to wait for their refitting to be completed.[67]

On 1/11 July the queen signed the third warrant.[68] This made no reference to the embargo, but declared that Drake 'hath made offer unto us of some special service to be by him executed, tending greatly to the benefit of us and our realm'. To this others had subscribed, 'yet upon some doubts conceived by them, that the same service shall not go forward, they are loath (as we are informed) to yield their contributions'. Therefore the queen announced 'our good liking of the offer of the said service and to assure our loving subjects that our meaning is not only that the said Sir Francis Drake shall proceed to the execution of the said service', but also that the contributors would receive their previously agreed profits from the voyage.

On 11/21 July the Privy Council issued a circular letter to all mayors of port towns empowering Drake to impress seamen 'for a voyage he intendeth . . . to make into foreign parts'.[69] He was expected to have left Woolwich with his ships on 15/25 July, but did not sign the indenture for the receipt of the queen's ordnance until 17/27 July, another indenture for further munitions until after 21/31 July, and a final one for the queen's ships and money until 30 July/9 August.[70] Precisely when he reached Plymouth is not clear, Spanish reports placed him off the Isle of Wight early in August, and in Plymouth by 6/16 August, but many of his ships were still in London on 11/21 August.[71] Nor is the long delay before his final departure from Plymouth on 14/24 September explained. The weather was probably chiefly responsible, both in delaying the voyage to Plymouth and in keeping Drake there, but hesitations by the queen (referred to both in the warrant of 1/11 July and in Drake's reported comments at Plymouth) may also have played a role.[72]

It is equally clear that the departure from London was made in great haste, and that a further halt in England was necessary to take in stores.[73] Also revealing is a second circular from the Privy Council of 11/21 August, rehearsing his powers of impressment, and ordering local authorities to imprison men deserting his fleet.[74] Drake was expected to have left England before the end of August; indeed he himself appears constantly worried that the queen might cancel the voyage entirely. For this reason even the final departure was made in haste.[75] There is, however, no evidence that the unexpected arrival of Sir Philip Sidney at Plymouth at the end of August made any difference one way or the other.[76]

III

The departure from Plymouth provides a suitable occasion for summarising what can be stated about Drake's instructions at that point. His 1596 account (albeit a posthumous one) refers to the voyage as being: 'so authorised and warranted successively from time to time by sundry her majesty's orders and directions as hereafter upon every occurence verbatim is rehearsed'.[77] It then recites the three warrants of 29 July/8 August 1584, 23 December 1584/2 January 1585 and 1/11 July 1585 discussed above. In none of these is the voyage described in anything but veiled terms; nor do they mention its destination or the release of English shipping held in Spain. At no later stage in the voyage is Drake recorded as referring to any now-missing commission or to written instructions, with the exception of his announcement at Bayona that he was under the queen's orders. This was in direct contrast to Bernard Drake, who was specifically granted a commission to seize Spanish shipping off Newfoundland in retaliation for the embargo, and may have been quite deliberate. In March 1586, when one of the earl of Leicester's followers defended his acceptance of the governor-generalship of the Netherlands on the grounds that Drake's voyage would be a greater provocation to Philip II, Elizabeth made the well-known answer, 'if need be the gentleman careth not if I should disavow him', which would have been impossible had he held a formal commission.[78] Her decision to proceed in this manner is probably best explained by her fear that Drake's activities might jeopardise a possible peace settlement, if one could be made with Philip II in the meantime.[79]

In the absence of either commission or instructions we are left with only the records of the voyage itself as a possible guide to its purpose. The key questions are two: the purpose of the landing at Bayona, and the role of the interception of the *flotas* in his plans. The answer to the first is a straightforward one: the anchoring in the roadstead of Bayona on 27 September/7 October was purely accidental. Drake had decided to shelter there from an approaching storm rather than risk the dispersal of his fleet. The fortnight the fleet remained there (from 27 September/7 October to 11/21 October) enabled him to redistribute stores and replenish supplies. The need to do so was a consequence of his hasty departure, but there is no evidence that had the weather been favourable he would have broken his journey at this point specifically to do so. Finally, according to Christopher Carleill, the commander of the soldiers, 'which was not the last, to make our proceedings known to the king of Spain, if he may find and see more apparently that we nothing fear any intelligence he hath gotten by all the espials he hath either in England or elsewhere'.[80] This act of bravado, of a type to which Drake was notoriously prone, clearly reflects English appreciation that the destination of his fleet was a matter of major concern in Spain. But Carleill was also writing after the fact; Drake did not stop to make a bravado, nor indeed would the circumstances for it would have arisen had not he encountered the governor of Bayona, Don Pedro Bermúdez de Santiso, on the day that he arrived.[81]

The governor's dispatch of a pinnace to contact the strangers forced Drake to reciprocate by sending one of his officers. The speech he was to deliver is curious: Drake was sent 'from Her Majesty' to demand the reasons why Philip II was embargoing English ships; if Philip meant by it an act of war then Drake would respond in like manner. The speech does not mention a specific commission to this effect, nor is it clear that Drake believed that any Englishmen were held in Bayona. While there was still genuine confusion in England over Philip's purpose, owing to the failure of a declaration of war to follow the embargo, it is difficult to see the speech as anything more than cobbled together to intimidate the Spanish audience.[82] As it was, Bermúdez defused the situation by declaring that he had no power to declare either war or peace, that English merchants in Bayona were under no restraint, and (possibly to rid himself of Drake) that Drake was free to obtain food and water.

A major storm that lasted for several days then intervened.

Immediately afterwards ships were sighted near Vigo. Drake ordered that they be investigated, 'wherein might be some good things for our relief'. It turned out that they were filled with the household belongings of the inhabitants of Vigo, then in the process of fleeing from his approach. In the meantime some of his men, who had been landed to take on water, had begun pillaging. At this point Bermúdez summoned a further meeting: this resulted in a formal truce and an exchange of hostages, under which the English were permitted to continue re-supplying so long as they returned all Spanish property. This truce lasted until Drake departed on 11/21 October.

The significance of the landing at Bayona has thus been greatly distorted. It had nothing to do with instructions to free embargoed English vessels, for there is no evidence that any were ever issued; Drake's arrival at Bayona was accidental; and neither Bayona nor Vigo was sacked or even threatened. As Philip II himself observed, the damage done by Drake's fleet was minimal.[83] But no attempt had been made to do more; Drake, if wary, was perfectly happy to reach a *modus vivendi* with the governor, as Grenville had been in the West Indies several months previously.

Nonetheless Drake had lost a further two weeks. Thereafter he made his way directly southward towards a destination identified to the fleet on 21/31 October as the Canaries.[84] At this point he also lost contact with England. Carleill's letter to Walsingham of the 11th/21st was the last received from the fleet until Drake himself wrote to Burghley on entering the Channel on 26 July/5 August 1586.[85] In the meantime all the English government learnt of his progress came from continental (i.e. ultimately Spanish) sources. This appears to have been expected, for in January 1586 Burghley wrote that no word had been received from Drake since he 'departed from the coast of Spain . . . neither do we look to hear afore March'.[86] In the Canaries Drake attempted to land at Palma (3/13 November), but was beaten off; a landing at Hierro on the following day was discussed and rejected. Thereafter he proceeded to the Cape Verdes and on the 17/27–18/28 November took Santiago, his first really hostile action, and possibly a response to the rebuff at Palma. On 29 November/9 December the fleet departed for the West Indies. This phase of the voyage is particularly curious. Drake was more aggressive than he had been in Spain, yet also unwilling to waste unnecessary time. Neither group of islands was particularly rich, and could not have been a high priority of the voyage. Drake's primary motive appears to have been the securing of further supplies for the westward journey.

The slender evidence for Drake's intentions in this and the later phase of the voyage comes from two difficult sources. His 1586 letter to Burghley adopts a defensive tone from the start: the expedition 'had lacked no possible travail or diligence which might anyway belong to the handling of so great a dispatch'. However, Drake then added: 'I will make it most apparent unto your honour that it escaped us but twelve hours the whole treasure which the King of Spain had out of the Indies this last year, the cause best known to God; and we had at that instant very foul weather'.[87] This comment raises the key question of the extent to which the interception of one of the *flotas* was intended, and, if so, where and when. Sir Julian Corbett suggested that Drake was referring to the period in May 1586 when he was hovering off Havana.[88] Yet 'this last year' would appear to apply more obviously to 1585. However, after leaving Bayona Drake set off directly south; he made no attempt to linger off the Spanish coast, nor did he display much interest in obtaining intelligence en route.[89]

On 28 October/7 November Drake encountered a French privateer off the Canaries, who informed him that one of the *flotas* had been sighted off Cape St. Vincent several weeks before.[90] The *flota* of New Spain had in fact arrived in August, but the *flota* of *Tierra Firme* was delayed by bad weather until 18 October. In September Philip II had expressed relief that Drake's continued presence in Plymouth would enable the *flotas* to escape him. The tone of Drake's comment certainly reads like an excuse for both the delay in Plymouth and at Bayona. Cardinal Granvelle later observed that Drake's halt at Bayona had saved the *flota* of *Tierra Firme*; but how Drake would have known he missed it by half a day is still not clear.[91]

The second document is no more straightforward. 'A Discourse of Sir Francis Drake's Voyage' is an anonymous itinerary dated 25 April/5 May 1586, which Corbett has described as 'the plan of the campaign'.[92] It is written in two different moods. The first section recites the events of the voyage to the sack of Santiago in the historic past tense and relatively accurately.[93] It could not have come from a member of the expedition, for no communication had been received since the departure from Bayona. On the other hand by April 1586 many of the events of the previous autumn could have been pieced together from Carleill's letter and general reports. The latter half of the letter is written in the subjunctive and describes a route round the West Indies which Drake 'might arrive and proceed by conjecture as follows'. It is considerably less accurate than the first section. Far from being a secret plan provided by an intimate of Drake's, it reads like a purely speculative essay on the route Drake might take, having arrived in the West Indies, written by someone (Hawkins?) with a competent knowledge of Caribbean navigation.

There is no reason to query the general conclusion that the epidemic that struck the fleet after its departure from the Cape Verdes may have forced Drake to revise his more ambitious plans.[94] Nevertheless, if the sacking of Santo Domingo, Cartagena and St. Augustine provided spectacular propaganda, the voyage overall was still a strategic failure. The earl of Leicester commented when the first reports reached him at the end of July: 'it cannot be that he should spoil so many places and get no more. He would never go any more voyages if it be so. . . .'[95] There is no doubt that profits similar to those of the Circumnavigation Voyage were expected, but the disappointment was more serious than that. Walsingham's earlier observation that on the success of Drake's voyage 'dependeth the life and death of the cause according to man's judgement' indicates its true significance.[96] The 'cause' was the English intervention in the Netherlands; only a major maritime success by Drake would justify the strategy on which the intervention was based.

IV

Given Drake's tendency to make up his strategy as he went along, it is doubtful whether a definitive account of the evolution of the West Indies Voyage will ever be possible. But the evidence discussed here suggests a general outline. We can be relatively certain that it began at the end of 1583 as a voyage to the East Indies that may have been primarily commercial. During 1584 it developed into something more aggressive — probably an attack on the Portuguese East Indies under the flag of Dom António. At the beginning of 1585 this voyage was suspended and the expedition was taken into the queen's control. It is probable at this stage that some plan for attacking the *flotas* during their assembly in the West Indies, in conjunction with a military intervention in the Netherlands, was developed. Leicester, Burghley and Walsingham all referred to it in 1585 as a voyage to the Indies.[97] However, the delay in Drake's departure from England may have led to an attempt to intercept the *flotas* off the Spanish coast. Had he done so successfully, there can be little doubt that he would have returned to England immediately with his booty. However, his enforced halt at Bayona prevented him from catching the *flota* of *Tierra Firme*; he had no alternative but to return to the original plan for a voyage to the West Indies, although the season was then not propitious for the interception of major shipping.

The relationship of Drake's voyage to the embargo was thus coincidental, and the Bayona incident an accident that was largely irrelevant to its aims. More significant was the role reports of Drake's intentions played in inspiring it. The embargo did not change English policy decisively, for the negotiations with the States-General of the Netherlands were well in train, and these made a maritime campaign almost unavoidable.[98] It did, however, confirm Walsingham's long-held conviction that there was a Catholic League in existence. He noticed the exemption of the French from the *cédula* the *Primrose* brought to England, and drew the conclusion that it: 'cannot but be interpretid as a manifest argument of secreat intelligence and mutuall concurrency lykely to be betwin the French and the Spaniard, for the ruyne and overthrow of the professours of the Ghospell'.[99] Such 'evidence' of the hostility of Spain made it possible to justify the English intervention in the Netherlands as an act of self-defence; it is also possible that had it not been for the embargo, Elizabeth might have been more hesitant about embarking on a maritime war against the Spanish empire.

In making the position of anyone in England who wished to defend good relations with Spain impossible, the embargo can legitimately be described as a major miscalculation on Philip's part. Yet he was panicked into it by reports that England had in effect already gone to war against him. If the affair is a chapter of accidents, these accidents drew their significance from a climate in which both sides had more or less accepted that some form of conflict between them was practically inevitable. The effects of the West Indies Voyage itself were not dissimilar. There are good grounds for regarding the voyage as a Spanish success, for Drake failed to inflict any serious or lasting damage on the empire. But the bravado at Bayona and the fear that this was only the beginning of a wider maritime campaign led Philip to re-examine the case for an Enterprise of England. It was the threat rather than the reality of a major English privateering war that inspired both the embargo and the assembly of the *Gran Armada*.

NOTES

1. An account of the 'escape of the *Primrose*' is published in Hakluyt, VI, 413-18. Hakluyt included a translation of the *cédula*, the original of which is now PRO SP 94/2/78. The claim that the corregidor himself was captured which appears in Hakluyt and later English accounts is an error. Guevara identified himself as the lieutenant-general in his interrogation (see n. 2 below); see also *BMO*, I, pp. 487, 506.

2. PRO SP 12/179/28-38. The report (dated 13/23 June) is in Atye's hand.

3. See, for example, PRO SP 94/2/92-v, a letter from Roger Howe, an English merchant in Seville, 5/15 June 1585. For the immediate response to the *Primrose*'s return, see PRO, SP 12/179/15, the earl of Sussex to Sir Francis Walsingham, 9/19 June 1585. Walsingham relayed the news to Edward Wotton, the English ambassador in Scotland, on the 11th/21st: J. Bain (ed.), *The Hamilton Papers* (2 vols, Edinburgh, 1890-92) II, p. 650.

4. *Monson Tracts* I, pp. 125-6.

5. The draft instructions for Ralegh are PRO SP 94/2/96; for Drake, SP 12/179/48-9. The phrase quoted was added by Walsingham. The English naval preparations are drawn from PRO E 351/2221, the account of the treasurer of the navy (John Hawkins) for 1585.

6. PRO SP 12/180/40-v, endorsed 9/19 July, and printed in Corbett, *Spanish War*, pp. 36-8. Copies of further related correspondence of 9/19-10/20 July are found in Magdalene College, Cambridge, Pepys MS 2871 [Miscellaneous Collections III], pp. 171-6.

7. PRO HCA 25 [Bonds and Recognizances]/1, pt. 2 [unfoliated]. The main series of recognizances bound the shipowners to obey the regulations governing the letters of reprisal; a second (smaller) series bound those who had not done so already to supply proof of the losses they claimed to have suffered from the embargo.

8. This appears in both English and Spanish accounts, see Corbett, *Spanish War*, pp. 3, 43-4, and *BMO* I, pp. 518, 529, 530, 533.

9. S. D'Ewes (ed.), *A Compleat Journal of the Votes. Speeches and Debates, Both of the House of Lords and House of Commons throughout the whole Reign of Queen Elizabeth* (London, 1693), p. 409. The embargo was not specifically mentioned in *A Declaration of the causes mooving the queene to give aide in the low countries* (published in October 1585), as stated in Martin and Parker, p. 102.

10. *Monson Tracts* I, pp. 121-2.

11. Pp. xiii-iv. The English ambassador in France, Sir Edward Stafford, claimed in July 1585 that the embargo was intended for the Enterprise of England, *CSPVen*, VIII, p. 118.

12. Corbett, *Drake*, II, pp. 9-11, 19. He was followed by Oppenheim in *Monson Tracts*, I, 126.

13. K. R. Andrews, *Elizabethan Privateering: English Privateering during the Spanish War 1585–1603* (Cambridge, 1964) pp. 15, 191–2.

14. *Drake's Voyages: A Re-Assessment of their Place in Elizabethan Maritime Expansion* (London, 1967) pp. 110–12, 116.

15. M. F. Keeler (ed.), *Sir Francis Drake's West Indian Voyage 1585–86* (Hakluyt Society, 2nd ser, CXLVIII: 1981) pp. 9–11. J. Sugden, *Sir Francis Drake* (London, 1990) pp. 176–7, adds nothing new.

16. Martin and Parker, pp. 100–2, 111.

17. P. Pierson, *Commander of the Armada: The Seventh Duke of Medina Sidonia* (New Haven and London, 1989) pp. 55–6.

18. Gómez-Centurión, *Comercio*, pp. 187–9, 226. F. Fernández-Armesto, *The Spanish Armada: The Experience of War in 1588* (Oxford, 1988) pp. 78–9, argues that it was Elizabeth's intervention in the Netherlands that led Philip to undertake the Enterprise of England and does not comment on the embargo or the West Indies Voyage.

19. For the *lacunae* in the records of contemporary naval administration, see S. Adams, 'New Light on the "Reformation" of John Hawkins: The Ellesmere Naval Survey of January 1584', *English Historical Review*, CV (1990) pp. 96–111.

20. Corbett, *Drake*, II, pp. 9, 11.

21. Keeler, *West Indian Voyage*, pp. 50–9.

22. PRO SP 46 [State Papers, Supplementary] /17/159–81.

23. PRO SP 94/2/78. Cf. Hakluyt, VI, 418.

24. A *cédula* issued on 25 May (*BMO* I, p. 476) refers to the ships of the 'rebeldes de todos mis Estados, y de los esterlides y de Alemania y los de Inglaterra'; the order of 22 June for the general embargo of the English in reprisal for the escape of the *Primrose* referred to the earlier embargo as being simply of all ships in Spanish ports except the French (*Ibid.*, p. 487).

25. *BMO* I, pp. 436, 494, 498, 502.

26. Elizabeth sent William Waad to Spain in at the beginning of 1584 to explain the expulsion of Mendoza, but Philip refused to give him an audience. In turn Elizabeth refused to see an envoy from the duke of Parma, Ascanio Cifani, in January 1585.

27. *BMO* I, p. 321.

28. His interrogation (PRO SP 12/178/114–v) also revealed his correspondence with Mendoza. For Mendoza's difficulties, see *BMO* I, pp. 481, 493, 519.

29. For the importance of Mendoza's Portuguese agents in 1587–8, see below, p. 178.

30. Discussed in general in S. Adams, 'The Spanish Armada: The Lurch into War', *History Today*, XXXVIII (May 1988) pp. 19–25; reprinted in *Historia 16*, CXLVIII (August 1988) pp. 43–52. A more detailed account, on which what follows is based, will appear in my forthcoming work, *The Protestant*

Cause: Religion and the Making of English Foreign Policy, 1559–1630.

31. Bodleian Library, MS Tanner 79 f. 207.
32. *BMO* I, pp. 395–6. Frobisher later became vice-admiral of the West Indies Voyage.
33. E. G. R. Taylor (ed.) *The Troublesome Voyage of Captain Edward Fenton 1582–3* (Hakluyt Society, 2nd ser, CXIII: 1959); E. S. Donno (ed.), *An Elizabethan in 1582. The Diary of Richard Maddox, Fellow of All Souls* (Hakluyt Society, 2nd ser, CXLVII: 1976).
34. *BMO* I, p. 438, cf. 439–40.
35. Taylor, *Fenton Voyage*, pp. xxvii–iii, 12. See also Andrews, *Drake's Voyages*, pp. 100–1.
36. The case for the importance of Portuguese naval resources is made in R. B. Wernham, *Before the Armada* (London, 1966), pp. 356–7. G. K. McBride, 'Elizabethan Foreign Policy in Microcosm: the Portuguese Pretender, 1580–1589', *Albion*, V (1973) pp. 193–210, is not very perceptive.
37. D. Digges (ed.), *The Compleat Ambassador* (London, 1655) p. 127, to Leicester, 12 Aug. 1571.
38. Magdalene College, Cambridge, Pepys MSS, Letters of State, II, p. 371, to Leicester, 4 June 1570.
39. To Leicester, 31 Mar./11 Apr. 1586, printed in J. Bruce (ed.), *Correspondence of Robert Dudley, Earl of Leycester during his Government of the Low Countries . . . 1585 and 1586* (Camden Society, XXVII: 1844) [hereafter *Leycester Corres.*] p. 199. For an exposition of this strategy by Humphrey Gilbert in 1577, see D. B. Quinn and A. N. Ryan, *England's Sea Empire, 1550–1642* (London, 1983) pp. 84–5. For its influence in the early seventeenth century, see S. Adams 'Spain or the Netherlands? The Dilemmas of Early Stuart Foreign Policy', in H. Tomlinson (ed.), *Before the English Civil War* (London, 1983) p. 83, and 'Foreign Policy and the Parliaments of 1621 and 1624' in K. Sharpe (ed.), *Faction and Parliament* (Oxford, 1978) p. 151.
40. Such calculations failed to take into account the fact that the Spaniards would draw similar conclusions and increase the defences of the empire. Cf. P. E. Hoffman, *The Spanish Crown and the Defense of the Caribbean, 1535–1585: Precedent, Patrimonialism and Royal Parsimony* (Baton Rouge and London, 1980) esp. pp. 196–99.
41. Quinn and Ryan, *England's Sea Empire*, p. 87.
42. PRO SP 12/168/4–6, 'Memorial of divers things necessary to be thought of and to be put into execution for this summer', 3/13 Feb. 1584. Two copies of the agreement with the Dutch (3/13 Mar. 1584) survive: PRO SP 103/33/91–92 and ARA, Eerste Afdeling, De Regeringsarchieven van de Geünieerde . . . Provinciën, I–97. For the panic, see HMC, *Manuscripts of . . . the Duke of Rutland*, I (London, 1888), p. 160, and PRO SP 12/167/134.

43. The most important of the many papers produced by this meeting is the resolution of the council: PRO SP 83/23/59–60.

44. The procurations for the Dutch commissioners were issued on 27 May/6 June 1585: ARA, Eerste Afdeling, Regeringsarchieven, I–96.

45. BL, Lansdowne MS 43, fos. 20–1, printed in T. Wright (ed.), *Queen Elizabeth and Her Times* (2 vols, London, 1838), II, 231–4.

46. PRO SP 12/167/11v, Hakluyt to Walsingham, 7/17 Jan. 1584; SP 83/23/art. 6, Edmund York to Walsingham, 22 Sept./2 Oct. 1584. One of the recipients was William Fenner, see his deposition of 30 Mar./10 Apr. 1585: PRO SP 12/177/123. It is probable that most English privateers active in early 1585 were operating under these commissions; their numbers should not be exaggerated.

47. For Prynne's earlier involvement with Dom António, see his letter to Leicester of 16 November 1581: BL Cottonian MS Vespasian C VII f. 386. He was in Dom António's service in 1584; in April 1585 he was sent by Leicester to escort Dom António to England and arrived with him in September. See *CSPFor*, XIX, pp. 75, 303; P. Durand-Lapie, 'Un Roi Détroné Réfugié en France: Dom Antoine Ier de Portugal (1580–1595)', *Revue d'Historie Diplomatique*, XVIII (1904) p. 640; BL Cottonian MS Caligula E VII f. 257, Ruy Lopez to Leicester, 16/26 Apr. 1585; and HMC, *Rutland MSS*, I, pp. 179.

48. PRO SP 12/168/120–2.

49. PRO SP 46/17/170v.

50. PRO SP 46/17/178.

51. BL, Lansdowne MS 41 f. 9. This memorandum also reveals that £5,000 of the queen's money assigned to Drake had not yet been paid out. On 16/26 November, Christopher Carleill, the commander of the soldiers on the expedition, was summoned from Ireland, *CSP Ireland, 1574–85* (London, 1867) p. 537.

52. *Drake's Voyages*, p. 110.

53. PRO SP 46/17/159.

54. The warrant is identified as a commission in Corbett, *Drake*, II, 9; *Monson Tracts*, I, 125; Keeler, *West Indian Voyage*, p. 10.

55. E. Elliott-Drake, *The Family and Heirs of Sir Francis Drake* (2 vols., London, 1911) I, p. 67.

56. PRO SP 83/23/61.

57. PRO SP 12/177/153–4.

58. On Grenville's voyage, see A. L. Rowse, *Sir Richard Grenville of the 'Revenge'* (London, 1940) pp. 203–20, and D. B. Quinn (ed.), *The Roanoke Voyages, 1584–1590* (2 vols., Hakluyt Society, 2nd. ser. CIV: 1955) I, pp. 158–73.

59. Quinn, *Roanoke Voyages*, I, p. 205.

60. *BMO* I, pp. 486–7, 489–90.

61. *BMO* I, pp. 467–8, 469–70, 475–6. The Spanish interest was reported by Hakluyt in April, Quinn, *Roanoke Voyages*, I, p. 155.
62. *BMO* I, pp. 471–2. This news was also reported by the Venetian ambassador in Spain on 4/14 April, *CSPVen*, VIII, p. 114.
63. *BMO* I, pp. 473–4.
64. *Ibid.*, pp. 487–8. See also Croft below, pp. 241–2.
65. This was the conclusion drawn by the French and Venetian ambassadors in Spain, both of whom were very much interested in the purpose of the embargo. See A. Mousset (ed.), *Dépêches Diplomatiques de M. de Longlée, resident de France en Espagne* (1582–1590) (Paris, 1912) pp. 148, 150; *CSPVen*, VIII, pp. 115–18.
66. *BMO* I, pp. 494–5, 498.
67. The ordnance warrant is printed in Corbett, *Spanish War*, p. 28. For the refitting of the ships, see PRO E 351/2221 [Hawkins' account for 1585]; no details of Drake's preparations are found there, however, nor does his own account [E 351/2222] supply any. Leicester visited the *Galleon Leicester* at Woolwich on 15/25 May and 5/15 July, it was probably also fitting out there then; see his household account for 1584–85, Christ Church, Oxford, Evelyn MS 258b [unfoliated].
68. PRO SP 46/17/160.
69. PRO SP 46/17/172.
70. The indentures are found in Corbett, *Spanish War*, pp. 27–33, and PRO SP 46/17/166. For Drake's expected departure on the 15th/25th, see HMC, *Rutland MSS*, I, p. 177. On 20/30 July Arthur Atye informed Jean Hotman that Drake had been given permission to leave London: Paris, Archives du Ministère des Relations Extérieures, Correspondence Politique, Hollande, II f. 89. According to a shipwrights' report of 1588 the 'setting forth' of his ships occurred on the last of July, see Laughton, I, p. 44.
71. *BMO* I, pp. 495, 497, 503.
72. For the effect of the weather, see *ibid.*, pp. 524–5, but this may refer to period after Drake left Plymouth.
73. On the state of the stores see C. Carleill to Walsingham, 11 Oct. 1585, Corbett, *Spanish War*, pp. 41–2.
74. PRO SP 46/17/176.
75. Corbett, *Spanish War*, pp. 41–2, and pp. 83–4, Drake to Burghley, 26 July 1586. Carleill's comments in the Journal of *Tiger* (Keeler, *West Indian Voyage*, p. 72), repeat those in his letter to Walsingham.
76. As suggested by Corbett, *Drake*, II, 15–19.
77. Keeler, *West Indies Voyage*, p. 51.
78. *Leycester Corres.*, p. 173.
79. On 22 August/1 September 1585, instructions were drafted for Sir John Smythe to propose a settlement in the Netherlands to the duke of Parma, see PRO SP 77/1/73–77. These were cancelled on the 26th/5th, following

confirmation of the fall of Antwerp, see HMC, *Calendar of the Manuscripts of . . . the Marquess of Bath*, V (London, 1980), p. 45 [misdated to 1583].

80. Corbett, *Spanish War*, pp. 41–2, cf. *BMO* I, p. 523.

81. The following account is drawn from Carleill, both the letter to Walsingham (Corbett, *Spanish War*, pp. 42–9) and the *Tiger* journal (Keeler, *West Indian Voyage*, pp. 78–90). The 'Summarie and True Discourse' (Keeler, p. 219) refers to an intention to take Bayona by surprise, but it is not reliable. Cf. the reports of Bermúdez, *BMO* I, pp. 518, 533, and *CSPVen*, VIII, p. 124.

82. For an example of the confusion over the absence of a declaration of war, see PRO SP 12/180/56, Sir G. Carey to Walsingham, 15/25 July 1585.

83. *BMO* I, pp. 550–1. See also Martin and Parker, p. 111.

84. Keeler, *West Indian Voyage*, p. 92.

85. Corbett, *Spanish War*, pp. 83–5.

86. *Leycester Corres.*, pp. 51–2. For examples of Spanish reports in wider circulation, see *CSPVen*, VIII, pp. 127–32.

87. Corbett, *Spanish War*, pp. 83–4.

88. *Ibid.*, p. 84, n. 1.

89. See, for example, Keeler, *West Indian Voyage*, pp. 90–2, 184.

90. *Ibid.*, p. 184.

91. *BMO* I, pp. 540, 551.

92. Corbett, *Spanish War*, pp. 69–-74.

93. Keeler, following Corbett, notes that the attack on Palma was 'not on the original plan', *West Indian Voyage*, p. 93, n. 1.

94. Corbett, *Drake*, II, pp. 33, 50; Andrews, *Drake's Voyages*, p. 120; Keeler, *West Indian Voyage*, p. 29.

95. *Leycester Corres.*, p. 381.

96. *Ibid.*, p. 341.

97. For Walsingham, PRO SP 12/177/154; Leicester, *Leycester Corres.*, p. 48; Burghley, 'Diary' published in S. Haynes and W. Murdin (edd.), *Collection of State Papers . . . left by William Cecil, Lord Burghley* (2 vols., London, 1740–59), II, p. 783.

98. Cf. Croft below, pp. 241–2.

99. To Wotton, 11/21 June 1585, *Hamilton Papers*, II, p. 650.

3

THE SPANISH ARMADA: NAVAL WARFARE BETWEEN THE MEDITERRANEAN AND THE ATLANTIC

I. A. A. Thompson

The 1588 Armada was a key event in the history of naval warfare and a decisive moment in the historic shift in the balance of power from the Mediterranean to the Atlantic. It was a clash between two military systems; a clash between a country that was placing itself in the van of new modes of Ocean warfare and a power whose naval forces had hitherto been concentrated mainly in the Mediterranean and which had operated in a very different framework of military imperatives. For Spain, therefore, the Armada marked a radical change in her military profile and presented her with serious logistical and administrative problems. Whether or not those problems were resolved, and the means adopted for their solution, had important implications not only for the configuration of the *Gran Armada* and the military outcome of the campaign, but also, by altering the balance of the Spanish military and political system, for the internal articulation of the Spanish Monarchy.

The first years of the reign of Philip II saw a spectacular expansion of Spanish naval power in the Mediterranean. Charles V never had more than about forty operational galleys in regular commission; between 1562 and 1574 Philip II tripled the Mediterranean fleet. In the peak years of the 1570s, around 1574, Philip II was maintaining a fleet of over 140 galleys in the Mediterranean (the equivalent of some 25,000 *toneladas* of shipping) with a supporting squadron of roundships (in 1572 consisting of 68 *naves* of 23,500 *toneladas*). This fleet carried in excess of 45,000 men (about 7,000 sailors, 25,000 rowers, 15,000 regular infantry — and many more for a major expedition), and mounted about 800–900 guns, firing 5,500–6,000 lbs of shot.[1]

The *Gran Armada*, in contrast — using the 'general muster' of 24 May 1588, not the unreliable printed inventory of 9 May — consisted of 66,000 tons of shipping, including four galleasses, four galleys and some ninety great ships, a total of 30,000 men (of whom 18,539 were soldiers, 7,666 seamen, and 2,088 oarsmen), 2,431 guns, firing about

13,000 lbs of shot, costing in all 256,588 ducats a month (282,247 *escudos*).[2] It was a force twenty times the size and cost of the only high-board squadron previously maintained by the Spanish crown in the Atlantic on a regular basis, the *Armada* of the Indies guard. In short, the Mediterranean fleet carried nearly 60% more men; the Armada had three times as many guns, two and a half times the firepower, 40% more tonnage, and consequently a greater quantity of stores (sails, cables and chandlery).

The Mediterranean war was a war of galleys, of more or less specialised warships, permanent instruments of the state, and in the 1570s mainly, though not always, state-owned; Atlantic war was a war of round-ships and galleons, mainly armed merchantmen, in great part privately owned and only temporary and occasional adjuncts of state power. Mediterranean war was a war of 'prowess',[3] though not without its skills, essentially a war of 'aristocratic dash',[4] like a seaborne cavalry charge. Atlantic war, though not without its valour, was a war of 'proficiency', of technical skill, of experience and expertise, a 'bourgeois' war.[5] Mediterranean warfare was labour intensive; Atlantic warfare was capital intensive. The Mediterranean war was a war of men, propelled by men and fought man to man; Atlantic war was a war of *matériel*, of sails and guns. Oarsmen made up about half the capital value of a galley, ordnance at least half the capital value of a galleon (c.10–12% of that of a galley). Only about one or two per cent of the running costs of a galley went on munitions, no more than a quarter of those of a galleon.[6] Mediterranean warfare was also relatively expensive. A galley cost as much to fit out and run as a 300-ton galleon nearly twice its size, carrying a similar number of soldiers and nearly four times its weight of ordnance.[7] It is worth noting, therefore, that the shift to the Atlantic coincided with, and reflected, the exhaustion of the traditional resources of Mediterranean warfare. It is perhaps no coincidence that the retreat from the Mediterranean took place at the moment when the demographic growth of the sixteenth century was faltering, and when the price differentials between foodstuffs and munitions most disfavoured the galley.[8]

Lacking most of the essential resources for naval power, Spain was in many ways ill-equipped for her maritime role. Practically everything needed for the galleys, except iron and timber, had to be imported: sails, oars, hemp and munitions from Naples and Milan; masts, spars, tar and pitch via Flanders; tin and lead from England; canvas and sailcloth from Brittany. And she was almost entirely dependent on Italian volunteers, especially Genoese, for seamen. Almost 90% of the material costs of a galley and over 30% of its running costs (excluding pay) were spent in Italy, Flanders and France.[9]

Philip II's Mediterranean power, therefore, had to be a 'Monarchial' enterprise, a cooperation between Spain and his other Mediterranean realms. Only fourteen of Philip II's seventy-eight galleys at Lepanto were Spanish and only 9,700 of his 24,800 infantry. Messina was the base, and Naples and Sicily the graneries and supply centres of the fleet. At Lepanto, Naples and Sicily contributed more than half the galleys, and more than one-third the costs.[10] In 1574, Naples supported fifty-three galleys and a *tercio* of infantry – the expansion of the Neapolitan and Sicilian squadrons being part of a deliberate royal policy 'so that correspondingly less of the extraordinary costs be provided by Spain'.[11]

But already by the mid 1570s the Spanish Monarchy was proving incapable of maintaining a naval force in the Mediterranean at the levels of the years of the Holy League. The spectacular expansion of the Mediterranean fleet, which was tripled in numbers within the twelve-year period 1562–74, had been achieved only by the exhaustion of resources and the sacrifice of standards. The new galleys were badly-built and ill-equipped, with inexperienced officers, chronic shortages of rowers and seamen, and high costs.[12] All this coincided with an acute financial crisis, which was to lead to the royal 'bankruptcy' of 1575. By 1574 three-quarters of the 420,000 ducats of the clerical *subsidio*, granted by the papacy in 1560 expressly to maintain sixty of the 100 galleys to which the king had committed himself, was being diverted to the war in the Netherlands.[13] By January 1575, thirty-one of the 146 galleys were unmanned and out of commission, and the forty-six galleys of the Spanish squadron needed 100,000 ducats spent on them to make them seaworthy.[14] In December 1576, after Philip II had recognised his inability to maintain a larger force, in view of the 'great expense' and 'considering how ill in order many of my galleys are and have been', the fleet was cut back to 102 galleys and committed to a purely defensive role, 'since it is not possible for my fleet to be numerous enough to be able to face the enemy'.[15]

The reduction of the fleet released perhaps half the scarce resources that had been tied up in the Mediterranean war and so might be seen to have facilitated the reappropriation of resources that the *Gran Armada* would require in 1588. The reality was not quite so easy. Mediterranean resources were not immediately transferable to other theatres, neither ships, seamen, nor soldiers were suitable, or available, for service in the Atlantic.[16]

Thus the run-down of the war in the Mediterranean meant less the release of resources than the displacement of the military burden from Italy to Spain. From 1578 the majority of the galleys, Italian no less than Spanish, were serving regularly in Spanish waters, with Spanish and Italian galleys regularly based in Puerto de Santa Maria, Sanlúcar, Cadiz and Gibraltar, and Andalucia was coming to displace Sicily as the centre for the provisioning of the galleys, with a new commissariat for victualling the *armadas* established in Seville in 1580 or 1581. Nonetheless, Andalucia was in many ways not a satisfactory alternative, not least because of the high level of prices prevalent there.[17]

Neither was the reduction of the Mediterranean fleet — ordered six months before news of the truce with the Turk reached Madrid — part of a planned restructuring of Spanish military force in preparation for a new set of strategic priorities, a conscious preparation for a decisive shift away from the Mediterranean to the Atlantic. The annexation of Portugal and the campaigns of 1582 and 1583 in the Azores had a great political impact internationally, but they were not the first steps in a new rearmament for an Atlantic military strategy. Santa Cruz's proposal in August 1583, after his victory in the Azores, that his fleet should be kept in being and sent against Elizabeth, was ignored. Instead, the military apparatus that had conquered Portugal and the Azores was dismantled. The last 3,000 German and Italian troops in Lisbon were finally sent home in March 1584. The programme for the construction of 15,000 tons of shipping in Guipuzcoa and Vizcaya to serve as a kind of naval militia, first put forward in 1581 when the pacification of Portugal was still uncertain and when it was believed that the French, the English and the Dutch were arming a great fleet to attack the King of Spain, was abandoned in October 1584 only a third completed. At the same time the crown was contemplating selling off the nine galleons that were being built for the Indies Guard to private owners. At the end of 1584 Philip II was actually in the process of reversing a policy that had been intended to begin the creation of a permanent, Spanish Royal high-seas fleet.[18]

Meanwhile, the reduction of the galley fleets continued. From their peak of about 146 in 1576, they had fallen to eighty-eight by 1587. Nor was anything done to reform munitions supply or to reverse the deterioration into which the arms industries were falling, despite the repeated admonitions of the captain general of the artillery. In 1584 a contract negotiated for the importation of 10,000 cwt of Hungarian copper for the casting of artillery was cut by 60%. The negotiations with the prince of Salerno — which had been going on sporadically since 1578 — to reopen the cannon-ball factory in Navarre, inoperative now for many years, were suspended in 1585 and the matter dropped until July 1586.[19]

The apparent continuity 1577–1580–1588 is, therefore, a false one. From the logistical point of view the 'enterprise of England' was not the culmination of a long-prepared military plan going back to the 1570s, but the abrupt reversal of a prolonged run-down of Spanish naval forces which had been temporarily interrupted, but not halted, by the campaigns of 1580–83. It was the end of what Chaunu calls, 'le calme militaire relatif des années 1582–1585'.[20]

The shift from Mediterranean to Atlantic brought, in round terms, an immediate doubling of military demand for men and *matériel*, but even more important, a logistical shift from areas of relative Spanish strength (men, morale, discipline) to areas of Spanish weakness, ships, guns, and technology (seamen, gunners, gun-founders).[21] Spanish round-ships played only a small part in the Mediterranean wars. Of the 33,000 *toneladas* projected for the attack on Algiers in 1573 no more than 4,000 were to come from Spain. Of the thirty-nine great ships assembled for the Portuguese campaign in 1580 not one was Spanish.[22] By around 1580, with shortages of masts, spars, planking and pitch, a decline of shipping, and little activity in the shipyards, men like the great advocate for a strong Spanish naval presence in the Atlantic, the *contador* Alonso Gutiérrez, were despairing of the possibility of assembling a native-built fleet.[23]

One of the reasons why it was thought so difficult was the problem of manning a Spanish fleet with sailors, pilots or gunners. Various schemes to conscript seamen or, failing that, to induce them to sign on voluntarily by offering them pay in advance, and a substantial bonus, proved largely ineffective, as did efforts to enlist and train gunners.[24] Spain was also chronically short of artillery for such a fleet. Not only was she dependent on imported copper and tin, but the cannon-founding facilities of Malaga and Seville were insufficient for the demands of naval warfare in the 1570s. In order to arm the forty-nine extra galleys fitted out in 1572, not even Spain's share of the prize-guns taken at Lepanto sufficed, and Philip had to try to borrow artillery from the petty states of Italy (Savoy, Genoa, Florence, Ferrara, Malta) and to negotiate the purchase of iron guns from England, via the earl of Leicester.[25]

However, it was the Spanish munitions industries which were in the worst position to meet the huge increase in demand. With the breakdown of the negotiations with the prince of Salerno there was no cannon-shot made at all in Spain, and the country's gunpowder manufacturing capacity was actually less in 1587 than it had been in 1580 (from a daily output of twenty cwt in 1580 to twelve cwt in 1587).[26] The only one of the war industries that was expanding in the 1580s was the small-arms industry in Guipuzcoa and Vizcaya, but this, like all the other munitions industries, was crippled by lack of money. When the captain general of the artillery took up his post in Lisbon in 1587 to start equipping the fleet, he reported major deficiencies in everything, right across the board:

> I have drawn Your Majesty's attention to the great shortage there is of all kinds of artillery, both for land and for sea. I have to say the same for gunpowder, matchcord, lead, iron, steel, rope, equipment and machinery, so Your Majesty can see to the great need that there is. It is apparent that for each of these items time is required, and there are problems which cannot be sorted out except by continuing the procurement of everything and making every effort to assemble large quantities in all provinces, especially of saltpetre and facilities for milling gunpowder, since everywhere there is such great need, and in all parts no less shortage of cast-iron shot for the guns.[27]

All these failings are well known, but what is important to note is that what was lacking was precisely the qualities required for the new warfare. As Leonardo Donà had noted in 1570, good ships were in short supply because those employed in Atlantic waters were small 'and so not suitable for the actions that are envisioned'; while those engaged on the Indies run, though large, were undergunned and short of seamen.[28] But in addition to these long-standing inadequacies, there were new ones arising. It seems that it was precisely at this moment that the apparently inexhaustible supply of volunteers for the *tercios* was beginning to run dry. In the early 1580s it was becoming increasingly difficult to recruit soldiers, a development perhaps connected with the levelling off of population growth and an upturn in the levels of real wages. Between 1571 and 1578 the average recruiting captain was raising 256 men; in the decade after 1580 (1580–91) the average slumped to 161, and even this was achieved only with inordinate expense to the crown and intolerable suffering to the villages through which the unpaid and undisciplined soldiery passed. In the years after 1580, the complaints of the *cortes* bear witness to the breakdown of the entire recruiting system.[29]

A similar breakdown is apparent in the supply services. Just as in recruiting, the 1580s were a period of constant complaint by the *cortes* about the extortions of the purveyors.[30] The problem of supply, particularly of grain and other agricultural produce, was made worse by the increasing difficulties of Castilian agriculture, exacerbated by a series of bad harvests between 1580 and 1584, the reduction of imports from northern Europe resulting from the Spanish embargo on English and Dutch shipping from May 1585, and the growing danger from piracy in Spanish waters.

It was, therefore, against the background of an almost total collapse of the administrative and supply system that the decision to embark on the invasion of England was taken. The Armada had to be created from scratch out of a logistical vacuum at the moment of a general crisis of procurement.

The first requirement was a system of military administration geared to the needs of large-scale ocean warfare. There was neither a permanent naval commissariat nor an established naval base on the Atlantic seaboard adequate for the needs of 1588. The council of war was expanded, its secretariat doubled with a separate office of naval administration under the ex-purveyor of the galleys. Andrés de Alva. The military governorship of Galicia was revived, a new governorship created in the Canaries, and the duke of Medina Sidonia appointed captain general of Andalucia. In April 1586, Francisco Duarte, factor of the Casa de Contratacíon of Seville, was made purveyor general of the high-board fleets maintained at Castilian expense in Portugal, and in October the councillor of finance, Antonio de Guevara, was appointed purveyor general in Andalucia.[31]

The lack of an established naval base on the Atlantic beyond Cadiz raised the problem of finding a site that would reconcile both the 'operative' (or strategic) and 'logistical' functions of a base. As long as war was in the north and provisions in the south, the problem remained intractable, and it remained unresolved thirty years later. Some consideration seems to have been given to fitting out the Armada on the more strategically placed Cantabrian coast (as in 1574), but the scale of the Armada's requirements and the importance of Lisbon's commercial nexus and its ordnance facilities determined the choice.[32] The logistical factor prevailed, therefore, but both for political and administrative reasons Lisbon was in other respects unsatisfactory. The limited jurisdiction of the Castilian commissariat meant that it was not possible to employ the arbitrary measures used in Castile and local purchases had to be made in cash; conflicts with the Portuguese commissariat, Portuguese hostility to Castilians, especially to the soldiers, even confusion between Castilian and Portuguese weights and measures, restricted control, impeded effectiveness, increased opportunities for fraud and deceit, and contributed a great deal to the provisioning failure in 1588.

In Castile the Armada preparations generated a stream of reforms during the summer of 1586 and throughout 1587 and 1588, intended to remedy the most glaring defects of the system of military organisation. New biscuit baking ovens were put up in Lisbon and Malaga. Measures were proposed to find 'a way to organise provisioning without so many complaints against the purveyors and their officials', schemes to get the lords and cities of Andalucia to contract to provide fixed quantities of their harvests, for example, or to get the town councils to do the buying of the grain and act as guarantors of payment, or to establish official grain quotas in accordance with the capacity of each village.[33]

A major reform of the recruiting system was undertaken. New regulations for recruiting captains were issued in 1584. A commissary general with judicial authority to coordinate billeting and supervise recruiting was appointed in 1587, and a second the following year, dividing their jurisdiction between Castile and Andalucia. A preliminary listing was made of veteran soldiers living in retirement, and initial investigations set up with a view to the establishment of a national militia. Of most significance, however, were a proposal in October 1586 to get the cities to take responsibility for raising soldiers, and a series of agreements with the lords and cities of Andalucia to raise quotas of men from their estates in order to avoid the problems caused by royal recruiting captains — both measures of a decentralizing nature analogous to those proposed for the provisioning of grain.[34] Although some thirty companies were recruited in 1587 by royal captains, a similar number of the companies serving in 1588 were levies of Andalucian, Extremaduran and Castilian cities and of lords like the count of Benavente, and the dukes of Bejar, Feria and Alburquerque.[35]

There were reforms also in munitions procurement. Surveys were begun to discover new mineral deposits; the Lérida saltpetre plant was put to work again (May 1587); the cannon foundries in Lisbon were expanded and brought into production; negotiations were resumed to open the shot-works in Navarre, and to take over for the crown the privately owned sulphur mines at Hellín in Murcia; and the agreement with the Basque shipbuilders, in suspension since 1584, seems to have been taken up again at the beginning of 1587.[36]

A plethora of reforms then, but to what extent was it possible to remedy in two years chronic inadequacies in the military–administrative structure? Was the very existence of the *Gran Armada* the vindication of Philip II's bureaucratic system, as some have claimed — if not a military victory, an administrative triumph?

There were assembled in the estuary of the Tagus on the eve of departure some 130 vessels — not counting the 10 caravels. Of these, nine galleons and two *pataches* of the royal squadron of Portugal (annexed to the crown in 1580), the same number of galleons and *pataches* of the squadron of Castile, and a further four galeasses and four galleys belonged to the king, and the remaining 100 or so *naves*, *urcas* and *pataches*, freighted or requisitioned for the occasion, were privately owned.[37] The make-up of the Armada suggests that there had been some late improvements in Spain's shipbuilding capacity, up to twenty-nine or thirty of the forty-five best private vessels in the fighting-squadrons were of Spanish origin, a good number of them built in accordance with agreements made with the royal superintendent, Cristóbal de Barros.[38] After the disaster, in October 1588, when the reconstruction of the royal fleet was being undertaken, it was claimed that no less than forty galleons of up to 500 *toneladas* could be built on the coast between San Sebastian and San Vicente de la Barquera within a year.[39] An exaggeration no doubt, but a much more optimistic comment than would have been possible only a few years before. The negative side, however, was that this quantitative success in 1588 was achieved only by creaming off the big ships from the Indies route. The result was a severe tonnage-crisis in the American trade. Tonnage sailing outward in 1587 was only 11.9% of the average of 1583–86, the lowest figure until 1650.[40]

There were ships enough in 1588, therefore, but the problem of manning them remained unsolved. There was still an acute shortage of seamen. One of the reasons for diverting the ships of the Indies *flotas* was to incorporate their sailors into the Armada, which even as late as the end of March 1588 was incapable of putting to sea 'because of the very great shortage there is of sailors'.[41] When it sailed at the end of May, it carried only 10.9 seamen per 100 *toneladas*, only two-thirds of the norm established for the navy in the seventeenth century, and it would not have got those without the press ganging of foreign mariners in Spanish ports.[42] Some of the problems of ship-handling that arose during the voyage no doubt had something to do with the shortage of seamen and the inequality of their distribution among the ships and the squadrons, some of which had three times more mariners pro rata to tonnage than others.[43] In all this there were serious operational dangers. Foreign pilots and sailors deserted at the first opportunity, and significantly the squadron which suffered the heaviest losses, the Levantine, was the one with the lowest ratio of seamen.

Something similar could be said of the shortage of gunners. Years later, the duke of Medina Sidonia was to say that to rely on German and Flemish gunners was to hold a lighted bomb in one's hand — he had in mind, perhaps, the tragic fate of the *San Salvador*.[44] Lacking too was the capacity to equip the ships with adequate artillery. There can be no doubt that the Armada was woefully undergunned. 'The whole Armada is short of guns', wrote the marquis of Santa Cruz.[45] Although new furnaces were set up in Lisbon, there were neither sufficient master founders, polishers, adjusters and ironsmiths, nor the materials (copper, iron, timber) and money. At the end of February 1588, the captain general of the artillery declared that in the year he had been in Lisbon he had been unable to cast more than sixty guns, about 180 cwt, 'since they are things which, even with a surplus of money, cannot be had nor made without a long lead-time'.[46] The new-cast pieces comprised a mere 2½% of the guns carried in the Armada, totally insufficient to remedy the shortage of artillery on the private vessels, three-quarters of whose guns were their original 'ship-guns', overwhelmingly small, cast-iron pieces, of little but defensive value.[47]

On the other hand, if we are to believe the inventory of 9 May 1588, the targets for munitions appear to have been met. However, there is reason to doubt the veracity of that inventory. The victualling account was certainly fraudulent, and the uniformity and exactness of the munitions listings simply do not accord with the data that we have from other and subsequent accounts. The squadron of Castile, for example, on 14 May, had more than enough powder for the sixty shot per gun with which it was credited in the inventory of 9 May, but each gun had no more than twenty-five shot. Here again, there was no uniformity from squadron to squadron. In mid-April, although the galleasses and the Andalucian squadron were well-munitioned, the Levant squadron was 383 cwt of gunpowder short, and the hulks had none at all.[48]

The attempts to reform munitions production had come too late. The first cannon-balls from the new shot-foundry at Eugui, in Navarre, did not come on stream until the end of 1588, at the earliest, and the bulk of the shot for the Armada came from abroad. Fifteen-thousand cwt of copper from Milan, requested by the council of war in May 1587, still had not arrived in Spain in September 1588, and the agreement over the Hellín sulphur mine was not concluded until 1589. Although the captain general of the artillery claimed he could produce 4,000 cwt of gunpowder within six months, Medina Sidonia found the Armada at the end of May 1588 with no more than 3,000 cwt, less than half it was thought to need, and 550 cwt had to be bought from German merchants in Lisbon at more than double the normal price.[49]

Yet, however well or ill the Armada was stocked, equipping it had left the defences of the peninsula dangerously denuded of munitions of all sorts. In September there were no more than 100 balls of shot and 15-20 cwt of powder in La Coruña, and the other arsenals and fortresses of Spain were 23,000 cwt of gunpowder short.[50]

The Armada was also weak in infantry. It was the lack of soldiers that had prevented Santa Cruz going out to intercept Drake off Lisbon in May 1587, and even at the end of March 1588 there were barely 10,000 soldiers on board.[51] It was only the arrival of 3,000 men from Extremadura, the withdrawal of troops from the Lisbon garrisons, and the last minute recruitment of 2,000 Portuguese in April and May which gave the Armada a degree of numerical respectability. It put to sea on 30 May with thirty-one soldiers for every 100 *toneladas* of shipping, more than the norm for the 1624 Armada, but less than the (perhaps unrealistic) figures projected by Santa Cruz in March 1586, or by Medina Sidonia in March 1587.[52]

However, what is in doubt is not so much the number as the quality of the troops involved. All were agreed the troops to be put ashore for invasion must be a trained and experienced elite of 'gente vieja'. Santa Cruz had wanted 27,000 mercenaries from Germany and Italy, and 11,000 veteran Spanish infantry from the *tercios* in Italy, the garrisons of Portugal and the Azores, and the Armada of the Indies Guard. In May 1588 the *Gran Armada* had less than 19,000 soldiers, none of them Germans or Italians, and at least twenty-nine of the 104 companies of the *tercios* of Pimentel from Sicily, Luzón from Naples, Toledo from Portugal, and Isla from the Indies galleons, were new companies raised in Spain in 1587. A minimum of 60%, and possibly as many as 75% of the infantry on the *Gran Armada* were raw recruits, many of them not even volunteers, but conscripts levied by the lords and cities of

Andalucia and Extremadura. The *Gran Armada* was the first time that Spaniards were conscripted for service overseas. This was the legacy of the collapse of the voluntary recruiting system after 1580.

Given that contemporary experts believed that it took three times as long to train a soldier for service at sea, one can only guess at the fitness, morale and military capacity of such men. Despite some satisfaction in court circles with both the number and the quality of the soldiers aboard,[53] the duke of Medina Sidonia was a good deal less impressed: 'the men are not as well-trained as they should be, nor are the officers'.[54] The 400 Galicians sent by the counts of Lemos and Monterrey were described by Medina Sidonia as

> so useless they cannot serve even as pioneers. Besides, they are all married, with numerous children, and most of them old and infirm . . . Even their own captains have not wanted to accept them, because apart from dying and taking up space on the ships, they are no good for anything, for none of them knows what an arquebus is, nor any sort of weapon. They have let themselves become like dead men, and some have not eaten for two days. In view of this I have dismissed them all, and they have gone back to their homes.[55]

The victualling requirements for the Armada called for twice the amount of wheat normally procured by the Castilian military commissariat in Andalucia in an ordinary year, a quantity itself considerably increased since 1580; and three times the amount of wine, in addition to all the provisions brought from Sicily, Naples and other parts of Castile. These demands were all the more difficult to meet because the 1587 harvest was poor and the very existence of the Armada and the fear of embargo or English interception inhibited grain shipments from the Baltic.

Ultimately, however, the failure was not one of procurement, though success in this respect was achieved only at the expense of Andalucia, Galicia and Portugal, and the victualling of the Indies fleets, but of the erosion of supplies by delay, wastage and fraud. Consuming nearly 15,000 quintals of biscuit and 1,500 pipes of wine a month, by the time it sailed the Armada had already consumed in normal rations half as much again as it took with it, in addition to the massive wastage caused by conditions of shipboard storage and by the processes of loading and unloading. In January 1588 bread and biscuit was being embarked for eight months; in April the Armada had five months supply; and it sailed at the end of May with enough for four months. The optimistic reports of the ministers, however, had been based on statements from the purveyors and quartermasters which were either fraudulent or incompetent.[56] On 14 June, only two weeks after sailing from Lisbon, Medina Sidonia was writing, 'I carry a great shortage of victuals', and some ships put in to La Coruña on 19 June without water.[57] The fleet restocked in La Coruña, but when the English captured the *Rosario* on 1 August, they found stinking fish, bread full of worms, leaky casks and sour wine. When the Armada sailed out of La Coruña on 22 July, it was carrying biscuit for only fifty-seven days, and less than three weeks later Medina Sidonia was forced to cut rations by two-thirds simply in order to enable the men to get back to Spain. After the disaster, on 28 September 1588, the council of state, complaining of 'the malice and corruption that there was in the provisioning', concluded 'the principal reason for the decision to return was the shortage of victuals'.[58]

It looks then as if it was the incompleteness of the solutions to the logistical problems raised by the demands of the Atlantic that determined the configuration of the Armada, and hence its strategy and fate.

The salient characteristic of the *Gran Armada* was its heterogeneity, a heterogeneity in ownership, manning, armament, and loyalties. Such heterogeneity was by no means unique but it was a characteristic that was of greater disadvantage for the effective conduct of a strategic offensive, in which unity of action and uniformity of purpose are of the essence, than it was for defence, as the English themselves found in the 'counter-Armada' of 1589. But in contrast with the situation in the English fleet in July 1588, many, if not most of the shipowners — like Andrés Felipe, the captain of the *Gran Grin*, who had invested 20,000 ducats in his ship in the expectation of doubling his money on the Indies run only two months before he was embargoed[59] — the empressed German, Dutch, Flemish and Portuguese sailors, and the conscripted soldiers on the Armada simply did not want to be there. As the *maestre de campo general*, the chief military staff officer, Don Francisco de Bobadilla, observed in a letter from the flagship to the king's confidant, Don Juan de Idiáquez, on 20 August 1588: 'The strength of our Armada was twenty or so vessels, and those fought very well, even better than was needed, but most of the rest fled whenever they saw the enemy attack'.[60]

The need to employ whatever ships were available regardless of sailing and handling qualities, the insufficiency of mariners and artillerymen, the inability to arm the fleet on a rational basis or with adequate firepower, meant the Armada lacked all the intensity factors needed to bring the English to battle or to destroy their fleet if it encountered it. The *Gran Armada* was not equipped for an offensive role *at sea*; its tactical imperative had, therefore, to be one of defence. The Armada had to be 'invincible', and that meant reliance on the one factor in which Spain was preponderant, size. The strategy of the fleet had to be a 'Mediterranean' strategy, the strategy of Lepanto in which a vast arc of over 200 vessels blasted its way through the enemy front, a strategy of mass. All the Spanish planners were of one voice in insisting that 'His Majesty's Armada must not be restricted, but the biggest and most powerful that it can be'.[61] The Armada had to be too big to be defeated, its ships too large and powerful, even if 'less nimble and less seaworthy', its soldiers too numerous, as much for the defensive firepower of their arquebuses and muskets as for boarding and landing, as they proved at Gravelines.

But a strategy of mass posed insuperable problems for sixteenth-century administrations. The greater the Armada, the more the ships and men, the more provisions and supplies that were needed, the longer the time it took to prepare and assemble; the longer it took to prepare and assemble the greater the wastage, the deterioration and the decay, and the more that was consumed merely to keep it in existence. There were soldiers being maintained on the Armada's account well over a year before it finally set sail. In the eleven months it was in Spain, between July 1587 and May 1588, the *tercio* of Naples lost 25% of its effectives, and the same thing was happening in the Netherlands to an even greater degree.[62] Similarly, provisions had begun to be assembled after the harvest of 1586. By May 1588, as we have seen, the Armada had already used in normal rations alone half as many victuals again as it was to carry with it out of Lisbon, in addition to all the wastage that we know to have occurred. The inadequacy of the administrative infra-structure — in Galicia there were not even storehouses for sorting the shot — simply accelerated the logistical instability inherent in all great sixteenth-century expeditions.

These problems of logistics and manpower made it impossible for the Spanish fleet to act as an independent force. So much was admitted by Philip II in the instruction of 14 September 1587, ordering a late change of strategy: 'the strength of the two fleets not being as great as was estimated to be desirable for the principal enterprise . . . not having been able to assemble this year everything projected in the plans'.[63] It was the impossibility of assembling a force large enough for direct action against England which made the fatal plan for a junction with Parma unavoidable, if for no other reason than the need to restock the Armada with water, provisions and munitions in the Netherlands.

Without enough 'gente vieja' or veterans, it was impossible to mount an invasion directly; without more powerful artillery it was impossible to destroy the enemy's fleet; without munitions it was impossible to resist their attacks; without victuals it was impossible to maintain the Armada as a fighting force at sea: 'from that (shortage of victuals) has followed not only the loss of so much treasure and the uncountable revenue Your Majesty has spent on this Armada, all fruitlessly, but the loss of the Armada itself, the men on it, and as a result everything else that we see'.[64]

Conclusion

The most fundamental problems faced in the creation of the Armada were consequences of the incomplete transition from Mediterranean to Atlantic modes of warfare. The Armada was the first stage in that transition; it was, in that sense, too early — administratively and culturally premature. The persistence of a 'Mediterranean mentality' can be seen, for instance, not only in the tactical dispositions adopted and in the 'cavalry' attitudes of men such as Don Alonso de Leiva, but, even more damagingly, in the status conflicts between sailors and soldiers, which, reinforced by social conflicts between gentlemen and commoners, and national conflicts between Castilians-Andalucians, on the one hand, and Basques-Cantabrians, on the other, must have had a shattering effect on morale. Don Pedro de Valdés, admiral of the Andalucian squadron, complained of the subordination of his sea-captains and ships' masters, men with years of experience on the Indies run, to 'men who have never been on the open sea nor understand its ways. For that they are held in disdain and have little desire to serve. This was not the least reason why the Armada was dispersed in the recent storm which scattered it' near La Coruña.[65] The Guipuzcoans, on their return, blamed the soldiers for causing many of the losses on the Irish coast by their violence towards the crews and by preventing the pilots and sailors from navigating freely.[66]

It was, of course, the failure of the Armada which then made necessary the regularisation and institutionalisation of Atlantic warfare in the years after 1588 with the establishment of a permanent *Armada del Mar Océano*, and that permanence in turn actualised the wider implications of the shift from the Mediterranean to the Atlantic.

The first implication was a long-term shift in the balance of military power. The Mediterranean system of warfare involved the control of an enclosed maritime space by the symbiotic operation of galley fleets and coastal fortifications.[67] It was a state war of permanent fleets and fortress outposts, maintained by the treasury and manned by the employment of state power — in Spain's case by the condemnation of criminals, prisoners of war and heretics to galley service by the royal courts. The Atlantic system of warfare was an ocean war on the 'open sea', a war not of control but of disruption, a 'little war' involving the raiding and defending of 'moving' targets (coasts, trade, routes), a war of sporadic and irregular action by part-time forces, sustained by independent capitalist activity and manned through market mechanisms by men with marketable skills. In this kind of war state power was not cost effective (not at least until there was a greater differentiation between warship and merchant ship) and the great monarchy had no military advantage over the small.[68] In the Atlantic all the more grandiose expeditions were spectacular failures, to a greater or lesser degree, for reasons not dissimilar to those which influenced the outcome in 1588 and because of the disassociation between sea and land.

The internal dimension of that shift was a shift from public to private in the organisation of war. Vicens Vives has drawn attention to the connection between the development of the state and the institutionalisation of war in the Mediterranean in the 1530s.[69] With war in the Atlantic and with the Atlantic war invading the Mediterranean from the 1580s that process was being reversed. The expansion of the Mediterranean war had involved an expansion of the role of the 'public sector' in military organisation. In 1560 the squadron of Naples comprised six royal galleys and ten private; in 1574 it had forty-nine royal and only four private. Only twenty-nine of the 146 galleys Philip II was maintaining in 1574 were privately owned, serving under contract. The heavy war galley, with in excess of 170 oarsmen, was not economically viable either as a merchant vessel or as a pirate unless it was 'salaried', and it was not mannable except with the help of the state.[70] The cut back in the galley fleets in 1576 was also, therefore, a cut back of the 'public sector' — that was explicit in the instruction of 27 December 1576. The economics of the round-ship, on the other hand, the little structural differentiation between the *nave* and the galleon, the relationship of crew space to cargo, the inability of the state to compete for free labour, favoured the private sector. The shift from galley to round-ship, therefore, was also a shift in the balance between the 'public' and 'private' share in war. If at Lepanto 80% of the galleys were the king's, in the fleet at Terceira in 1583 only three of thirty-six capital round-ships were the king's (excepting the two galeasses and twelve galleys), and in 1588 only thirty of the 130 vessels and less than one-third of the front-line ships. Philip II's creation of a large, permanent ocean fleet in the 1590s was an attempt to translate into the Atlantic the predominance of the 'public sector' in the Mediterranean. As such it did not succeed — the royal galleons never exceeded one-third of the ships in the expeditionary fleets of 1596 and 1597.

The logistics of the high seas fleets also promoted a more general movement of privatisation as the state was unable to employ its coercive power to import *matériel* for naval warfare from outside its jurisdiction, or to counteract the exhaustion of local resources and technical skill shortages. The maintenance and supplying of fleets by contracts with private entrepreneurs and the reforms in the system of grain procurement and recruiting, referred to above, were the administrative dimension of this public-private shift.

At the same time, however, the greatly increased demand for the fleets — the Armada in 1597 required 7,000 cwt of powder and 8,000 cwt of hemp,[71] four times more than the total requirement of the galleys of Spain and Portugal and the Armadas de Indias — by increasing Spain's negative foreign trade balance and exposing Spain's naval forces to the risk of an interruption of supplies from overseas, promoted more state intervention in the strategic sectors of the economy, mining, munitions, manufactures and shipbuilding, and an extension of controls over the arms industries. Royal shot and armour factories were set up, the output of gunpowder in the royal powder mills doubled and the treasury budget for domestic arms and munitions expenditure tripled between the early 1580s and 1600.[72]

In economic and fiscal terms the shift from Mediterranean to Atlantic meant also a shift, in both benefits and burdens, from east to west. The beneficiaries of war in the Mediterranean were the Catalans, the Neapolitans, the Sicilians and the Genoese. It was there that the galleys were built and where the greater part of the two and a half million ducats a year that the war in the Mediterranean was costing was spent. The beneficiaries of war in the Atlantic were rather the sea-board provinces on the western and northern peripheries. The more than

40,000 *toneladas* of shipping built in the Basque yards between 1588 and 1599 cost in excess of one million ducats, to which has to be added annual payments for freightage and wages for officers and mariners which, in 1590, amounted to some 250,000 ducats. A rough estimate would put some 20% of gross income in the Basque country in those years as coming direct from the royal treasury. Galicia, which had remained on the margins of military spending during the 1560s and 1570s, was another beneficiary of the 1590s, recovering in wages and purchases for the fleet perhaps half of what it paid in taxes. Even Andalucia, ravaged by naval purveyors and their commissaries, may have recovered as much as a third of its enormous tax burden by way of military spending in the province. All this, both before and after 1580, but even more so thereafter, meant a huge payments transfer from the Castiles to the peripheries — Portugal, Aragon, Cantabria, Vizcaya, Navarre — the greater part of them contributing little, or nothing, to disposable royal revenues.

The shift from Mediterranean to Atlantic is also a shift in the balance of the Monarquía Hispánica. The shift to the Atlantic led to the progressive hispanisation of war. In 1580 all the large sailing ships employed in the conquest of Portugal came from the Levant; in 1583 at Terceira, half the ships were of Mediterranean origin; in 1588, only one in eight of the major vessels were.[73] At Lepanto only 40% of Philip II's troops were Spaniards; in the *Gran Armada*, Spaniards comprised 90%, and the rest were Portuguese.

The war in the Mediterranean had been an instrument for the integration of the Spanish Monarchy and for the maintenance of Spanish dominance in Italy. As Don García de Toledo explained in November 1571, only one month after Lepanto, the importance of the victory lay in 'demonstrating to friends and enemies that when there is true union with His Majesty there must needs be very great success in everything'.[74] In the Mediterranean, Castile, Aragon and Italy were interdependent. In 1574 thirty-eight of the galleys maintained by Castile were in Italian waters, and Castile between 1571 and 1576 was sending on average 800,000 ducats a year to Italy. By the early 1580s the current was reversed; the galleys of Naples and Sicily were serving in Spain and both Naples and Sicily were contributing men and money to the Armada.[75]

The point is not that this represented a greater burden than in the 1570s — by the early 1580s Naples's expenditure on the galleys was only half that in 1574 and fiscal pressure in the 1590s was less severe than it had been in the 1570s[76] — but that it now represented an expatriation of *servicios*, whilst Italy was left to sustain the cost of its own defence largely unaided. During the 1560s and 1570s the Mediterranean kingdoms got the protection of Spain and the economic benefits of military spending in return for political subordination to Madrid; after 1580 they had not only to protect themselves, they had also to protect Spain.

One is getting the sense, in the last years of the century, of a distancing of the Mediterranean kingdoms from the Monarchy. Reglà has contrasted the participation of the Catalans in 1571 and their absence in 1588, and Koenigsberger has noted the reluctance of Sicilians in 1589 to contribute to 'causes not their own'.[77] Whereas the threat to the Spanish Mediterranean from the Sicilian channel seems to have had a cohesive function, the threat from the Straits of Gibraltar seems to have been disjunctive. The Atlanticisation of war in the 1580s changed the framework of association between Castile and Spain and between Spain and the Mediterranean kingdoms, and that in turn contributed to the acute Castilian sense of isolation which is the leitmotiv of the history of the 'Monarquía' in the seventeenth century.

NOTES

1. There were, for example, 24,800 soldiers paid by the King of Spain on the galleys at the battle of Lepanto in 1571.
2. AGS GA 221 f. 158 'Relación sumaria del estado de la Real Armada', referring to the 'French-style muster' of 24 May, sent to the king with a letter dated 28 May 1588; AGS GA 223 f. 99 Francisco Duarte to the King, Lisbon 30 May referring to the 'general' muster of 24 May. See Casado Soto below for a discussion of tonnages.
3. M. D. Feld, 'Middle-class society and the rise of military professionalism: the Dutch Army 1589–1609' in *The structure of violence. Armed forces as social systems* (Beverly Hills/London, 1977) pp. 169–203 at p. 169.
4. P. W. Bamford, *Fighting ships and prisons. The Mediterranean galleys of France in the age of Louis XIV* (Minneapolis, 1973) p. 24.
5. See Feld, note 3.
6. Slaves on the galleys were valued at 700 *reales* in the 1570s, and *forzados* at 330 *reales*; a gun cost c.176 *reales* per cwt. A galley had (at that time) a

crew of 164 oarsmen, and carried about 100 cwt of cannon. An account of 1570 (AGS E 453 'Relación de lo que vale una galera ordinaria') put the total cost of a galley at 142,830 *reales*, including 63,370 for the crew. According to a document of 1591, the ideal armament for a galleon of 1,300 *toneladas*, valued at 32,500 ducats, would cost 18,656 ducats, AGS GA 347 s.f.

7. Fully armed with crew and artillery, a galley cost 13,000 ducats; that would have fitted out and gunned a ship of about 317 *toneladas*; in 1624, on the 65 ducat per *tonelada* estimate of the secretary of the Navy, Martín de Aroztegui, the running-costs of a galley were the same as those of a 300-*tonelada* light-galleon, AGS GA 899 s.f., 18 Nov. 1624.

8. J. F. Guilmartin, Jr., *Gunpowder and galleys. Changing technology and Mediterranean warfare at sea in the sixteenth century* (Cambridge, 1974) pp. 222–5. Whilst the price of biscuit increased fourfold between 1523 and 1587, the price of gunpowder only doubled, and that of bronze guns between 1544 and 1587 rose by one-third, A. Carrasco, 'Apuntes para la historia de la fundición de artillería de bronce en España', *Memorial de Artillería*, XV (1887) p. 182.

9. I. Bauer Landauer, *La marina española en el siglo xvi* (Madrid, 1921) pp. 453–8.

10. G. Parker and I. A. A. Thompson, 'The Battle of Lepanto 1571. The costs of victory', *MM*, LXIV (1978) pp. 13–21.

11. AGS E 448 Philip to Don Juan de Austria, 26 Jan. 1572.

12. AGS E 453 'Relacion que Marcelo Doria dio al Sr Don Juan sobre el dar Su Md las Galeras por asiento', n.d.

13. I. Cloulas, 'Le "subsidio de las galeras" contribution du clergé espagnol à la guerre navale contre les Infidèles de 1563 à 1574', *Mélenges de la Casa de Velázquez*, III (1967) pp. 289–326, p. 319 and Table 1; AGS GA 78 f. 58.

14. AGS E 453 'Lo que ha parecido en consejo', 22 Jan 1575; AGS GA 80 f. 129.

15. BPU Geneva, Coll. Favre t. 28 ff. 83–7, 97–101v (courtesy of Professor Geoffrey Parker).

16. J. Alcalá-Zamora, *España, Flanders y el Mar del Norte (1618–1639)* (Barcelona, 1975) p. 81; Italians, noted Tomé Cano, 'are not high sea sailors', *Arte para fabricar y aparejar naos* (1611, edn E. Marcos Dorta, La Laguna, 1964) p. 50; Guilmartin, *Gunpowder and Galleys*, pp. 64–6 on the different requirements of Mediterranean and Atlantic seamanship; and Philip II's comment to Medina Sidonia on the Ragusan ships, 'I can see very well that, as you say, the levant ships are less nimble and more weatherly for these waters than the ones we build here', Herrera Oria, *Armada* p. 217.

17. Codoin II p. 173, J. A. Doria argued (12 May 1594) that Spanish galleys

should be sent to Italy every other year for refit, 'because there they could be provided with better and cheaper things than here'.

18. Thompson, *War*, pp. 190–1.
19. Thompson, *War*, p. 252.
20. VIII/ii/1 p. 701.
21. But cf. Rodríguez-Salgado on navigation and cartography, below pp. 142–3 and Casado Soto on shipbuilding, below pp. 107–9 (edd.).
22. J. Suárez Inclán, *Guerra de anexión en Portugal durante el reinado de don Felipe II* (2 vols., Madrid, 1897–8) II p. 363.
23. BNM mss 1749 ff. 361–70, Gutiérrez's memorandum 23 Oct 1577 where he stated that it would be impossible to raise a fleet in Spain 'as navigation and the use of the sea have declined in our coasts', and because of the difficulties getting seamen, ships, etc.; port of Bilbao to Philip II complaining that 'it has no ships or sailors', T. Guiard y Larrauri, *La industria naval vizcaína* (Bilbao, 1917) p. 69; AGS GA 91 f. 74, Francisco Duarte, 24 Nov 1579: 'I detect such little enthusiasm and spirit among the people who could exercise these tasks that I doubt if it will be possible to carry out what we intend in a long time . . . and they assure me that in Vizcaya and Guipuzcoa no more than four or five ships are being built', despite a bounty of two ducats per *tonelada* over 300 *toneladas*. On the shortage of masts, spars, planking and pitch in Cantabria, Cristóbal de Eraso, 17 Nov 1577, AGS GA 82 f. 215; Cristóbal de Barros, 15 Feb 1581 X, MNM Navarrete XXII, doc. 76, f. 292v, and Juan Martínez de Recalde, 25 May 1581, MNM Navarrete XII, doc. 76 ff. 297v–99v.
24. A form of maritime conscription was instituted in Vizcaya and Guipuzcoa in 1581 to man the Indies fleets, but it was not successful. In 1583 in order to raise seamen in Guipuzcoa recruits were offered three ducats a month, four months in advance, plus three ducats bonus 'so that they may come and serve more willingly', Guiard, *Industria naval vizcaina*, p. 306; AGS GA 214, 'Recuerdo de García de Arce', 1587; AGS GA 199 f. 49, Juan de Acuña Vela, captain general of the artillery, 24 July 1587: 'no one seeks to become a gunner anywhere, and many of those who are offered such posts refuse them and do not want them, and so there are many vacant positions everywhere, which, unless we give them to people who are no good, cannot be filled'.
25. Leonardo Donato's report of 1573 on the lack of artillery in Spain, E. Alberi *Relazioni degli ambasciatori Veneti al senato durante il secolo decimosesto* (15 vols, Florence, 1839–63) serie 1, vol. VI p. 399; AGS E 448 R.C. to Don Juan of Austria, 30 Nov 1572; AGS GA 82 f. 163 negotiations for the purchase of 200 iron guns from England 1577.
26. Thompson, *War* p. 241.
27. AGS GA 199 f. 49 to the king, 24 July 1587.
28. 15 Nov 1570, M. Brunetti and E. Vitale, *La corrispondenza da Madrid*

dell'ambasciatore Leonardo Donà (1570-73) (Venice-Rome, n.d.) vol. I no. 56 p. 144.

29. Thompson, *War* pp. 104-5, 112-15.
30. *Ibid.*, pp. 211-17.
31. I. A. A. Thompson, 'The Armada and administrative reform: the Spanish council of war in the reign of Philip II', *English Historical Review*, LXXXII (1967) pp. 698-725.
32. M. Bustamente Callejo, 'Consejos del capitán laredano Don Lope de Ocina y de la Obra al rey Felipe II para la conquista de Inglaterra', *Altamira* I (1952) pp. 75-82, at p. 77.
33. Thompson, *War* pp. 218-20.
34. *Ibid.*, pp. 115-16, 123-4.
35. Herrera Oria, *Armada* p. 4; AGS GA 199 f. 83; GA 221 ff. 6, 17, 18, 19; GA 223 ff. 79, 230.
36. AGS GA 1299 'Relacion sobre lo que toca a la fabrica de las naos que se hazen en Vizcaya', and the Junta de Galeras, 25 Sept 1584 with the king's decision, 11 Oct 1584; AGS GA 233 f. 155 *cuenta* of the paymaster of Avellaneda's *asiento*, Hernando de Aguirre, 20 April 1588: 20,000 ducats paid to seven outfitters for construction of eight ships, totalling 5,175 *toneladas*.
37. AGS GA 221 f. 158, 28 May 1588.
38. See Casado Soto below pp. 99-101, 111, 113.
39. AGS GA 347 Orduño de Zamudio, 3 Oct 1588.
40. Chaunu VIII/ii/1. p. 754.
41. FD I p. 475 Medina Sidonia, 26 March.
42. For the 1624 norms, AGS GA 899 Martín de Aróztegui, 18 Nov 1624; on the shortage of mariners, Rodríguez-Salgado below pp. 144-8.
43. AGS GA 221 f. 158, 28 May 1588: 6,766 mariners for 62,278 *toneladas* (excluding galeasses, galleys, *zabras* and *pataches*), only 2/3 of the 16/100 norm of 1624. The Portuguese squadron had a ratio of 1,134 men for 7,373 tons (= 15.4); the Castilian 1,216/8,144 (= 14.9); Biscay squadron 810/6,562 (= 12.3); Andalucian 775/8,402 (= 9.2); Guipuzcoan 644/6,937 (= 9.3); Levantine 837/9,537 (= 8.8). A few individual examples will serve to emphasise the differences in manning within each squadron: in the Levantine squadron the *Rata* had 10.2, and the *Regazona* 6.4; in the Guipuzcoan squadron the *Santa Maria* had 11.5, and the *Santa Cruz* 5.3; in the Biscay squadron, the *Santa María de Montemayor* had 6.4, and the *María Juan* 15; the Portuguese galleons averaged 16, the *Florencia* had 9.
44. P. Pierson, *Commander of the Armada* (New Haven & London, 1989) p. 222.
45. Herrera Oria, *Armada* p. 97, 29 Dec 1587; individual captains also complained about the inadequacy of ordnance, e.g. AGS GA 222 f. 60

Oquendo, 19 March 1588 declared it to be deficient; GA 220 f. 55, Recalde, 6 Feb 1588 said it was too little and too small; GA 222 f. 7 Valdes, 19 March 1588 that it was too small.

46. AGS GA 220 f. 224, 27 Feb 1588; and AGS GA 199 ff. 47, 52, 15 July 1587.

47. Only 46% of the Armada's guns were 'countable' in Michael Lewis's terms (= 4lb shot), and only 6.8% threw a ball of 15 lbs or over (162, cf. 251 English); I. A. A. Thompson, 'Spanish Armada gun procurement and policy', in *God's obvious design*, ed. P. Gallagher and D. G. Cruickshank (London, 1990) pp. 69–84 at p. 70.

48. On 14 May 1588 the Castilian squadron with 295 guns had 566 quintals of powder; even deducting 80 quintals for the infantry, it had 77 quintals more than it needed for its guns at 60 shot per gun; but it only had 25.3 balls per gun (7,474 balls, including stone and fancy shot), AGS GA 221 ff. 148, 152. On 17 April 1588 the other squadrons (excluding that of Portugal), with 1,750 guns, were short by 21,700 iron and 2,340 stone balls and by 1,268 quintals of powder — but distribution was uneven: the galeasses and Andalucian squadron were more or less supplied up to scratch; the Levant squadron was 38,363 lbs of powder short; the hulks had none, and needed 43,575 lbs, AGS GA 221 f. 143 (9 May 1588), f. 127 (10 April 1588), f. 129 (17 April 1588).

49. FD I pp. 482, 527 (23 April 1588), 195 *reales* per quintal; contractors in Granada were supplying it for 84 *reales.*

50. Herrera Oria, *Armada* p. 283, Governor Cerralbo 12 Sept 1588; AGS GA 365 'Relacion general de la artilleria que ay en España', 17 Nov 1588; fortresses and arsenals needed 23,423 quintals of powder, which was 70% of requirement, 7,731½ quintals of lead (66.5% of requirement), 7,757 quintals of match (63%), 774 guns (60%), but 545 or 77% of naval gun types (demi-cannon, demi-culverin, sakers, *pedreros*) and 23,968 shot (10.75%). On the bad quality of Spanish gunpowder, AGS GA 191 Alonso Moreno, pilot of Seville, 13 Nov 1586; GA 302 'Relacion tocante a la polvora' of 1589; *ACC* XI p. 518 petition 12, of 1588.

51. FD I p. 475.

52. In the 1624 fleet there were 26 soldiers per 100 *toneladas*; Santa Cruz wanted a ratio of 50 men to 100 *toneladas*, Medina Sidonia wanted 100 per 100 (5 March 1587), Maura, p. 169. In 1588 the soldiers averaged 31 per 100 *toneladas* (20,181 men — 873 on the galeasses for 62,278 *toneladas*). The soldiers for the campaign have been the subject of two recent monographs in the Naval Institute's *Gran Armada* series: M. Gracia Rivas, *Los tercios de la Gran Armada (1587–1588)* (vol. VI, Madrid, 1989) deals with the men on the fleet; H. O'Donnell y Duque de Estrada, *La fuerza de desembarco de la Gran Armada contra Inglaterra (1588)* (vol. V, Madrid, 1989) with the forces in the Netherlands under Parma.

53. FD II p. 100, 21 May 1588; and Herrera Oria, *Armada*, p. 210, 1 July 1588; *ibid.* p. 249 Andrés de Alva, 19 July 1588; also AGS GA 225 f. 68.

54. FD II p. 137, letter of 24 June 1588.

55. FD II p. 204, letter of 19 July 1588. Most of the veteran troops were with the duke of Parma in the Netherlands.

56. Andrés de Alva, La Coruña, 19 July 1588, thought there was bread and wine for four months and other things for two or more, 'it honestly has enough victuals which are absolutely essential, that is bread and wine' — Herrera Oria, *Armada* p. 250; Bernavé de Pedroso, La Coruña, 6 July 1588 said: 'I do not think that it will be short of water, and what they have taken is good quality', he thought they had sufficient supplies for four and a half months, AGS GA 225 f. 58; FD II p. 152 letter 5 July 1588.

57. FD II pp. 118, 119 letters of 14 and 19 June 1588.

58. Marquis of Almazán in the council of state meeting. With some exaggeration for effect he went on, 'when the fleet left Lisbon on 30 May we were informed that it had provisions for six months, and that is what those in charge of victualling and provisioning wrote; on 24 June when it took shelter in La Coruña the wastage and fraud in victualling was discovered, and after taking on new provisions, it was said and confirmed that it was now better provided than before, with more than six month's provisions, and now we have seen that in the twenty-seven days it sailed — for that is the length of time that elapsed between 23 July when it left La Coruña to 20 August when the duke of Medina Sidonia wrote to say he had cut down rations so that they would have enough to last for a month — the shortage of victuals was evident'. AGS E 1945.

59. AGS GA 343, petition of Doña Ana de Avila, 26 June 1591.

60. F. Pérez Mínguez, *Don Juan de Idiáquez, embajador y consejero de Felipe II* (San Sebastián, 1934) p. 237 note 256.

61. Don Juan de Idiáquez, 28 Feb 1587 in Maura, p. 167.

62. The *tercio* of Naples, listed with 2,889 men in twenty-six companies at the Lisbon muster, had 1,864 in ten companies in July 1587, 1,803 at the end of August, and 1,396 in May 1588, FD I p. 387, AGS GA 221 f. 37; there were a total of 11,389 soldiers on 2 December 1587, and 1,053 fewer on 8 January 1588. See Gracia Rivas below pp. 204–5 for an explanation of some of these losses.

63. Herrera Oria, *Armada* p. 34.

64. AGS E 1945 council of state, 28 Sept 1588.

65. AGS GA 225 f. 55, 15 July 1588; Rodríguez-Salgado below p. 146 for a further discussion of this letter.

66. FD II pp. 469–76; Rodríguez-Salgado below pp. 154–5.

67. Guilmartin, *Gunpowder and galleys*, ch. 3.

68. AGS E 165 f. 229 Alonso Gutiérrez, 9 June 1587.

69. J. Vicens Vives, 'The administrative structure of the state in the sixteenth

and seventeenth centuries' in H. J. Cohn (ed.), *Government in Reformation Europe 1520–1560* (London, 1971) pp. 58–87.

70. The king provided the galley contractors with a number of *forzados* specified in the contract, usually fifteen a year.

71. AGS GA 482 Santa Gadea writing from Ferrol, 27 Feb 1597.

72. Thompson, *War* pp. 242–8.

73. 26 Feb 1580, 'there are thirty-nine large Levantine ships and not a single one from these realms', Suárez Inclán, *Guerra de anexión en Portugal* II p. 363; in 1583 about half the Terceira fleet was of Mediterranean origin (17 vessels out of 36, 11,000 out of 20,000 *toneladas*), *CSPVen* VIII no. 148 p. 60, in 1588 only one in eight of the larger ships.

74. Codoin III p. 30.

75. Codoin II p. 173, J. A. Doria, 12 May 1594: 'the galleys of Spain used not only to come to Italy but to stay there for years on end'. The *cortes* were wont to complain that the coasts of Spain were unguarded because all the galleys were in Italy, *ACC* II p. 428 (1566); now Sicilian and Neapolitan galleys were serving in Spain (11 of the 16 Sicilian galleys in 1588, 12 of the Neapolitan in 1596), and both Naples and Sicily contributed with men and money to the *Gran Armada* (e.g. the *tercio de Sicilia* and six vessels from the Levant were charged to Sicilian revenues, FD I p. 308; Viceroy Alva de Liste claimed Sicily spent 533,000 *scudi* in 1588, H. G. Koenigsberger, *The government of Sicily under Philip II of Spain* (London, 1951) p. 132.

76. A. Calabria, *State finance in the kingdom of Naples in the age of Philip II* (Ann Arbor, 1978) ch. 5.

77. J. Reglà, *Felip II i Catalunya* (Barcelona, 1956) p. 205; Koenigsberger, *Government of Sicily* p. 56.

4

ATLANTIC SHIPPING IN SIXTEENTH-CENTURY SPAIN AND THE 1588 ARMADA

José Luis Casado Soto

War at sea is more dangerous and exposed than war on land, because of the great misfortunes that can arise and occur.
— Alfonso X: *Leyes de Partida*, II, XXIII (1256–63)

The Castilians are building ships of all shapes and sizes, large and small, in this and that style, in an attempt to sail all the world's seas and to provide everything which is provided by the ships of all other kingdoms.
— Juan Escalante de Mendoza, *Itinerario de las tierras y mares occidentales* (1575)

1. How current opinions have been formed

Historians throughout the world have long expressed reservations about the quality of Spanish shipping in the sixteenth century; at times indeed they have pronounced frankly unfavourable judgements on it, and have not hesitated to make adverse comparisons with shipping of other Atlantic states. Broadly speaking, Spanish ships have been totally identified with contemporary large Mediterranean cargo vessels. Consequently their design has been dismissed as obsolete and much has been made of their awkward displacement, and the clumsy manoeuvring ostensibly caused by their huge superstructures — all this being in stark contrast to the supposedly advanced development of English and Dutch shipping.[1]

These arguments simply do not fit with another equally undisputed fact which is far more important and carries much greater weight: during the sixteenth century Spain was precisely the one power that built and maintained the first truly world-wide empire in history, despite encountering considerable resistance and having to face foreign aggression. There is no doubt that in order to do so it was essential for

Spain to control communication routes across several oceans. Technically (and logically) this would not have been possible unless Spain had by this time possessed the necessary organisation, seamanship, armament, and quite specifically, shipping.

A more recent and persistent trend has been to limit discussions of Spanish shipbuilding and naval activity to a purely Mediterranean context.[2] This shows complete ignorance of — or at the very least a willingness to set aside — the powerful pull of the Atlantic on Castile, evident from the middle ages, as well as of the widespread and permanent presence of its multiple fleets around Europe's Atlantic waters during the whole of the sixteenth century; not to mention the impressive achievements in the fields of exploration, conquest, defence, and the intensive commercial exchanges with the whole of the American continent, from Newfoundland to Tierra del Fuego and the Pacific Ocean.

This distortion can be attributed principally to two significant factors: first, the great scarcity of Spanish research into shipbuilding during the period of its greatest geographical discoveries;[3] second, in stark contrast to what has just been said, the wealth of publications dealing with contemporary English naval matters.[4] Without a doubt the pejorative opinion of Spanish shipping has been created by Anglo-Saxon historiography. A careful examination of the references given in these texts reveals that they have based their assertions on a very small number of books dealing with the 1588 Armada, and quite specifically those published as a result of the great celebrations held one hundred years ago, at the time of the tricentenary of the event.[5] These celebrations served to circulate and to fix in the popular imagination opinions which had their origin in the propaganda campaign and psychological warfare that ensued as the protestant world attempted to take advantage of the strategic failure of Philip II's invasion. This propaganda was re-used whenever relations with Spain worsened during the intervening four hundred years. In effect the *Gran Armada* campaign quickly became both a contributory cause and a mainstay of the so-called Black Legend in England, which condemned Spain for greed and tyranny, as well as of cowardice and incompetence, two adjectives that propagandists prior to 1588 had never dared to conceive, let alone use against the Spaniards.[6]

After the Second World War came the first — albeit qualified — challenges to the axiom that the defeat of the Armada had been one of the turning points of universal and European history.[7] In a parallel development, works appeared on the technical aspects of the campaign, subjecting the shipping, ordnance and the tactics of both sides to a seemingly rigorous scientific examination.[8] The conclusions reached, however, were largely in agreement with traditional views, which now had the added advantage of being confirmed by strict 'scientific' research. Consequently, while the most recent and original works on the Armada have re-examined many well-known aspects of the campaign, its consequences and effects on subsequent history, they continue to repeat almost without exception (as if it were an immutable truth) the common consensus regarding the differences and diverging quality of the technological development of the two combatants.[9]

Notwithstanding their scientific character, these works (which have done so much to consolidate the traditional picture) will not stand up to a thorough examination; it soon becomes evident that they suffer from serious and very basic methodological deficiencies which totally undermine their conclusions. The most important of these are:

(a) Lack of clarity and uncertainty over the Spanish system of measurements in the sixteenth century[10]
(b) Ignorance of the different ways of measuring tonnage in the Atlantic regions of Spain during that century[11]
(c) Lack of statistical data (of the size and dimensions) of individual ships before the seventeenth century[12]
(d) Ignorance of the existence in Spanish archives of several treatises, memoranda, discussions of prototypes and naval architecture for the historical period under consideration[13]
(e) Complete ignorance of the systematic and consistent policy of Philip II to build more and better ships in order to meet the needs of his empire.[14]

Discussions of Spanish shipping have also been based on the biased interpretation of highly dubious iconography without respect for chronology,[15] and on a handful of statements made after 1588 either by those who needed to justify a strategic failure in which they had taken part; or by those who wanted to make the more than dubious claim that this had been a naval, that is, a tactical victory.[16]

2. Aspects of Philip II's naval policy

Philip II has enjoyed little favour among historians in general, but in the specific field of naval policy he has been sentenced without any mitigating circumstances being taken into account, thanks largely to the failure of the *Gran Armada* and the subsequent manipulation of the event by patriots on both sides, but also because of a forthright judgement issued from the pen of the most distinguished historian of the Spanish navy, who condemned Philip II of being lukewarm and indifferent to naval matters, in contrast to his father, the Emperor Charles V.[17] No historian familiar with the Spanish archives of the period can maintain such a claim now.[18] Nevertheless, some very significant aspects of naval affairs to which the king and the councils of War, Indies and Finance devoted so much attention to remain little known or ignored.

2.1 Legislation

Philip II's concern to regulate important matters through legislation has long been acknowledged, but little attention has been paid to the constant efforts he made to legislate on naval affairs. He began early, in 1550 during his last regency, with the proclamation of new ordinances reforming and systematizing security arrangements in the Indies Trade.[19] Even more far-reaching were the ordinances of 1552 which, among other things, stipulated the ordnance to be carried on board and gave the shipowner a fixed time limit in which to acquire the necessary guns.[20]

Shortly after becoming king, between 1561 and 1564, Philip instituted the system of two annual *flotas* or convoys, one for New Spain, the other for *Tierra Firme*. He ordered that the flagship and vice-flagship should carry 100 tons less than their ordinary weight capacity to facilitate the handling of the guns, and to give them greater manoeuvrability.[21] In 1565 he decreed that henceforth a galleon of 300 tons or more should serve as flagship; it was not to be laden at all with merchandise, but instead to carry even more artillery.[22] The following year he imposed the same conditions for the vice-flagships of the *flotas*.[23]

To this we should add the updating of mercantilist legislation, which reinforced the decrees of previous monarchs giving Spanish ships preference over foreign vessels, and prohibiting the sale of Spanish ships to foreigners — thus withdrawing some of the generous concessions Charles V had made to the Italians and the Netherlanders. There were also a variety of technical specifications applied to improve the safety of shipping: for example, orders were issued that all vessels must have two pumps and set aside a cabin at the bow for the powder (1552); that old vessels should not be altered and made bigger (1557); that each ship should have two rudders (1575); that ships sailing to the Indies should not be fitted with oak masts (1577), and many others.[24] These rules applied not only to the Indies fleets, but also to ships plying trade to the Netherlands.[25]

2.2 The Promotion of Shipbuilding

Least known of all the government's naval activities was the complex and determined policy of incentives to promote shipbuilding, especially warships and ocean-going vessels. The crown worked towards this end in a variety of ways. As well as the imposition of the mercantilist policies described above, its activities covered the following major areas:

(a) Intensification of the programme for the plantation of oaks along the coast of Biscay in strips of land 12 kilometres deep stretching from the coast and the river banks, particularly after 1563.

(b) The amendment of the controversial 'ley de la mayoría' giving preference to ships of more than 600 tons over smaller cargo vessels; now it was reduced to 300 tons.

(c) Whereas before the *acostamiento* or annual payment to ship-builders of 10,000 *maravedis* per ship was granted for each 100 tons over the 600 ton mark, its ceiling was now reduced and it could be claimed by those who constructed vessels of over 300 tons.

(d) All purchases of naval stores were exempt from sales taxes comprehended in the *alcabala*, as were sales of ships between Spaniards.[26]

(e) A fund was set up to give interest-free credit to shipbuilders; these funds were repayable two years after the ship had been launched, and lent out again to other shipbuilders. The fund started with a capital of 20,000 ducats in 1563 but it was increased in 1568, 1578 and 1583 when it was over 42,000 ducats. The funds granted under this scheme, which was managed throughout by Cristóbal de Barros, were calculated at two ducats per ton. In return for the loan, the shipbuilders had to agree to construct these vessels according to government specifications provided by royal officials, which affected its size, strength, fittings, and armament. Thanks to these, the ships built were equally suitable for commerce and for war.[27] Running parallel to this scheme was another similar project run by Lope de Avellaneda with a capital of 60,000 ducats: in exchange for following even stricter building regulations, and undertaking to serve in the royal fleets whenever required, shipbuilders were lent four ducats per ton.[28] A year before his death, Philip II issued further decrees greatly improving the system of naval loans and subsidies, raising the figure to a maximum of 4,000 ducats per ship, which was to be returned three years after the ship was launched, during which time the crown undertook not to embargo it.[29]

2.3 The Creation of a New Bureaucracy

During Philip II's reign the crown decided to administer its Atlantic navy directly, in contrast to Charles V's decision to use a contract system. An immediate consequence of this was the creation of a number of administrative and technical offices which were, on the whole, exercised by efficient and well-qualified staff. The usual procedure followed by the government was to deal with naval matters in a formal meeting or *consulta*. This might also involve bringing into the discussions technical or specialist officials. Once a decision had been made, orders would be transmitted to the chief magistrates in the towns (*corregidores*), and to commissioners of the two main commercial centres, the consulate of Burgos and the Casa de Contratación of Seville.

The key figure in the construction of Atlantic shipping throughout practically the whole of Philip's reign was Cristóbal de Barros, who was a salaried royal official and specialised in naval affairs from 1562 to his death in 1596. He was the recipient of a number of decrees in 1563 which formally inaugurated the king's naval policy, and he was charged to see to their execution. Until 1574 when he was given the formal title of *Superintendente de Plantíos* with wide-ranging powers even over the *corregidores*, he was described merely as a 'criado del rey', servant of the king. His responsibilities were extensive, ranging from the implementation and control of the crown's policy on plantations, the measurement of ships built in the ports of Biscay, running the shipping loan scheme, drawing up a register of the ships available in northern Spain, overseeing the construction of warships paid directly by the royal fisc, as well as drawing up (under direct instructions from the king and his councillors) frequent memoranda, reports and analysis of all such naval and related activities. The bulk of the legislation on naval matters was a direct consequence of his zealous work; indeed it was often merely a textual copy of his recommendations.

There is one other facet that has not received due attention: the organization and provision of specialised, permanent fleets at different points in the extensive Spanish empire.[30] In 1562 a squadron of eight galleys was formed to ensure the safety of shipping by keeping the corsairs out of the seas around Cape St. Vincent and the gulf of Cadiz.[31] In 1568 what would soon be called the *Armada para la guarda de la Carrera de las Indias* was created with twelve specially constructed galleons built at the Deusto shipyards.[32] Two years later eight frigates were built at Havana to use in the defence of the Caribbean.[33] From 1575 the defence of the West Indies and the mainland was covered by two galley squadrons; one based in Cartagena, the other around the Greater Antilles, collectively known as the *Armada de Barlovento*. A few years later the galleys were replaced by galleons.[34] From 1578 another fleet was gradually put together in Peru to defend the South Pacific.[35] With the galleons of Portugal, and the gradual incorporation of *naos* and *pataches* from the coast of Biscay, a formidable and permament fleet operated after 1580 with its base in Lisbon, which not only made possible the conquest of the Azores, but also guaranteed the safe arrival of the Indies fleets during that whole decade. In the 1590s it was formally instituted as the *Armada del Océano*.[36]

Apart from the usual hierarchy of military and naval command all these fleets had efficient administrative infrastructures, which included accountants, overseers, purveyors, clerks and other personnel who usually exercised their charges over long periods of time. This completely contradicts the traditional notion that Spain had no permanent Atlantic fleets until after the *Gran Armada*. This erroneous belief stems largely from the fact that most of the ships' soldiers and sailors were disbanded during the winter months, but this was common practice in all navies of the period. While there were occasional setbacks, and a temporary slowdown during the mid 1580s, and while the size of the administrative machinery was small in comparison to that created during and after the

Gran Armada campaign, this in no way undermines the argument that Spain did possess fully-functioning Atlantic fleets on both sides of the ocean with the necessary administrative infrastructure long before the *Gran Armada*.[37]

3. Basic Facts on Atlantic Ship Construction in Iberia during the Sixteenth Century

Our team was one of several participating in the *Gran Armada* research project sponsored by the Instituto de Historia y Cultura Naval in Madrid; we undertook to study the basic *matériel* of the enterprise, the ships and ordnance. It was soon evident, however, that we could not tackle these subjects from the limited perspective of a concrete event, owing to the level of confusion and lack of definition that characterised the study of so many aspects of our themes. We had no choice but to widen our analysis.

No attempt at unravelling the complex problems of Spanish naval architecture in the sixteenth century could be done without a major effort to find additional documentation in the vast archives created by the elaborate and efficient bureaucracy which evolved to meet the administrative and defensive needs of the growing Spanish empire. Among the enormous quantity of documents there are many thousands which make possible the reconstruction of different facets of naval architecture and logistics, although these are dispersed in a multitude of different collections and have scarcely been used.[38]

3.1 Measuring Ships

Until now the few writers who have attempted a definition of Spanish ship measurements in the Age of Discovery have belonged to one of two historiographical schools, which curiously enough are not as incompatible as they appear. The one has focussed on the reconstruction of Colombus' ships;[39] the other has been concerned with quantifying the volume of Indies trade and is properly the realm of the economic historian.[40] The notable discrepancies in the figures produced arise largely from the fact that these studies have been based on a very limited number of contemporary references, often taken out of context. Not only has a basic conceptual confusion between cargo capacity and displacement weight been created, but simple arithmetical errors have been repeated. In order to reach a firm definition of the measuring system used in the Spanish Atlantic coast it has been necessary not merely to expand the range of research, but also to compare the information obtained with a statistically valid sample of measurements of individual ships.

The Atlantic coast of Spain during this period used the *codo* as the basic linear measurement in the construction and evaluation of shipping, but the term meant different things in different areas, and consequently it had different mathematical values. There were two main standards of measurement which concern us here, that used in the major shipbuilding centre of Spain, the Cantabrian coast (coast of Biscay) and the slightly less common measurement of the Andalucian coast which primarily affected Indies commerce.

From the middle ages the *tonel* — the basic unit of measurement for the cargo volume of a vessel — was the equivalent of two *pipas* of wine, or eight cubic *codos*. However, because of the different value given to the *codo*, this meant that measurements in the Cantabrian and Andalucian coasts were out by almost 10% (See table below).

Worse still is the confusion surrounding the *tonelada*. Virtually all those who have touched on this subject have found the problem of defining its metrical value by far the most difficult to solve. Their conclusions have been wrong, mainly because they have failed to perceive a crucial semantic change during the sixteenth century that led to the use of the same word for two quite different things. In its original form, the *tonelada* was a *unit of account*, which was obtained by adding 20% or 25% to the estimated tonnage of the ship, that is to the objective dimensions of the vessel which were reckoned in *toneles*; the 20% or 25% was a bonus to top up the basic rate of pay for the ships hired by the crown which had not been raised since 1509 despite the general increase in prices. It also served as an incentive and additional compensation for the proprietors since their ships would run much greater risks while in the service of the crown, especially in a war. Thus there was a clear distinction between the *tonel* and the *tonelada*. From the mid century, however, the distinction gradually became blurred in the southern Spanish ports, where the word *tonelada* was increasingly used also to describe the dimensions of a ship. It was almost always made clear what type of *tonelada* was in use by adding the words '*de carga*' (cargo tonnage), to distinguish it from the *tonelada* proper, the *tonelada de sueldo* (that is the accounting unit made up of cargo tonnage plus 20%–25%).

Table 1   Naval Metrology in the Spanish Atlantic During the Sixteenth Century

---

Vara Castellana = 3 *pies* = 4 *palmos* = 48 *dedos* = 0.8359m

---

Units of Longitude

Codo Castellano (cC) = 32 *dedos* = 0.55726m
Codo Cantabrico (cR) = 33 *dedos* = 0.57468m (= c.ribera = c.real)

Units of Volume or Tonnage

Tonelada de carga (Seville) = 8 (cC)^3 = Tn
Tonel macho (Cantabrian) = 8 (cR)^3 = TM

Units of Account

Tonelada de sueldo = *tonel macho* or *tonelada de carga* plus 20% − 25% bonus payment

---

It is important to take into account the powerful interests at stake when it came to gauging the size of ships. It could make a great deal of difference to the customs dues charged, and the amount which might be claimed when the crown hired a vessel, and as a result there were many fraudulent and contradictory statements made about a ship's tonnage.[41] In fact we have a great deal of evidence of the many different ploys used to manipulate the figures, for instance by the deliberate substitution of *toneles mayores* and *menores*, or *toneladas de carga* and *toneladas de sueldo*; as well as confusing the measurements taken in the north with those taken in the south. In order to put an end to the abuses, the confusion, and the many law suits they gave rise to, as well as to safeguard the interests of the royal fisc, Philip decreed in 1590 — it was his third attempt at this — that all naval measurements should be reconciled. Henceforth all shipwrights were to use the *codo de ribera* used in the Cantabrian coast, and the *tonel macho* or gross tonnage which resulted from this. Somewhat confusingly, however, this new measure was called a *tonelada*, and the word would in the future retain this specific meaning.[42]

3.2 Estimating the Tonnage of Ships

There is a consensus among naval experts that the tonnage of ships during the middle ages and even in the sixteenth century was estimated in an empirical fashion. A final decision was not reached until the ship had been launched and loaded more than once, because of the great difficulty then, as now, of quantifying the amount of useful cargo space that can be used in the very irregular shape of a ship's hull. Nevertheless, this does not mean that expert shipwrights were incapable of giving an approximate estimate based on the basic dimensions of the ship, in other words of the beam, keel, height (depth of the hold) and length.

Spain was the first European country to confront the pressing necessity of establishing a rigorous and objective system of measuring ships. The subsidies for naval construction, the payment of wages to embargoed shipping, the customs dues on Indian commerce and maintenance of its monopoly, even the security measures decreed for the commerce with the New World, were all based on the tonnage of a ship. Consequently, from the beginning of the sixteenth century special officials were appointed to establish the tonnage of the many ships which fell under one or more of these categories, with sufficient authority and skill to avoid lawsuits and conflicts between those concerned.[43]

As has been noted earlier, until now we had no knowledge of any mathematical formulae employed in calculating the capacity of Spanish ships in the sixteenth century.[44] In the course of our research we have discovered a formula which was used in the Cantabrian coast throughout the century,[45] as well as three other formulae used in the Atlantic coast of Andalucia between 1550 and 1590. Together these prove how far the measurement and tonnage of ships had proceeded towards a mathematical definition in the two areas where most of the Atlantic and oceanic shipping of Spain was concentrated during the sixteenth century. It was never a question of simply applying a fixed arithmetical formula, however. Once calculated the figures were adjusted to take into account a number of related factors such as the different type of ship, and the different shape of the hull above and below the water-line. Thus we can state without hesitation that the mathematical formulation of the useful capacity of a ship was pioneered in the Spanish Atlantic ports, and they developed far more rigorous and exact systems of calculation than those adapted many years later by the rest of the European maritime states.[46]

3.3 Naval Typology

Thanks to these formulae and the more than two hundred dimensions of individual ships we have found, it has been possible to classify the

Table 2   Formulae used to Estimate Tonnage in the Spanish Atlantic During the Sixteenth Century

L=length   B=beam   K=keel   H=height, i.e. depth of hold

Cantabrian: in cR (codo ribera/real)

$$\text{(1520–1590)} \;=\; \frac{L\sqrt{\dfrac{\left(\dfrac{B}{2}+H\right)^{2}}{2}}}{8} \quad \frac{19}{20}=\frac{19}{640}\,L\left(\frac{B}{2}+H\right)^{2} \quad =TM \;\text{(Toneles Machos)}$$

Seville & Cadiz: in cC (codo castellano)

$$\text{(c.1560)} \;=\; \frac{\dfrac{2}{3}\,K.B.H.}{8} \;=\; \frac{K.B.H.}{12} \;=\; \text{Toneles}=Tn$$

$$\text{(1570–1590)} \;=\; \frac{L\sqrt{\dfrac{\left(\dfrac{B}{2}+H\right)^{2}}{2}}}{8} \;=\; \frac{1}{32}\,L\left(\frac{B}{2}+H\right)^{2} \;=\; Tn \;\text{Toneles}$$

different types of ships used by the Spanish crown during the sixteenth century. Their typology has been tested and refined by reference to shipbuilding treatises, memoranda and the various contemporary prototypes produced.

The vast majority of Spanish ships plying the Atlantic were built on the Cantabrian coast, to be precise in the provinces of Cantabria, Vizcaya and Guipúzcoa. Some Mediterranean and Baltic ships were used from the 1570s onwards, but they were few until the very end of the century.[47] Contemporary documentation leaves no doubt as to the very high esteem in which Cantabrian shipping was held. It should be stressed that one of the reasons for the acute shortage of Cantabrian shipping was the need to meet the constantly rising demand for more and bigger ships for the Mediterranean, which drained a significant portion of total Cantabrian production as the price of shipping in the Mediterranean was fifty per cent higher than in Spain. If mercantile sectors in Seville put a great deal of pressure on the government to allow Flemish and German hulks to be used in the Indies routes it was for the simple reason that they cost half the price of a Cantabrian ship of the same tonnage.[48] The high regard and reputation for quality of Cantabrian shipping was sustained throughout Philip's reign, which is sufficient proof of its excellence: these ships were truly seaworthy and structurally sound. It was no mean achievement to maintain such standards, as this lengthy period was one of constant evolution and structural adaptation in order to respond to the pressing needs of the Atlantic.

It is important to bear in mind that increased demand meant not only the production of more ships, but also a marked growth in size and tonnage.

Clearly such an increase in tonnage required a whole series of structural changes in the construction of ships. Broadly speaking it led to alteration of the shape of the ribs, a reduction of the superstructure, and the reinforcement of the frame, and it affected the fittings (more sails, and therefore more masts and more complex standing rigging and sheets). This process was not limited to the *nao* — which was the most frequently used ship for mercantile and military purposes — but was applied to the other different types of ships from the Cantabrian yards, which we can now begin to classify with some accuracy. The table below summarises the basic measurements of each of these types of vessel.

Spanish Atlantic Galleon from the last quarter of the sixteenth century. Note the small superstructure. Ref. Archivo General de Indias *Patronato* 175 R. 41.

Table 3   Tonnage Increase in the Spanish Fleets During the Reign of Philip II

Year	Fleet	Number of ships	Average weight in *toneles*	Index
1557	Fitted out in Laredo to take 6,000 soldiers to the Netherlands.[49]	23	246	100
1567	Fitted out in Santander to take Philip II to the Netherlands; disbanded.[50]	24	392	159
1572	Fitted out in Laredo to take the duke of Medinaceli to the Netherlands.[51]	7	475	193
1588	Cantabrian ships in the *Gran Armada*.[52]	29	553	225

Table 4   Proportions and Capacity of the Major Types of Ships in the Atlantic Coast of Spain During the Second Half of the Sixteenth Century

Ship type	Toneles	Beam	Keel	Length
Naos	150–700	1	2 – 2.25	3.2
Navios	40–150	1	—	3.6
Galleons	300–700	1	2.3 – 2.5	3.3 – 3.66
Galleasses	100–200	1	2.13 – 2.47	3.2 – 3.8
Zabras	30– 80	1	—	3.75
Pinazas	20– 40	1	—	3.88

These proportions are in stark contrast to those of foreign shipping, whether Italian, Flemish or German, used by the crown to complement the fleets, as shown in Table 5.

All contemporary memoranda and Spanish construction treatises are unanimous that Spanish ships were built with small superstructures, quite contrary to foreign ships. Even in the very largest vessels the superstructure consisted merely of a wooden deck for the forecastle and another for the quarter-deck or poop, on which at the very end, one might find an awning for the captain's cabin.[53]

Table 5   Proportions and Capacity of 'foreign' shipping

Ship type	Toneles	Beam	Length
Adriatic ships	600–1,100	1	2.8
Tyrrhenian ships	400– 800	1	3
Flemish hulks	200– 700	1	2.8
German hulks	300– 700	1	3.1

3.4 Calculating the Size of the Spanish Fleet and Ship Production

Until now, only one attempt had been made to calculate the global volume of the Spanish fleet during the sixteenth century. Usher based his estimate on a paragraph from Tomé Cano written at the beginning of the seventeenth century which is absolutely worthless for such a complex calculation.[54] We do have the partial, although in some ways exhaustive, accounts of the ships sailing to the New World between 1504 and 1650 compiled by Huguette and Pierre Chaunu. Unfortunately the Chaunus' work is seriously flawed: firstly, it gives no indication of the overall number of ships from which these samples were taken; second and most importantly, they have made a grave error when computing tonnage by following the entirely mistaken theory that there was a transition from the *tonelada corta* to a (fictitious) *tonelada larga* in Spain during the sixteenth century.[55]

There are definitely many factors which complicate the task of estimating the global volume of shipping whether of Spain or other countries during the sixteenth century. The vast majority of port books have disappeared, and those extant are extremely selective; these factors alone justify the complaints that we lack sufficient documentation. Nevertheless the discovery of a number of accounts of shipping in this period makes possible an approximate estimate for three separate periods of the sixteenth century: that is for the second half of the 1530s, the mid century, and the beginning of the 1570s.[56]

The figures given above are the best we can provide for the time being, but they must be considered only as rough indicators because of the very uneven and varied documentation from which they have been collated, the partial and selective nature of those documents, and the limited projections made to reach the final figures. What they do establish beyond question is the great increase in tonnage during the first two decades of Philip II's reign.

Table 6   The Volume of Shipping in the Spanish Atlantic During the Sixteenth Century (in Toneles)

Period	Cantabrian Fleet	Indies Fleet	Total
c.1536	35,000	10,000	45,000
c.1555	38,000	12,000	50,000
1572	45,000	20,000	65,000

The various measures adopted by the king and his councils to promote shipbuilding from the beginning of the reign, and extended and consolidated as the years passed, clearly gave a powerful stimulus to the construction of more and bigger ships, made to the rigorous technical specifications drawn up by the crown's officials whose aim was to create ships equally suitable for commerce and for war. We know that in 1567 alone twelve ships were built in Cantabria and Guipuzcoa, with an average size of 385 *toneles machos*; together with some four or five others built in Vizcaya, they amounted to some 6,000 *toneles*.[57] We also know that the new measures implemented that same year had truly impressive results, because in a mere five years, more than sixty ships with an average of over 400 *toneles* were built with the help of government subsidies, apart from another sixty averaging 250 *toneles* built without subsidies; in other words, a little under 40,000 *toneles* of shipping were added to the existing fleets.[58] Naturally we have to deduct from this total a considerable number of ships which went to the Mediterranean via Andalucian intermediaries, as well as the ordinary losses in the oceanic routes and the North Sea.

It is evident that notwithstanding such success the government was not satisfied with its original measures, and decided to extend them. In 1582 Cristóbal de Barros undertook to organise the construction of seventeen *naos* of over 350 *toneles*;[59] and that same year Avellaneda started his contract for the construction of seventeen more ships of over 500 *toneles* each.[60] In 1586, shortly before his death, Avellaneda informed the council that he had organized the construction of three great ships, of a combined tonnage of 2,065 *toneles machos*, and that their construction was well advanced.[61] These figures refer only to mercantile vessels and should be supplemented by another series of ships built specifically for fighting in Atlantic waters. At the beginning of the 1560s for example, Alvaro de Bazán built at least six *zabras* in the Cantabrian coast which were to serve in the royal fleet. In 1568

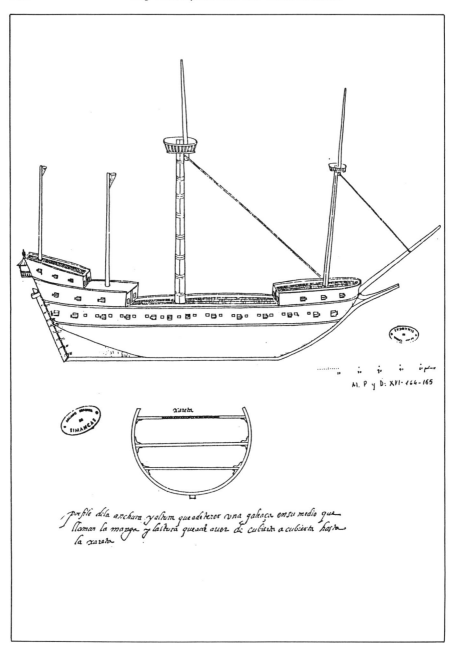

Profile and central rib section of a *nao agaleazada*, or Galleon, drawn in 1589. Note how small the superstructure is, and the marked launching. Ref. AGS MPD XVI — 164–5.

Pedro Menéndez de Avilés built twelve galleons of 250 tons in Deusto by royal command; these formed the defensive Indies squadron, *La Armada para la Guarda de la Carrera de Indias*. During the first half of 1574 the royal fisc took charge of the construction of ninety-three light vessels in the Cantabrian ports; they included *zabras, pinazas, galeotas*, and ships' boats which were intended to take part in the abortive expedition against the rebels in the Netherlands. Four years later Cristóbal de Barros built another two *galeazas* of 800 tons to serve as the flagship and vice-flagship of the Indies fleets.

After the annexation of Portugal the royal fleet incorporated the nine Portuguese royal galleons. Philip II also ordered that another eight galleons should be built, along with two *galeoncetes*. Meanwhile in the yards of Santander nine galleons were built between 1582 and 1584. There was a brief gap after this, which contrasted sharply with the great activity in the two years following the return of the *Gran Armada* from the British isles when another twenty one galleons were launched — six at Santander, six at Bilbao, six at Portugal, two at Gibraltar, and one at Vinaroz.[62]

All these different types of ships were conceived and constructed according to rigorous and rational criteria rather uncommon in that period. They were homogenous prototypes, designed to carry out very specific and well defined tasks; consequently there was great variation in their relative strength, speed, and manoeuvrability; each being developed in a manner best suited to its particular function and the level of armament required.[63]

4. Spanish Ships in the *Gran Armada* of 1588

As noted at the beginning of this article, the 1588 campaign and the *Gran Armada* in particular require special consideration because of the prevalence of the distorted accounts of the event which make up much of its ample historiography. It is our intention to restrict our analysis strictly to an assessment of the figures which have been used to justify and support the current negative judgements on the Spanish fleet — figures which have been accepted uncritically and repeated in the majority of the books published both in Britain and in Spain to commemorate the four hundred anniversary of the event.[64]

4.1. The Opposing Fleets

The constant reliance on the same limited documentary sources printed at the turn of the century[65] has at best created considerable confusion in respect of the figures given in the published estimates — not just of the numbers in the Spanish and English fleets fighting in 1588, but also the number of ships lost in the Channel and in the return journey.[66] Another key factor in the ensuing muddle is the failure to distinguish between the number of ships mobilised and those which actually participated in the fighting.

It has proved necessary to search for documentation relating to each ship which took part in the *Gran Armada* in order to proceed beyond mere guesswork. What we did was to create a dossier for each vessel with details from the moment it was launched, or embargoed, until it was disbanded, re-used, or lost. As a result we have been able to state with certainty the exact number of ships that sailed, their provenance, type, their place in the various squadrons, how they performed, and what happened to them.[67]

More work needs to be done on the English side to match this depth of documentation and analysis, but by dint of careful reading of the few documents available, we have come to the same conclusions as the most recent estimate published in Britain, that is a final figure of 226 English ships mobilized.[68]

The very different levels of research and information now available on the two fleets becomes even more of a restriction as we attempt to calculate and contrast their respective tonnages and to create an equivalent list of weights and measures — which must be done before any valid comparison can be made. While we now have the dimensions and tonnage of every single ship in the Spanish fleet, we only have those of thirty English vessels. Matters are made worse by the fact that the method of estimating tonnage in England was considerably more primitive than that used in Spain, particularly in its mathematical formulation, and therefore its results more approximate and uncertain.[69] Notwithstanding these limitations we decided to employ the dimensions of such English ships as are known and estimated their tonnage by using the formula applied in the Spanish Atlantic; at the same time we used Spanish ship dimensions and made calculations according to English rules, all this after making the necessary conversion of the different units of measurement used on each side. This dual procedure has shown that the English ton (burden) was approximately 30%

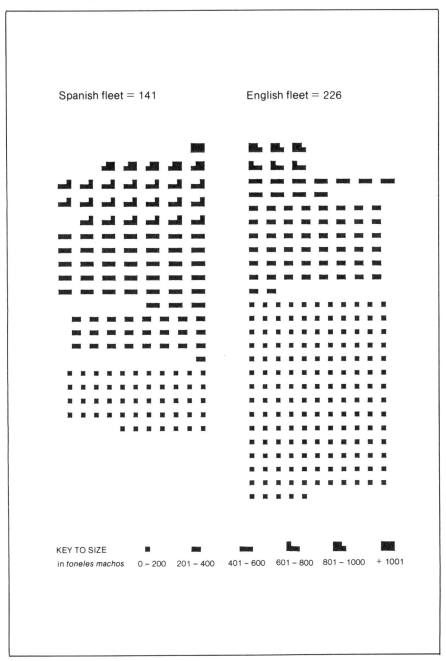

Comparative graph of the ships mobilised in England and Spain for the 1588 campaign.

greater than its Spanish equivalent. Armed with this information we have made a comparative exercise summarised in the following table. While it should be taken with some caution, we feel that this comparison is the closest to the reality of 1588, and the best indication of the size of the fleets confronting each other as yet available in print.

Out of this mass of shipping, only 122 ships from the Spanish fleet made it to the Channel. The 4 galleys, 1 *nao*, 5 *pataches* and the 10 Portuguese caravels had all left the fleet before the first encounters with the enemy.[70] A further 5 *pataches* should be deducted from the total because they were dispatched by Medina Sidonia to the Netherlands with messages to Parma. Thus Philip II could count on 117 ships to oppose the 180-strong English fleet.

To give these figures some meaning, however, we have to break them down into the different categories, function and operative capacity of the ships which made up the opposing fleets. Unfortunately we are once again seriously hampered in this exercise by the scarce and uncertain information we have for the English ships, compared to the vast documentary sources available for the Spanish fleet. After due consideration we decided that it was possible to subject only the Armada squadrons to a rigorous analysis. Our findings of the type, size, function and operative capacity of the 137 ships that sailed from La Coruña can be summarised as shown in Table 8.

4.2. The Encounters in the Channel

The *Gran Armada*, as can be seen, was essentially a well-defended convoy; only half of this force was Spanish, the other half was made up of large Italian, Flemish and German cargo vessels hired to transport the huge quantities of victuals and *matériel* needed for an action so far from its home base with no friendly deep-water port near the theatre of operations to succour the fleet, which had the added problem of having to provide everything necessary for the troops coming from Flanders to carry out the invasion. These huge cargo vessels were much slower and awkward to manoeuvre than the galleons or *naos* from Cantabria. They determined the disciplined and effective tactical formation adopted in the Channel by the Spaniards; equally important, perhaps, is the role these great vessels played in the distortion of the true image of the *Gran Armada*, which almost immediately became identified as a fleet made up entirely of colossal and clumsy 'warships'. By contrast the English

Table 7   Comparative Tonnages of Spanish and English Ships Mobilised for the 1588 Campaign

Toneles Machos	Gran Armada	English fleet
1001 – 1100	1	—
901 – 1000	1	2
801 – 900	5	1
701 – 800	7	2
601 – 700	13	1
501 – 600	18	7
401 – 500	20	4
301 – 400	13	11
201 – 300	12	38
101 – 200	7	72
1 – 100	40	87
Galleys	4	1
Total: Number of Ships	141	226
Total: Toneles	51,005	40,021

Table 8   Summary of Type, Size Function and Operative Capacity of the 137 Ships that sailed from Coruña.

Warships: Total 24
    20 galleons
    4 galleasses

Armed Merchantmen: Total 44
    29 Cantabrian *naos*
    13 Mediterranean *naves*
    2 hulks

Auxiliary Vessels: Total 38
    1 *nao*
    2 hulks
    4 galleys
    2 *galeoncetes*
    20 *pataches*
    7 *zabras*
    2 *pinazas*

Ships with Victuals: Total 31
    21 hulks
    10 caravels

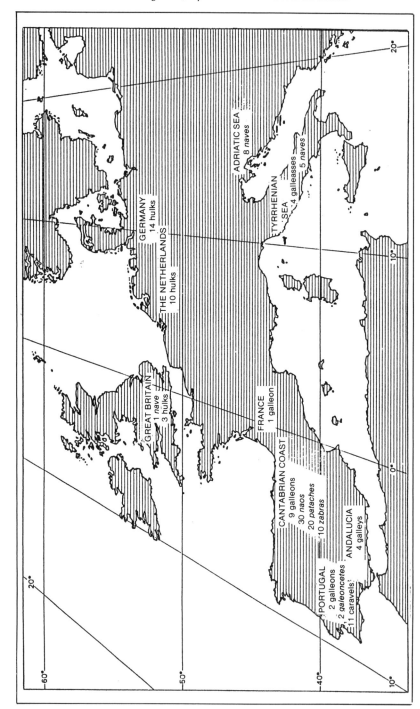

GERMANY
14 hulks

THE NETHERLANDS
10 hulks

ADRIATIC SEA
8 *naves*

TYRRHENIAN
SEA
4 galleasses   5 *naves*

GREAT BRITAIN
1 *nave*
3 hulks

FRANCE
1 galleon

CANTABRIAN COAST
9 galleons
30 *naos*
20 *pataches*
10 *zabras*

ANDALUCIA
4 galleys

PORTUGAL
2 galleons
2 *galeoncetes*
11 caravels

Provenance of the 141 ships mobilised for the Gran Armada of 1588. Note that only 117 participated in the fights in the Channel.

had the inestimable advantage of operating very close to their home base, so they could take provisions regularly without having to weigh down their ships, which were in any case more manoeuvrable because they tended to be considerably smaller than their rivals.

Slowly but surely new evidence has been amassed which proves that during the rather distant skirmishes that took place as the fleets moved up the Channel — Plymouth 31 July; Portland Bill 2 August; Isle of Wight 3-4 August — the opposing fleets did not inflict any substantial damage on each other,[71] and this enables us to challenge the persistent (and sometimes biased) efforts of writers to add — often in the form of more or less fictional attempts at dramatization — material which is nowhere supported by the documentation.[72] Even the battle of Gravelines which witnessed serious fighting did not give either side victory. Medina Sidonia had no option but to anchor off Calais, to await the arrival of Parma's *tercios*. The disadvantages of the anchorage, so exposed and liable to strong currents and winds, were seized upon by the English in order to destroy the formation which had forced them to remain at a distance during the previous week. Eight fire ships were sent against the Armada; three were successfully dispersed by the *pataches*, but to avoid catching fire, the Spanish fleet was forced to weigh anchor or cut cables. In the ensuing confusion, and carried by the current, most of the *Gran Armada* was driven towards the dangerous shifting shoals of the Flemish coast. Medina Sidonia with some eighteen ships had to face the entire English fleet. After hours of this uneven confrontation, the result was strikingly meagre: one Spanish ship (the *nao María Juan*) was sunk, and two Portuguese galleons were so badly damaged that they were forced to head for the coast and run aground.

When the Spanish fleet had recovered its formation, however, the English were forced to maintain their distance while the strong south-west winds pushed the still formidable and disciplined Armada northwards. On three different occasions a group of about one dozen vessels from the Armada hove to and challenged the English fleet to give battle; three times the English evaded a confrontation without firing a shot, by rapidly shortening sails and dropping further behind.

4.3. *The Terrible Return Journey*

On the 11 August, off the Scottish coast, the *Gran Armada* lost sight of the English fleet, which had to leave its pursuit of the feared Spanish forces due to lack of victuals and to the ravages of a typhus epidemic on board. Six days later the Armada faced the first of many storms and dense fog.

Out of the 117 Armada ships which fought in the Channel, three had been lost through accidents — the *naos Nuestra Señora del Rosario* and the *San Salvador*, and the galleass *San Lorenzo*. Another *nao*, the *María Juan* had been sunk, and two Portuguese galleons were grounded after Gravelines. One *patache* returned to Spain with news of what had happened. The Spanish fleet as it rounded the British isles on 20 August at about 60 degrees consisted therefore of only 110 vessels.

From that day onwards, the ships endured more than a month of constant violent storms and gales. The wild winds rent the sails, tore the rigging, and even wrenched spars and masts. The huge waves opened the weaker hulls and so much water poured in that the pumps could not clear it. The continuous physical exertions and the low temperatures which the ill-provided seamen and sailors had to endure in these northern latitudes were compounded by the successive cuts in their rations after the 11 August, so that the health of many men was grievously undermined. Then came typhus and scurvy; the able men in the fleet were decimated.

The combination of adverse circumstances forced the commanders of the worst-affected ships to seek refuge and provisions, especially water, in the rugged, dangerous, and little known western coast of Ireland. That broken coastline full of jagged and steep rocks was the trap into which most of the 28 ships lost in those tempests fell. The majority of those lost in this area were Italian ships and German and Flemish hulks, but not the Iberian vessels which were more sturdily built.

On the 21 September, after five weeks of being the playthings of the waves and the unleashed winds, the first ships of the *Gran Armada* arrived in the Cantabrian ports. The largest group — some fifty ships which had somehow managed to follow Medina Sidonia's flagship — entered Santander and Laredo. Eight *naves* and one *patache* went to Pasajes, and another nine *naves* and six *pataches* headed for Galician ports. One hulk anchored at Gijón, and a Guipuzcoan *nao* made it to Lisbon. The smaller ships continued to arrive up to the end of November, and some did not return until the following year.[73]

Propagandist and historian alike have until now estimated losses of the *Gran Armada* at between 60 and 70 ships, counting as lost all those ships for which they had no published documentation. But the detailed accounts of the campaign and the administrative documents for later

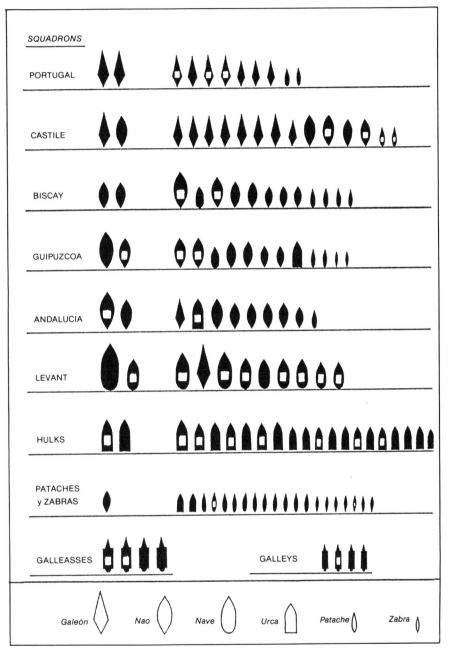

The Gran Armada which set sail from La Coruña on 22 July 1588, showing the different types of ships within each squadron. The ships marked with a square were lost before returning home. The size of the ships is represented in units of 200 *toneles*.

fleets have allowed us to prove that the total number of losses in the campaign was no more than 34 or 35 ships. As has been mentioned, it is striking that most of the ships lost in the journey through the North Atlantic back to Spain were Mediterranean vessels (71% of their total tonnage was lost), or northern hulks, particularly Flemish (62%) and German (51%). Few Spanish ships were lost, only 20% of their tonnage; casualties were also very low among the *pataches* and *zabras* (10%) and the galleons (6%), and none of those lost in these categories was Spanish.[74]

It is hardly daring therefore to conclude from these figures that the Iberian ships proved sturdier and more seaworthy — even when pitted against such hostile elements — than shipping from the inland seas, whether the Mediterranean, North Sea or the Baltic.

4.4. Some Remarks on the Guns of the Gran Armada

Wild and unsupported statements have also been made about the naval ordnance used by both sides, which have invariably exaggerated the excellence and high quality of English cast-iron guns, particularly the English-speaking historians, who have dealt with this matter in detail. The works of Laughton and Corbett at the end of the last century created what we might term the 'first orthodoxy' — that the English fleet was carrying more long-range guns than the Spanish ships which had on board light pieces, quite inadequate for the purpose. The theory was not challenged for over half a century.

In the early 1940s, however, came the 'second orthodoxy', as Lewis turned the argument on its head and claimed that while the English had three times more long-range, medium-calibre pieces of the culverin type, the Spaniards had three times more of the medium-range, heavy guns, which gave it one-third greater fire-power than the English. Using highly suspect documentation, but making a great deal of fuss about the ingenuity it had required to reconstruct the artillery complement of each Armada vessel, Lewis went on to make some sophisticated statistical projections. In fact he had based his figures for the Armada on the artillery inventories of only eight ships — most of them Mediterranean — drawn up several months before they set sail. This was nevertheless a more solid research base than that available for the opposite side. Since he had no inventories at all for the English fleet, Lewis simply used the figures he found for normal shipboard armament given in documents from before and after the event.

Despite the authority, notoriety and wide diffusion of Lewis' works, it proved as easy for Thompson to destroy this carefully constructed edifice as it is to bring down a house of cards. He did it by the admirably simple expedient of testing Lewis' figures against original documentary evidence provided by the artillery inventories of some 40% of the *Gran Armada* ships. Thompson's reconstruction of the ordnance aboard the Armada ships was far weightier than any other to date, but it can now be further adjusted by incorporating the data provided by the minute inventories for almost every ship which have now been found and made available.[75]

The problem that has resurfaced and with greater force is that we can not make a coherent, balanced, and therefore scientifically viable comparison between Spanish and English guns. The inbalance between the volume and quality of information available for the two fleets becomes more and more apparent.

The contentious issue of the guns used during the 1588 campaign ought to be tackled in all its complexity. During this period gun production had not been standardised and there were very different procedures and systems in use which are very difficult to evaluate nowadays. Note for instance one aspect not considered in discussions of the efficiency of these guns, and that is the quality of the materials used to make them, whether bronze or cast-iron. Cast-iron English guns appear to have been more highly valued than German ones, for instance, but bronze ones were incomparably better if much more expensive; they were also safer and could take more powder for the same calibre shot, with the result that they had a greater range and penetration. We should not forget that two thirds of the cannon used by the Spanish in 1588 were bronze.

Recently another factor has been brought into the debate — the quality of the gun carriages.[76] While the far-fetched claims that the four-wheeled English carriage allowed for an absolutely disproportionate speed of manoeuvre compared to the Spanish carriages were quickly dismissed, further (and *balanced*) research needs to be carried out into the efficiency of different types of carriages used in the Spanish fleet, beginning from the premiss that we need to define first the various elements and materials used in construction, as well as their manoeuvrability and capacity to absorb the recoil. Other aspects which must be studied before an adequate comparison can be made include the different systems of retention, the different types of gunpowder in use, and the quality of the ammunition among others. Only then can we begin to made adequate comparisons.

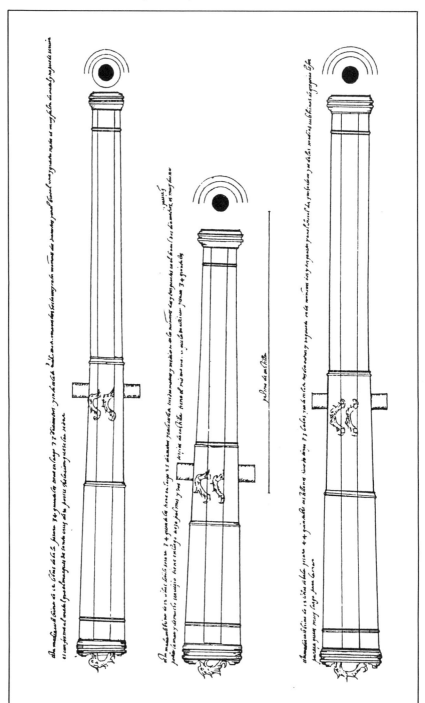

Three different types of bronze half culverins on board the Gran Armada ships. Ref. AGS MPyD V–16.

5. Conclusion

Far from having a transcendental importance as has so often been claimed for it, the Armada campaign of 1588 did not alter the balance of power which existed before the fleet was launched. While it is true that the Spaniards did not secure control of the Channel route as they wished, nor the end of English intervention in the Netherlands, nor the cessation of the official and unofficial English attacks against transatlantic commerce; it is no less true that the English failed to capture the Indies *flotas* despite sending large fleets to do so during the sixteen years the war lasted. Nor did England's direct attacks and encouragement of dissidents provoke a rebellion in Portugal or secure its secession from the Spanish Monarchy.

Spanish naval power maintained its hegemony over the most important routes, and indeed increased its domination thanks mainly to the large increase in shipbuilding both for commerce and war, and to the reinforcement of the permanent specialist squadrons already in existence, such as the ones for the Atlantic ocean, the Indies trade convoys, the Caribbean and the Pacific. At the same time a significant effort was made to strengthen the fortification of ports on both sides of the Atlantic which at times prevented, and at all times impeded the repetition of the much-vaunted English attacks against poorly defended settlements carried out by Drake and his cohorts during the previous years.

Despite the difficulties, errors and problems, Spanish hegemony would endure for many decades more. Using basic logic and common sense alone we should realise that such a feat could not have been possible given the widespread hostility towards the Spanish Monarchy and the attempts to dismember it, unless Spain possessed an impressive financial and organisational capacity, as well as the naval technology and military might that made it more effective than the enemy.

New research on the 1588 Armada campaign and the results of intensive investigation into Spanish naval construction during Philip II's reign clearly discountenance the deeply-rooted, traditional and wholly negative views of Spanish shipping in that period. Spanish naval architecture was probably at the forefront of the most sophisticated technological movement of the time. These are surely ample reasons for discarding the still current and simplistic views of Spanish naval technology which have so distorted and impoverished a rich and complex reality, especially as the information available in the archives allows us to analyse and reconstruct in great detail most aspects of these important questions.

Finally a word of caution and encouragement: comparative studies will only be free of lingering suspicion of nationalist bias and lack of scientific method when they begin from an equivalent research base on both sides, quantitatively and qualitatively, and homogeneous methodological criteria are used. It is therefore of the greatest interest to us to encourage more research in English local and national archives to add to the rather meagre documentary corpus available on English shipping during this period. We also need to have further studies and critical editions of treatises on naval construction, English and Spanish, particularly of those which have become known almost solely for their illustrations.

NOTES

1. This opinion is so unanimous there is no point in citing even the most important books which promote it. The key works which have established this notion will be referred to in the notes as the argument unfolds. But as an example of these views the reader can turn to C. M. Cipolla, *Guns and sail in the early phase of European expansion, 1400–1700* (London, 1965). It is east to test the contention that these views are widespread; one need only consult the relevant entries in the major encyclopedias, such as the Britannica, Larousse, and Espasa.

2. English historians have been unanimous on this issue, and have influenced others as a result; the most influential works are cited in the following footnotes.

3. Only three books could be found of any use for our topic: C. Fernández Duro, *Disquisiciones* vol. V. T. Guiard y Larrauri, *La industria naval vizcaina* (Bilbao, 1917); G. Artiñano y Galdacano, *La arquitectura naval española (en madera)* (Barcelona, 1920). All of them are characterised by the lack of technical specifications and abundance of anachronistic references.

4. The most influential works are: G. L. Clowes, *Sailing ships. Their history and development* (2 vols, London, 1932); R. & R. C. Anderson, *The sailing ships* (London, 1947); F. Howard, *Sailing ships of war, 1400–1860* (Greenwich, 1979). Many articles on the subject have appeared in the pages of *The Mariner's Mirror* from 1911 to the present day, among whom we should mention particularly those by Carr Laughton, De Courcy Ireland, Glasgow, Lander, Lewis, Martin, Munro, Salisbury, Waters etc.

5. Almost all the printed primary sources in English were produced shortly after the tricentenary, along with the translations — not always very accurate — of a handful of Spanish documents: see Laughton and Corbett; also J. S. Corbett, *The successors of Drake* (London, 1900); M. A. Oppenheim, *History of the administration of the Royal Navy and of merchant shipping in relation to the navy from MDIX to MDCLX* (London, 1896).

6. W. S. Maltby, *La Leyenda Negra en Inglaterra. Desarrollo del sentimiento antihispánico, 1588-1660* (Durham, N.C. 1971; Sp. trans. Mexico, 1982) pp. 97-111; L. Newton, 'La Leyenda Negra y la historia de la fuerza naval española. Algunos comentarios.', *Archivo Hispalense*, CLXXI-CLXXIII (1973) pp. 219-232. This theme is more fully explored in M. J. Rodríguez-Salgado, *'This little isle': English patriotism and the Armada myth, 1588-1988* (forthcoming).

7. Here pride of place goes to G. Mattingly's *The Armada* (Boston, 1959) which was conveniently re-titled for its English edition that same year as *The defeat of the Spanish Armada*. While dismissing many commonly-held opinions, Mattingly concludes nevertheless that the failure of the campaign ensured the survival of protestantism.

8. The most influential works are perhaps those of M. Lewis, 'Armada guns. A comparative study of English and Spanish armaments', *MM* 28 (1942) pp. 41-72, 105-147, 231-245, 259-290, and 29 (1943) pp. 3-39, 100-122, 163-178, 203-231 subsequently reprinted as *Armada Guns* (London, 1961); D. W. Waters, 'The Elizabethan Navy and the Armada campaign', *MM* 35 (1949) pp. 90-138 reprinted with documentary appendices as no. 17 of the National Maritime Museum's *Maritime Monographs and Reports* (1975). Both have published books of even greater importance in shaping public and specialist opinions, for example Water's *The art of navigation in England in elizabethan and early stuart times* (London, 1958), but most particularly Lewis' *The Spanish Armada* (London, 1960). See also note 4 above.

9. K. R. Andrews, *Drake's voyages: a reassessment of their place in Elizabethan naval expansion* (London, 1967); R. Stenuit, *Treasures of the Armada* (London, 1974); C. Martin, *Full Fathom Five. Wrecks of the Spanish Armada* (London, 1975); N. Fallon, *The Armada in Ireland* (London, 1978); also Martin and Parker.

10. The Spanish *tonelada* is variously estimated in these works ranging from 1,40 to 2,63 cubic metres; and often there is total confusion between the cargo capacity of a ship and the displacement tonnage or weight, the latter being a concept totally alien to the sixteenth century. For a full discussion of these estimates and clarification of the measurements, see Casado Soto, *Barcos*.

11. Fernández Duro *Disquisiciones* V pp. 150-2 published an anonymous

memorandum of 1618 which contains a formula for measuring the tonnage of ships attributed to the Cantabrian shipwright Cristóbal de Barros. This formula was interpreted and applied in the works of L. B. Carr Laughton, 'English and Spanish tonnage in 1588', *MM*, 44 (1958) p. 153; E. K. Thompson, 'English and Spanish tonnage in 1588', *MM*, 45 (1959), p. 154; M. Morineau, *Jauges et methodes de jaugage anciennes et modernes* (Paris 1966); and C. Martin, 'Spanish Armada tonnages', *MM*, 63 (1977) pp. 365–7. As I have amply demonstrated (in *Barcos* pp. 84–94), however, this formula was not used at the time of the Armada.

12. As far as we know the measurements of only six sixteenth-century ships connected with Spain have been published, but these were Italian ships hired by Philip II's officials for the occasion; see Martin, 'Spanish Armada tonnages'.

13. Only a few paragraphs of T. Cano's book *Arte para fabricar, fortificar y aparaejar naos* (Seville, 1611) have been taken into account, and the engravings illustrating D. García de Palacio, *Instrucción náutica para el buen uso y regimiento de las naos* (Mexico, 1587; ed. facs. Madrid, 1944); García de Palacio's works have not been assimilated, not even those published by Fernández Duro in volumes V and VI of *Disquisiciones*.

14. Some progress has been made in this field by two English-speaking historians, D. C. Goodman, *Power and penury. Government, technology and science in Philip II's Spain* (Cambridge, 1988), and C. R. Phillips, *Six galleons for the king of Spain* (London, 1986).

15. A primary example of this is the depiction of the galleon *San Martin* which can be seen in the murals of the so-called Sala de las Batallas in El Escorial. Considered as the archetype of the battleships in the Armada, it was painted in 1590 by Granello, who copied it from an engraving by F. Huys of 1565, who in turn had based it on a drawing of a ship by Breugel the elder c.1560. The Italian painter adapted his model to fit the aesthetic needs of composition, reducing the length of the ship by more than a third, and exaggerating the superstructure. Elizabeth I's famous *Armada Portrait* now preserved in Woburn Abbey, attrib. to George Gower), shows two naval scenes which are also based on the engravings of Huys as taken from Breugel drawings, that is fully thirty years before the Armada. The Dutch engravings and paintings of the event which were done several years after the event, do not depict Spanish ships of the period either, but typical vessels from the Netherlands. As for the ships depicted in the well-known Pine engravings of 1739, they do not even merit a comment from the point of view of naval architecture. A good selection of paintings and engravings have been reproduced in Rodríguez-Salgado, *Catalogue*. Casado Soto, *Barcos* pp. 188–9 discusses the specific case of the *San Martin*.

16. For the former, there is no doubt of the influence of the accounts in FD II; as for the latter, pejorative remarks about the Spaniards are wholly absent

from contemporary correspondence but make an early appearance in the pamphlet literature, e.g. P. Ubaldino, *A discourse concerninge the Spanish Fleete* (London, A. Ryther, 1590) and Lord Burghley's *The Copie of a Letter* (London, 1588). The propaganda produced at the time of the Thirty Years' War and later was to emphasise these points.

17. FD II pp. 173-201. The first English-speaking historian to have popularised this was perhaps C. H. Haring, *Trade and navigation between Spain and the Indies in the time of the Habsburgs* (Cambridge, Mass., 1918).

18. It suffices to turn to A. Heredia Herrera, *Catálogo del Consejo de Indias. Consultas* (vols I (1529-91) and II (1591-99), Madrid, 1972). The king's annotations of many documents reveal the frequency with which he dealt with such matters, and the considerable interest and understanding he had of them.

19. *Colección de documentos inéditos relativos al descubrimiento, conquista y organización de las antíguas posesiones españolas de Ultramar* XXV (Madrid, 1932).

20. MNM CN XX f. 106.

21. FD II p. 464.

22. FD II pp. 466-7.

23. H. and P. Chaunu, *Seville et l'Atlantique (1504-1650)* (12 vols., Paris, 1955-60) III pp. 42, 103, 146.

24. These and many other regulations can be found in the *Cedulario Indiano recopilado por Diego de Encinas* (1565) publ. by A. García Gallo (Madrid, 1945); in J. Veitia Linaje, *Norte de la Contratación* (Madrid, 1672); and in *Recopilación de Leyes de los Reynos de las Indias* (Madrid, 1681) IV.

25. M. Basas Fernández, *El Consulado de Burgos en el siglo XVI* (Madrid, 1963) *passim.*

26. For a fuller discussion of all these measures, see Casado Soto, *Barcos* pp. 101-118.

27. AGS CMC 3e 3532 n. 3. Accounts of the loans negotiated by Cristóbal de Barros.

28. AGI RP 260 (1) r°8, Lisbon 15 July 1582.

29. *Recopilación de Leyes de los Reynos de las Indias* IV f. 17.

30. See I. A. A. Thompson, *Guerra y decadencia. Gobierno y administración en la España de los Austrias, 1560-1620* (Spanish edn. Barcelona, 1981) pp. 225-241.

31. MNM CN 22 f. 277.

32. Chaunu III pp. 160-225.

33. AGS GA 82 ff. 187 and 215.

34. B. Torres Ramirez, *La Armada de Barlovento* (Seville, 1981).

35. P. E. Pérez Mallaina & B. Torres Ramirez, *La Armada del Mar del Sur* (Seville, 1987).

36. Casado Soto, *Barcos* pp. 44–54.

37. Thompson's article above gives a gloomier picture, placing great stress on the inefficiencies of the administrative structure prior to the war and emphasising the shortage of shipping.

38. We have already published a monograph based on these documentary sources: Casado Soto, *Barcos*, but we have continued our research and are still discovering new and important material, which has been incorporated into the arguments advanced in this article.

39. C. Fernández Duro, *La nao Santa Maria en 1892* (Madrid, s.a. [1893]); E. A. D'Albertis, 'Le construzione navali e l'arte della navegassione al tempo di Cristoforo Colombo', *Racolta di documenti e studi publicati dalle Reale Commisione Colombina* IV/i (Rome, 1893); J. Guillén Tato, *La carabela Santa María* (Madrid, 1927); C. Etayo, *La Santa María, la Niña y la Pinta* (Pamplona, 1962); J. M. Martínez Hidalgo, *Las naves de Colon* (Barcelona, 1969).

40. A. P. Usher, 'Spanish ships and shipping in the sixteenth and seventeenth century', in *Facts and factors in economic history* (Cambridge, Mass, 1932); E. Schäfer, *El Consejo Real y Supremo de las Indias. I: Historia y organización del Consejo y de la Casa de Contratación de Indias* (Seville, 1937); Chaunu, I; F. C. Lane, 'Tonnage, medieval and modern', *Economic History Review*, 2nd ser., XVI (1964) pp. 213–33 and Morineau, *Jauges et methodes de jaugage.*

41. AGS GA 186 f. 16 — report to ensure that the interest-free royal loans were calculated on real tonnage, not on the 20% greater *tonelada de sueldo* (1586); AGS CMC 2e 772 s.f.; AGS CS 280 — different measurements for Lizardi's *nao*, the *San Francisco* (1587–91); AGS CMC 2e 942 s.f., discussion of the different measurements given for Meléndez's *nao* the *Santa María de la Blanca* (1589–91).

42. A study and description of all this in Casado Soto *Barcos* pp. 58–71.

43. J. Pulido Rubio, *El piloto mayor de la Casa de Contratación* (Seville, 1950) pp. 766–772.

44. See note 11.

45. It is now possible to state that the formula used by Cristóbal de Barros in 1580 was the same one used by Pedro de Busturria in 1568 (see AGS GA 347 f. 23) which in turn is very similar to the dimensions and measurements used in 1523, and published by T. Guiard, *La industria naval vizcaina* (Bilbao, 1917) p. 76.

46. Casado Soto, *Barcos* pp. 73–94, 226–30.

47. Chaunu VIII pp. 255–6 have calculated that between 1504 and 1580 ninety per cent of the ships sailing from Seville and Cadiz to the New World had been constructed in the Cantabrian coast. The proportion increased to one hundred per cent in the Spain-Netherlands routes.

48. Casado Soto, *Barcos* pp. 118–153.

49. AGS CS le 141 s.f.

50. AGS CS le 197 s.f.

51. FD II pp. 266–74.

52. Casado Soto, *Barcos* pp. 208–21.

53. Casado Soto, *Barcos* pp. 118–153, 186–204.

54. Casado Soto, *Barcos* pp. 210–11. The extreme and nostalgic comment by Cano recalling the situation in the ship yards during his youth from the elegiac vantage point of his old age can be found in *Arte para fabricar y aparejar naos* (Seville, 1611); we have used the edition by E. Marco Dorta (La Laguna, 1964) pp. 94–5.

55. Chaunu, I, II, III and VIII. As M. Morineau has already shown in his article 'Un curieux cas de deontologie: la tonelada española' in *Historiens et Géographes* CCLXII (1977) pp. 510–12, the Chaunus followed Schäfer and the mistaken definition given in the *Diccionario de la Real Academia de la Lengua*, and took the sum of the square (Castilian) *codo* as if it was a cubic *codo*, with the result that instead of reaching the correct result of 1.3844 m³ per *tonelada* of Seville, they invented their *tonelada larga* of 2.612 m³. The discrepancy forced them to apply progressively greater adjustments to try to reconcile the tonnage given in the documentation with their theoretical tonnage; the final result is a major distortion of reality.

56. Casado Soto, *Barcos* pp. 94–118.

57. AGS CJH 90 no. 312, 322, 323.

58. AGI RP 260–2 r° 29 f. 6.

59. AGI IG 2,661 (16 July 1582).

60. AGS GA 130 f. 157 (Burgos 30 Sept 1582).

61. AGS GA 186 ff. 15 & 16 (Bilbao 13 and 18 July 1586).

62. The acquisition of the nine Portuguese galleons and the additional nine ships built in Guarnizo in 1582–3, along with the successful implementation of the subsidy policy in effect covered the crown's needs for shipping and permitted the relative slow-down in construction that Thompson has noted above, p. 73. Details of all these projects in *Barcos*.

63. Casado Soto, *Barcos* pp. 294–375.

64. Out of the more than thirty books published by British presses during 1988 only two have contributed original material and gone beyond the reiteration of well-known facts: Rodríguez-Salgado, *Catalogue*, and Martin and Parker. Even the few books published in Spain have shown the same uncritical acceptance of the figures for shipping and losses given in traditional accounts, see for example Gómez-Centurión, *Comercio* and *ibid.*, *La Invencible y la empresa de Inglaterra* (both Madrid, 1988); and M. González-Arnao, *Los naufragios de la Armada Invencible* (Madrid, 1988).

65. Notably FD, Herrera Oria, and Laughton.

66. See notes 4, 5 and 7 above.

67. Casado Soto, *Barcos* pp. 186–226, 376–84.

68. Casado Soto, *Barcos* pp. 226–31, 385–8; Rodríguez-Salgado, *Catalogue* pp. 156–8.

69. G. Robinson, *The Elizabethan Ship* (London, 1956); L. B. C. Laughton, 'English and Spanish tonnage in 1588', pp. 151–4; Glasgow, 'The shape of the ships etc.', pp. 177–87; W. Salisbury, 'Early tonnage measurement in England', *MM*, 52 (1966) pp. 41–51; R. J. Lander, 'An assessment of the numbers, sizes and types of English and Spanish ships mobilized for the Armada campaign', *MM*, 63 (1977) pp. 359–67.

70. The fate of the four galleys and the *nao Santa Ana* which took refuge in Le Havre are all well known; the vicissitudes of the five *pataches* sent to Parma can also be followed in the accounts published in FD and Herrera Oria, *Armada*. The caravels simply disappear from the documentation after the fleet's departure from La Coruña. Lord Howard did not mention them in the report he sent Walsingham on 30 June either, see N. A. M. Roger, *The Armada in the Public Records* (London, 1988) pp. 52–3.

71. Thompson, 'Spanish Armada guns', pp. 355–6; Rodríguez-Salgado, *Catalogue* pp. 237–49; Casada Soto, *Barcos* pp. 232–5.

72. It is lamentable that Martin and Parker should have shown the same weakness in their otherwise stimulating book.

73. Casado Soto, *Barcos* pp. 232–47.

74. Casado Soto, *Barcos* pp. 248–9, 379–84.

75. Thompson, 'Spanish Armada guns', pp. 355–71; references to Laughton, Corbett and Lewis in notes 5 and 7 above.

76. C. Martin, 'A sixteenth-century siege train: the battery ordnance of the 1588 Spanish Armada', *The International Journal of Nautical Archaeology and Underwater Exploration* XVII (1988) pp. 57–73. The discussion of the guns on the opposing fleets is highly dubious, and we certainly cannot accept the anachronistic and utterly disproportionate visual evidence provided in p. 210 of Martin and Parker, which seeks to disqualify *Spanish* gun-carriages with a false comparison between two wheels from a large Venetian siege-gun carriage, and a four-wheeled carriage for a much smaller gun mounted on the Swedish ship, *Vasa* forty years later!

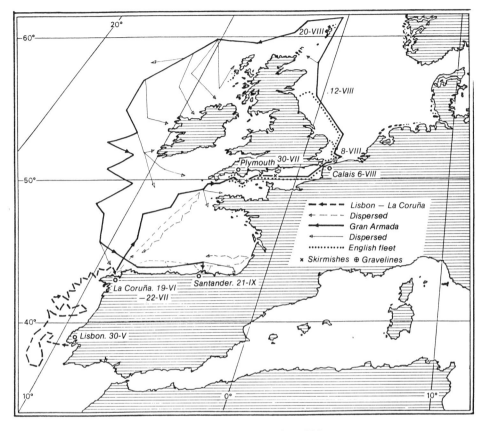

Route of the Gran Armada, 1588.

5

PILOTS, NAVIGATION AND STRATEGY IN THE *GRAN ARMADA*.[1]

M. J. Rodríguez-Salgado

My wind cooling my broth
Would blow me to an ague, when I thought
What harm a wind too great at sea might do.
I should not see the sandy hour-glass run,
But I should think of shallows and of flats,
And see my wealthy Andrew dock'd in sand,
Vailing her high-top lower than her ribs
To kiss her burial. Should I go to church
And see the holy edifice of stone,
And not bethink me straight of dangerous rocks,
Which touching but my gentle vessel's side,
Would scatter all her spices on the stream,
Enrobe the roaring waters with my silks,
And in a word, but even now worth this,
And now worth nothing?[2]

The fearful images which haunt the merchant awaiting news of his ships create a sombre mood at the start of Shakespeare's *Merchant of Venice*. The risks of maritime ventures in distant seas are amply demonstrated in this tale of the wealthy man reduced to penury through the loss of his ships. Philip II had far more to lose than money and merchandise when he sent his fleet against England in 1588. At stake were his honour, his reputation, and the defence of his vast empire. If he won, the catholic faith would be considerably strengthened; some believed it would turn the tide of protestant victories and herald the recovery of christian unity under the Church of Rome. If he lost, the protestants would gain heart and might form a league against him and the English would continue meddling in the Netherlands and Portugal, multiplying his internal as well as his external problems. With so much at stake, it is easy to imagine him,

> Plucking the grass, to know where sits the wind,
> Peering in maps for ports and piers and roads;
> And every object that might make me fear
> Misfortune to my ventures, out of doubt
> Would make me sad.[3]

He had certainly been morose for much of the year. The effort to organise the campaign had made him ill with anxiety and overwork. But waiting for news of the fate of his fleet must have been agonising. Every scrap of information was scrutinised. Being cautious and thoroughly accustomed to discount the wild rumours of his day, Philip would believe neither good nor bad reports until confirmed by several trustworthy informants. But he was only human, and when letters arrived from, among others, his ambassador in France congratulating him on a considerable victory, his hopes were raised. It made the disaster all the harder to bear subsequently.[4]

The reasons for that disaster have long been heatedly debated. The important role of the weather was acknowledged at the time, and has been given considerable attention in recent research. Nevertheless Philip II continues to receive much of the blame for what happened. Recent works by Thompson and Parker have emphasised the king's role in the tragedy. Thompson blames Philip for attempting something which he could not organise adequately, and is scathing of the preparations for the campaign. Parker accuses him of being an armchair strategist and tactician who failed to appreciate the implications of his ambitious plan.[5] The logical conclusion of both these lines of argument is that the king sent his men on an impossible mission. 'The king had created the Armada', Parker states emphatically, 'and in the end the king destroyed it'.[6] The duke of Medina Sidonia has been rehabilitated and exonerated.[7] Yet one vital aspect of the campaign which sheds light on the role of the king and his commanders, and could have had some bearing on its failure, has not been studied: the level of technical knowledge and skill in the fleet. This paper touches on this important topic by exploring the problems of providing the Armada with the technical expertise it required to execute its mission and survive.

1. The Strategy

Philip II drew up his strategy for the invasion of England with the benefit of a vast fund of information. Since 1559 he had received detailed reports and plans, many from English exiles. He had also studied carefully the detailed report on the anchorages, ports and coasts of England which Alexander Farnese, duke of Parma, produced in November 1583 when an invasion was seriously mooted.[8] Thorough to a fault, Philip also sent Juan Martínez de Recalde, one of his leading seamen, to take soundings of the Channel and report on its ports and navigation before making the final decision to attack in 1585.[9] Once that decision had been made, Philip set in motion large-scale preparations for the campaign. As was frequently the case in this period, due to the slow pace of military preparations, these preceded a decision on a specific target or strategy. While his servants were busy raising men and money, and gathering victuals, the king pondered over maps, charts, rutters and reports. He was an avid map collector, and his library contained some of the best atlasses and textbooks on navigation. Two extant notes exchanged between the king and a secretary reveal that he was using two charts and a rutter to fix the position of Channel ports and establish exact distances between them. One of the works he consulted was Abraham Ortelius's *Theatrum Orbis Terrarum.*[10]

The two most significant proposals laid before Philip in 1586 for an invasion of England were those of the marquis of Santa Cruz and the duke of Parma, his two most distinguished commanders. Both sought command of the enterprise and suggested plans that made the best of their skills and strengths. Santa Cruz, the leading naval expert, naturally wanted a naval expedition from Spain which may have been inspired by his successful campaign in Terceira, but on an infinitely larger scale. He proposed a truly Great Fleet of nearly 800 vessels, with more than 94,000 men. Besides the awesome task of gathering such huge forces from Iberia, his plan was unlikely to win favour with the king as it required the participation of most of the monarchy's galley fleet, which would leave the sensitive and vulnerable Mediterranean front dangerously exposed. Philip was subsequently put under great pressure by his naval commanders to allow more galleys to participate in the English campaign, but he refused: he was afraid the Ottoman and North African powers would attack if he reduced his defences. Without galleys, as will be seen, the expedition was severely limited, both in terms of where it might land, and in its capacity to manoeuvre and isolate enemy ships in battle.[11] Parma suggested a dash across the Channel by an army of 30,000 men from Flanders. They would cross over from the Flemish coast in small boats and effect a surprise landing, probably in the Thames estuary, so that they could march on London and besiege it within days of their arrival.[12]

Philip devised his own plan. It was heavily influenced by Parma, but it made better use of his resources: his best men, who were in the Netherlands, and his ships, which were in Spain.[13] Recently it has been argued that he combined the two plans because there was enough money to pay for both.[14] This is not the case. Philip combined the two forces, not the plans; moreover he was, as always, short of money and desperate to keep costs low. His strategy was founded on the premiss that he did not have sufficient forces in Spain or the Netherlands for a major invasion. England's chief defence was her navy but Philip had no warships in the Netherlands, where his veteran troops were stationed. It was inconceivable to mount a major invasion successfully without these troops, but his warships were in Iberia and the Mediterranean. There were other reasons conditioning his choice, not least that Philip could look back to the highly successful combined operations in the invasion of Portugal, particularly the attack on Lisbon.[15] This plan also enabled him to leave adequate defence cover both in the Netherlands and Iberia, both areas he considered to be particularly vulnerable.

Naturally, neither Parma nor Santa Cruz liked the king's proposal, since each was deprived of the honour of single command. Nevertheless, once Philip had assured them of his favour and gratitude, and given them both grants, he made it clear that they must accept joint command or pull out. Santa Cruz and Parma grumbled, but they got down to work and did their best to increase their part in the enterprise. Over the next few months they experienced periods of depression and despondency when they criticised the king's strategy — which he altered several times in response to the time of year and English activities. Yet Santa Cruz, Parma and Medina Sidonia also wrote enthusiastically about the plan and expressed their firm conviction that it would be successful. As late as January 1588 Parma described the king's plan as admirable, and would not accept any changes.[16]

The final strategy, outlined in September 1587, and more or less restated in February 1588, was to send a large fleet from Lisbon to 'cape Margate': it would either wait for Parma and his troops at the anchorage in the Downs, or might proceed up to the mouth of the Thames if the situation was favourable. From either position, the Spanish fleet was to disrupt all shipping, and hopefully block the English fleet in the Thames estuary. But the king made it very clear that the Armada was an auxiliary force. Its main task was to cover Parma's passage and landing. Defeating the English fleet was not even to be attempted unless they tried to impede the landing. Strict limitations were imposed on the fleet's commander to ensure that he did not undertake independent action until Parma had set foot in England, and then only if Parma did not require further naval support.[17]

Philip did not involve commanders or experts directly in the final process of decision-making: this was standard procedure. He collected information and opinions, then retired to mull over them and make a final decision. In this instance, apart from a wealth of material on paper, he could draw on his own experiences. He had sailed the Channel on four occasions between 1554 and 1559, and lived in England, as well as commanded in battle. He had learnt to distrust the English, and this also affected the strategy: despite the wild promises of the exiles, he did not expect much help from the catholics.[18] Moreover, secrecy was of the essence. Unless the process of consultation was strictly limited, the plan would be leaked. Once he had chosen his strategy, he took secret, unofficial soundings from Santa Cruz and two other expert naval commanders, Miguel de Oquendo and Juan Martínez de Recalde.[19] Whatever they said did not prompt him to change the plan.

Nevertheless we know that Recalde, along with military experts such as Bernardino de Escalante, believed that the strategy chosen by the king was too risky. Without a deep-water port in the Channel to shelter and repair the fleet, they thought it would be better to attack one of the western English ports, which were near to Spain, easily accessible, and had weak defences. Falmouth, Plymouth and Dartmouth were three of the sites suggested by Recalde; Escalante favoured Milford Haven among others. The journey from Spain was relatively easy, and the Spanish fleet could maintain a clear passage without much difficulty. Proposals varied as to whether the conquest should then proceed towards Bristol, or along the southern coast: there were good reasons for both.[20] Similar strategic considerations lay behind the suggestion that Philip should invade Ireland rather than attempt a direct attack on England. Philip was fully conscious of the importance of a Channel port: indeed at one stage he was convinced that an invasion was impossible without it, whether the target was in Scotland, Ireland or southern England.[21] But there were serious drawbacks to what, for the sake of convenience, one might call a 'western strategy'. Advocates of an attack on ports in south-western England or southern Ireland proposed that the invasion should be organised from Iberia. The army of Flanders could not be taken away so far or for so long from their stations. Apart from the heavier burden on one area of the empire, these plans entailed a long-term military and naval commitment — precisely what the hard-pressed king was anxious to avoid. While those in favour assured Philip that his forces would eventually reach London, they all admitted that the conquest of England would be slow. Parma's plan of a direct strike against the capital had the great advantage that it promised immediate results. Even partial success would bring Elizabeth to the negotiating table in one campaign. The army of Flanders would be operating close to its base, and would be able to beat a hasty retreat if necessary. Moreover, an attack on the enemy's capital was also far more prestigious. While Philip seriously thought of putting into effect one of these 'western' plans during 1585 to 1588, particularly as setbacks endangered the preparations for a major invasion, he finally settled for the original plan of a dual attack.

The king realised that he had devised a difficult strategy which required perfect timing and the favourable combination of many international and internal factors. Yet he was convinced that it would work, so long as he acted quickly and retained that all-important element of surprise. When he gave the order to attack in September 1587, however, the first of many conflicts between the king, his commanders and naval experts ensued. Whereas his decision was conditioned by political and not just military factors, theirs was firmly grounded on the practical needs of men, ships and *matériel*. Philip wanted immediate action because the international situation was favourable, and because he had been promised a sizeable loan from Rome if he acted before December. He was desperate to recover his prestige after the latest English aggression against Spain and the New World and most anxious to avert another English attack in the spring of 1588. Impressive as these reasons were, Santa Cruz and Parma opposed the order because neither force was ready. It took months of painstaking organisation to levy and transport troops, fit out ships and gather victuals.[22] Neither man wanted to risk failure by fielding inadequate and ill-prepared forces; both feared the treacherous winter gales. In his instructions to Santa Cruz, Philip acknowledged the dangers of sailing to England in winter, 'particularly in the Channel, and without a secure port', but he argued that God, whose cause he was defending, would surely help. Moreover, at this stage Philip enjoyed undoubted numerical strength and the advantage of surprise. He also tried to reassure his Iberian commanders that the fleet was perfectly equipped to sail safely:

'the papers and special charts which the marquis [of Santa Cruz] has of that coast will furnish the necessary information, and the pilots of Oquendo's squadron have the required experience'.[23]

That brief, almost casual comment is extremely important. It suggests that doubts had been voiced about the technical preparations of the fleet, which the king was dismissing with bland assurances that could hardly have convinced his men. It was all very well for the Admiral to have charts and one squadron to have pilots, but what of the rest of the fleet? How would they fare when dispersed by the inevitable winter gales? Most of the ships gathered in Lisbon were commercial vessels embargoed or hired by the crown, usually with a full crew. Many of them, whether from Northern or Mediterranean waters, made their living from sailing across the Channel, as Philip reminded Medina Sidonia later. Ships from the levant sailed regularly to France and England, while the German and Flemish hulks traded between the Baltic and the Mediterranean.[24] It may be assumed that most had pilots and masters on board who could navigate to the appointed place, but the number of mariners who knew the route was clearly small. The king was aware of the problem but unwilling to solve it since this would mean delaying the fleet's departure while more men were found.

The need to have technical information and expertise for an invasion of England had been amply discussed since 1583 when the duke of Guise had proposed a campaign with Philip and the papacy. One of the reasons Philip gave for not acting quickly and decisively when he was approached was that he had 'no news of the native [English] pilots we would need to guide it [the fleet]'.[25] Guise promised to remedy this by sending ships with experienced sailors to meet the Spanish fleet.[26] This failed to satisfy the king, who continued to harp on the lack of information, ports and pilots when accounting for his inactivity. He insisted in September 1583 that no fleet from Spain could successfully reach England without having catholic English pilots — preferably on board; if not at least they must come to meet the fleet.[27] His commander in the Netherlands, the duke of Parma, came forward with a solution: 'up to twenty-five or thirty mariners and navigators with experience of these seas and channels could be sent when the time came, either to Spain or to . . . the Scilly isles, where other Spanish fleets crossing the Channel have usually been met'.[28] Recalde's reconnoitring expedition had partially remedied the lack of trustworthy information at Philip's disposal, but there is no evidence that Philip had secured, or even attempted to secure, English, French or Flemish pilots.

When the duke of Parma presented his detailed commentary on the proposed invasion of England in April 1586, he sounded a cautionary note. Parma expected Elizabeth to get help from Holland, Zealand, Germany and France, thus giving England numerical superiority. But this was not the only reason he believed they would prove superior at sea. The English would have the inestimable advantage of local knowledge and of 'mariners with greater experience of these waters than those in your majesty's service. Should it come to a direct encounter with them, they have the advantage of knowing the banks, the tides, the ports and anchorages all along the coast'.[29] Philip must therefore have a Channel port to shelter his fleet, and above all, he must have skilled navigators — a point reiterated in memoranda produced by experts such as Fernando Gutierrez de Ureña, who stressed the very particular skills required to sail the Channel. Ureña insisted that a campaign against England or Ireland could not be undertaken without having one experienced pilot and two practiced mariners per ship. These men must have practical experience of sounding and specific knowledge of the Channel tides and ports.[30] This raises two important questions; first, why Iberia, which was undoubtedly the most advanced state in navigation technology at that time, could not readily provide the necessary expertise for the campaign; second, whether these deficiencies were remedied in time, or if they contributed to its failure.

2. Pilots and Navigation in Sixteenth-century Iberia

The sixteenth century witnessed a remarkable change in the status and training of pilots in Europe. There is little information about the most common pilots, those who guided shipping into ports, or commercial pilots outside the Indies routes. This reflects the low esteem in which they were held. The navigational skills required for most maritime journeys were limited and had changed little over the previous century. They could be exercised either by specialised pilots, masters or lower officials.[31] What mattered was the ability to memorise landmarks and to know the tides and waters in which they sailed. Very simple estimates of ship's speed were applied. Practical experience and instruction by old pilots — as the writer Michiel Coignet stated in his 1581 textbook on pilotage — were the prerequisites of effective coastal navigation, and sufficed for most shipping, which plied well-established routes.[32]

Magnetic needles, portolan charts and celestial observation were known and increasingly used on more lengthy journeys.[33]

The Portuguese exploration of Africa and subsequent discoveries of new continents reflected the gradual improvements in navigation and ship design, and gave a powerful boost to further inventions and refinements of instruments and techniques. The training of pilots for the new long-distance oceanic runs became a matter of the greatest importance for governments, and the Iberian powers quickly established special institutions for this. It was not merely a question of safety, although ships with skilled navigators were naturally less likely to be lost; what really concerned monarchs was how to control this vital information. Discovery was a sufficient justification to claim new lands, but so was settlement. Good pilots could find new lands; they might also take enemies there. Along with cartographers, pilots could establish who possessed which territories, especially after the Iberian powers and the papacy divided the world with their arbitrary lines. The long and unedifying struggles over the Moluccas and the Philippines illustrate the value of these men, and the way in which governments exploited the new knowledge.[34] The increasing valuation of the skills of pilots was evident in legislation and in new rates of pay. Contracts show that during the sixteenth century pilots in the longer northern and Indies voyages were paid more than the masters. After 1573 pilots were allowed to become masters, and from the 1580s men without knowledge of navigation were allowed to act as masters of their own vessels as long as they had at least two pilots on board. Clearly pilots were now considered experienced enough to do the work previously done by the master and pilot; that is to set the course, navigate and manoeuvre the ship.[35]

The transformation in the status of the pilot and the nature of his art owed a great deal to royal patronage, and specifically to Philip II. When Philip II returned to Spain in 1551 he spearheaded a thorough reform of the technical training offered to pilots and masters in the Casa de Contratación in Seville. He established a chair of navigation and cosmography in 1552, and regulated the content of the courses. Aspiring pilots received good theoretical grounding on the sphere and astronomical observations, as well as basic instruction on the use of instruments such as the compass, astrolabe, quadrant, cross-staff and clocks. They learned how to set a course with chart and dividers, and much about tides. In 1582 the king set up a new Academy of Mathematics in Madrid, and navigation was a major part of the curriculum.[36] The theoretical elements of navigation were considerably expanded in the course of the century. The Iberians led the way in all this, as well as in cartography, and gradually in the making and use of instruments. Their navigational textbooks were rapidly disseminated and translated.[37] By the mid-sixteenth century two of the leading teachers at Seville, Pedro de Medina and Rodrigo Zamorano, proudly claimed that now pilots could navigate with the use of arithmetic, geometry and astrology, and did not require landmarks for guidance. In fact the most renowned writers and teachers of the art of navigation had no practical naval experience.[38] Although García de Palacio in his *Instrucción Náutica para Navegar* (Mexico, 1587) put practical experience of the sea before mathematical, astrological and cosmographical knowledge for the ideal pilot, those with theoretical skills were accorded greater respect than those with only practical experience. The crown kept things in proportion by insisting that pilots for the Indies should not be licenced before acquiring practical experience of sailing those waters to complement their theoretical training. But perhaps the most effective barrier towards the transformation of pilotage into a profession dominated by books and instruments was commercial pressure. The Indies trade required a constant supply of pilots, consequently the time they could spend on formal training was dramatically reduced. Whereas it had been intended that pilots should undergo a one-year course, in 1555 it was reduced to three months, and in 1567 to two months counting feast-days. Teachers complained of lower standards among the trainee pilots, but it seems to me that this was essentially directed at the lack of reading and writing skills of some aspiring pilots and their lack of interest in the more theoretical aspects of the course.[39] The trained pilots who worked for the Indies trade were considered the finest practitioners of the art. Foreign powers consistently sought to entice Spanish and Portuguese pilots to their service. The problem was that there were never enough of them to satisfy demand.

It is tempting to generalise from the Indies experience and assume that pilotage in all areas developed into a more academic and instrument-based science. But pilotage on most routes continued much as before, with primary observations of land and sea, and on-the-job training. By the 1580s the naval writer Bernardino de Escalante made a broad if clear distinction between 'marineros de costa y derrota y otros de alta mar', that is those who navigated with the aid of coastal markings and rutters, and 'open sea' sailing requiring charts, instruments and celestial navigation.[40] Royal patronage was almost entirely devoted to the latter, and specifically the Indies routes. Conscious of the growing divide between them and the more traditional skills of northern navigators, Philip tried to improve the situation by appointing a professor, Andrés de Poza, to travel and teach the new navigational skills to pilots in the north coast of Spain in 1575.[41]

By then there was a crisis in northern Iberia. Trade between Spain, Portugal and northern Europe had suffered seriously from the wars in France and the Netherlands, and the hostility of the English since the 1560s. Convinced that maritime insurance cushioned the merchants and retarded the adoption of adequate defence — either by individual armament or convoy system — Philip prohibited insurance of mercantile shipping on the Spain-Netherlands route in 1572. That same year the rebels seized many of the ports of Holland, and English and French pirates joined in the attacks against Spanish shipping. Such adverse commercial and political conditions provoked the withdrawal of many Spaniards from direct trade to northern Europe. In 1574 Dutch rebels captured Middleburg and the Spanish wool fleet. When Philip organised a fleet to counter the rebel offensive in 1574, he was told that there were too few Spanish pilots; pilots from Zealand, Dunkirk and Le Conquet would be needed to guide the fleet.[42] His failure to mount a successful counter-offensive sealed the fate of native trade between Iberia and the Netherlands and drastically reduced the number of local mariners and pilots with experience of the Channel, so that by the 1580s few Spanish pilots knew the Channel or northern routes.[43]

3. Pilots and Mariners in the Armada of 1588

Santa Cruz was adamant that his fleet did not have sufficient experts on board to sail in the winter of 1587. Indeed he was short even of common sailors. Despite strenuous efforts to recruit more, he made little progress. The musters revealed 4,898 seamen in December 1587, and only 5,124 in February 1588.[44] The only way to attain tolerable manning levels was to reduce the number of ships, although this did not solve the problem of pilots. For Philip such practical problems were greatly outweighed by urgent political considerations. Reducing the number of ships would give England numerical superiority, and thereby greater reputation. More importantly, further delay would be dishonourable and suggest that Philip was too weak to avenge enemy attacks. Despite Santa Cruz's complaints that the fleet was not ready,

Philip decided in January 1588 that it must sail by early February. Faced with the king's displeasure Santa Cruz dared not oppose the order, but he continued to request experienced mariners. As late as February 4 he begged the king to transfer the pilot Cristóbal Sánchez from the galley fleet.[45] Philip would no more remove key personnel than galleys from the Mediterranean front, but he finally accepted that something had to be done quickly to remedy the shortage of sailors and pilots. His solution was surprising: Santa Cruz should organise a secret raid on French and other foreign ships in Lisbon and Setubal the night before the Armada sailed.[46] The Admiral's death put paid to this plan.

Kidnapping foreign seamen in a secret raid was extraordinary even in the sixteenth century, when monarchs regularly used force to obtain whatever they needed for war. It was not so much a question of ethics, but of trust. Men violently taken to serve a foreign master were not expected to do so with loyalty or valour. On the contrary, they would surely try to defect and might sabotage the enterprise. Moreover, there would be important political and commercial repercussions. Rather belatedly, Philip also ordered officials in northern Spain to search and send with the utmost urgency all the pilots and seamen who knew the Channel. The response was not heartening: only one pilot could be found in Galicia, and he had only navigated the Channel twice. It was no consolation to learn that there was a more experienced Galician pilot who was out of the country.[47] There was a better response from the coast of Biscay, although here too there were problems as the *corregidor*, Don Ordoño de Zamudio, explained to the king. Commerce between Biscay and the Netherlands had ceased years ago, Zamudio stated, so experienced Channel pilots and mariners moved to the lucrative commerce with France (the Biscay-Nantes-Rouen routes), or abandoned seafaring altogether. He found six 'famous pilots' relatively quickly in Laredo and Castro de Urdiales, along with some fifty experienced sailors. Further efforts raised the figure to nine experienced pilots and one hundred seamen. Unfortunately it proved necessary to employ both bribery and compulsion to make the pilots join the Armada. They were given substantial financial inducements: cash payments of 100 ducats, very good salaries, and promises of honourable treatment. It did not suffice: Zamudio had to report that 'they are going by force and cursing me'.[48] While all of the pilots were thoroughly experienced, only four were described as disgruntled but reasonable — implying that the others, angry at being made to leave their homes, could not be trusted. These pilots and mariners set off in March 1588.[49] Three of these pilots

(Lope de Ocina, Juan de Escalante and Martín Vélez de Liendo) were designated 'de los mas principales' as soon as they joined the Armada.[50]

Medina Sidonia had considerable experience of fitting out New World fleets and this was to prove a great advantage when he was appointed to command the *Gran Armada.* Under his firm guidance, the fleet increased in size, and the worst deficiencies were remedied. Between February and May the number of ships grew from 114 to 151, and the number of seamen from 5,124 to 7,666.[51] Without minimising his role and unquestionable initiative, it should be said, however, that he also benefitted from the extra time which allowed projects made earlier by the king and Santa Cruz — as in the case of the northern mariners — to be completed. Medina Sidonia initially believed that Indies pilots were superior and should be treated accordingly. When Philip informed him of the search for pilots in northern Spain, the duke merely replied that he would try to find pilots in Andalucia. He did not think it mattered that these men were only trained to navigate to the New World: 'even if they have not sailed to Flanders, they will be more useful than others who lack their experience'.[52] Once in Lisbon he realised that this was not necessarily true. By July Pedro de Valdés complained to Philip that the captains and masters in his squadron — men of proven honesty, wealth, and 'of great experience and practice in naval affairs, for they were raised in the Indies run' — were unhappy because Medina Sidonia did not consult them on naval matters.[53] Relations between Valdés and Medina Sidonia were already strained, and the snub — if that is what it was — may have been intended against Valdés rather than his squadron. Nevertheless, it is important to stress that the skills of Indies mariners were not as valuable for the campaign as those of Channel pilots, learned or otherwise. Indies pilots regained their superior position during the return journey, when their thorough grounding in celestial navigation, experience of open sea sailing, and ability to use charts were crucial for the survival of many ships.

The situation by early March 1588 was still alarming. Only the Portuguese squadron had experienced pilots on every ship. Despite Philip's initial assurances, only half of Oquendo's ships were well equipped, and only three of the Levant vessels had 'a good pilot', although the others had sailors who knew the Channel but who could not navigate the ship. Juan Martínez de Recalde's Biscay squadron had pilots skilled only in navigation to Newfoundland. Ironically, it was the main-line ships that were worst off. Most of the pinnaces and *zabras* had experienced pilots, perhaps because these were the only types of ship still regularly used between Spain and the Netherlands, mainly to bring mail and information. However only two of these pilots had sailed the Channel in a large vessel. The rest could not be transferred to the first-rate ships because navigating a deep-draught vessel of anything from 500 to over 1000 tons along dangerous waters was very different from handling a swift, shallow vessel usually of less than 50 tons along the same route. Moreover, even the northern pilots trained in the wool fleets of earlier decades were unlikely to have managed ships of more than 300 tons. The squadrons of Castile, Andalucia and the hulks were not included in this list, so we cannot tell how well equipped they were; presumably the hulks would have had one or more Channel experts,[54] but even here the situation was precarious. An Emden shipmaster whose ship had been embargoed wrote to his wife that his vessel had been filled with 800 men, but 'not one of them capable of steering a course at sea, himself excepted, who is both master and pilot as many are'.[55] Little wonder Medina Sidonia was so anxious to have the northern pilots in Lisbon at once — he did not trust local officials to deal with their journey for fear that there would be the slightest delay.[56] It seemed like a losing battle: as the *Gran Armada* grew, so did his need for pilots, some of whom succumbed to the epidemics ravaging the fleet.[57] Meanwhile, Philip's demand for pilots from the Netherlands remained a dead letter. Parma was having great difficulties in manning his own ships. In the end he dared not disobey orders, but he sent only two pilots at the close of March 1588. He assured Philip that they were the best, and that no more could be sent from the Netherlands.[58]

Medina Sidonia was far from achieving his dream to provide every ship in the *Gran Armada* with an experienced pilot. Meanwhile there were still shortages of common seamen. It was natural under the circumstances that more radical measures should have been considered. Perhaps the easiest way to increase the skilled contingent in the fleet was by seizing more German ships, which were in abundant supply along the Iberian coast, but Philip risked provoking a major diplomatic and commercial crisis by doing so. He had sworn not to embargo Hanseatic shipping as part of an agreement recently concluded with the Hanseatic League, who undertook (in exchange for commercial privileges) to supply him with vital naval stores and grain.[59] As the time for sailing drew nearer, Medina Sidonia came to the same conclusion as his predecessor: he would have to leave several ships behind in order to bring the rest to adequate manning levels. Just as before, the king insisted on the maximum number of vessels so as to match the English fleet, and renewed his licence to kidnap foreign seamen the night before the departure of the fleet. Medina Sidonia was grateful for the option, but the desperate expedient was not used. The timely arrival of embargoed merchant ships from Andalucia provided him with an easier source of supply.[60] When the Armada sailed from La Coruña in July 1588 it had just over 7000 mariners in 138 ships, giving manning levels which the commanders found acceptable.[61]

The duke had also come up with imaginative and less violent remedies to the unsolved problem of skilled personnel. Having identified the problem as a lack of specific knowledge rather than general navigational skills, it was decided to provide information of the Channel which experienced pilots from other routes could use. In March 1588 he ordered six of the most experienced pilots in the fleet — two Basques, two Portuguese and two from the Indies — to meet in the house of Martínez de Recalde every morning and afternoon. Their task was to produce a rutter for the Channel that would reconcile the various sailing instructions available, adding information that might help the fleet; they also had to produce navigational charts.[62]

These were difficult tasks, especially given the limited time available. The rutters consulted in Lisbon contained contradictory material. While Indies rutters were regularly studied and reconciled by experienced officials in Lisbon and Seville, rutters on other routes were still primarily private accounts and observations.[63] There were a few printed rutters, among them Pierre Garcie's *Le Grand Routier*, which covered much of the area that would be crossed by the *Gran Armada*.[64] It was not available in Spanish or Portuguese, but the French original may have been used by the committee. Medina Sidonia brought the printer Antonio Alvarez — who produced naval texts in Seville — to Lisbon where he took charge of the printing of the rutter produced by the pilots at the end of March 1588.[65] The duke wanted to provide each ship with a rutter and sailing instructions, although this may not have been the only rutter he distributed, since he stated at one point that 'the best rutters' would be given to ships without pilots or charts.[66] Philip was delighted with this intiative and demanded copies of all the navigational material produced.[67]

The official rutter included detailed information of depth measurements and soundings necessary to navigate the Channel safely: 'you must be governed by sounding' is the constant and wise refrain. It was admirably clear, and comfortingly reassuring throughout. The navigator is told not to worry, and to have the confidence that by taking frequent sounding and identifying the sediment, it was always possible to fix one's position in the Channel.[68] The sediment is described simply throughout: thus around Portland, at thirty-five fathoms, the pilot would find 'pebbles the size of black beans'. If it was 35-37 fathoms, and the pebbles white 'resembling chick-peas' the navigator would know that he had passed Portland and was near the Isle of Wight. Landmarks were also clearly identified, and instructions were given on how to enter many English ports. Having navigated by given sounding, distance and depth, the navigator could confirm his position by sight.[69] Several pages are dedicated to descriptions of the mouth of the Channel, between The Lizard and Ushant. It was essential that the ships should be able to identify their position at the start, and then set their course accordingly. The rutter ended with details of the tides along the coast.[70]

Impressive as all this appears at first sight, there are some very curious features in the rutter. Why, for instance, did it include detailed instructions about navigation to Belle Isle, Morbihan and other parts of neutral France? Or instructions to get into ports too shallow for most of the Armada? The area covered is odd, as can be seen from the map, as are some of the instructions. The rutter reflects the king's orders by getting the pilot as far as the coast between Romney and Dover. The ships are instructed to anchor anywhere between Dover and The Downs, since it is a clear coastline, but are warned to hold their course between eight to nine fathoms; any deeper, and they will be heading towards the Goodwin Sands. Once here, the rutter rather surprisingly informs the navigator to 'wait for a pilot to take you to London or Dover'. Similarly, to find the way from Cape Gris-Nez to Dunkirk, where Parma's troops were gathering, the pilot is advised to hire a pilot at Calais. Access to the ports beyond Blankenberg was to be gained by firing a shot outside the town, and a pilot would — so the rutter assures the sailor — automatically emerge and take the ship to Flushing (under English control) or Sluys (recently retaken by Parma).

Of course in such difficult waters, local pilots would normally be essential, but such cooperation from enemy pilots was inconceivable, which was why the rutter had been produced in the first place. There were sailing instructions here to the southern Irish coast and the Isle of Wight where the Armada might be sent once Parma's troops had landed in England, but the odd coverage, the limitations precisely in the areas Dover-London, Calais-Flushing which mattered most for the fleet's strategic deployment, and the internal evidence suggest that it is a hastily-converted, if first-rate commercial rutter. The best sailing

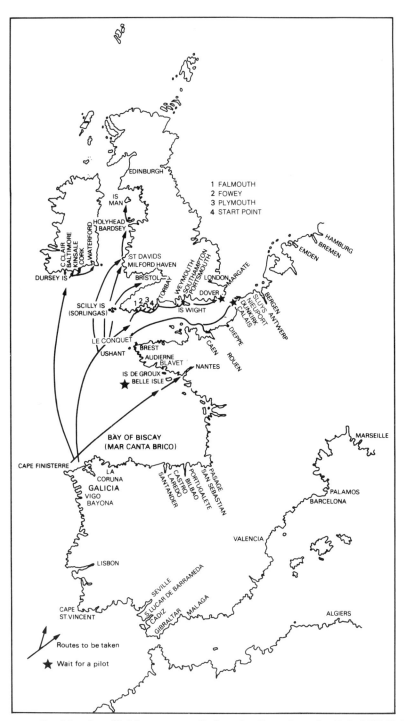

Routes outlined by the official rutter supplied to the Gran Armada. Ref. AGS E 431
p. 17. Map outline taken from *The Mariners Mirror* (1588), Anthony Ashley's translation
of *Spieghel der Zeevaerdt*.

instructions correspond to the areas of France, southern Ireland and western England most frequently used by commercial shipping trading between Iberia and these countries. It would be quite natural for a merchant ship to fire guns and call for pilots outside a port; and even, as the rutter suggests in two instances, to take shelter in bays beneath the guns of the English fortifications.

Medina Sidonia wisely did not confine his efforts to written sailing instructions, he provided charts for the fleet. At least sixty, and perhaps as many as eighty-five of the large ships were issued with a standard chart Medina Sidonia ordered from the cartographers at Lisbon. Again this was a striking demonstration of his authority since the Portuguese had a long tradition of secrecy regarding the production of maps as well as rutters.[71] Unfortunately there is no evidence to show what this chart covered: it may have been a general chart of the British Isles, or a detailed one of the crucial areas round the Channel. Two charts thought to have come from Armada ships do describe in detail parts of the English Channel and coast. The most important one — reproduced here — depicts the Dover Straits: it shows the Downs as well as the dangerous Goodwin Sands and Flemish shoals, that is the most crucial areas for the Armada, and ones not covered by the rutter.[72] But these were luxury items, as were marine Atlases such as the *Spieghel der Zeevaerdt*, Lafreri's *Isole del Mar*, and Ortelius's *Theatrum*. The ships that plied the Channel route would have charts of the area, but it is impossible to assess whether the fleet was adequately supplied with charts. The recovery of dividers, compasses, astrolabes, sounding leads and other navigational instruments from the wrecks testifies to the advanced skills of the pilots aboard the ships, and their ability to use charts.[73]

These admirable provisions did not suffice. From his study Philip and his advisers despaired of making sense of the still contradictory information. In an undated exchange we can glimpse their earnest efforts to make sense of the rutters and charts. 'In order to reconcile the difference between the two charts I have here', Philip asked for 'the rutter' — possibly the one published in Lisbon. The results were not entirely conclusive: 'the larger chart seems to give a distance of some 35 to 40 leagues between the Isle of Wight and Dunkirk,' he noted, 'and the smaller one a distance of 50 leagues, which seems closer to the distance given in the rutter'.[74] There were other problems; when his secretary told him that he had looked up one of the places mentioned in the rutter (Le Conquet) in Ortelius's *Theatrum* and found that it was in

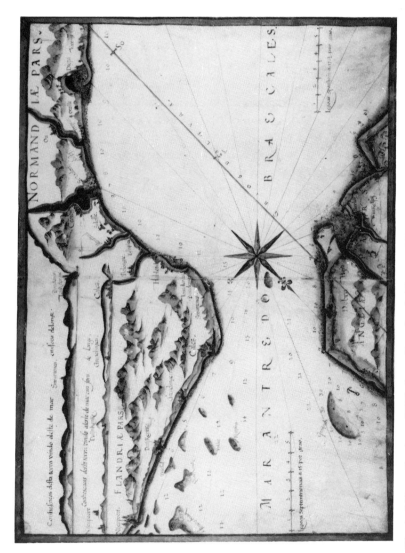

Chart of Dover Straits c. 1587–8, attributed to L. Texeira. NMM G218 6721. Reproduced by courtesy of the National Maritime Museum, Greenwich, London.

the mouth of the bay near Brest, Philip consulted his own charts: 'I can't find Conquet in the smallest chart, but they tell me that the large one shows it to be where you say. I've just looked at the small chart to see where Montanart is, but I can't find it there or in the rutter, which only mentions Ontandot — perhaps this is the same place.'[75] It is not surprising therefore, that Medina Sidonia should have decided that unless the Armada stayed together, many ships would be lost for lack of adequate technical knowledge and information. He was right. The rutter was extremely useful once the ships reached the Channel, and until they passed the Isle of Wight, but it did not obviate the need for a pilot, and the ships without charts needed one even more. When the pinnace of Diego de Salinas was separated from the fleet, he was unable to rejoin it because he did not have a pilot. Inadequate pilotage seems to have caused the galley *Santa Ana* to lose its way, and was certainly to blame for its failure to rejoin the fleet.[76] Rigid discipline was vital for the survival of the *Gran Armada*, and not just to ensure a successful outcome; hence the savage penalties which were imposed for anyone who diverged from the course ordered by the captain general.

These tough measures were also considered necessary in view of the large numbers of foreign pilots and masters. The Iberian commanders were worried that the impressed men would flee, and their worst fears seemed confirmed when the Armada was dispersed in the storms off La Coruña on 19-20 June 1588. Medina Sidonia and Pedro de Valdés accused foreign seamen of deliberately separating from the rest of the fleet. Their reaction owed more to fear of royal retribution, however, than xenophobia. They were trying to cover up a serious mistake and disobedience. Medina Sidonia had been instructed to head straight for England without delay. He decided, however, to wait in the open sea, seven leagues off the Galician coast for urgently needed supplies being sent from Lisbon. The pilots advised against it, and urged that the fleet put into La Coruña or Ferrol. Medina Sidonia was afraid of Philip's reactions, although he merely admitted to being afraid his men would defect if they put into a home port after their horrendous experiences at sea since embarking at Lisbon. Finally, on 19 June, with the weather conditions deteriorating, he capitulated, but too late to transmit the change of plan to all the fleet. Some of the ships proceeded up to the Channel as ordered earlier; these and the vessels which failed to reach port before nightfall were caught by violent, unseasonal storms and dispersed.[77] Even before he was fully apprised of the facts Philip was sceptical of the allegations. As always he requested an investigation, but he was confident that there were sufficient controls on the foreign seamen to preclude sabotage:

> the suspicion that the foreign seamen in the hulks have done this deliberately should prove unfounded if, as you have always been warned to do, you have taken adequate security measures. This is easy, given the many soldiers on board. I am confident that you have taken sufficient care and attention and put at least a pair of experienced and trustworthy Iberian mariners in each of these ships, so that if they suspect that the strangers are setting a different course, they can tell the soldiers to constrain them.[78]

It was soon evident that he was right. All the ships except the few too severely damaged to rejoin the fleet regrouped at La Coruña. What is really striking is the high degree of discipline and order the *Gran Armada* maintained. In 1589 almost half the Dutch ships that had been embargoed by Elizabeth had escaped, soldiers and all, before the English saw action in Spain.[79]

The tension between the different 'nations' in the Armada should not be over-estimated or dramatised. Philip's empire was multi-national, his military forces always so; his subjects were well accustomed to work alongside people of many different states. While there were tensions on board the ships, the only account of a fatal confrontation between a foreign pilot and the men on his ship, the murder of a Genoese pilot off the coast of Ireland, comes from a totally untrustworthy source.[80] It is inconceivable that soldiers would have killed the only man on board ship who could get them safely home. The reverse happened in another ship, and this incident is more likely to have been repeated during the harrowing return journey. After enduring abuse from Portuguese soldiers, Flemish mariners tried to escape from a hulk to the Irish coast; the soldiers sensibly forced them back on board.[81] The conflict was not so much between different 'nations', as between soldiers and sailors. The province of Guipúzcoa complained to Philip afterwards that some Armada ships had been lost 'because the pilots and mariners were not free to navigate as they needed'.[82] One of the chief pilots graphically described their differences to the king: 'when one of them says attack, the other says no, and the one who has no experience of the sea meddles, although [naval war] is very different from that on land'.[83] These accusations seem plausible; one can imagine a soldier wishing to attack without taking into account if the ship has the weathergage, or is capable of manoeuvring rapidly into position. But there was not a single specific example given in these two reports (both by naval men). Naturally mariners disliked taking orders from military commanders and resented taking risks with their ships, but the Armada was a warfleet, and like all such fleets it was bound to act as the generals and the strategic needs of the campaign required.

Medina Sidonia chose three men to provide him constantly with naval advice: Diego Flores de Valdés and captains Marolín de Juan and Ojeda. The pilot he seems to have trusted most was Domingo Ochoa. As the fleet approached the Flemish coast Ochoa was sent to discuss the situation with Parma, and Captain Marolín was blown off course while transmitting orders for the fleet to avoid the fireships and regroup. Although there were no pilots on board, Marolín successfully navigated the pinnace to friendly Flemish waters.[84] Neither man was able to rejoin the fleet, thus on the worst stage of the journey, Medina Sidonia had to put his trust on others. He had French and Flemish pilots aboard the flagship, *San Martín*, and took Scottish pilots also. In August 1588, the man who had extolled the superiority of Iberian Indies pilots and criticised foreign seamen was reduced to offering the French pilot a reward of 2,000 ducats if he succeeded in navigating the fleet safely back to Spain.[85]

Pilots of all nations gained a more important role as the campaign got underway. At first most were consulted unofficially by captains and commanders, who reported their opinions to the commanders in the council of war, but soon the pilots were consulted formally, especially when Medina Sidonia received contradictory advice. After an inconclusive council meeting on 20 July to determine when the Armada should sail, the leading military officer, Don Fransisco de Bobadilla, was baffled by disagreements between 'the naval generals and the pilots'; the duke may have shared this confusion since he insisted afterwards that 'the most important pilots in the fleet' should come to give their opinion before the council. Twelve pilots are named in an account of the meeting, although more were present. All the names appear to be Iberian, with pride of place going to Fernan Gabriel, *Piloto Mayor* of the Portuguese squadron.[86] The majority declared in favour of an immediate departure if the conditions of the previous day were repeated, and this decided the matter.

4. The Journey

Owing to delays caused by bad weather and supply problems, all element of surprise had been lost by the time the Armada arrived in the Channel. The original strategy could not be followed since the English had a large fleet at Plymouth and were determined to use it offensively. This shattered any hope of taking shelter in a port west of Dover if the weather again worsened, as the Armada might be blockaded by the English navy. In any case, the pilots who suggested this plan had not been told what the ultimate destination of the Armada was; all Medina Sidonia was willing to tell them now was that they must not stop until joining up with Parma.[87] When Philip read this he congratulated the duke on his answer, and felt sure that Medina Sidonia would follow orders. In fact the duke showed little sign of wishing to abide by the royal injunction not to engage the enemy fleet unless it could be avoided. The circumstances on arrival in the Channel were of course very different from what they had been when Philip drew up his original plan, and even there battle was not prohibited, merely discouraged. Although Medina Sidonia refused to attack the English fleet in Plymouth as some had urged him to do, confidence in his forces, and the conviction that the English navy was divided prompted him to attempt a general engagement shortly after sighting the English.[88] But the English fleet got to windward of the Armada and refused to give battle at close quarters. Unless he could engineer a boarding action Medina Sidonia knew he had no chance of victory against the swift and soon numerically superior enemy force. Philip's soldiers remained his chief weapon, as the English well knew. Sensibly, the English used their advantages — swifter, lighter vessels and intimate knowledge of the sea — to avoid boarding. Disappointed, the duke proceeded relentlessly up the Channel, aided by good weather. Lamenting the lack of galleys, he found an alternative solution: he asked Parma to send him some fifty small, manoeuvrable vessels, intending to use them to isolate and engage some of the English ships and thus force the enemy to close in a boarding action.[89] The ships never came.

Between them, the pilots, rutter and charts allowed the fleet to sail safely. The closer the fleet got to Flanders without confirmation that Parma was ready to sail, the more preoccupied Medina Sidonia became by the lack of shelter and anchorage. With the enemy fleet undefeated and in sight, the Armada must wait to escort Parma. Parma's only chance of a safe passage was to attach himself to the Armada which would have to protect his vessels and cover the landing. With mounting panic the duke informed Parma of his position and demanded experienced pilots of the coast of Flanders to guide them to a suitable port.[90] No news or pilots arrived, so the duke ordered the fleet to stop at Calais, the anchorage nearest the Flemish coast, on 6 August.

Finally, the following day news came that Parma was not yet ready to sail. Controversy continues over this. Recently Martin and Parker argued that he was ready, but pretended he was not in a clever subterfuge to confuse the enemy. Be that as it may, he certainly succeeded in convincing his own side. Later, when Philip quoted evidence proving Parma's inadequate preparations, and failure to obey royal orders to remain in the coastline, Parma admitted these accusations, having denied them previously. Nevertheless, it seems perfectly plausible that — as Parma claimed — he had so prepared his departure that it only required a couple of days to get the bulk of the army on the boats, and that if he had received Medina Sidonia's messages earlier, a junction of their forces would have occurred. Of course this scenario conveniently omits the one major impediment to Parma's departure — the presence of a Dutch rebel fleet blocking the sea passages. Parma had not warned of this until January 1588, and he knew that the casualties from an encounter between his largely unarmed flotilla and the heavily armed rebel ships would have been horrendous. His reluctance to sail is quite comprehensible.[91] Faced with reports of an expected waiting time between two days and two weeks, the council of war aboard the Armada heatedly debated what to do next. The pilots were unanimous that the fleet must not remain in the exposed Calais roads. A change of wind, combined with the strong currents, would at best rapidly disperse the fleet and send it out to the North Sea; or at worst, to certain destruction in the dangerous Flemish shoals. While he appreciated the risk, Medina Sidonia refused to take their advice because, as the pilots candidly admitted, if they left the anchorage for the relative safety of the North Sea it would be almost impossible to return to the Flemish coast and join Parma later: 'the difficulty of returning here means the whole expedition would be jeopardised'.[92] And Medina Sidonia was not willing to give up just yet.

The English realised the dilemma faced by the Armada in Calais and intended to take full advantage of it. They knew that a few fireships, with the aid of the strong currents and a prevailing wind, could dislodge the enemy fleet from its anchorage and disperse it. The stratagem was so obvious that pilots and generals warned Medina Sidonia to expect the attack, which came on the night of August 7. While there was no wild panic in the Armada, as was commonly thought, the ships hastily cut their cables and dispersed in all directions, with inevitable consequences, graphically described by one of the ships' masters:

> by dawn we were scattered among the shoals. As we knew so little of those shallows, and they were so familiar with them, being (as-it-were) their homeland, they were able to profit so well from our dispersal that despite refusing to board us, and fleeing every time we attacked, yet they defeated us.[93]

This bleak reflection made after the *Gran Armada* had returned does not take into account the extraordinary feat of discipline and seamanship during the arduous battle of 8 August off Gravelines. The scattered fleet somehow sailed away from the shoals and regained formation. The English assailed them furiously. It has been suggested recently that this was because they had realised the weakness of the Spanish artillery.[94] Whatever their opinion of the much-debated power of the Armada guns — and there is no proof that they had formed a cogent opinion of the multifarious naval armament of their opponents — the English still dared not board even a sinking ship. There were perfectly sound strategic reasons for redoubling their efforts against the Armada at this point which need not involve speculation on guns. The first was the undoubted superiority of the English, numerically and strategically. The Armada was dispersed, and ships could be picked off and pounded by effective massed cannonades. It was also imperative to continue the work of the previous night — to keep the Armada separated, and push it towards the Flemish shoals where nature rather than men would destroy the invaders. The Dutch rebels had removed the barrels and markers which signalled shoals and other dangers to shipping along the treacherous Flemish waters. Even the ships with experienced pilots and charts could not navigate safely without these markers.[95]

Throughout the battle Medina Sidonia was as concerned by the shoals as by the enemy ships. The few Flemish pilots in the fleet now proved their worth as they sailed continuously in small boats keeping a lookout and warning vessels that got too close to the shallow waters. The pilots urged the duke to call off the battle and make for the North Sea. They spelt out the danger: unless the fleet made for open water, it would be lost in the shoals. But Medina Sidonia could only reiterate that to sail north was to imperil the whole enterprise. They had to stay until Parma sailed out. On August 9 the battered Armada felt the wind change, and just as the pilots had warned, they began to drift inexorably towards the sands. The pilots told the duke 'that not one ship in the fleet would be saved. They were all drifting towards the shallow waters of Zealand, and nothing could be done . . . only God could save them'.[96] When the leadsmen called out six and a half fathoms, the men braced themselves. Some prayed, others wept; a few demanded to die fighting. In a short time the first great ship would be grounded. The English held back perhaps as much out of fear as curiosity for the outcome. Then came the miracle the Armada had hoped for: the wind veered WSW, blowing the Armada out towards the North Sea. They were not yet out of danger: all ships were told to follow the flagship closely as so few of the pilots knew where to set their course in those waters. By dint of strict discipline and tireless activity of the expert pilots, Medina Sidonia kept the fleet together and navigated northwards. Not a single ship was lost in the shoals that day. The printers had named the fleet 'La Felicissima Armada', the most happy or most fortunate fleet — it seemed rather appropriate now.

The problem was what to do next. Despite the danger, the reports of serious shortages of ammunition in the front-line ships and the knowledge that Parma was not quite ready to sail, it was unanimously decided in the council of war that they would attempt to turn back to the Channel to pick up Parma's flotilla. If the weather continued to drive the fleet northwards, however, they agreed that they must return to Spain by the north-about route.[97] This is traditionally seen as the final stage of the campaign, an impression confirmed by Medina Sidonia's correspondence. But it is a false impression; other options had been discussed by the king and his officials in case the two forces failed to meet. Once the Armada had made every effort to escort Parma and failed, it was allowed to act independently, and it was widely rumoured in Europe that it had done so. Medina Sidonia might have sheltered in Scottish waters until the weather changed and allowed the fleet to return south, but this would have alienated James VI who had been neutral in the conflict, and led to the disintegration of the fleet. It is curious, however, that there is no mention of a descent on Ireland, which had been the most popular alternative to an attack on England, or of heading for the Isle of Wight. Again it could be fear of losing control over the demoralised fleet that deterred the duke, who was himself deeply depressed after leaving the Channel. At this stage in the campaign, there is no sign of a wider strategic vision. Medina Sidonia's refusal to attack the English ships in Plymouth and stubborn insistence on remaining near the Flemish coast even at the risk of losing the whole fleet do point to his inability to look beyond the main (but not sole) task of covering Parma's passage. Nevertheless, it must be emphasised that while the Armada was still virtually intact, as the duke admitted to the king, it was seriously weakened by food shortages, and an alarming depletion of ammunition in the front-line ships.[98] They had to return or land where they might secure victuals and ammunition.

There is no suggestion that the king or his commanders had considered this outcome or made any provision for the fleet to sail over 750 leagues 'through rough seas little known to us'.[99] Few of the pilots had ever navigated these northern waters, and it is unlikely that many had even basic charts of the area, which were rare in any case. Even most of the maritime atlases included Ireland only in general maps, and had little accurate information of its western coast. There is no evidence that the German pilots — who were most likely to have known that route as Hanseatic ships were regularly using it as an alternative to the pirate-infested Channel in the 1580s — were consulted.[100] On 24 August, only twelve days after losing sight of the English fleet, the Armada commanders were already uncertain of their whereabouts. There was a violent row aboard the *San Martín* as the French pilot, Diego Flores de Valdés and Coco Calderón argued, 'with the chart in hand' over the exact position of the fleet, and what would be the best course to follow around Ireland. In the end, Calderón and the French pilot persuaded Medina Sidonia of the importance of sailing as far west of Ireland as possible. Valdés wanted to stay close to the coast, and given some of the losses around Ireland later, it would appear that other pilots agreed with him.[101]

The pilots and masters were instructed to set a course NNE until it reached 61 degrees and a half, then (giving Ireland a wide berth) to double the cape and run WSW to under 58 degrees, thence SW to 53 degrees, then taking a course SSW they would get to Cape Finisterre and head for La Coruña or another Galician port. Now, more than ever it was imperative for the fleet to stay together and follow the few ships with expert mariners who could make sense of this, and bring them back on course if the winds changed. But the weather turned, and the destruction of the *Gran Armada* began in earnest. Violent gales scattered it in all directions. Some ships managed to round Scotland before the worst of the storms and returned to Spain with seemingly miraculous speed. Heavy cargo, battle damage and inadequate manpower slowed the bulk of the fleet which took the full brunt of the fierce and unseasonal gales. The journey tested naval skills to the maximum. Sounding was used, but it was of very limited use in these waters. The few who did have charts were frequently unable to use them: fog and heavy rain prevented celestial observations and made it impossible to fix an accurate position. Whenever they met other Armada ships, commanders would seek information and help each other, and they tried desperately to keep in groups, but violent storms repeatedly separated the battered vessels.[102] The high mortality rate, caused largely by exposure and putrid victuals, threatened the survival of ships. Many mariners died, and either the soldiers learnt how to hoist sails or they perished. On one Biscay ship, the pilot, master and captain all died, leaving the men bereft of leadership and expertise. When they encountered another ship off the Irish coast they were lost and had no idea what course to follow.[103]

For those who lived to see the longed-for Iberian coast, their joy was almost immediately compounded with despair. Contrary winds prevented them from entering La Coruña or other Galician ports. The mariners were no more familiar with parts of the Iberian than the Channel coast. When Philip considered diverting the Indies *flota* in 1584 from Seville to Lisbon due to similar adverse conditions, he was informed that at least twelve Portuguese pilots had to be sent to guide them, since probably 'not one' of the Indies pilots knew the Portuguese or Galician coast. Now the problem was how to get the fleet through the dangerous waters of Biscay to safety. When Coco Calderón advised the *Nuestra Señora del Juncal* to follow him to Santander, the pilot refused to do so because he did not know the port and was frightened of losing the ship in the fast currents which characterised this coast.[104]

Given these most difficult circumstances, it is quite extraordinary that so many of the Armada ships docked safely: eighty-seven returned after their nightmarish round-about journey. A good many of the ships which sailed this route — Hanseatic and Dutch hulks, as well as Levantine ships — were lost in the attempt. This underlines the importance of the weather conditions in the disaster; the faster front-line ships were able to evade the worst storms.[105] It may also reflect — as Casado Soto and Thompson have argued — the quality of the ships and the manning levels. Above all, however, it reflects the excellence of the Iberian navigators and impressed foreign seamen who navigated the stricken ships to safety.

5. Conclusion

The campaign of 1588 was remarkable in every sense. Philip II, who had few Atlantic vessels and no deep-water Channel port, had launched a vast sea-borne invasion of England. By dint of extraordinary efforts he gathered shipping, provisions and men from every corner of the globe. Philip reaped a welcome harvest from his long-term policy of encouraging navigation and shipbuilding in Iberia. Decades of royal patronage had created a small, but important pool of skilled men and shipping of the highest quality. Thanks in part to the initiatives of Medina Sidonia most of the fleet was equipped with sufficient information to navigate the Channel safely, but they had failed to provide for the contingencies which almost overwhelmed the fleet. While they succeeded in sending good pilots, their use was limited by the specific nature of their training. Both at the planning stage and throughout the campaign, however, the commanders had access to excellent naval advice. Nevertheless, when this technical advice conflicted with political or broader strategic requirements, both Philip and his admirals ignored it, and took enormous risks which could have destroyed the fleet. From the moment the king was willing to hazard his ill-equipped fleet in the depths of the 1587 winter, to the botched stop-over in La Coruña, and worse still, the decision to wait in Calais, the fleet was exposed to grave dangers for the sake of reputation and in order to achieve its ultimate goal. The number of close escapes, culminating in the providential change of wind direction which saved it from the Flemish shoals, are almost as striking as the repeated misfortunes that assailed the *Gran Armada.*

The defeat made Philip intensify his efforts to expand his naval forces in northern European and Atlantic waters. Orders were given to build ships and again the king had to debate how they would be manned. The shortage of skilled mariners had been aggravated by the heavy casualties in the Armada. The king was forced to relax regulations restricting Iberian naval instruction to his own subjects; in 1589–90 'good Catholic men' from allied powers were invited to come for training.[106] Without the impetus provided by trade and piracy, however, Philip found it almost impossible to create the conditions for a thriving naval life in northern Spain. Even protectionist legislation failed to improve the position of the Iberians in northern trade, and consquently Philip was forced to review his prohibition of privateering. The 1590s saw a very moderate participation of Iberian vessels in the privateering industry,[107] but Philip's distaste of unregulated activity, and fear that his own privateers would further disrupt the vital trade with northern Europe, made him reluctant to issue licences. When he came to plan the next major invasion in 1596, he found it easier to gather good ships, yet more difficult to find skilled manpower. To solve the problem the pilot Lope de Ocina suggested that royal patronage for shipbuilding in Biscay should be accompanied by some form of naval conscription.[108] This was never attempted. The political and legal problems that would be raised by such a measure, as well as the opposition from competing commercial interests consigned it to gather dust in the royal archives.

Philip never again attempted a joint campaign from Spain and the Netherlands. Subsequent invasion attempts were limited to Iberian-based, seaborne campaigns. These attacks come under what I have termed a 'western strategy': they were smaller-scale and directed against southern Irish and English ports.[109] The shift in policy can be explained in two ways: the problems encountered in coordinating two distant forces in Spain and the Netherlands were starkly exposed in 1586–8 and may have persuaded the government that this strategy was too complex for the technical and administrative means of the Spanish Monarchy. It could be argued, however, that the campaign also proved that a powerful invasion force could be mounted in the heartland of the Monarchy, Iberia. This certainly impressed the protestant powers; while they celebrated England's salvation, which they interpreted as a victory for the protestant cause, the strategic implications for the Netherlands, Germany and France were very considerable. Although he experienced great bitterness and despair at the outcome of the invasion, Philip was right to believe that even failure would bring dividends and restore some of the honour and prestige he had lost.

NOTES

1. My work on pilotage and navigation owes a great debt to Robert Baldwin of the National Maritime Museum, Greenwich, who over the years has communicated his enthusiasm and shared his extensive knowledge of navigation with me.
2. William Shakespeare, *The Merchant of Venice*, act 1, scene 1. Salarino's speech.
3. Ibid., Salarino to Antonio.
4. Rodríguez-Salgado, *Catalogue* p. 12; Martin and Parker pp. 255–8.

5. I. A. A. Thompson, 'The Invincible Armada', in *Royal Armada. 400 Years* (London, 1988) pp. 160–179. His book, *War*, remains essential reading for Philip II's military establishment. See also his article 'The Armada and administrative reform: the Spanish council of war in the reign of Philip II'. *The English Historical Review*, LXXXIII (1967). G. Parker, 'Why the Armada failed', in *History Today* XXXVIII (1988) pp. 26–33. These ideas are expanded in Martin and Parker.

6. 'Why the Armada failed' p. 33.

7. I. A. A. Thompson, 'The appointment of the Duke of Medina Sidonia to the command of the Spanish Armada' *Historical Journal* XII (1969) pp. 197–216; P. Pierson, 'A commander for the Armada', *MM* LV (November 1969) pp. 383–99, and his recent biography: *Commander of the Armada. The Seventh Duke of Medina Sidonia* (New Haven & London, 1989).

8. AGS E 590 f. 125 Parma reminded Philip of this three years later. The original has not been found.

9. L. Cabrera de Córdoba, *Felipe II. Rey de España* (2nd edn., 4 vols., Madrid 1876–7) III p. 228.

10. AGS E 431 ff. 15 & 16. Philip had long been fascinated by geography, and was a patron of Ortelius, even after he settled in the rebel city of Antwerp. He gave three copies of the *Theatrum* to the Escorial library; the contents of another Atlas were displayed on the wall of one of the antechambers in the monastery-palace. P. Guillermo Antolín, 'La librería de Felipe II. Datos para su reconstitución', in *Reinvindicación histórica del siglo XVI*, (*Boletín de la Real Academia*, Madrid, 1928) pp. 335–426. B. Rekers, *Benito Arias Montano 1527–1598* (Groningen, 1961), esp. pp. 127, 147, 157.

11. Different versions of the plan in AGS GA 221 f. 1(bis), and FD I pp. 250–319; it is summarised and discussed in Rodríguez-Salgado, *Catalogue* pp. 17–18. Cf. p. 156 for Medina Sidonia's alternative of using small Netherlands boats.

12. Rodríguez-Salgado, *Catalogue*, pp. 17, 19; AGS E 590 f. 125.

13. Rodríguez-Salgado, *Catalogue*, pp. 17–20.

14. Martin and Parker, p. 119.

15. Political and dynastic considerations also affected his strategy. He had to appoint the duke of Parma as commander of the enterprise because the duke was his best military commander, and acceptable to the pope, whose help Philip considered vital. Yet the king did not trust Parma entirely, largely because they had conflicting claims to the English throne. Cf. above Rodríguez-Salgado p. 15 and Thompson, pp. 83–4, who stresses the constraints of limited resources. On the Portuguese invasion, W. S. Maltby, *Alba* (Berkeley, 1983) ch. 14.

16. For a more extended discussion of this see the Introduction by Rodríguez-Salgado, *Catalogue* pp. 24–7. Parma's letter to Philip AGS E 594 f. 8.

17. The strategy was refined and changed in the lengthy period before the Armada reached the Channel, see Rodríguez-Salgado, *Catalogue* pp. 27–8, 125; and Adams below, pp. 173–9.
18. Details of Philip's experiences as king in England can be found in M. J. Rodríguez-Salgado, *The changing face of empire. Charles V, Philip II and Habsburg authority, 1551–1559* (Cambridge, 1988) and D. M. Loades, *The reign of Mary Tudor* (London, 1979).
19. AGS E 165 f. 11 Philip to Santa Cruz.
20. FD II pp. 169–172 Recalde's opinion. Escalante's negative evaluation of the plan, AGS E 165 f. 223, Seville 3 April 1588.
21. AGS E 589 f. 15; all these areas had been considered in the course of discussions in 1583–4, see *BMO* I esp. pp. 397–8, 399, 408.
22. Thompson, above pp. 76–7, 81 and O'Donnell below pp. 220–31 for the problems of provisions of troops; Santa Cruz's difficulties with the king in E. Herrera Oria, *Felipe II y el marques de Santa Cruz en la empresa de Inglaterra* (Madrid, 1946).
23. AGS E 165 ff. 6–7 *minuta*.
24. AGS E 165 ff. 133–4 Philip to Medina Sidonia, 5 July 1588.
25. AGS E 944 f. 147 printed in *BMO* I p. 406.
26. *BMO* I p. 397.
27. *BMO* I p. 406 and 408.
28. AGS 586 f. 46, Parma to Philip, 11 Oct 1586, pubd *BMO* I p. 413.
29. AGS E 590 f. 125.
30. 'To navigate these waters', he added in his pedantic and repetitive epistle, 'they need to take constant soundings, and each pilot must have two other good mariners of great experience of that coast, acquired by frequently sailing those waters'. AGS GA 225 f. 112, 8 July 1588. Ureña had served in Philip's fleets since 1558, and the letter was intended both to advise the king, and to request favour for past services.
31. For examples see F. F. Olesa Muñido, *La organización naval de los estados Mediterraneos y en especial de España durante los siglos xvi y xvii* (2 vols., Madrid 1968) esp. II pp. 701–2, 848.
32. Michiel Coignet, *Instruction nouvelle des poincts plus excellents et necessaires touchant l'art de naviger* (Antwerp, 1581) cited by D. W. Waters, *The Art of Navigation in England in Elizabethan and Early Stuart Times* (London, 1958) p. 4.
33. E. G. R. Taylor, *The Haven-finding art* (London, 1956), esp. parts III and IV.
34. D. C. Goodman, *Power and Penury. Government, Technology and Science in Philip II's Spain* (Cambridge, 1988) pp. 53–65; R. C. D. Baldwin, 'The development and interchange of navigational information and technology between the maritime communities of Iberia and North-Western Europe and Asia, 1500–1620' (M. Litt Thesis University of Durham, 1980) pp.

120–153. Deliberate falsification of maps was also used to confuse the enemy, and access to information strictly limited.

35. Olesa Muñido, *La organización naval*, II pp. 886–9.
36. Goodman, *Power and Penury* pp. 73–4, p. 85 n. 53; Baldwin, 'The development and interchange of navigational information', pp. 120–53. The academy was intended to be a model for provincial and urban institutions, but since the crown would not finance them, they did not materialise.
37. Pedro de Medina's *Arte de Navegar* published in 1545 was already available in French translation in 1554, and in most European languages subsequently. Martin Cortes' navigational textbook, *Breve compendio de la sphera y del arte de navegar*, was published in Seville in 1551, and adopted as the set text by the Casa de Contratación. It did much to increase interest in and knowledge of celestial navigation, and was translated into English by Richard Eden and published in London in 1561, the first of nine editions before 1630. Similarly, the next textbook adopted by the Casa — Rodrigo de Zamorano's *Compendio del Arte de Navegar* (Seville, 1582) — was soon translated into Dutch as well as English. Details of the impact of Iberian skills on European development in Baldwin, op. cit.
38. Goodman, *Power and Penury* p. 85 n. 53.
39. Goodman, *Power and Penury* p. 78; Baldwin, op. cit., pp. 143–4.
40. H. Lapeyre, *Une famille de marchands: Les Ruiz* (Paris, 1955) p. 194. Musing on an eighteenth century text (*Abrégé de Pilotage*), which recommended that to estimate speed the pilot should take into consideration the quality of the vessel, the wind and water speed, and tide, Lapeyre (p. 192) concluded 'autrement dit, on se fiait à des impressions'.
41. Goodman, *Power and Penury* p. 73.
42. M. Pi Corrales, *La Otra Invencible* (Madrid, 1986) p. 98.
43. The wool incident has been admirably described by William D. Phillips jr. and Carla Rahn Phillips, 'Spanish wool and Dutch rebels: the Middleburg incident of 1574'. *American Historical Review*, vol. LXXXII (1977) pp. 312–330. Details of trade between Spain and the Netherlands in Gómez-Centurión, *Comercio*; Casado Soto, *Barcos* pp. 36–43 discusses some of the fleets sent from Spain after 1513.
44. AGS GA 221 f. 46; GA 221 f. 59.
45. AGS GA 220 f. 4, Lisbon 4 February 1588.
46. FD I pp. 450–1.
47. AGS GA 220 f. 91, the marquis of Cerralbo to the king, 29 February 1588; GA 222 f. 148 *ibid.*, 24 March.
48. AGS GA 220 f. 94, 24 February 1588; quote from GA 222 f. 134, 1 March 1588. Some of the Guipuzcoan pilots who served in the Armada of

1588 continued to serve in subsequent royal fleets, see L. Martínez Guitian, 'Aportación a la historia de Santander. Construcción naval y navegación en corso durante el reinado de Felipe II', *Altamira. Revista del Centro de Estudios Montañeses* (Santander) III (1934) pp. 199–238. I am very grateful to José Luis Casado Soto for bringing a number of articles in this journal to my attention.

49. AGS GA 222 f. 6, Medina Sidonia to Philip, 15 March 1588.
50. FD II p. 210; Ocina continued to play a major role in Philip's northern naval policies, see M. Bustamente Callejo, 'Consejo del Capitán laredano D. Lope de Ocina y de la Obra, al Rey Felipe II para la conquista de Inglaterra' *Altamira* I (1952) pp. 75–82.
51. More guns, ammunition and victuals were taken aboard, and the number of soldiers increased from 12,604 to 18,539. May figures AGS GA 221 f. 158.
52. AGS GA 220 f. 168, to Philip, San Lucar 28 February 1588.
53. AGS GA 225 f. 55, 15 July 1588.
54. FD II pp. 201–3.
55. *CSPFor* XXII p. 156.
56. AGS GA 222 f. 126 (21 March 1588) Duarte de Acuña handed over 2,000 ds for the journey. Philip knew of their departure in mid-April and immediately informed Medina Sidonia, FD I pp. 520–1.
57. FD I p. 484 Medina Sidonia to Philip, 23 March 1588 reporting the death of two of his best pilots and begging for conditions to be improved.
58. Parma reported that most of the skilled mariners had taken service with the rebel provinces of Holland and Zealand, and were prevented on pain of severe penalties from taking service elsewhere, and that his efforts to attract skilled sailors from neighbouring states had failed. None had come from Scotland although he had sent some money in 1587, and English diplomatic pressure scotched his attempt to get ships and mariners from Denmark. 'There is such a shortage of good pilots and even of sailors here — he wrote in May 1588 — that if the crossing were any longer, we would not have hazarded an attempt'. AGS E 594 f. 26 to Philip, 20 March 1588; E 594 f. 49 ibid., 13 May; E 592 f. 110, ibid., 22 August 1587 giving details of his naval needs; E 592 f. 73 — the Scottish plan. *CSPFor* XXII pp. 75–6, Daniel Rogers to Walsingham; AGS E 594 f. 62 Parma to Philip, 13 May 1588 on Denmark. Details of the types of ships he used in F. Riaño Lozano, *Los medios navales de Alejandro Farnese* (Serie *Gran Armada* VII, Madrid, 1989).
59. Philip could not afford to alienate these German merchants more than he had already done by seizing a few of their hulks to transport the fleet's victuals and equipment. Aware of the king's difficulties, one of the German shipmasters affected thought he might secure the release of his ship by promising to bring back essential naval stores and 100

experienced mariners and artillerymen. He claimed he needed nine months to do this. AGS GA 221 f. 197. C. Gómez-Centurión, 'Las relaciones Hispano-Hanseaticas durante el reinado de Felipe II', *Revista de Historia Naval* XV (1986) pp. 65–83, further discussed in his *Comercio* esp. pp. 221ff.

60. FD I p. 451 Philip to Medina Sidonia, 20 March 1588; ibid., pp. 475–80 reply from Lisbon, 26 March 88; p. 486 Medina Sidonia to Philip, 27 March 1588.

61. GA 221 f. 181 for 15 July gives 7,050 mariners, with a further 358 still missing. Some may have joined the fleet before sailing; see Rodríguez-Salgado, *Catalogue* p. 36 a fuller discussion of the figures; also Casado Soto, above pp. 166–7, and his *Barcos*, esp. pp. 172, 177 — he reckons one more ship sailed — and that the fleet now had optimum manning levels, p. 182. Thompson, pp. 78–9 above, and note 43, stresses the extremely uneven distribution of men, and questions the adequacy of manning levels.

62. AGS GA 222 f. 9 to Philip, 23 March 1588.

63. New World pilots had a duty to provide the Casa officials with their rutters after each voyage, so as to allow the government to keep careful records of the new lands, and to improve safety on these hazardous routes. Licenced and approved pilots and mariners were given access to the information, but foreigners and others were kept out. Maps and rutters were lent out to licenced masters, but the Portuguese were extremely hostile to printing this valuable information. In Castile — particularly under Philip II — printing rutters and navigational information was approved.

64. *Le Grand Routier, pilotage et encrage de mer, tant des parties de France, Bretaigne, Angleterre, Espaigne, Flandre que des hautes Alemaignes, avec les dangers des portz, havres, rivières et chanalz et régions dessus dictes.* Written *c.*1483 and published more than twenty years later, it was translated into English and printed in 1528, going through several editions subsequently. Lapeyre, *Les Ruiz* pp. 194–5; Baldwin, 'The Development and interchange of navigational information' p. 210.

65. *Derrotero de las costas de Bretaña, Normandia, Picardia, hasta Flandes, y de la de Inglaterra, Manga de Bristol y Sant Iorge, y parte de la Costa de Irlanda.* AGS E 431 f. 17; a printed version has long been available in Herrera Oria, *Armada*, pp. 156–180.

66. AGS GA 222 f. 9.

67. FD I p. 493, p. 499. He must have received them around the middle of April.

68. Thus if a ship had sailed from Finisterre N for 20-25 leagues, and NE for another 100-110 leagues, the soundings should reveal a depth of 90-95 fathoms, and the sediment from the sea bed should be like 'a pilgrim's

shell, envelopped in coarse white sand'.

69. For instance, he would recognise Fowey by the broken church tower, and make doubly sure by identifying an island to the east with another church in a promontory, and a sandy beach to the SE.

70. AGS E 431 f. 17.

71. AGS GA 222 f. 9; FD I p. 493, 499. The higher figure has been suggested by Martin and Parker, p. 285 n. 30.

72. National Maritime Museum, Greenwich, G218:6721. I am very grateful to Robert Baldwin for his comments on these charts. The 'Dover Straits' is thought to have been seized by Drake from Don Pedro de Valdés's ship, the *Nuestra Señora del Rosario*. It appears to be a copy of Lucas Waghenaer's engraving from the *Spieghel der Zeevaerdt* (1584), and may have been made by the famous Portuguese cartographer Luis Teixeira, or his associates. A limited facsimile edition entitled 'Portolan Chart of the Dover Straits' has been published by Editions Alecto in conjunction with the National Maritime Museum (London, 1988). The attribution to Teixeira and its Armada provenance are highly likely but not proven, as Martin and Parker claim (p. 192 colour reproduction 43); and there is certainly no proof that the chart was the one ordered by Medina Sidonia as they assert there. Baldwin is convinced that a chart now in the Dr. Englebrecht collection, Prinz Hendrik Museum, may also have been taken by the Dutch from one of the Armada ships. It covers, though in much less detail, the coast from Poole to Dover, giving details of depth, shallows and anchorages.

73. See for example, Rodríguez-Salgado, *Catalogue* section 12, p. 213ff., esp. nn. 12, 13, 16, 19, 21.

74. AGS E 431 f. 15.

75. AGS E 431 f. 16 s.d. This scrutiny of the maps may have been prompted by news (reported by the secretary) that the English fleet had sailed out as far as Brest. But Philip's remark that 'It is therefore a bad thing that they should have returned from there' also suggests he may have been trying to establish where some of the Armada ships had gone after the storm off La Coruña.

76. AGS GA 226 f. 104 (Salinas), E 594 f. 131 (galley).

77. FD II p. 108, p. 119.

78. AGS E 165 ff. 133 & 134. Philip to Medina Sidonia, min, 5 July 1588; FD II p. 145.

79. R. B. Wernham, *After the Armada. Elizabethan England and the struggle for Western Europe* (Oxford, 1984) pp. 75, 111. About twenty-four of the transport vessels with some 3,000 men on board had left before they reached La Coruña, and several ships with some 2,000 men escaped as the fleet left the city.

80. The young man's story is riddled with lies and inconsistencies and

Fernández Duro dismissed it as pure fabrication in his introduction to *La Armada Invencible* I pp. 195–7. Colin Martin, *Full Fathom Five* (London, 1975) pp. 45–53 claims that the young man was at first misunderstood, then fabricated part of his story.

81. AGS E 165 f. 251 Relacion del sargento Alonso de Porres, 4 October 1588.

82. FD II p. 476.

83. Bustamente Callejo, 'Consejos . . . de Ocina', p. 76.

84. The prince of Ascoli was on board the ship. AGS E 165 ff. 296–7; E 594 f. 182.

85. Report by Coco Calderón, AGS GA 221 f. 190; AGS E 431 f. 37.

86. FD II pp. 205–11, pilots named p. 210: Fernan Gabriel, Juan Ramos, Andres de Urquiza, Domingo Ochoa, Lope de Ocina, Juan de Llatado, Antonio Francisco, Juan Alvarez de Proa, Jeronimo Perez, Sebastian Muñoz, Martin Velez, Juan de Escalante. Of these, only Ochoa had been included in the March list of experienced pilots, from which one may deduce that with the exception of the three pilots from Guipúzcoa who had joined subsequently (above pp. 145–6), the rest belonged to the Portuguese and Castilian squadrons not included in that list.

87. AGS E 165 f. 125 Philip to Medina Sidonia, 21 June 1588. Also FD II p. 114, and pp. 101–5 for the duke's view of the strategy in May and June.

88. Adams below pp. 183–6 offers a detailed reconstruction of the duke's decision. Longer narratives of the battle in Pierson, *Commander*, pp. 134ff. and appendix pp. 235–43; Martin and Parker, chapters 9 & 10; more briefly in Rodríguez-Salgado, *Catalogue* section 14; the most vivid account in G. Mattingly, *The defeat of the Spanish Armada* (London, 1983) chapters 21 to 28.

89. AGS E 594 f. 117 Medina Sidonia to Parma, 5 August 1588; see also Rodríguez-Salgado, *Catalogue* pp. 239–40.

90. AGS E 594 ff. 114, 117, 122, letters from Medina Sidonia to Parma 1, 5 and 7 August.

91. Martin and Parker, p. 185; Rodríguez-Salgado, *Catalogue* p. 37. In his paper to the Anglo-Spanish conference in London, O'Donnell argued that if the fleet had been able to stay in Calais for a few more hours, the two forces would have met; other historians opt for a longer time span, but no one denies that the fusion was possible. Logically we can conclude that having a deep-water port in which to shelter was ideal, but Philip's strategy could have worked without it in optimum circumstances. Details of Parma's forces and strategy can be found in G. Parente, H. O'Donnell, F. Fernández, M-C. Couceiro, M-A. Armada, *Los sucesos de Flandes de 1588 en relación con la empresa de Inglaterra* (Madrid, 1988); H. J. O'Donnell y Duque de Estrada, *La fuerza de desembarco de la Gran Armada contra Inglaterra (1588)* (Madrid, 1989) and his article pp. 216–20, 232–3 below.

92. AGS E 594 f. 177, account of Jorge Manrique.
93. FD II pp. 273–8, relacion del maestre de una de las naos de Sevilla, quote pp. 276–7.
94. Martin and Parker pp. 195ff. The gun debate continues. In a BBC2 television documentary (August 1988) a test with replica English and Spanish-style sea-carriages showed that the English carriages were easier to move, but both guns were reloaded in a matter of minutes. Moreover, it is impossible to generalise about the Armada guns, given the immensely varied provenance of guns, carriages and gunners. Cf. Casado Soto pp. 122–3 above. I. A. A. Thompson 'Spanish Armada gun procurement and policy', in P. Gallagher and D. W. Cruickshank, *God's obvious design* (London, 1990) pp. 69–84 gives a succinct account of the lack of procurement policy and inability to equip the fleet adequately, and he argues that these factors were decisive since the Armada was incapable of winning an outright naval battle against the English. Nevertheless it should be stressed that Medina Sidonia did try to fight such a battle, considering his men to be superior to his guns.
95. AGS E 693 f. 30 Guillén San Clemente, Philip's ambassador to the Emperor, Prague 13 September 1588, reporting a complaint by the city of Emden whose citizens were seriously affected by this. The Dutch had to offer them compensation for loss of trade. Ironically, some weeks earlier, the city of Emden itself had considered removing these markers for fear that the Armada might try to anchor in the port! *CSPFor* XXII p. 157, August 12/22.
96. AGS E 431 f. 47.
97. AGS E 431 f. 47, and GA 221 f. 190.
98. Thompson pp. 81–2 above makes clear the high level of spoilage as well as corruption. Martin and Parker, pp. 199–200 claim that there was plenty of ammunition, but the Armada commanders repeatedly complained of shortages, and they cannot all have been lying or deceived. Captain González Aller in his paper to the third Anglo-Spanish conference, stated that some ships returned with many cannon balls, but others had used them all, so it is not possible to generalise — a point emphasised recently in Thompson, 'Spanish Armada gun procurement' esp. p. 75. Pierson is inclined to think that if Medina Sidonia had shown any more initiative, the outcome might have been even worse, *Commander* p. 223.
99. AGS GA 221 f. 190, Coco Calderón.
100. It was widely feared that the pilots from Hamburg would navigate the Armada there after their dispersal from Calais, BNM mss 979 ff. 77–82 Giulio Sauorgnano to Filippo Pigafetta, Venice 23 September 1588. There is a chart dating from 1588 — Chart of the North Sea and the Baltic — made by Thomas Laton (probably copied illicitly from information available in Danzig) showing the Baltic and North Sea in some detail, but even this does not get much beyond northern Ireland;

another chart would have been necessary to avoid shipwreck in the west coast of Ireland where many met their death. I am most grateful to Peter Barber of the British Museum for bringing this interesting chart to my attention. He examined it before its sale at Christie's (13 April 1988) and found that it had compass holes and pencilled circles in the area between Flushing and East Anglia, suggesting it was used to navigate this area.

101. AGS GA 221 f. 190.
102. AGS GA 227 f. 157 Aramburu's account is a carefully annotated report which shows what a skilled navigator was able to do despite these conditions — with a great deal of inspired guesswork and prayer.
103. AGS E 165 f. 251; AGS GA 227 f. 45 Medina Sidonia to Philip, 27 September 1588 with details of how the soldiers helped to sail the ships.
104. AGS GA 221 f. 190. Goodman, *Power and Penury* p. 80 for the 1584 incident.
105. Casado Soto, *Barcos* p. 245, 249, and his article above, pp. 120, 122.
106. Goodman, *Power and Penury*, p. 80.
107. Gómez-Centurión, *Comercio* pp. 56, 242–4.
108. Bustamente Callejo, 'Consejos . . . de Ocina' p. 76, who erroneously dates the document to 1588.
109. Lope de Ocina was still urging an assault against Falmouth, Dartmouth and Plymouth in 1596; Bustamente Callejo, p. 79. W. Graham, *The Spanish Armadas* (London, 1972) for a brief account of the later attempts.

6

THE BATTLE THAT NEVER WAS:
THE DOWNS AND THE ARMADA CAMPAIGN

Simon Adams

If there is one aspect of the voyage of the *Gran Armada* upon which there has been practically universal agreement, it is that the decisive flaw in Philip II's strategy was the absence of a port on the North Sea where the Armada could take shelter, reform or embark the duke of Parma's army. From this general conclusion there is no reason to dissent. Yet the focus on the issue of a port in the Netherlands has led to another aspect of the question receiving only cursory attention. If a large fleet was to be sent from Spain to take part in an amphibious invasion of England, it would need a suitable anchorage on the English coast as well, and for all the apparent openness of the coastline, the number of large estuaries or roadsteads is a limited one.[1] The range of potential invasion beaches was in practice quite restricted.

This point was addressed directly by the panel of military and naval officers commissioned to survey the coastal defences of England in their report of 27 November/7 December 1587.[2] They identified four major anchorages: Milford Haven, Plymouth, Portland and the Solent, and 'the Downs, Margate and the Thames'. Milford Haven was considered too remote to be of use to an invading army; the choice of the others would depend on the strategy that Philip II adopted. Plymouth was 'thought to be the most likely place . . . for that it is unlikely that the king of Spain will engage his fleet too far within the Sleeve before he have some good harbour'; Portland offered 'a great harbour for all his ships to ride in, good landing for men, the Isle [of Wight] being won is a strong place of retreat'; the Downs, Margate and the Thames 'are thought so fit landing places . . . in respect of the commodity of landing and nearness of the prince of Parma in whose forces the king of Spain reposeth especial trust'. As will be seen, English strategy was in large part shaped by this appreciation. More complicated was the influence of English anchorages on Spanish strategy, for any discussion of this question leads directly to one of the longest-running disputes arising

173

from the campaign: what has been rightly described as the 'confusion [that] still surrounds the Armada's real destination'.[3] For this reason, the way in which English anchorages affected Spanish planning deserves extensive re-examination.

Our principal concern will be with the Downs. This was possibly the best-known anchorage in the North Sea, 'where thousands of ships may ride as safely as any harbour of Europe'.[4] Moreover, excellent beaches were available immediately to the north of Sandwich, within easy reach of the Flemish coast. On the other hand, it also possessed some disadvantages for an invader. It was an established anchorage for English ships patrolling the Narrow Seas. It was not easy of access, for the Goodwin Sands limited entrance to two channels. The southern entrance opposite Dover was defended by Henry VIII's 'castles' at Walmer, Deal and Sandown.[5] The northern channel involved an awkward entry round the North Foreland.[6] Lastly, the cliffs and the Downlands themselves offered excellent vantage points a defender.[7]

Serious discussion of anchorages in England was initiated on the Spanish side in the autumn of 1583, once the recapture of Dunkirk and Nieuport earlier in the summer made an invasion of England from Flanders possible. In September 1583 Philip II raised two important issues with the duke of Parma, the general question of an invasion of England and the possibility of sending him by sea rather than overland a reinforcement of Spanish infantry made available by the recent capture of Terceira. Parma was asked specifically if the Flemish ports would be able to handle large ships, or whether the troops should be transferred to local coastal shipping at the Downs ['las Dunas'].[8] A month later Parma supplied a description of the Flemish ports. Dunkirk and Nieuport were able to accommodate ships of 150 *toneladas* (200 at high tide) and there were anchorages off Mardyke and Dunkirk where the troops could be transferred to smaller craft. The Downs, however, were undoubtedly a superior anchorage, being 'very deep and big enough for any fleet'.[9]

Parma also reported that he was seeking the advice of English exiles about an invasion — according to Léon van der Essen it was in fact the Welsh catholic Hugh Owen who proposed a landing in Kent.[10] On 30 November Parma sent the king a detailed survey of the English coastline, and recommended two landing areas: Milford Haven in the West and 'Ravenspergt' in the East.[11] The latter was chosen 'both for past examples and for other respects that appear most commodious, easy, short and secure'. The 'other examples' have been taken to refer to the

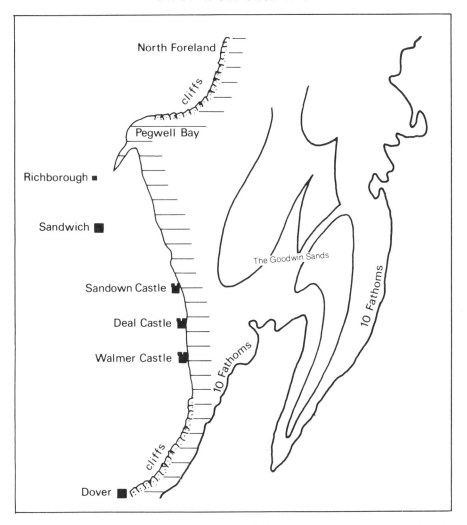

The anchorage at the Downs. Drawn from H. M. Colvin (ed.), *The History of the King's Works*, IV, pt. ii (H.M.S.O., 1982), fig. 32, with permission of the Controller of H.M. Stationery Office.

invasions of Julius Caesar and Hengist Horsa, and by 'Ravenspergt' Parma is assumed to have meant Richborough by the mouth of the Stour between Sandwich and the North Foreland.

Although it was received in Madrid in January 1584, Parma's survey has not since been traced.[12] Some idea of its contents can be deduced, however, from a similar survey produced in October 1597 for the Adelantado of Castile, which may even have been based on it.[13] This too described Milford Haven as 'the finest port in England' and then commented on the size of Plymouth, Southampton and Portsmouth. The Downs were considered a good anchorage, 'the water is deep and [it is] a clean anchorage', but the defences of the southern entrance and the awkwardness of the northern were also noted. When Philip resumed discussion of an invasion in December 1585, it was to his earlier survey that Parma in his delayed answer of 20 April 1586 initially referred him.[14] It is clear that by this stage Parma considered that the limitations of the Flemish ports had been fully exposed, and that Philip, who noted twice in the margin of the draft of his letter of 29 December 1585 that 'without a port, nothing can be done', appreciated this as well.

The invasion plan that Parma finally produced in April 1586 was limited to a surprise landing employing Flemish coastal craft, which had the advantage of being able to transport troops directly onto the chosen beaches. Since the English would be taken unawares only the minimal provision of twenty armed vessels for defence against naval interception was necessary. The landing area was to be the coast 'from Dover to Margate, which is at the mouth of the River Thames'; it was chosen both for the brevity of the passage and because it was believed that the wooded and rolling terrain of the countryside would provide protection against English cavalry. The risk of landing so close to the centre of government was accepted in the hope that the moral effect of a successful Spanish landing might cause Elizabeth to capitulate.

Parma's letter was brought to Spain by the Italian engineer Giovanni Battista Piatti. Piatti's verbal report filled out some further details but it also included two important points that are difficult to reconcile either with each other or with Parma's plan.[15] The first of these is the description of the landing place as 'next to the mouth of the River Thames in the sea, which is that of London' ['junto al desembocadero del rio Tamise en la mar que es el de Londres'], which could mean Richborough, or possibly even Margate itself. The second, however, is the statement that the landing-place was 'no more than eighteen miles' from London, enabling the army to reach the city within two or three days after landing. Assuming Piatti had not got his distances completely wrong, this can only mean a landing quite far up the Thames estuary, which in turn is difficult to square with the emphasis on the brevity of the passage. Piatti also raised a new issue: an invasion south of the Thames left the river as an obstacle to an assault on London. However, the easier approach via the Essex bank was too vulnerable to attack by cavalry. He proposed, therefore, that this question be resolved after the landing, and the army possibly transported to the Essex bank during the march on London.[16]

The capture of Sluys in August 1587 did not affect the invasion of England in any material way. Parma was expected to have besieged Ostend, but at the last minute he chose Sluys because he believed it to be less well defended. The unexpectedly stout English defence and the major, if unsuccessful, Anglo-Dutch efforts to relieve it delayed the surrender sufficiently to prevent Parma from moving on to Ostend before the end of the summer. It is possible that he deliberately exaggerated the importance of Sluys to counter the charge of having wasted his efforts on a secondary objective.[17] More significant was his complaint during that summer that since the essential secrecy had now been lost his invasion fleet could no longer operate without naval protection. This led Philip to draw up what became the ultimate version of the invasion: the combined operation that was imparted first to Parma and then to the marquis of Santa Cruz in September 1587.[18] The attack was to take place immediately, despite the risks attending a major naval operation in the Narrow Seas late in the year, in the hope that it would still catch the English unawares. The fleet was to sail up the Channel and 'anchor off the Cape of Margate' ['dar fondo en el cabo de Margata']. The duke, 'thus seeing that his passage was safe, with the fleet posted at the Cape, or sailing to and from the mouth of the river of London if the weather permits', would then make his crossing.

The description 'el cabo de Margata' identifies it as the North Foreland (also known as St. Margaret's Head), rather than the roadstead at Margate itself. With luck (or divine providence) the fleet's arrival would catch the English shipping dispersed and the queen's warships immobilised in their anchorages in the Thames. By stationing itself off 'el cabo de Margata' the Armada would act as a screen, preventing an English sortie from the Thames from interfering with the landing, which by implication would take place in Kent according to Parma's proposal of 1586.[19] It was a strategic position — 'from that post it is possible to block the passage so that the ships of the river of London and of the east will not be able to join those of the south' — that would permit the defeat of the English navy in detail. It was to be held only so long as it took to get the army across; thereafter Santa Cruz was free to attack the English in their ports. The instructions concluded with a recognition of the fact that winter weather would probably force the Armada to seek a sheltered anchorage. There was no question of the fleet sailing to Flanders: Margate Roads was suggested in the first instance, or if necessary Santa Cruz could proceed further into the Thames estuary. Either position would enable him to maintain his blockade of London.

The delayed departure of the Armada during the winter of 1587/8 brought another factor into play: the deployment of the English fleet. Spanish intelligence of English maritime activity still depended on the espionage network run by Bernardino de Mendoza from Paris.[20] His best agent at this stage was a member of the household of Dom António in London, António de Viegas. The relative accuracy of Viegas's reports probably owes much to the close involvement of Dom António with Drake and the other English commanders.[21] However, since his 'avisos' had to be relayed through Mendoza to the Escorial, by the time they reached the commanders of the fleet they were out of date by several weeks, a delay of no small significance.

In November 1587 Mendoza began reporting a new English deployment. The fleet Sir Francis Drake had brought back from Cadiz that summer had remained at Plymouth; it was now to be reinforced and employed in some form of diversionary attack against Spain itself.[22] In January 1588 the possibility of an English diversion inspired a second set of instructions for Santa Cruz.[23] With the example of the marquis's chase after Drake in 1587 in mind, no doubt, Philip was adamant that any diversion be ignored; only if Drake tried to stop the Armada on the open seas or if he was encountered at the mouth of the Channel was he to be fought, for such an encounter would provide an excellent opportunity to defeat the English in detail.[24] The diversion might even be an advantage, for then Santa Cruz would only have to face the 'Almirante de Inglaterra' at Cape Margate. Even should he encounter both English fleets there, he would be superior to them. After the landing had taken place Santa Cruz should take the fleet into the Thames to assist the army (possibly to cross the river for the assault on London), leaving part of it to guard communications with Flanders. In case storms were encountered en route, two rendezvous were recommended: the Scillies at the mouth of the Channel, and the Isle of Wight (i.e. the Solent) halfway up.

Philip did not regard the destination of the fleet as changed in any way. The text of the instructions refers simply to the 'plan agreed upon [traça accordada]', and he noted in the margin of the draft:

> It would be well to remind him about the cape of 'Margat', which I believe is what the duke of Parma is referring to, although he does not name the place; and it would be good also to inform the duke of Parma of this.

However, in view of the new English deployment, a screen or blockade at 'Cape Margate' was no longer relevant. It would now be the site of a major battle. To deal with this eventuality Philip revised the strategy of the invasion in a major way. If the English fleet combined to fight the Armada off the Kentish coast, he wished Parma to send to Santa Cruz 'the greatest number of ships and men possible'. A later note on the English ability to reinforce their fleet with both men and small craft 'as their fleet will be so close to land', and the need for Parma to be ready to supply both to the Armada is equally revealing. It was no longer a question of the fleet making possible an invasion, rather Parma was to join the fleet for a major battle in English coastal waters before the invasion took place.

Santa Cruz may not have received these instructions, but they are not irrelevant because they became the basis of those given to the duke of Medina Sidonia on 1 April.[25] Medina Sidonia was also sent a copy of those of 14 September to which he was referred for general advice as to the enterprise, but it is not clear whether he also received copies of Parma's 1583 survey or his description of the Flemish ports as well. The overall strategy remained unchanged in the new instructions, but there were some important revisions. In the section of advice about storms en route Medina Sidonia was specifically warned to avoid the coasts of France and Flanders owing to shoals and sandbanks. He was to sail 'as far as Cape Margate, in order to unite with the duke of Parma there'. As in the January version there was advice on how to conduct a battle with the English at Cape Margate, over which there was now some confusion. The king's earlier marginal notes about Parma assisting the fleet were not embodied in the text, but, while the battle was envisaged as taking place before the juncture with Parma, Medina Sidonia was also advised to try and get Parma across without fighting, 'by diverting the enemy or some other way'. A further new issue was raised: the supplying to Parma of the soldiers carried by the Armada if the battle had not been fought. This point was addressed more fully in an accompanying set of secret instructions, which informed Medina Sidonia that, 'stationed off Cape Margate', he was to learn from the duke where these reinforcements were to be landed.[26] Philip then raised the question of a failure of the landing. In that eventuality Medina Sidonia was to attempt to occupy the Isle of Wight, though it was emphasised that this was only to be undertaken on the return from Cape Margate, not on the outward voyage.

No further formal instructions have been discovered, and the question of the destination of Armada was not specifically raised in the later surviving correspondence between Medina Sidonia and the king. However, two important pieces of evidence suggest that the question was regarded as settled at the time the fleet departed from Lisbon. The printed rutter supplied to the fleet concludes its survey of the English coastline with the entry to the Downs; no advice was provided about sailing to Margate, let alone to Flanders. The anchorage in the Downs is also clearly marked in 'Teixeira chart' of the Dover Straits.[27] Equally revealing is the advice of Bernardino de Escalante to the king of 3 April.[28] Escalante understood that the Armada would enter between the Goodwins and the coast, be joined by Parma's shipping and then make the assault from the anchorage in Downs and the shore between St. Margaret's Head and Margate. He disliked this plan and advised instead that the fleet be used for an independent invasion via Milford Haven. His numerous objections to the Downs were significant ones: the anchorage was not usable in storms; it could only be entered through a defended passage from the south; there was no alternative port in England after the Isle of Wight; the Armada's ships were too large to go to Flanders later and collect Parma's horses. Lastly, it was too obvious; it was too easy for the English to concentrate their forces there.

By May the question of whether Medina Sidonia was expected to fight the English en route had assumed a greater importance. On this point the instructions to ignore any English diversion, and not to be deflected from his course, have caused no small confusion.[29] Yet Philip was equally clear that Drake if encountered en route could be engaged.[30] Moreover, although the king would have liked Medina Sidonia to have occupied the Downs without a fight, the detailed advice on conducting such an engagement supplied in both the April instructions and later letters suggests that there was considerable doubt as to whether this would be possible.

The period between the issuing of Medina Sidonia's instructions and the final departure for the Channel on 22 July was divided into two distinct phases by the voyage from Lisbon to La Coruña (30 May to 19 June). During the first phase the intelligence picture underwent several major revisions. Since January Drake's squadron had remained at Plymouth and had not gone to sea; the majority of the English ships were still either in the Thames or the straits of Dover.[31] On 16/26 April Mendoza's London source reported a major re-deployment. The lord admiral, Howard of Effingham, was to join Drake at Plymouth with the main fleet, leaving only forty-odd ships in the straits. On 8 May Mendoza himself wrote that the combined fleet of Drake and Howard (eighty ships) was intending to attack the Armada in Spanish waters. Later reports included an invasion of Portugal by Dom António.[32] If this intelligence was true, then some important consequences would follow. Should the combined English fleet depart on a diversion to Spain, the Armada had the opportunity of reaching the Downs with only the small Dover squadron in its path. On the other hand, if Medina Sidonia were to encounter both Howard and Drake at the mouth of the Channel he would have to face a major battle much earlier than had been planned for.

There was, however, a further complication. On 23 May/2 June the London source reported that Howard was not in fact going to Plymouth but was remaining in the straits (this was quite inaccurate for Howard arrived in Plymouth that very day). The news was relayed by Mendoza to Philip on 14 June. Shortly afterwards this assessment was again revised, and from 26 June onwards Mendoza's reports contained the correct information that the combined fleet was operating from Plymouth.[33] How much of this intelligence reached Medina Sidonia and how it affected his plans is therefore a major question. Nor is it an academic one; whether the Spaniards knew that Howard was at Plymouth before they left La Coruña on the final voyage was among the questions put to Don Pedro de Valdés by the English council after his capture.[34] Here a final difficulty arises. On 18 July Philip informed Mendoza that he had not received any of his dispatches since that of 14 June.[35] Therefore when Medina Sidonia ultimately left La Coruña on 22 July he may have known of the initial report of the combining of the English fleets, and then the revision, but not the later confirmation of the first report.

Shortly before the fleet left Lisbon an important exchange of letters took place between Medina Sidonia and the king. On 21 May Philip drew the duke's attention to the fact that Drake had not left Plymouth.[36] Although he now felt that the Armada would be so superior in strength that the English probably would not fight, he speculated that Drake might be planning to fortify himself in Plymouth, let Medina Sidonia pass, and then fall on his rear, while Howard attacked the Spanish vanguard from the straits. Conversely, he wondered whether the English might be intending to attack the Armada en masse at the invasion area after the landing had taken place and the soldiers had been handed over to Parma. In the first instance he advised Medina Sidonia to deploy the fleet to deal with a simultaneous attack; in the second he advised him that he should retain sufficient troops on board and also warned that since the enemy would be stationed off his own coast Medina Sidonia was to beware of attacks by fireships and infernal machines. In conclusion he was again reminded of his instructions not to respond to any diversions off the Spanish coast. Medina Sidonia answered on the 28th.[37] He would prefer to defeat the enemy en route, but appreciated the need to join Parma as soon as possible rather than seek out the opposing forces. He then outlined his intended deployment of the Armada to meet a possible attack from both front and rear. To deal with an attack after the landing, he intended to unite with the duke first and then defeat the English before landing a single man.

This correspondence makes it clear that prior to the departure from Lisbon Philip and the duke still believed the English fleet to be divided. More importantly it reveals Medina Sidonia's crucial assumption that he and Parma would fight the battle for the landing place jointly, rather than the fleet doing so on its own before Parma's flotilla emerged. It is in this context that his letter to Parma en route to La Coruña (10 June), which for the first time raised the destination of the fleet, should be read.[38] Medina Sidonia stated his intention of making his way directly to the English coast and requested that Parma then inform him where they could join forces. From the context this can only have been a site on the English coast for Parma was expected to 'come out with his fleet'. It is possible that Escalante's (or similar) observations on the Downs in bad weather may have had their effect, for most of the letter is taken up by Medina Sidonia's concern that the coast to the west of Dover did not provide him with a safe port to retire to should he need a refuge from storms. Not only was the 'junction of the fleets' to take place before the battle, but Parma was also to be prepared to supply the fleet with fresh water from Dunkirk.

This letter provoked a horrified response from Parma, but his answer never reached Medina Sidonia. Philip was also sent a copy of the letter, however, and on 21 June he did attempt to correct his admiral's mis-impression. The duke should push on to Cape Margate rather than worry about ports to the west of Dover, because until the passage was cleared Parma could not venture out, since his shipping consisted of 'small cargo vessels, not warships'.[39] Medina Sidonia's response to this is not known, but the king's letter does not appear to have been forceful enough to persuade him to revise his intention of joining forces before the battle. The verbal message he sent to Parma by Captain Don Rodrigo Tello on 25 July, shortly after leaving La Coruña on the final voyage, was, according to his own record, a request for Parma to designate the best place for him to unite with the Armada.[40]

The correspondence from La Coruña is dominated by the state of the fleet and its food supplies. On 27 June, however, a council of war was summoned to decide whether the Armada should proceed before all the ships had been reassembled and repaired.[41] The minutes identify two opinions, that of Don Jorge Manrique, who opposed an immediate departure, and that of Don Pedro de Valdés who recommended one. Both based their arguments in part on intelligence of the English fleet: Manrique referred to 'the last reports of 26 April, which his majesty had sent to the duke', while Valdés opined that 'the enemy's fleet has to be divided in two or three parts in order to prevent the passage of the duke of Parma and bar the entrance of the Channel to this fleet'. Since the report from London of the 26 April was the first to announce the impending union of the two English fleets, it is difficult to avoid the conclusion that there may have been a serious disagreement over the possible English deployment. Valdés's later answer to his English questioner that the Spaniards 'had received advertisements in Spain' that the English fleet was at Plymouth and expected it to let them pass suggests that Philip's warning of an attack in the rear by Drake had been circulated.[42] Valdés also seems to have told Petruccio Ubaldini that he thought it would have been easy to capture Plymouth since he did not expect to meet any force there that the Armada could not overcome.[43]

It would appear, therefore, that the intelligence the Armada received at La Coruña may have included the news that Howard was to join Drake, but not in sufficiently conclusive form. A further report that might have tipped the balance seems to have arrived too late. A Coruña fisherman named Domingo de Lago, who had been captured by the English in May, had seen Howard with forty ships in Plymouth during June. He made his way back to Spain in July, but was not interviewed until after the Armada had sailed.[44]

That no major reappraisal of the Armada's strategy took place is revealed by Juan Martínez de Recalde's letter to the king of 11 July.[45] Recalde's main concern was the state of the Armada's food supplies, particularly in view of what he appears to have believed would be a long military campaign in England. Although the Armada could base itself in the Thames after the army had landed, shortages in Flanders would make it difficult to obtain supplies there. These could only come from

Spain, and in view of the absence of any large harbours between Southampton and the Thames, he recommended the seizure of one of the major ports in the West Country (Falmouth, Plymouth or Dartmouth) to provide a staging post, even at the risk of separating the fleet from the army. What, however, is particularly revealing is his offhand reference to the Downs as the objective of the Armada. If the English did not give battle the fleet was to 'proceed to the Downs and from there assist and help the [forces] in Dunkirk'; it would thus provide security for the transport of the army 'to whatever place has been chosen as the most convenient, which would have to involve the shortest route to one or other bank of the Thames'. This passage would also suggest, however, that he was not privy to Medina Sidonia's intention of joining Parma before the battle.

With one exception, Recalde's letter is the last surviving reference to the Armada's intended destination. The exception is the letter that Pedro de Valdés sent to the king from captivity, which survives only in an English translation; this is the only known Spanish statement that the destination of the fleet was Dunkirk.[46] In view of its context it is a document to be handled with great care; unfortunately, it has had a major impact on much of the modern literature on the Armada because it was taken as evidence in the early but still influential study of the Armada's strategy by the American historian W. F. Tilton that prior to the departure from Lisbon Medina Sidonia had altered the destination from Margate to Dunkirk, and only discovered at Calais that reaching Dunkirk was impossible.[47] To reach this conclusion, however, Tilton was forced to suggest that 'It is possible that [Recalde's use of] the phrase 'Dunas' referred to the Flemish coast', a gloss that flies not only in the face of the general sense of Recalde's letter, but is also difficult to reconcile with the contemporary Spanish usage of 'las Dunas', and the earlier discussions of navigation in the Narrow Seas.[48] It is possible that this view of the Armada's destination was peculiar to Valdés's ship, for the English learnt by 25 July/4 August 'from some Spaniards that are taken' that they intended to 'come down into the narrow seas to have taken in their forces at Dunkirk and Sluys, whose flatt botham boats and other shipping their fleet would sufficientlie have wrested into the Temes mouth'.[49]

When he arrived at the mouth of the Channel, Medina Sidonia was therefore still unsure of the disposition of the English fleet, but there is no evidence that the original intention of making for the Downs had been changed. On 29 and 30 July, however, a number of important events took place on the *San Martín*, which have caused considerable debate. The English coastline near the Lizard was sighted and celebrated by the hoisting of the royal standard and the saying of prayers; almost all of the scattered ships of the Armada were reassembled; Medina Sidonia wrote two letters to the king (the last he would write before the battle); a council of war was held; English sails discovered to leeward; and Alférez Juan Gil was dispatched to reconnoitre. When Gil returned with several English fishermen, he provided the first definite confirmation of the fact that Howard and Drake had combined forces and were then in the process of leaving Plymouth.

The chronology of these events has been variously reconstructed, and there is much confusion over their relationship to each other. For this the sources are in part to blame; even Captain Alonso Vanegas of the *San Martín*, whose journal is considered the fullest and most reliable of the voyage, simply includes all the events in his entry for the 30th.[50] Least controversial is the time of the return of Alférez Gil with his fishermen, which is established as about one o'clock in the morning of the 31st. He had been despatched the previous evening, possibly about the time the English sails were sighted, which Vanegas gives as dusk. Therefore one major point is certain — that full knowledge of the deployment of the English was not obtained until after the previous decisions had been taken.[51] Equally clear is the starting point: the Lizard was sighted in the afternoon of the 29th.[52] The central question is what occurred in the meantime, particularly the connection between the letters sent to the king and the council of war.

The letters can be described conveniently as the long and the short. The long letter exists in two versions, one dated the 29th, the other on the 30th and located 'á vista del cabo de Lisarte'.[53] Both recount the events of the 29th: the sighting of land, the celebrations, and the state of the fleet. That of the 29th states that it is being written at six in the evening; that of the 30th includes a passage beginning 'and until now, Saturday the 30th of July' and commenting on the damage to the *capitana* of the galleases. The latter is clearly a second version of the former completed in the morning of the following day. The short letter is dated the 30th and also located off the Lizard; it states specifically that it was written after the first one.[54] It is also the more important of the two, for it outlines the duke's immediate intentions, particularly his decision not to proceed beyond the Isle of Wight before making contact with Parma. Having received no information from Parma as to where he would come out to, Medina Sidonia was concerned that he was expected to take the Armada to the coast of Flanders, which was too dangerous. He also complained about not having seen a ship or man since leaving La Coruña, 'it is like groping in the dark', but when the Armada approached Plymouth he hoped to send a pinnace to capture a prisoner.

There is no reason not to conclude that this letter was written immediately after the second version of the long letter, i.e. in the morning of the 30th — nearly twenty-four hours before Alférez Gil reported the presence of the combined English fleet. More difficult is the chronology of the council of war. Only three sources for the council are known, the Vanegas narrative and two statements made by Pedro de Valdés after his capture.[55] Vanegas places the council on the 30th immediately after the sighting of land; Valdés after the interrogation of the fishermen. On the other hand, Valdés also states that the sighting of the English sails occurred two hours after the council meeting, which would place it clearly in the afternoon of the 30th. According to Vanegas, the purpose of the council meeting was the straight-forward one of resolving the order of battle. However, during its course Don Alonso de Leiva and others proposed a surprise attack on Plymouth as a means of eliminating any English ships that happened to be there. The proposal was rejected by Medina Sidonia on the grounds that it was against the king's orders, too risky and too time-consuming.

The relationship between the short letter and the council meeting is the key point. If the council was held first, then the decision not to proceed beyond the Isle of Wight might have been a consequence of it. This has been the conclusion drawn in some of the best studies of the Armada.[56] However, the absence of any reference to the council in either letter, and the overall chain of events in both the Vanegas and Valdés accounts suggests the council was held in the afternoon of the 30th, after the letters were written. This suggests the following reconstruction: in the morning Medina Sidonia, seriously worried by the absence both of intelligence in general and of news from Parma, intended to gain time by holding the fleet in the western end of the Channel. These considerations underlay his rejection of the attack on Plymouth in the afternoon; in the event that the expected word came from Parma, he could not afford to be caught in the middle of a complicated assault. Alférez Gil's fishermen, however, transformed the whole situation. By the first hours of the 31st it was now clear that the Armada was about to be engaged by the greater part of the English fleet. Any attempt to remain west of the Isle of Wight would risk disaster. Medina Sidonia's Isle of Wight plan, therefore, did not survive the 30th and there was no attempt to enter the Solent in the following days.[57]

The Armada was remarkably successful in making its way up the Channel — although it owed much to generally favourable weather. The main sources for Medina Sidonia's plans during this phase of the voyage are the letters he sent to Parma on the 1st, 4th and 5th of August. All refer to his intention of continuing his journey and to English attempts to halt him. All demand the identification of the place of rendezvous, but on the 1st he also requested 'pilots of the coast of Flanders' in case a major storm was encountered, and by the 4th he was worried that the winds would bring him 'to that coast' before an answer was received.[58] On the 4th and 5th he also asked for ammunition and a reinforcement of flyboats to be sent out to him.[59]

On the 6th he made his decision to halt in Calais roads. Calais itself was not a suitable port, for as early as the 1520s its harbour had become too silted for use by large ships.[60] Moreover Philip had instructed Medina Sidonia to avoid the French coast, and informed Henry III that Spanish ships would only enter French ports in an emergency.[61] The accounts of the decision to halt — apart from those that mention it only in passing — are quite clear as to what happened. A major discussion took place on the *San Martín* over whether to stop or to proceed. The very fact that one occurred is itself significant, for it suggests that no earlier decision to halt at Calais had been taken. According to Medina Sidonia's *Diario* many of those present wished to proceed further ['adelante'], but he was warned by the pilots that the currents would force him out of the Channel and into the North Sea.[62] Precisely where those who wished to proceed further intended to go is a mystery. It is interesting to note that although some accounts refer to the danger of the Flemish banks, those originating from the *San Martín* do not. In other words, there was no sudden discovery that the Armada could not reach Dunkirk.

Medina Sidonia's intention in halting was made clear in his first letter to Parma on the 6th; he had got as near as he could and would now hold off the enemy 'until Your Excellency comes with all the rest and we go and take a port [vamos a tomar algun puerto] where this fleet may anchor safely'.[63] 'Taking' a port could only mean doing so in England. The king's plan would thus have been carried out, although in so doing Medina Sidonia had completely reversed the initial plan of campaign. Instead of the fleet securing a landing place for the army, the army was to assist the fleet to find a safe anchorage. The duke of

Parma's complaints that Medina Sidonia had completely misinterpreted the function of his invasion fleet have some justice in them, but the initial suggestion that the army should aid the fleet had been made by the king himself.[64]

The English fireship attack on Sunday the 7th renders unnecessary any further speculation as to what the Armada might have done. It does, on the other hand, raise the final question of the role a potential battle in the Downs played in English strategy. Given that the main anchorages for the queen's ships lay in the Thames, and that the most significant concentration of merchant shipping was to be found in London, assembling a large fleet in the Downs posed no difficulty. The problem lay in identifying the site for the intended invasion. In the memorandum he drafted during the temporary invasion panic at the beginning of 1584, Burghley considered a landing in Milford Haven a strong possibility.[65] The fleet was to be divided between the Scillies, the Isle of Wight and Harwich or the Downs; the first squadron to sight the enemy was to summon the others and they would concentrate on his landing area. However, 'if the adversary will quietly proceed [up the Channel] all these three companies shall fall into one consort at the Downs'. For all its defensiveness this plan also recognised what became a key feature of the English strategy, the primary necessity to 'take advantage in their tails' or gain the weathergage.

The 1587 survey of the landing sites eliminated Milford Haven and concentrated on the Channel anchorages. Common sense, however, suggested that the capture of Zealand, which Parma had always advised, and which Howard considered the Spanish intention as late as February 1588, might still be the initial Spanish goal.[66] Moreover, the English commanders also had a healthy respect for Parma's well-known gift for strategic deception and opportunism, which made a two-pronged attack from Flanders and Spain or a diversionary campaign probable.[67] As the questions they posed to their prisoners reveal, even after the battle the English council suspected that two separate landings had been planned.[68] Although a surprise from Flanders could be easily parried by a limited Dover squadron, given the wider range of possibilities for a two-pronged invasion, the stationing of the main fleet was a more difficult question. As Howard wrote in May 1588, 'God knoweth which way the Spanish fleet will bend, either to England, Scotland or Ireland'. The possibility of a landing in Ireland or Scotland made a close deployment along the Channel coast of England questionable.[69]

A further complication arose from the enthusiasm for an offensive strike against Spain — in its most ambitious form an invasion of Portugal by Dom António — shared by Drake and most of the English commanders. Moreover, at the beginning of 1588 Drake appears to have believed that the Spanish preparations were still at a relatively early stage and that therefore another raid on their maritime communications similar to that of 1587 would set the Armada back a further year.[70] The rump of the fleet he had brought back from Cadiz to Plymouth was reinforced in January by six recently refitted queen's ships.[71] However, the queen's desire to avoid a provocation while seeking a settlement with Philip at the Bourbourg negotiations caused a suspension of hostilities and it was not until the end of February that doubts about Spanish sincerity in the negotiations led a committee of senior privy councillors to reopen the question of a naval offensive. On 25 February/6 March 1588 a complicated deployment of two fleets in home waters (Dover and 'on the west towards Irland and Spayn'), with possible diversionary expeditions to Portugal and the Azores (to intercept the Silver Fleet) was outlined.[72] In the end it was decided to send Drake 'to the coast of Spaine to withstand that nothing can be attempted against Ireland or Scotland', and to leave Howard 'to encounter them with his strength' should 'they have a meaning to come into the narrowe seas'.[73]

By this stage, however, the extent of the Spanish concentration at Lisbon was becoming apparent, which made Drake's earlier plan redundant. On 30 March/9 April he argued that sixty ships would now be necessary and over the next fortnight a debate ensued over whether a fleet of this size would be better employed in an attack on the Armada in Lisbon. On Drake's advice (it would appear), the direct attack was abandoned and on 17/27 April the decision (so accurately reported by Mendoza's agent) was taken to combine Howard's and Drake's fleets and to give Howard a broad commission to do what in his judgement seemed best to 'empeach any attempt on Scotland, Ireland or England'.[74] The Downs would be watched by a smaller squadron — the criticism directed at the decision to include in this squadron the new galleons *Rainbow* and *Vanguard* overlooks the fact that they were designed for operations in Flemish waters.[75] The new forward deployment can be attributed in part to the desire to seek a quick decision in order to avoid the financial effects of a prolonged mobilisation, but also to fears that whatever winds brought the Armada out would trap the English in their ports, and to the difficulty of deploying the fleet effectively to cover the range of possible invasion sites.

Howard expounded the aims of the new strategy in his answer to Elizabeth's famous instruction in June for the fleet to form a screen across the Bay of Biscay in case the Armada should evade a close blockade of Lisbon.[76] A blockade was not in fact his intention, but rather the gaining of the weathergage off the coast of Spain and the pursuit of the Armada to its destination. Howard even expected that the fear of having the English 'on their backs' would prevent the Armada from leaving at all. The same argument was made by the commanders of the Dover squadron, when they were criticised for sitting in the Downs and not mounting a close blockade of the Flemish coast.[77]

The immediate cause for the failure of the offensive was the unseasonably bad weather that both trapped Howard and Drake in port for much of June and July and played havoc with their already complicated logistics. The upshot was the surprise of the English fleet at Plymouth on the 19th/29th of July, a surprise made more dramatic because opinion in the fleet had held that it was now too late in the year for the Armada to sail.[78] Its hasty exit left the fleet short on supplies, and if the weathergage was successfully obtained, Howard was still faced with an unexpected running battle up the Channel, for which no tactical provision appears to have been made. His immediate aim appears to have been to prevent a landing in the other major Channel anchorages.[79] No small amount of the confusion that surrounds the engagements off the Isle of Wight may have been caused by the fact that the English were attempting to prevent an entry into the Solent that the Spaniards had no intention of making.

However, once the Solent had been passed only the Downs remained, which accounts for Howard's relaxed pursuit on Friday and Saturday. For Howard the Downs had many advantages: he would be close to his bases, he could unite with the Dover squadron, and he could replenish supplies. He appears to have made his intention known to the council earlier in the week, for on 25 July/4 August Robert Cecil wrote from the court that Howard had found the Spaniards unwilling to fight:

> but kepinge themselves close in a plumpe together, still doe fall downe the coast towardes the seas here betwixt Dover and Calles. My Lord Admyrall hathe the wind of them, and keepes it, havinge written hither that he thinks not safe to fight with them till he hathe brought them and lodged them into these seas wither their course is, and where my Lord Henry Seymour shall be redie to joyne with him, and the shipps of Flushinge and townes of Holland shall lye towardes Dunkirk, to keepe in the forces their.[80]

Further ammunition was sent from London to Dover on 26 July/5 August, some of which (at least) was received by the fleet before Sunday 28 July/7 August.[81] Thus Howard too had every reason to expect a decisive battle in the Downs. According to Mendoza's Portuguese agent, he had warned the queen to expect such a battle: 'the intention being that at the arrival of our Armada at the Downs, it should be attacked on all sides'. So sure was Viegas that the battle was to be fought in the Downs that he even reported that the Gravelines battle was fought there.[82] The decision to halt at Calais came as just as much a surprise to the English. They saw it as a clever device to employ the tides of the straits of Dover to carry them into the North Sea and thus throw off their pursuit.[83]

If the halt at Calais finally enabled the English to disrupt the Armada's formation, it also turned the potential battle of the Downs from the first of the great series of seventeenth-century engagements fought there into the battle that never was. This does not mean, however, the importance of the Downs to the campaign should be discounted. It was the one anchorage where the combined invasion from Spain and Flanders could take place. The dispatch of the Armada directly to Flanders was never intended and if the Armada never reached the Downs this was the result of Medina Sidonia's fixed belief that he and Parma should join forces first and then the unexpected discovery of the combined English fleet at Plymouth. Precisely how Medina Sidonia came to misinterpret Parma's role so disastrously is unclear, but, as we have seen, the suggestion that Parma should aid the fleet in a battle in English waters was first made by Philip in January 1588. For the English the strategic alternative lay between a concentration in the Downs or an offensive in Spanish waters; any intermediate deployment would serve no useful purpose. The encounter off Plymouth was completely accidental. If neither fleet obtained any real advantage in the Channel engagements this was because neither fleet had either planned, or was prepared, to fight a battle of that kind.

NOTES

1. This point is also made, *mutatis mutandis* for the conditions of the 1940s, in C. B. A. Behrens, *Merchant Shipping and the Demands of War* (London, 1955) p. 11. The absence of a suitable deep-water anchorage caused Santa

Cruz to reject plans for a landing in Scotland, see K. Brown, 'The Making of a *Politique*: the Counter-Reformation and the Regional Politics of John, Eighth Lord Maxwell', *Scottish Historical Review*, LXVI (1987) p. 164.

2. There are many copies of this report, which is also printed in Monson, *Tracts*, II, pp. 276ff; the one employed here is BL, Harleian MS 187 f. 110. Monson considered Falmouth more important than the commissioners did, but otherwise agreed with the report. On this point, see also Rodríguez-Salgado above, p. 138.

3. Martin and Parker, p. 137, n. 11, see also pp. 140, 157–8, and the observations in Rodríguez-Salgado, *Catalogue*, pp. 28, 125.

4. Monson, *Tracts*, III, p. 31.

5. Described in H. M. Colvin *et al.*, *The History of Kings Works*, IV *(1485–1660)*, pt. ii (London, 1982) pp. 455–65. See also the map of the Downs on p. 456.

6. See the contemporary accounts of navigating the Downs in William Borrough's letter to Walsingham of 28 July/7 August 1588 in Laughton, I, pp. 336–7, J. A. Williamson (ed.), *The Observations of Sir Richard Hawkins* (London, 1933) p. 12ff, and E. S. Donno, *An Elizabethan in 1582*, pp. 109–11.

7. See the description of the sighting of the Armada in PRO SP 12/213/78, Sir Thomas Scott to Burghley, 27 July/6 August 1588.

8. *BMO* I, pp. 405–6, 12 September 1583.

9. *Ibid.*, pp. 411–13, 11 October 1583.

10. L. van der Essen, *Alexandre Farnèse, Prince de Parme* (5 vols., Brussels, 1933–37) V, p. 166. His source is not given, it may have been in the now-destroyed Farnese archive.

11. *BMO* I, pp. 420–1.

12. *Ibid.*, p. 425, 17 January 1584. See also Rodríguez-Salgado above, p. 136.

13. A. J. Loomie, 'An Armada Pilot's Survey of the English Coastline, October 1597', *MM*, XLIX (1963) pp. 288–300. The identity of the compiler is not known and, while Loomie speculates (pp. 288, 290) that the survey was based on recent atlases supplemented by personal knowledge, there is no reason why Parma's survey could not have been employed as well.

14. *BMO* I, p. 550. Parma's letter of 20 April is AGS E 590 f. 125. I am most grateful to M. J. Rodríguez-Salgado for photocopies of these documents and those from *legajo* 594.

15. AGS E 590 f. 126.

16. The English took the common sense view that Parma would choose the Essex bank and entrenched their main army at Tilbury, though taking the precaution of constructing a bridge of boats to allow its rapid deployment in Kent.

17. Essen, *Farnèse*, V, pp. 129–30, 139–40, 186. For Parma's difficulties with Sluys as a port, see F. Riaño Lozano, *Los Medios Navales de Alejandro Farnesio (1587–88)* (Serie Gran Armada, VII: Madrid, 1989)

pp. 183–4, 202, 213, 218–19, 252. See also the observation of Lord Henry Seymour in 1588, Laughton, I, p. 207.

18. Essen, *Farnèse*, V, pp. 186–7. Herrera Oria, *Armada*, pp. 33–42, esp. 36. On the abandoning of an earlier two-pronged attack against England and Ireland, see Martin and Parker, pp. 118–19, 137.

19. As also noted by Rodríguez-Salgado, *Catalogue*, p. 28. P. Pierson, *Commander of the Armada: the Seventh Duke of Medina Sidonia* (New Haven and London, 1989) p. 129, refers to the 'Cape of Margate' as being 'between the Kentish coast and the Goodwin Sands'.

20. See Adams above, p. 50.

21. *CSPSp*, IV, p. 12. For Drake's association with Dom António see S. Adams, 'The Spanish Armada: The Lurch into War', *History Today*, XXXVIII (May 1988) pp. 19–25. There is a passing reference to Viegas in Delamar Jensen, *Diplomacy and Dogmatism: Bernardino de Mendoza and the French Catholic League* (Cambridge, Mass., 1964) p. 106, but this work does not discuss Mendoza's English intelligence in any detail. Cf. pp. 153–7.

22. *CSPSp*, IV, pp. 162–3, 166, 174.

23. Herrera Oria, *Armada*, pp. 130–3.

24. See the discussion of the effects of Santa Cruz's pursuit of Drake to the Azores in Martin and Parker, pp. 131–2.

25. FD II, pp. 5–13. A translation of these instructions (from a different source) can be found in G. P. B. Naish (ed.) 'Documents Illustrating the Spanish Armada', *Naval Miscellany IV* (Navy Records Society, XCII, 1952) pp. 15–17. On the fate of the January instructions for Santa Cruz, see Martin and Parker, p. 286, n. 2.

26. FD, II, pp. 13–15.

27. For the rutter, see Herrera Oria, *Armada*, p. 168. For a full discussion of the 'Teixeira chart' and its relevance to the Armada, see Rodríguez-Salgado above, p. 169, n. 72. It is difficult to see how Martin and Parker (p. 284) can conclude on the basis of this chart that Margate Roads was nominated as the final anchorage, when it does not even appear there.

28. Herrera Oria, *Armada* pp. 372–5.

29. See the offhand reference to Medina Sidonia's instructions 'not to fight until he reached the Downs, unless attacked' in Corbett, *Drake*, II, p. 212. The argument that Medina Sidonia was not expected to fight his way up the Channel is more fully developed in Maura, pp. 248–50, and I. A. A. Thompson, 'The Appointment of the Duke of Medina Sidonia to the Command of the Spanish Armada', *Historical Journal*, XII (1969) p. 205. See also Pierson, *Medina Sidonia*, pp. 82, 109, 129.

30. The version of Medina Sidonia's instructions printed in Maura, p. 250, omits the passage on dealing with Drake if encountered in the Channel. Cf. the versions cited in n. 25 above.

31. *CSPSpan*, IV, pp. 274, 279, 298. See also the *noticias de Inglaterra* of

February 1588 sent to Medina Sidonia and printed in Maura, pp. 245–6.

32. *CSPSp*, IV, pp. 307, 311.
33. *Ibid.*, pp. 319, 333–4, 352–3.
34. Laughton, II, p. 26.
35. *CSPSpan*, IV, p. 347.
36. Herrera Oria, *Armada*, pp. 196–8.
37. FD, II, pp. 101–4, esp. 103.
38. *Ibid.*, pp. 112–15.
39. Herrera Oria, *Armada*, p. 202. For Parma's reaction, see Essen, *Farnèse*, V, pp. 219–20, and Martin and Parker, pp. 183–4.
40. *Diario* of Medina Sidonia in Herrera Oria, *Armada*, p. 233. See AGS E 594 f. 114 for the letter sent with Tello.
41. FD, II, pp. 141–7.
42. Laughton, II, p. 28.
43. See Ubaldini's 'Narrative', printed in D. W. Waters, *The Elizabethan Navy and the Armada of Spain* (National Maritime Museum, Monograph Series, XVII: 1975) p. 90.
44. Herrera Oria, *Armada*, pp. 230–2. Pierson (*Medina Sidonia*, p. 129, n. 8) speculates that Medina Sidonia did interview Lago. I am very grateful to Professor Geoffrey Parker for a useful correspondence on the dating of this document and of Medina Sidonia's letters of 30 July.
45. FD, II, pp. 169–72.
46. PRO SP 12/215/66-v (printed in Laughton, II, p. 133), 21/31 August 1588.
47. W. F. Tilton, *Die Katastrophe der Spanischen Armada, 31. Juli – 8. August 1588* (Freiburg im Breisgau, 1894) pp. 12–13. Tilton's influence can be detected in Martin and Parker, see p. 284, n. 11. F. Fernández Armesto, *The Spanish Armada: The Experience of War in 1588* (Oxford, 1988) pp. 126, 182–3, advances a similar argument.
48. Tilton, p. 11, n. 3.
49. HMC, *Twelfth Report. Appendix Pt. IV: The Manuscripts of the Duke of Rutland, I* (London, 1888), p. 253, Robert Cecil to ? Manners, 25 July/4 August 1588.
50. FD, II, pp. 371–6.
51. As noted by Martin and Parker, pp. 28–9.
52. *Diario*, Herrera Oria, *Armada*, p. 234.
53. The version of the 29th is found in *Ibid.*, pp. 252–5; that of the 30th in FD, II, pp. 219–21.
54. FD, II, pp. 221–2. This is referred to as the 'postscript' in Martin and Parker, see p. 28.
55. Valdés's two accounts of the council meeting are found in his interrogation (Laughton, II, p. 28), and his letter to the king of 21/31 August, see n. 46 above.
56. G. Mattingly, *The Armada* (Boston, 1959) p. 270, places the council

meeting in the morning of the 30th; Martin and Parker, pp. 23–5, in the afternoon of the 29th; Pierson, (*Medina Sidonia*, p. 129) 'Friday evening or sometime Saturday', but prior to the letter to Philip. He also speculates that Medina Sidonia's decision to wait at the Isle of Wight was discussed by the council.

57. Cf. the conclusions of Martin and Parker, p. 286, n. 10. I find Pierson's argument (*Medina Sidonia*, chapter 8) that Medina Sidonia both intended and attempted an entry into the Solent unconvincing, particularly in view of his reconstruction of the events of the 30th.

58. AGS E 594 ff. 115 and 116, Medina Sidonia to Parma, 1 (dated 31 July, but not sent till the following day) and 4 August. The phrase quoted from the latter is mistranslated in *CSPSp*, IV, p. 360 as 'I expect to be on the Flemish coast very soon'.

59. AGS E 594 ff. 116–17. The account of the letter of the 5th in Medina Sidonia's *Diario* (Herrera Oria, *Armada*, p. 240–1) refers to a request to Parma to be ready to sortie 'as soon as we come in sight of Dunkirk'.

60. The silting of Calais had prevented Henry VIII from travelling to the Field of the Cloth of Gold in his great ship *Henri Grace à Dieu*, J. G. Russell, *The Field of the Cloth of Gold* (London, 1969) pp. 62–3.

61. *CSPSp*, IV, p. 273.

62. *Diario*, Herrera Oria, *Armada*, p. 241. Cf. *CSPSpan*, IV, p. 374 and FD, II, p. 260. Captain Vanegas (FD, II, p. 367) refers to Calais as the nearest point to where Parma was waiting. The argument, ultimately derived from Tilton (*Katastrophe*, p. 13), that Medina Sidonia only discovered at Calais that reaching Dunkirk was impossible overlooks his earlier appreciation of that very problem. Thus the references in Martin and Parker, p. 129, to 'the advance to Calais' and Pierson, *Medina Sidonia*, p. 156, to setting 'course for Calais' on the 5th do not make sense.

63. AGS E 594 f. 120.

64. AGS E 594 f. 124, Parma to Philip, 8 August. For further discussions of his response, see Essen, *Farnése*, V, pp. 224–7 and Martin and Parker, pp. 181–4, though they refer to the issue as one of escort rather than taking part in a battle.

65. PRO SP 12/168/5-v, 'A memorial of divers things necessary . . . for martial defence', also discussed in Adams above, p. 52.

66. Laughton, I, p. 65. The survey of 1587 is discussed at the beginning of this essay, see p. 173 above. Its dismissal of Milford Haven was followed by Ralegh in 1596 when he advised ignoring an invasion via the western ports and concentrating in the Thames. Sir W. Ralegh, *Works* (8 vols., Oxford, 1829) VIII, pp. 677–80, 'Observations' on "Articles propounded . . . upon the Alarum given by the Spaniards in the year 1596"'.

67. See the comments of Lord Henry Seymour, Laughton, I, pp. 206–8, 309–10.

68. *Ibid.*, II, p. 36, question 9.

69. *Ibid.*, I, pp. 186–7, cf. pp. 56–8, 103, 231–3. See also BL, Cottonian MS Vespasian C VIII f. 12ff, privy council memorandum of 25 February/6 March 1588, printed in part by W. F. Tilton, 'Lord Burghley on the Spanish Invasion', *American Historical Review*, II (1896), pp. 93–98.

70. See Magdalene College, Pepys MS 2876, pp. 240–1 (a copy of the now-damaged BL, Cottonian MS Otho E IX f. 164), T. Fenner to the earl of Leicester, 4/14 February 1588.

71. The most valuable source for the precise deployment of the English ships are the accounts of Sir John Hawkins for 1588 (PRO E 351/2225) and the naval victuallers James Quarles (E 351/2386) and Marmaduke Darell (E 351/2496). Drake had only eight ships in Plymouth in December 1587, but thirty by the end of February. Ubaldino's account ('Narrative', 83–4) of Drake's commission of December 1587 suggests that he was further prepared than he was in reality.

72. BL, Cottonian MS Vespasian C VIII f. 12.

73. HMC, *Calendar of the Manuscripts of . . . the Marquess of Bath*, V (London, 1980) p. 86, Sir Francis Walsingham to the earl of Shrewsbury, 27 February/8 March 1588.

74. Laughton, I, pp. 123–6, 159, 170. Ubaldino, 'Narrative', pp. 85–6, compresses the chronology considerably.

75. For the building of the *Rainbow* and the *Vanguard*, see BL, Cottonian MS Galba C VIII f. 41, Howard to Leicester, 26 February [1586]. Compare Seymour's comments in 1588, Laughton, II, pp. 128–9.

76. Laughton, I, pp. 192–3, 195–6, 202–5.

77. *Ibid.*, I, 330–1, 333.

78. Ubaldino 'Narrative', p. 88. Compare Leicester's observation to Sir Edward Norris on 10/20 July 1588, 'for anything that is hitherto known, the Spanish fleet is rather returned back, and the opinion now is doubtful whether they will come or not forward [*sic*]', *CSPFor*, XXII, p. 25. For earlier worries about Plymouth, see Laughton, I, pp. 172, 212-15.

79. Laughton, I, 299.

80. HMC, *Rutland MSS*, I, p. 253.

81. BL, Cottonian MS Otho E IX f. 214v, Walsingham to Leicester, 26 July/5 August 1588 (printed in part in Laughton, I, p. 327 and mis-addressed to Burghley). There is an account of ammunition being shipped to Howard from Dover on Saturday the 27th/6th in *CSPSp*, IV, p. 412.

82. *CSPSp*, IV, pp. 390–1.

83. Laughton, I, p. 345.

7

THE MEDICAL SERVICES OF THE *GRAN ARMADA*[1]

Manuel Gracia Rivas

Introduction

Until very recently, our knowledge of health provisions in the sixteenth century Spanish navy was extremely limited.[2] The decision to study different aspects of the *Gran Armada* for the commemoration of its quartocentenary enabled us to have access to a considerable volume of documentation, mostly in the Archivo General de Simancas, and until now unpublished.[3] With these documents it has been possible to reconstruct in considerable detail what happened in Lisbon in the months before the departure of the Armada, as well as the measures that were taken on its return. Most importantly, they have yielded specific data about the men on board, and the health provisions for the army and the fleet. This rich vein of documentation has also provided the starting point for studies currently being completed of other military events closely related — at least from the point of view of health provisions and personnel — with the *Gran Armada*.[4]

Health Provisions for the Troops in the Armada

The army and navy enjoyed the benefits of a royal concern for good health provisions and institutions since the end of the fifteenth century. The army had a royal field hospital called the *Hospital Real del Ejercito y Armada de S.M.* which served in all the major military campaigns of the early-modern period. The hospital was not an alternative to the normal health provisions which ensured basic medical attention for even the lowest military personnel. Even the smallest permanent army units had independent practitioners: each company had a barber, and each *tercio* a physician and a surgeon, to attend to its needs. Every warship in the royal fleet tended to employ a surgeon or a barber while on campaign, but it was rare to find them in the armed merchantmen

197

which were embargoed and used in all campaigns. This medical system had been laid down in early medieval ordinances which specified that there should be a physician and a surgeon, or at least the latter, in each active military unit.[5] Naval squadrons usually employed an apothecary as well. This was the basic model for health provision, and it had evolved in the galley squadrons. As the oldest permanent naval units of the empire, the galleys had the longest traditions. It was normal for them to be administered by a centralised structure which covered all aspects of the galley's functions. At the top of the medical hierarchy there was a *Protomedico* (Royal Physician) and *Cirujano Mayor* (Surgeon-in-chief) who would oversee and control the medical provisions for the royal fleet.[6]

Both in the army and navy therefore, there were three levels of medical provision and each should be analysed in turn. At the lowest level was the barber, who in theory at least, was expected to have passed an exam or paid specific dues before exercising his profession. He had no academic education, little formal training, and usually even less capital. Through daily contact with patients he would gradually acquire the basic knowledge to carry out his tasks, which included shaving the men and tending to their hair, as well as dealing in the first instance with any of the injured within his unit. His social status was very low, and his pay even lower than that of other 'minor officials' in the army and navy. Nevertheless his proximity to the sick and wounded, who in many instances had no other professionals to turn to, gave him certain privileges. His pitiable wages were supplemented by voluntary contributions from soldiers and sailors, who had an obvious interest in employing experienced and able barbers for their companies, and to ensure that sound, if basic, medical provision was available to all members of the unit.

The surgeon had a more elevated status than the barber, although there were major differences between the surgeons trained at a university and those who had acquired their skills outside a formal education and were known as *cirujanos romancistas*, literally vernacular surgeons. Both groups were able to carry out quite major operations and tended to be career professionals, who served and gained experience in a number of campaigns and having done so, expected these services to provide a stepping-stone to a higher position. They were assisted by empirics who were sometimes directly paid by the surgeon, who would provide them with the necessary instruments.

At the top of the medical pyramid was the physician, who was always university trained, and often had knowledge of surgery too; he almost always enjoyed considerable prestige. Unlike the others, he was seldom employed outside the hospital.[7]

The Hospital at Sea

The very concept of a field hospital as a body that dispenses aid and attends immediately to those wounded in an armed conflict, is a genuinely Spanish invention. It was Ferdinand and Isabella who organised the first field hospital in 1476, during the siege of Toro. In the final stages of the war of Granada, there were field hospitals in Baza, Malaga, and the best known one in Santa Fe. Later the principle was applied to the navy: all the major naval campaigns included a hospital ship.[8] Broadly speaking, the main characteristics and structure of these hospitals at sea were as follows:

1. The Ships

The hospital was put aboard one or two hulks — cargo vessels where the medicines and diets were carefully stored. It is important to stress that the naval hospital could not operate at sea. It should not be thought of as a hospital ship in the modern sense of the word, but merely as a specialised medical cargo vessel. It could not operate effectively until the troops had landed. Putting medicines and personnel on one or two vessels was a highly risky practice: if these cargo ships were lost, as happened on several occasions,[9] the forces were left without medical provisions when they reached their target, when they most needed them.

2. Setting up the Hospital

The provisions for the hospital included tents which could be used in the absence of suitable buildings; but the norm was to instal the hospital in several houses requisitioned for this purpose. Adjoining buildings would be chosen which could be adapted to create both large and individual wards to accommodate the sick and wounded.

The number of 'beds' would vary. Each unit consisted of: (a) the bed itself, which might be a simple low wooden bedstead — the wood to build them was also part of the hospital complement, (b) a straw mattress, (c) a straw pillow, (d) one or two blankets per bed, (e) four linen sheets per bed. The more illustrious patients were accommodated in the few wooden beds with hangings, and they had wool mattresses and pillows. Usually the beds had to be shared, and according to need, the wooden boards might be placed together to increase capacity.

3. Personnel

The number also varied according to need, but it always included the following officials:

(i) *The General Administrator* who was responsible for the running of the hospital. He was appointed by the king and usually a cleric of some prestige was chosen.

(ii) *The medical specialists.* The number of physicians always varied, but the norm was between two and five. If there were four or more, a royal physician would be appointed as well. There was always a chief surgeon, with a variable number of surgeons below him, usually the same number as physicians. They were assisted by one or two *platicantes* each. The apothecary also took one or several assistants.

(iii) *The administration.* These men were collectively known as the hospital officials. At the top of the hierarchy was the *mayordomo*, the overseer, in charge of the finances, and of providing the diets, medicines and other things necessary for the hospital. Below him was the *veedor*, or comptroller, whose task was to implement and check the financial affairs of the hospital; along with the overseer he had to sign the accounts book and justify expenditure. There was also a caterer and his assistant. The scrivener would write down details of all daily expenditure in a special book, kept by the *mayordomo* who in theory checked it every night; he was also responsible for making wills and taking down the final instructions and testaments of the dying men.[10] The bedding and other materials were the respondibility of the keeper of the wardrobe, who had 'to look after the beds, sheets, blankets and other things' given to him by royal officials for the use of the hospital, as well as the clothing used for the sick who were cured there.[11] There was a clerk who kept a list of all deaths and discharges. He noted who came and who left the hospital, primarily so as to allow for careful distribution of rations and so avoid fraud. The *tinelero* was in charge of the dining room, while the *botiller-dietero* had control of all the solid and liquid nourishment required. These two functions might be discharged by the same person or by two individuals. There was a cook who would have at least one assistant, and an *alguacil* to police and keep order inside the hospital, as well as a sacristan, and of course, a gravedigger.

(iv) *Nursing staff.* These consisted of a chief nurse and a varying number of nurses and assistant nurses, usually one nurse and assistant per ward. Among the nursing staff we usually find some clerics from the Orders of Juan de Dios and Obregón.

(v) *Chaplains.* Some four or five of these were attached to the hospital to look after the spiritual needs of the sick.

(vi) *Other clerics.* There were occasions, as in the Armada of 1588, when clerics from different orders embarked in order to attend to the spiritual needs of the sailors and soldiers. These were also considered as part of the medical corps.

4. Appointments and Pay

The general administrator, the royal physician, the chief surgeon, and some of the most important physicians were appointed by the king, in the final instance, but they were selected from the recommendations sent by the most senior royal physician at court to the council of war. The king might also appoint some of the chaplains directly. The rest of the hospital personnel were appointed by the captain general of the campaign on recommendation from the chief hospital administrator. In both cases, their formal appointment would carry details of their wages, which varied according to their experience and status, as well as whether they were expected to serve at sea or on land. Naval service was better paid. Table 1 gives details of the wages — in *escudos* — assigned to hospital personnel in 1587 and 1588.

5. Hospital Equipment

This included materials to set up the hospital wards, cooking implements, crockery and utensils for the dining-room, all that was necessary for saying mass — from altars to candles and cloths — and finally the medical utensils themselves, usually syringes, cupping-glasses, chamber-pots, and dishes.

Table 1　Wages assigned to Hospital Personnel in 1587 and 1588.

Office	Land	Navy
Physician	30	50
Surgeon	20	30–25
Assistant surgeon	—	6
Barber	6	8
Apothecary	12–8	20
Apothecary's assistant	4	—
Overseer	15	25
Comptroller	15	18
Keeper of the wardrobe	10	12
Scrivener	6	10
Caterer	6	6
Botiller y dietero (cellar & diets)	6	8
Tinelero (Dining room)	6	8
Assistants	3	4
Nurse	6–4	6–4
Assistant nurse	3	3
Cook	4	6
Assistant cook	2	3
Chaplains	10	20–10
Sacristan	3	5
Gravedigger	3	3
Clerk registering deaths and discharges	8	—

6. Therapeutic Remedies

A great variety of products were taken to cure the sick and wounded, including medicines, potions, material for bandages — oakum and rags packed in huge bales — and the so-called 'diets' — foodstuffs for the sick and wounded.

Great care and attention was given to the provision of medicines. Before the departure of the fleet one or several apothecaries were charged with the preparation and purchase of specific medicines which would have been found in any pharmacy of the period. They were classified into simples, syrups, lozenges, pills, oils, unguents, waters, electuaries, powders, poultices, preserves and herbs, and they were all packed in especially-made wooden boxes. Their delivery to the chief apothecary of the fleet was supervised by several physicians and done in the presence of a scrivener; all had to testify to the 'quality and necessity' of these items.

Even if the quantity and quality of the medicines proved satisfactory there was a major impediment to their effective use. As mentioned above, they would be stored aboard one ship and were therefore not always easily available. In order to deal with problems that might arise on board other vessels, the physicians and surgeons habitually took with them small quantities of medicines at their own cost and risk. The flagship also took a box with medicines.

It was the tragic experiences of the *Gran Armada* that proved the catalyst for radical changes in the medical provision of the Spanish navy. After 1588 every ship, however small, was provided with a certain quantity of medicines.

Besides the use of medicines, healing relied heavily on the consumption of special foodstuffs. Consequently the hospital was assigned a number of items, the 'diets', considered essential for a return to health. They included lamb (instead of the salt beef of the usual rations), chicken, eggs, raisins, sugar, almonds, and a host of items we might describe as treats, such as cakes made with sugar and eggs, vegetable preserves, candied and fresh fruit.

7. Finances

To cover expenditure the paymaster-general of the fleet assigned a monthly sum to the overseer. In effect this was an advance provided by the king, since the hospital was paid for by the beneficiaries themselves, through contributions deducted directly from the men's pay. The *real de limosna* (as it was called), was a proportional levy: while the common soldiers paid just one *real*, sergeants paid three, lieutenants five, and captains ten.

The First Hospitals of the *Gran Armada*

In a famous memorandum of 1586 the marquis of Santa Cruz outlined in detail what would be required for an invasion of England.[12] He reckoned that they would need a hospital with a capacity for 2,000 patients for which he estimated fifty-five officials would suffice. Nevertheless, by mid-1587, when the preparations for the campaign against England were well advanced, no steps had been taken to create a hospital for the fleet. The only hospital facilities for the troops that were gathering in Lisbon were in the small hospital belonging to the city's garrison — the San Felipe y Santiago — which was housed within the castle.[13]

In the summer of 1587 Santa Cruz was ordered to set sail at once with all available forces to protect the Indies fleets from Drake. It was that July when he hastily created a hospital 'for the royal army and fleet', which was duly embarked on the fleet in its mission to the New World.[14] The hospital administrator was Fray Fransisco de Salazar, and there were some twenty-eight officials under his supervision, including two physicians and seven surgeons. They were all aboard the ship *La Concepción Mayor* of Recalde's squadron, which was also carrying the medicines and other provisions.

While Santa Cruz was at sea, troops and sailors continued to arrive in Lisbon where Don Alonso Martínez de Leiva was in charge. The first serious epidemics broke out in the galleasses which had recently arrived from Naples and affected both soldiers and oarsmen.[15] It is difficult to give precise details of this epidemic, but taking into account the lateness of the season, the overcrowded conditions on board, as well as the state of the food and drink, it has been suggested that it might have been an outbreak of salmonella or food poisoning. Martínez de Leiva was forced to create another hospital to deal with this outbreak, and he did so with great difficulty, as most of the medical personnel and materials had been taken by Santa Cruz. Only eight officials were registered in the new hospital.

When Santa Cruz returned to Lisbon, the situation had worsened. He decided to leave the hospital set up by Leiva, and to create a new hospital on land with the officials who had been at sea with him. These were the origins of the two hospitals known as the hospital of the Xabonería and the hospital of the Vizcaínos, which continued to treat both sailors and soldiers in Lisbon until the Armada sailed. These developments forced the commanders to organise adequate funding for medical provisions and to appoint more medical officials. By early 1588 there were some seventy-six people serving in these hospitals.[16]

The Medical Situation in Lisbon

Until recently, the concentration of a large number of people in one place automatically carried grave health risks. The outbreak of disease in one company could destroy a whole army. We could give numerous examples of campaigns where this happened: the *Gran Armada* was certainly no exception, but until now we did not have information of what had happened before its departure.

The first outbreak of enteritis in the Neapolitan galleasses was quickly followed by others in different units. At the end of 1587 the situation deteriorated as spotted fever spread among the troops, causing the royal officials to order the infantry that had already embarked to disembark again. This seriously delayed the departure of the Armada.[17]

We can judge the severity of the outbreak by looking at Don Augustín de Mexia's *tercio*, which had 1,400 men sick out of a total of 3,600 soldiers — a contagion rate of 39%.[18] The worst affected was Oquendo's squadron. Even after the soldiers had been sent ashore, the sickness decimated his sailors. At considerable personal risk, Oquendo refused to leave his flagship, 'so that they will not be able to say that I abandoned them when they were sick'.[19] This crisis brought into sharp relief the paucity of the health care provided and inadequate supply of physicians in the hospitals. There were sufficient surgeons, barbers and nursing staff, but too few experienced physicians. Oquendo commented in a letter to the king, 'the [new] physician has not arrived, and the Portuguese hope to finish us off and dare to say so, may God convert them!'.[20]

From the very precise documentation that survives about the number of sick and dead, we can demonstrate that in the six months or so from the arrival of the men in Lisbon to the end of November 1587, 328 soldiers and 154 sailors had died in the city.[21] The epidemic peaked in December, when some 1,180 men were registered in the hospitals, that is 7.25% of the total military effectives. We need to add to this figure an unspecified number of men who were forced to remain in their quarters aboard ship either because they were less seriously ill, or simply because there was no space for them in the hospitals.[22] As the new year dawned, there was a remission which held until the departure of the fleet, with a brief but intensive new outbreak during February and March 1588 that led to the highest mortality rates, and affected the captain general himself, causing Santa Cruz's death on 9 February. Several authors have maintained that Santa Cruz died as a result of cumulative tension caused by his increasingly frequent and bitter quarrels with the king over the delays and departure of the fleet. Now we can confidently ascribe a good deal of that delay to the same epidemic that caused his death.[23] We should note, however, that such epidemics were quite common in this period, and often they led to a far higher mortality than that experienced by the *Gran Armada* personnel.

The Hospital for the Gran Armada Campaign

Shortly before his death, the marquis of Santa Cruz had started to organise the hospital which was to embark on the *Gran Armada*; it was the duke of Medina Sidonia, however, who took charge and finalised the preparations. At the end of January 1588 Philip II had named Don Martín de Alarcón as general administrator of the hospital.[24] The appointments of the principal physicians and surgeons were also drawn up.[25] On 5 April, following the recommendations of the general administrator, Medina Sidonia signed the appointments of all the personnel who were to embark with the hospital, giving details of their salaries.[26] Later, before the fleet sailed, there were further additions, so that on 28 May 1588 there were ninety-three people attached to the Armada hospital.

I have been able to identify almost all of the men who made up the medical staff of the fleet.[27] They can be divided into the following categories:

Chaplains: 4 Spanish, 2 Irish
Sacristan: 1
Physicians: 5
Chief Surgeon: 1
Surgeons: 12
Assistants: 13
Barbers: 7
Apothecary: 1 with 5 assistants
Overseer: 1
Comptroller: 1

Keeper of the Wardrobe: 1 with 1 assistant
Scrivener: 1
Caterer: 1 with 1 assistant
Botiller y dietero: 1 with 2 assistants
Tinelero y repostero: 1 with 2 assistants
Repartidor: 1
Cook: 2 with 3 assistants
Nurses: 6
Assistant nurses: 3
Gravedigger: 1.

The remaining officials were servants of the general administrator and monks. Twenty-one monks embarked with the hospital, fourteen from the Order of Juan de Dios, and seven from the Order of Bernardino de Obregón.[28] There were other members of the clergy on board the Armada — 198 of them to be precise, from different orders, and distributed throughout the fleet. Their primary function was to provide spiritual care for the soldiers and sailors, but during combat they were expected to play a medical role, and consequently, they were included in the hospital accounts.[29]

During the last week of April the medicines which had been prepared by three apothecaries in Lisbon were delivered. All of them were neatly packed into twenty-five wooden boxes of which we have the most detailed inventories.[30] The provisions received by the keeper of the wardrobe, Francisco de Medina, between 6 and 9 May were similarly noted in minute detail.[31]

At the same time the hospital staff were taken on board with their possessions. Two ships had been chosen for the hospital: the hulks *La Casa de Paz Grande* of 650 *toneladas*, and the *San Pedro el Mayor* of 580 *toneladas*. All the hulks in the fleet were from northern Europe, and had been embargoed for the campaign.[32] A few infantry were also put aboard these ships. There were soon serious problems with the hospital ships. The *San Pedro el Mayor* started leaking on the way from Lisbon to La Coruña. Although it was straggling, it did manage to make it into the port, where it was repaired. The *Casa de Paz Grande* was not quite so fortunate. It was dispersed in the fearful storm that struck the fleet as it reached La Coruña and beached in Laredo, so seriously damaged that it was impossible to set it afloat once more. The cargo and personnel were rescued and dispatched to La Coruña. It has proved impossible to find out whether the hospital was then put solely on board the *San Pedro el Mayor* or if another hulk was used as well.

In any case, the hulk *San Pedro* came to a tragic end. During the journey back, after successfully overcoming the dangers of the Irish coast, it reached the Channel, only to run aground near Plymouth where it was surrounded by local shipping. The vessel was sacked and its crew imprisoned. Further adventures awaited the medical staff of the Armada, which have come down to us in the account of one of the surgeons and two officials who managed to escape.[33]

Health and Medicine during the Journey

It is not necessary for our purpose to include a detailed account of what occurred after the *Gran Armada* sailed from Lisbon. What concerns us here is to focus on those events that touch on major medical issues. To facilitate our task we have divided the campaign into four phases: (a) The journey from Lisbon to La Coruña; (b) the fighting in the Channel; (c) the journey back to Spain; (d) the fleet's arrival in the Cantabrian ports of Santander, San Sebastian and Pasajes.

(a) From Lisbon to La Coruña. On the 30 May 1588 the fleet left Lisbon, and on the night of the 19 June, the duke of Medina Sidonia decided it was necessary to put into La Coruña. Unfortunately his order coincided with a sudden deterioration of the weather conditions, and

this prevented many of the ships from coming into port. Many suffered severely from the tempest, which caused considerable damage and delayed the sailing of the fleet to England until the 22 of July.

It was not the weather, however, which had forced the captain general of the fleet to take such a major step; a step which compromised the expedition. There were serious problems with the victuals, which were rotting, and water supplies were scarce. This, one of the Armada's most acute problems, was blamed by some on fraudulent suppliers, and they undoubtedly existed; but the real reason for the poor quality of the victuals was the lengthy period of time that had elapsed between purchase and consumption. Some victuals had already been thrown overboard in Lisbon because they were rotten.[34] Once the fleet had set sail it became apparent that the victuals were neither as abundant nor of such good quality as had been reported, in fact much of it was 'deteriorating very quickly'.[35] Consequently, Medina Sidonia demanded the immediate dispatch of further provisions, which he hoped would reach him as he approached La Coruña — initially he had no intention of entering the harbour and delaying his journey.

Sickness was soon apparent on board some ships, but this was only to be expected as most of the men were not used to the sea, and were soon suffering from the additional effects of harsh sailing condition and poor victuals. When they finally reached La Coruña it proved necessary to put the sick ashore and to establish a hospital on land. The first medical statistics we have are dated 6 July, when there were over 200 patients in the hospital. Worse still, it was reported that on the ships, 'many are sick, well over 2000 men'.[36] Up to 500 patients were taken into the hospital during the following days, the majority diagnosed as suffering from 'fevers' and apparently not gravely ill, since there were few deaths.[37] With the help of fresh and plentiful food they recovered fully, and when the fleet once again set sail, there were only 293 men too sick to re-embark.[38]

The most serious drawback for the campaign after this was not the number of men who were sick, or who needed to be put ashore, but the shortage of victuals. Despite strenuous efforts it proved impossible to provision the fleet adequately. The supply convoy which finally left Lisbon with victuals for the Armada that summer failed to reach the fleet in time.

(b) The fights in the Channel. A number of partial accounts survive which enable us to provide a rough sketch of the medical impact of the encounters in the Channel.[39] There were only five days of fighting, and

we have estimated that the *Gran Armada* suffered the following losses: 1000 dead, 1500 wounded, and a further 1500 who were either taken prisoner or disappeared. These are strikingly low figures, particularly when we take into account that one accident alone — the explosion in the *San Salvador* from Oquendo's squadron before the fighting started — accounted for 200 dead and many wounded. According to one contemporary observer[40] the Armada sustained the following losses: 207 dead on 31 July; 52 on 2 August; 60 on the 3 August; another fifty the following day; and 600 on the 8 August. The figures prove the relative lack of contact in the encounters before the battle of Gravelines on 8 August. Once the fireships had dispersed the Armada and caused it to lose its anchors the English attacked the dispersed ships. The battle of Gravelines involved most of the fleet until it regained its powerful formation.

(c) The journey back. The forty-five days that lapsed between Medina Sidonia's decision to return to Spain round the British Isles and the arrival in Santander of the first ships were undoubtedly the most dramatic of the campaign. Several factors contributed to the men's suffering, not least the quantity and quality of the victuals during the return voyage. The journey up to La Coruña had already revealed grave deficiencies in the provision of water and food; these were aggravated after the fleet's departure from Galicia, although while they were stationed there additional stores had been taken on board. It is now clear that when they set sail once again, the fleet only had sufficient victuals for the journey to England — and that with only a small margin. Once on shore, they would need to feed off the land, and rely on the convoys sent from Spain.

For this reason, it is striking that the duke of Medina Sidonia chose such a long journey back. It is evident that he was fully apprised of the scarcity of provisions, since he immediately ordered a reduction in the daily rations and got rid of the horses and mules in order to preserve water supplies. The situation was already precarious, and, to make matters worse, the weather conditions encountered by the fleet proved exceptionally harsh. The Armada was seriously delayed by storms: there are truly harrowing accounts of the difficulties some ships encountered navigating the coasts of Scotland and Ireland. These storms affected the victuals as they caused leaks which spoilt the stores in many of the ships, and of course they extended the journey. Some of the ships were forced to land in Ireland because of their desperate need for water and food, and it was here that the most serious casualties were registered, not only from the wrecks but in direct combat.

The sorry state of the fleet is clear from a fascinating account of the victuals remaining aboard the ships when they arrived at Santander. The *San Martin*, the duke of Medina Sidonia's flag-ship, had only 'eighty *quintales* of rotten biscuit and biscuit crums, and two *pipas* of vinegar'; the *San Cristobal* had 'one hundred and sixty *quintales* of rotten biscuit, and four *pipas* of wine'. Juan Martínez de Recalde's ship, *La Manuela*, was almost privileged by comparison; it had 'one hundred and fifty *quintales* of spoilt biscuit, eight *pipas* of wine, ten *quintales* of bacon, six *quintales* of cheese, and three barrels of putrid tuna'. The shortage of food affected all ships, large and small; even very small ones like the *zabra Julia* only had 'sixty *quintales* of broken biscuit and fourteen *quintales* of rotten bacon, and five *fanegas* of putrid chickpeas'.[41]

(d) The Armada's arrival at the Cantabrian ports. The bulk of the fleet reached the northern Spanish coast on and after 21 September. Every ship was in grave difficulties. After such a long and arduous journey, the men were weak. 'Every day, in every ship, three or four men would die before my eyes of hunger and thirst', Father de la Victoria stated.[42] The duke of Medina Sidonia reported that in the flagship: '180 men died of disease and three out of the four pilots died'. He was also very ill, 'after twenty-five days of fevers and fluxion'.[43] None of this should surprise us, knowing as we do, that some of the ships had run out of water a fortnight earlier, and some of the captains reported that for twenty-six days their daily rations had consisted of ground chickpeas and half a pint of water.

Most of the ships docked in Santander, but a substantial number of them sailed into Pasajes and San Sebastian, while a few others made for Asturian and Galician ports. The reports sent from these various areas alarmed the court. The king himself from the start spoke of between 3,000–4,000 sick.[44] But we know from the more accurate documentation that was drawn up later that of the 2,475 men who arrived in San Sebastian and Pasajes, only 327 of them were sick;[45] and of the more than 8,000 survivors in Santander, there were approximately 1,000 sick.[46] The majority of them were suffering from intestinal disorders caused by the putrid state of the water and the victuals, as well as the natural consequences of malnutrition. Some had contracted typhus. To deal with all of them it was imperative to devise quick solutions. The measures which were taken show clearly the ability of the Spanish Monarchy to respond to such a crisis.

The Situation on the Return of the Armada

Weather conditions had propelled most of the fleet to Santander, Pasajes and San Sebastian, which were then very small ports incapable of dealing with large numbers of people, let alone the hordes of men who arrived without warning, and who required major medical support. At once measures were taken to secure the necessary supplies to feed the men and repair the ships. Hospitals were created to accommodate the large number of sick and wounded. It should be said that after a very brief period of confusion, the response was extremely effective.

The king asked the cities to send aid for the sick, and in Santander officials were appointed to distribute the royal and individual donations that soon arrived. Thanks to the survival of most of the documentation we have minute details of what each area contributed, from clothing and medicines to specific foodstuffs for the sick. We also know that three hospitals were set up, one each in La Coruña, San Sebastian, and Santander. The latter was the most important, and given the status of Royal Naval Hospital. An administrator, Dr Manso, was appointed. He was a canon of Burgos, a most humane man, who discharged this important task and went on to manage the hospital in the port of Ferrol, and the Royal Military Hospital for the campaign in Aragon. All medical personnel from the Armada hospital were assigned to the Santander hospital, but there were very few of them left, since most had been captured in the hulk *San Pedro el Mayor* and would not return to Spain until 1590.[47]

An epidemic of spotted fever broke out in Santander causing the death of 200 patients in the hospital and spread to the civil population with devastating effects. A later account speaks of 'the grave epidemic it caused which led to the death of much of the population . . . More than six hundred people died, both rich and poor'.[48] Meanwhile, an outbreak of the much-feared yellow fever spread in San Sebastian — Admiral Oquendo was among its victims. On top of this affliction came others: the tragic fire in the ship *Santa Ana* which caused the death of 130 men, both soldiers and sailors; and the fire in the hospital. Although the patients were evacuated, everything else was consumed by the flames which reduced the building to its foundations.

The Human Cost of the 1588 Campaign

After the Armada, the king ordered the *corregidores* of the places of origin of both sailors and soldiers who had taken part in the campaign so as to draw up detailed accounts of local losses. Only one of these, drawn up in 1589 in the province of Guipuzcoa, has been found. It provides us with exceptional details not only of losses — 502 men from this area died — but also of the men who had participated.[49] In the absence of similarly detailed accounts for other areas, we have adopted an indirect method of estimating casualties. Since we know the number of men who left La Coruña, and the number who returned to the ports mentioned above, we can give approximate figures of losses. I must stress that it is only approximate, since the men who remained captive in England and Ireland are not counted here, and some of them, after extraordinary experiences, were able to return to Spain.

The following table summarises our findings and estimates for the campaign:

	Departed	Returned	Losses	% Total
Mariners	7,408	3,834	3,574	48.2
Soldiers	18,288	9,565	8,723	47.6
Total	25,696	13,399	12,297	47.8

There are further reservations to be made when considering these figures. Those for departure are exact, but those marked 'returned' are deficient in a number of respects. First, they do not take into account the Portuguese soldiers who were dispatched to Lisbon as soon as they landed.[50] This would bring down the difference between the two figures to 11,750. We can continue the downward revision by taking into account the prisoners already mentioned, for which we have no data, not even a working estimate. By piecing together a number of accounts written after the event, and bearing in mind the numbers involved in various escapes, we believe that no fewer than 2,000 men fall into this category.[51]

Taking all these disparate factors into account, we are left with a total of **9,000 men lost on the campaign**, that is 35% of the total. This then was the human cost of the *Gran Armada* expedition. Undoubtedly it was a sizeable figure, but it was no more, indeed probably a good deal less, than the number of deaths registered in various army epidemics of the period.

This brief resumé of the health provisions and medical aspects of the *Gran Armada* has shown that despite grave problems and danger, a medical service of considerable dimensions was provided for the fleet. Although hampered by the levels of medical knowledge attained at the time, the system had a very advanced structure, and sufficient flexibility to respond to new challenges — this can be seen most clearly in the measures adopted after the fleet had returned. The fact that four hundred years later we have sufficient documentation to reconstruct the Armada hospitals with considerable precision also reflects the powerful administrative infrastructure of which they were but a small part.

NOTES

1. This article summarises some of the main points included in my monograph *La sanidad en la jornada de Inglaterra (1587-8)* (Serie *Gran Armada* II, Madrid, 1988).
2. Indeed it was limited to fragmentary information provided in the documents published by Fernández Duro, despite the existence of a work by Juan Redondo entitled *El Servicio Sanitario de la Armada Invencible* (Madrid, 1903).
3. The documents in the vast holdings of the *Contaduría del Sueldo 2a época* (AGS CS 2e) were particularly important.
4. The hospitals of the fleet in El Ferrol (1589), Blavet (Brittany) in 1590, and Philip II's army in Aragon (1591).
5. The *Libro del Consulado* (1270) and *Ordenanzas Navales* (1354) of Bernardo de Cabrera are among the most ancient texts.
6. It was normal for the Spanish Galleys to have a royal physician in the sixteenth century. Perhaps the most famous of them was Cristobal Pérez de Herrera.
7. Gracia Rivas, M. *La vida a bordo. Problemática sanitaria de las navegaciones oceánicas* (forthcoming).
8. These were certainly included in the Tunis, Lepanto, and the Azores campaigns.
9. The Azores campaign, and again events in 1588, proved the grave danger of continuing with this practice.
10. AGS CS 2e 287 f. 534.
11. AGS CS 2e 287 f. 12.
12. FD I pp. 250ff.
13. AGS GA 301 f. 134.
14. AGS CS 2e 281 f. 25.
15. AGS CS 2e 287 f. 534.

16. AGS CS 2e 281 ff. 18 & 20.
17. Herrera Oria, *Armada*, documents no. xxxviii, xl, xli, xliii.
18. Op. cit., doc. xxxvi.
19. AGS GA 219 f. 38.
20. AGS GA 219 f. 40.
21. AGS CS 2e 278 f. 36.
22. AGS GA 221 ff. 44 & 46.
23. AGS GA 220 f.32. This document first discovered during our research in Simancas, specifies quite clearly that: 'the sickness has been diagnosed today, and it is typhus with coloured spots'. (*tabardillo de pintas coloradas*).
24. FA I doc. no. 67.
25. For example, that of Dr Francisco Segastibarría, Dr Diego de Santander, Licenciado Juán de Zárata and Licenciado José Vizconde, all on 30 January; Dr Antonio Pérez on 1 February, and Dr Juan del Rubio 5 February.
26. AGS CS 2e 281 f. 29.
27. AGS CS 2e 281: *Libro del contador Alameda*. This book preserves the contracts of all the personnel. I have published a summary of these contracts in Appendix II of my book *La sanidad en la jornada de Inglaterra*.
28. These two orders were created to provide hospital care; Juan de Dios was canonized and his order continues to provide invaluable medical care in our own days. The Congregation of the Minim Brothers, or of Obregón, was founded by Bernardino de Obregón in Madrid, in 1565. They did excellent work all over the world, but were dissolved during the French Revolution.
29. This has allowed us to identify them. Apart from these medical and religious functions, the clergy aboard the *Gran Armada* had another, less publicized but more delicate mission, which was to take charge of the English convents that had once belonged to their orders. This is why all of them had sent their representatives.
30. AGS CS 2e 278 ff. 1136ff.
31. AGS CS 2e 278 ff. 559ff.
32. AGS CS 2e 278 s.f.
33. AGS GA 245 ff. 187, 188.
34. M. Gracia Rivas, 'Aportación al estudio económico de la Gran Armada. Las libranzas del pagador Juán de la Huerta.' *Revista de Historia Naval* 13 (1986) pp. 51–78. See also Thompson above, pp. 81–2 and nn. 56 and 57.
35. FD II doc. 116.
36. AGS GA 225 f. 61.
37. FD II doc. 141.
38. AGS GA 225 f. 77.

39. The most interesting are the accounts of Luís de Miranda and captain Alonso de Venegas, both in FD II pp. 265–73 and 370–99 respectively.
40. Capitan Alonso de Venegas.
41. AGS CS 2e 278 f. 993ff. See Gracia Rivas, *La sanidad en la jornada de Inglaterra*, pp. 310–12. I am currently preparing a full and critical edition of this document which gives a great deal of detail on artillery and munitions.
42. FD II doc. 186.
43. FD II doc. 173.
44. T. López Mata 'Burgos en las tristezas de la Invencible', *Boletín de la Comisión Provincial de Monumentos Históricos y Artísticos* (Burgos, 1933) pp. 508–20.
45. M. Gracia Rivas, 'La asistencia sanitaria a los buques de la Gran Armada a su retorno a los puertos guipuzcoanos'. *Revista de Historia Naval* I (Madrid, 1983) pp. 111–22.
46. AGS GA 227 f. 227.
47. Some had escaped earlier, but most waited to be rescued and were incorporated into the naval hospital which was then established in Ferrol.
48. AGS GA 289 f. 102.
49. The name of the deceased is given, along with his occupation, his place of birth, the cause of death, and the family he left behind, AGS GA 302 f. 148.
50. The aim was to reduce pressure on Santander. Soon after the Spanish infantry were quartered further inland too.
51. The duke of Parma negotiated from the Netherlands for the return of these men. Some had a most tragic end nevertheless, such as the convoy intercepted by the Dutch near Dunkirk. They killed 270 soldiers who had been ransomed and were on their way to the loyal provinces, FD I p. 23. In February 1590 Pedro de Zubiaur led another convoy to Spain with at least 500 survivors, AGS GA 281 ff. 3 and 5.

8

THE ARMY OF FLANDERS AND THE
INVASION OF ENGLAND 1586–8

Hugo O'Donnell y Duque de Estrada

One of the least known aspects of the attempted invasion of England which led to the expedition of the 'Invincible Armada', is the fate and composition of the army that waited in the Netherlands, hoping to cross the English Channel — as William the Conqueror had done nearly five centuries earlier — under the protection of the Spanish fleet. The failure of the campaign, the lack of information, and the initial reluctance of the duke of Parma, commander-in-chief of these forces, to involve them in any military action other than the repression of the Dutch revolt, has led to widespread debate over the size of the invading army, and even to whether it existed at all. In this paper we will analyse the Armada campaign from the little-known perspective of the expeditionary force; from the viewpoint of those who prepared and waited in vain.[1]

1. Frantic Preparations

In the summer of 1588 even the least informed peasant along the Flemish coast knew of the vast forces being prepared in Nieuport and Dunkirk to punish the English queen. For a year now, the drums and fifes had sounded across the country calling for recruits to join the companies of well-known local lords. It was impossible to find a ship-wright or caulker; and the masters and owners of river and coastal vessels had been hired along with their ships and crews by the marquis of Renty, Admiral of the Netherlands, for an indefinite period of time. Recently, even day labourers and other untrained men had been recruited as pioneers, to cut down trees and dig canals. No one believed that all these preparations were against neighbouring rebels; and hopes of besieging Ostend, which would have ended the nightmarish enemy raids, had long since disappeared.

Over the previous months, the infantry had been stationed near the coast, and the price of victuals had risen sharply. The provision of hay and cereals for the cavalry, recently arrived from its Rhenish winter quarters, had created a scarcity of goods until then abundant. At the beginning of August 1588 German mercenaries had come to Nieuport via Bruges, with their strange and diverse armaments, and in very bad humour as their pay was several months in arrears. A month earlier, an Italian contingent had set up a well-organised camp on the outskirts of the city, happy to see the end of a harsh winter to which they were not accustomed. The local soldiers, seven regiments of Walloons, sought out kinsmen and friends among the city dwellers, hoping to get shelter, bedding and fire, or perhaps some food to supplement their ration of biscuit. Along with these eighteen thousand men, now ready to board, there was another army — of victuallers, merchants and prostitutes. In Dunkirk, less than two leagues away, it was a similar situation. Although there were only half the number of soldiers, the officials attached to the court and the expedition's headquarters had been assigned to embark here, and they had been joined by a large number of merchants, who gathered in expectation of buying cheaply the horses, household goods, embroideries and other booty taken by the soldiers, particularly the Spaniards, who had to get rid of their impedimenta as they set out for new, and hopefully richer, conquests.

The Spanish troops were the best: the most experienced, efficient and loyal. Four powerful tercios had just arrived from the lands near Artois and Hainault. They were well dressed and armed, and had full supporting services, as befitted the troops which the duke of Parma, their captain general and supreme commander of the expedition, called 'the main artery, the right arm, the ones who will ensure success'.[2] With them came the Irish *tercio*, who were also assigned to the vanguard because they were catholics who could be trusted and who got along well with the Spaniards, and the Burgundian regiment from the Franche-Comté, which had been thoroughly tested and had suffered heavy casualties in all previous campaigns. The cavalry were also instructed to embark from Dunkirk, but they had taken things easier. There was no space in the ships for them, so they would have to wait until a second journey could be made to England. By then, it was hoped that the special hoists and cranes for the horses would be ready, and then the transport vessels could be stripped of their decks for the horses to embark.

The army's store-houses in both towns had provided the small arms needed, as well as the tools and utensils for the pioneers. The heavy artillery, the cannons that were required to smash city walls, were aboard the great ships of the Armada. Some smaller guns, demi-cannon and quarter-cannon, as well as field guns, had been loaded into the Netherlands ships earlier, along with a curious palisade of wooden spikes designed to defend the troops from the attacks of the English cavalry.[3]

Huge crates of biscuit and barrels of local beer were stacked in the bilges. A snack was considered sufficient for the long-suffering troops since they were expected to be on board only some eight to ten hours. They would not even have to row since the currents would drag them into the landing beaches. Later, the hulks with the victuals under the duke of Medina Sidonia would bring them food. The fertile enemy lands would provide the rest; that was why they had chosen to land at harvest-time. There was one cloud in the generally bright and optimistic horizon: the flagship of this flotilla, built in Antwerp — a beautiful galleon with a carved, golden stern, streamers, pennants, the royal standard and railings hung with crimson damask — was unable to sail with the fleet, as it was blockaded in the Scheldt by Justin of Nassau's fleet. It had only been possible to move the smallest ships from the inland waterways to the coast, and that with great effort. A new canal was cut to enable one hundred and thirty barges to be moved to Ghent, and from there by the river Lieve to Damme, and by the Iperlee to Nieuport.

Despite all the problems that had been encountered, the army was now in place, and the time seemed right. Sufficient reserves had been left to counter any attack by the Dutch during the absence of the bulk of the army. The northern and north-western fronts had been stabilised recently after the Spanish occupation of two key positions along the river crossings. France, potentially the worst enemy, was consumed by its civil war; and the recently strengthened electorate of Cologne provided a useful bulwark against the protestant German princes. In the distant Mediterranean front, the Turks were quiet, and far too busy with the Persians along their exposed eastern flank to turn west. And while the negotiations for an alliance with James VI of Scotland had not been finalised, there were good hopes that this able and irresolute monarch might attack Elizabeth Tudor from the north at the same time that the victorious Spaniards landed in England. True, England had been alerted — the secrecy Parma considered so necessary to the success of the invasion had not been observed — but Elizabeth was isolated. The expense of the enterprise would also be lessened by the offer of one million ducats by the pope the moment the first Spanish soldier set foot in England.

Never had there been such a favourable conjuncture; everything seemed to suggest that the last Tudor monarch would pay for her daring policies once and for all — the seizure of Alba's payships, the persecution of the Catholics, the illegal commerce with the Spanish colonies, Drake's depredations, her financial and military support for the rebels in the Netherlands, the execution of Mary Stuart . . . it seemed that the lengthy account would soon be paid in full. Hopes were high after it was known in the Netherlands in June 1588 that a great fleet of 130 ships with 30,000 men on board had set sail from Lisbon heading for the Channel. No one knew better than Alexander Farnese, duke of Parma, and the principal designer as well as ultimate commander of this expedition, what an extraordinary effort had been required to bring all this to fruition.

2. The Defence of the Netherlands

From 1586, when Philip decided to launch the campaign, his councillors had to consider whether it was possible to do this without endangering the Netherlands. Parma was instructed to organise the complex defence of the area, which required measures against the rebels, against France, and against the protestant insurgents in the archbishopric of Cologne. From the spring of 1586 Parma sought to gain control of the strategic routes used by the rebels within the Netherlands, seizing Grave and Venlo which gave him control of navigation along the Meuse (June 1586), and secured the Spanish northern outpost at Zutphen (September–October 1586). Equally successful diplomatic moves led to the acquisition of the redoubt of Wouw and the city of Deventer (January 1587), which gave Parma control over most of the valley of the river Ijssel. On the secondary front in Gelderland, he was able to counter the incursions from Wachtendonck by taking Geldern in August 1587. That same month, the capture of Sluys on the coast provided him with another port and helped to neutralise the threat from Ostend. These successes effectively stabilised the various Netherlands fronts and gave sufficient security to undertake the operation against England.

More subtle methods were required to neutralise the French. It was imperative to prevent the warring parties from making peace. Generous subsidies were sent to the Catholic League which managed a short-lived victory over Henry III and the Huguenots just when the Armada sailed in 1588. If the king of France had won, or persuaded the two sides to make peace, he would undoubtedly have taken this excellent opportunity to have attacked the weak Netherlands with an army which was estimated at 60,000 infantry and 6,000 horse.[4] To oppose them, Philip II had only the garrisons of a string of frontier fortresses stretching from the Channel to the Meuse, supported by some Wallon heavy cavalry. Other dangers threatened, particularly from Elizabeth's German allies, headed by the prince Palatine. In Cologne, Dutch and Palatine aid had enabled the calvinists to raise the banner of revolt through half the archbishopric. Parma appreciated the danger to Brabant, and from 1586 diverted troops against the protestant strongholds of Neuss, Meurs, Alphen and Bonn. This military intervention served to reduce the internal violence in Cologne, and quelled the civil war, thereby eliminating a grave political and military danger for the Netherlands.

Apart from these preventive actions, Parma raised a field army of 10,000 infantry and 1,000 light cavalry, under his lieutenant, the count of Mansfelt. These troops, together with the Netherlands cavalry and the newly-recruited German mercenaries would support the 16,000-strong garrisons. Jointly, these measures gave the required minimum security for the Netherlands during Parma's absence in England.

3. The Painful Process of Gathering an Invasion Force

(a) Northern Troops

The plans drawn up in Madrid and Ghent specified the need for an army which, once joined to the forces aboard the fleet, would suffice to win, conquer and occupy England. The army would need to have at least 30,000 infantry and 500 horse. It would be made up of various nations, not only because the expedition was seen as a joint effort by the whole of the Spanish Monarchy, but also because they would need German and other troops to reach the required number. Additionally, hiring Germans was the best way of ensuring that the enemy was deprived of mercenaries, and for a time it was thought that the English would attempt to levy troops on the continent. Parma wanted 6,000 Spaniards, 6,000 Italians, 6,000 Walloons, 9,000 Germans, and 3,000 Burgundians.[5] The cavalry were to take along their saddles and bridles, but not their horses; it was hoped that these would be available in

England. In the two years it took to raise this army, there were no substantial changes in the overall figures for the infantry. Perhaps the most significant alteration in the plan was the inclusion of Irish troops, which proved necessary since there were insufficient Burgundians; and an increase in the number of Walloons and Germans in order to make up the losses among the Spanish and Italian troops. Fresh reports about the terrain in England and the size of Elizabeth's forces persuaded Parma to double the number of cavalry, however, and to take horses.

Parma needed money and trusted officers to levy the necessary Walloon, Burgundian and German troops. Mercenary leaders for whom war was a profession took charge of the process, but they needed money. Philip II doubled the usual monthly payments to the Netherlands to cover the extra costs: Parma now had 300,000 ducats per month to maintain the existing forces and raise new ones. Since the German soldiers had been severely reduced by the recent campaign on the Rhine, the emperor Rudolf II was asked to allow fresh levies in the Empire and give them free passage, as were the relevant authorities in the territories affected: Cologne, Westphalia, Bavaria, Brunswick, Swabia, Trier and Innsbruck. These were the 'High-German' troops, so-called to distinguish them from the Low Germans, that is the groups from the German-speaking lands of the Netherlands and Rhenish areas. Troops were also raised in these regions, but they were destined to join the Netherlands garrisons, not the invasion forces.

The colonels in charge were carefully selected; one of them was none other than the margrave of Burgau, son of the Archduke Ferdinand of Austria. His appointment had the added advantage of eliminating any problems he might have posed to the levy of 6,000 men from his lands. Another distinguished noble, close to the imperial throne, who was given command of German levies was Baron Eggenberg. Many of the existing German companies needed to fill vacant positions, and their experienced colonels set out to do so from their usual recruiting grounds. By the time the fleet was expected to sail from Spain, there were four German regiments with 8,000 men at the ready. They were tried and experienced troops, entirely loyal although their loyalty was purchased, and marked by a notable stoicism which impressed the chronicler Alonso Vázquez.[6] They were the single largest contingent of foreign troops in the invasion army.

It was easier to levy Walloons: they were nearer and so their levy and transport could be left to local royal officials. But there were disadvantages too: desertion was a major problem as the soldiers could be easily protected by their own countrymen. They were good soldiers, however, and much cheaper than any others. They were levied both for the invasion forces and the garrisons left behind. No new regiments were created; the new recruits were incorporated into existing regiments. Special care was taken with the veteran regiment which Parma himself commanded. Out of the ten Walloon regiments in the Netherlands, seven, with a thousand men apiece, were chosen to cross the Channel.

Making up the losses of the only Burgundian regiment proved impossible. None could be taken from the garrisons of the Franche-Comté itself because they would not suffice for defence of the area if the French or the calvinists from Geneva decided to attack; and as it was the time to gather the grape harvest, few volunteers answered the call. Eight hundred men were enlisted by the colonel, the marquis of Varambon, but only half actually joined their compatriots in the Netherlands. Of the rest, the majority deserted, and some died on arrival due to the harsh climate, poor quarters and epidemics. The Burgundians were highly prized, particularly as arquebusiers, but with only one thousand instead of the three thousand planned, it was decided to make up numbers by including Irish soldiers in the invasion force.

The Irish regiment had served since the defection of the Englishman, Sir William Stanley, at Deventer on 28 January 1587. The bravery and zeal of these men became proverbial. They became completely identified with their Spanish counterparts, and adopted the military structure of the *tercio*. General Zubiaur advised Philip II to allow 'the Irish to name captains of their own nation, and serve with the Spaniards because they are so deeply attached to Your Majesty'.[7] But the new *tercio* did not even reach one thousand men, so they were reinforced with some Scotsmen who had joined Philip's armies under similar circumstances and for similar reasons, having delivered Geldern to Parma.

(b) The Italian Troops

Money and good officers had succeeded in securing a substantial number of mercenary troops from the northern lands for the invasion, but the best known representatives of Philip II's regime, the Spanish and Italian soldiers, had to be recruited much further afield, and marched across Europe in order to join the invading army. There were two Italian levies: one of Neapolitans, organised by the viceroy, the count of

Miranda; the other, entrusted to Captain Capizucca, Parma's envoy, was to consist of men from different Italian states, including the papal lands. The Neapolitan levy attracted aristocrats and nobles, and was consequently so well armed and disciplined they did not resemble new recruits. Moreover, with their golden breast-plates and plumed helmets, they looked, according to Antonio Carnero, 'more like knights at a tournament than soldiers ready for war'.[8] The second Italian levy was composed of men from the Romagna, Urbino, Parma, Ferrara and Corsica. They were more poorly dressed and armed, and far less cohesive: 'since these men have been levied in small groups and different areas, they will not be as good as we thought, certainly not as useful as the Neapolitans who will be far superior'.[9] Both groups, totalling some 9,500 men, were transported in the Neapolitan galleys to Genoa. There they began the long and arduous journey also followed by Spanish troops along the so-called Spanish Road.

The journey from Italy to the Netherlands was the *Via Crucis* of the Spanish and Italian soldiers. The English and Dutch having command of the Channel, there was no alternative but to send troops from Genoa to Namur, a route planned by Cardinal Granvelle for the journey Philip II and his court should have made in 1563. It passed through the king's territories and allied lands. The route — going from Milan, to Piedmont, Savoy, Burgundy, Lorraine, Luxemburg and the Netherlands — had been used by nine armies since 1567 when Alba had taken the first Spanish contingent across. There were fixed stages along the way for the troops to rest and get provisions, but the conditions were harsh. The weather was often extreme and the Alpine passes very cold and difficult. It was hard to handle the baggage carts, and along parts of the route there was danger of attack from nearby enemies. Added to this, the king was invariably in a hurry to deploy the troops and insisted on a speedy journey. His orders to the governor of Milan and the commanders of the levies for the invasion were clear: 'you will make them follow their route with the greatest diligence, without allowing the least delay'. As the pace quickened, the roads were littered with exhausted stragglers who were picked up by medical teams and cared for in hastily improvised hospitals. Many soldiers deserted along the way, evading the mounted patrols.

Worse was still to come for the Italians when they reached the Netherlands. They had to endure a bitter Flemish winter in poor accommodation and damp conditions, without wood to warm themselves. An epidemic spread among them and a third of those who had

The Spanish road.

survived the forced march now died. From these and existing units in the Netherlands, Parma selected 3,000 Italians for the invasion of England.

The light cavalry was composed both of mounted arquebusiers and lancers. In effect it was made up of mounted footsoldiers, along with some Italian companies which had come with the infantry. It is worth mentioning in passing that there were also companies of Albanians, famous horsemen from the Balkans, who had fought in Habsburg armies since the days of Charles V. The 1,000 cavalry of the expedition were formed into twenty-three companies: six were arquebusiers, the rest lancers.

(c) The Spanish Infantry

Spanish infantry was widely recognised as the best fighting force in the early modern world. When Parma proposed his invasion plan in 1586 he naturally laid particular stress on the participation of Spanish soldiers. Parma insisted that Philip must supply him with some 6,500 men to bring the total number of Spaniards in the Netherlands to 10,800.[10] In the spring of 1586 there were three *tercios* in the north with a total of 4,305 Spaniards. Parma wanted to take 6,500 Spanish troops for the invasion; 3,000 more were required to campaign in the Netherlands, and a further 1,800 were to be left in the most important garrisons, including the one recently established in the castle of Antwerp.[11] Don Juan de Aguila, *maestre de campo* of one of the *tercios* justified Parma's demands for extra Spaniards on the grounds that the Spanish infantry alone could guarantee success.[12] In view of their importance, it is worth examining their recruitment at greater length.

Additional levies had already been raised in the spring of 1586 in Castile. After a long journey by sea from Barcelona to Genoa they had been stationed in Lombardy because of the instability in France. It was feared that the French were about to make peace and invade the Netherlands or the Franche-Comté, closing the Spanish Road through Lorraine and thus impeding the movement of troops and money to the Netherlands. In view of the urgency of mounting the invasion, however, it was decided that this unit of 2,000 men under Don Antonio Manrique — who were now partially trained — should be sent from Milan to the Netherlands. Parma suggested that five Spanish companies serving aboard the galley fleet could be used as temporary substitutes if the situation deteriorated in Milan, although he knew these men were indisciplined and would desert easily.[13]

The duke of Terranova, governor of Milan, received the order to prepare and send Manrique's men north in September 1586. Provided with the necessary licences for transit through Savoyard territories, they set off, but by then Parma was anxious to delay their arrival until the spring of 1587. A devastating epidemic had broken out in Burgundy, and the rains had started. A bad harvest that year added to the difficulties of collecting and storing sufficient provisions for the troops. His letters arrived too late to halt the march, however, and the troops under Manrique went first to Luxemburg and then to Namur where they were split up and used to reinforce the existing *tercios*. Precise instructions were given so as not to break up the *camaradas* — groups of friends who promised to help each other until death in war or peace. The redistribution was complete by May 1587. Some of the captains were now left without companies, and calling for satisfaction; but there was little fuss or disorder, and the captains seem to have been pacified with various diversions, promises and paid leave.

This *tercio*, which had such a brief history as a distinct unit, nevertheless made a deep impression through the areas which it passed. It was nicknamed the 'Tercio of the Saraband' due to its fine humour and penchant for guitar music. Soon the hardships of war made the men lose their joy in such pursuits. Alonso Vázquez commented 'they amused themselves as if they were in Spain, but they soon forgot the music and the dancing; the troubles and misfortunes they had to endure in Flanders left no time for such diversions.'[14]

The Spanish troops from Milan were the first of the levies to arrive. Parma put pressure on the king to send more, informing him on 22 March 1587 that

> the small number of infantry we have here is as good as any, but there are so few men that even with the new troops I can not fill a dozen companies. Many of the men have returned to Italy despite good treatment from us and our efforts to stop them deserting.[15]

The council of war in Madrid had already drawn up a detailed plan for new levies in the peninsula, recommending that up to 7,000 men (divided into twenty-eight companies of 250 each) should be raised. They calculated that after the usual losses through death and desertion this would give Parma an effective force of 6,000 infantry.[16]

As can be seen from figure 2, the council had chosen recruiting areas near to the eastern coast where troops could easily be transported by ship to Italy. In Aragon they designated lands within the kingdoms of

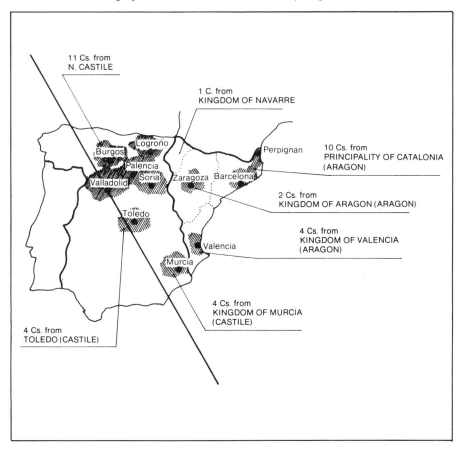

11 Cs. from
N. CASTILE

1 C. from
KINGDOM OF NAVARRE

Perpignan

10 Cs. from
PRINCIPALITY OF CATALONIA
(ARAGON)

Logroño

Burgos

Palencia

Soria   Zaragoza   Barcelona

Valladolid

2 Cs. from
KINGDOM OF ARAGON (ARAGON)

Toledo

4 Cs. from
KINGDOM OF VALENCIA
(ARAGON)

Valencia

Murcia

4 Cs. from
KINGDOM OF MURCIA
(CASTILE)

4 Cs. from
TOLEDO (CASTILE)

Recruiting areas of Spanish reinforcements for the Netherlands, 1587.

Aragon and Valencia. The principality of Cataluña was reserved for the levies of Don Luis de Queralt, a Catalan noble who had offered to raise men from his domains. The nearest Castilian province designated for levies was the kingdom of Murcia, with reasonable access to the port of Cartagena. Since more troops were needed than could be raised there, Toledo and its neighbouring villages, along with some towns of northern or Old Castile were also assigned. In the end, 19 companies went from the Castilian kingdoms: 11 from Old Castile, 4 from Toledo, 4 from Murcia; while 16 companies were sent from the Aragonese kingdoms: 2 from the kingdom of Aragon itself, 4 from Valencia and 10 from Cataluña. Navarre also contributed one company, bringing the total to

36 companies. Queralt was in command of the Catalans, and Don Antonio de Zúñiga of the rest.

The routes they followed can be seen in figure 3. The troops from Castile followed the valley of the river Ebro and embarked in Tortosa on the Genoese galleys commanded by Agabito Grillo. When they arrived in Barcelona, they were trans-shipped to the galleys of Naples. They were joined in Barcelona by the Aragonese and Navarre companies. The men from Murcia and most of the men from Toledo were taken to Cartagena where they also boarded Genoese galleys. The four companies of Valencia embarked in the port of Denia, and the Catalan troops were put on the galleys from Naples at four different ports — Salou, Palamos, Barcelona and Colibre. Weapons and ammunition were provided from the factories of Guipuzcoa, and from the stores sent up the Ebro to Barcelona by boat. Not all went smoothly. It proved more difficult than expected to raise men for the Netherlands, because at the same time troops were also being levied for the Armada. To make up numbers it proved necessary to accept some undesirable elements, including Catalan bandits, pardoned on condition of joining the army. When the viceroy of Cataluña was told that there was a possibility that these men might have to return to the principality as bad weather had made it impossible for the galleys to sail, he begged the king not to do this as it would be tantamount to 'allowing two thousand thieves to land'. Although some one thousand men short of their original total, there were still insufficient galleys to transport them. Agabito Grillo could not fit as many aboard his galleys as had been assigned, and he left a large group of men on the coast. These levies had already travelled more than one hundred leagues without proper leaders or victuals, and at the sight of the ships setting sail 'they wept'.[17]

At the end of May 1587 Philip II informed the duke of Terranova that he was increasing the number of Spanish soldiers in the Netherlands and that adequate measures should be taken for their passage. Terranova was warned to expedite these men, but he was not told why they were dispatched; and he did not seem to have guessed at this stage the real reason for the additional troop movements. He commented that it was 'sensible to take troops to Flanders as early as possible' in view of the rumours about France and their levies in Germany.[18] The Spaniards landed in Genoa as planned, and permission was obtained for their passage through Saona and Finale. But at the last minute grave difficulties arose. The duke of Savoy had granted them passage through the Mount Cenis pass, but with an epidemic ravaging his lands

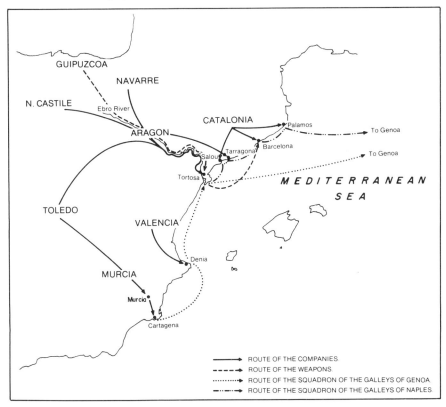

Dispatch of Spanish reinforcements to the Netherlands in 1587.

he was afraid these troops would spread it, and he informed Philip's officials they would have to change their route to the valley of Aosta and the Little St. Bernard pass. With victuals and stages already organized on the original route, all had to be changed and new stages organized.

On 20 August 1587 Don Antonio de Zúñiga landed in Saona. Five days later there was a muster which showed that there were 2,662 men distributed in seventeen companies. The soldiers had arrived in a bad condition, and all but naked. The governor of Milan distributed 800 sets of clothing among the most needy, and paid them part of their wages in cash. They were allowed to rest and refit, staying in the outskirts of Alexandria (duchy of Milan), and set out again on 6 September. Philip was still urging all speed. The troops crossed the Jura Mountains with great caution due to the proximity of protestant Swiss cantons. Having left behind the dangerous area of the Massif, they had to endure harsh weather, and inadequate provisions and resting places. They crossed into Savoy on 24 September and headed for Burgundy. They entered Lorraine on 13 October but by now their condition was pitiable. All were showing symptoms of exhaustion and falling sick at an alarming rate. Parma reported on their arrival at Namur on 14 November that 'they arrived unarmed and in rags, and so shattered that it is a dreadful sight. I do not think anyone has ever seen such misery in the [Spanish] nation. It is a pity that they should be seen in such condition, in rags, skinny and disfigured. These men will not be able to serve actively for a long time'.[19] The muster showed that fewer than 2,000 had survived, and of these 200 were sick. While the latter were distributed into hospitals, the rest were sent on to Antwerp and provided there with adequate clothing. Six hundred were chosen to garrison the castle, and the rest were distributed among the garrisons of Dendermonde, Sluys, Nieuport, Dunkirk, and Ghent.

The Catalan *tercio* set off from Lombardy on 7 October and immediately caused trouble. Don Pedro de Mendoza informed the king from Genoa that they were so indisciplined and unruly that 'I fear some disorder might occur'.[20] Although the duke of Savoy had given permission for them to cross his lands, rumours made him and his officials act very coolly as they approached. To satisfy him and to ensure his continued cooperation, the governor of Milan had to arrange compensation for all the damage caused by the troops, and promised payment for any future damage. It cost Philip II 30,000 *escudos* in compensation alone. As winter was setting in and Parma was becoming desperate to have his full complement of troops for the invasion, the speed of the march was quickened. This, together with the usual hardships of the route, caused widespread desertion. Terranova had to organise a round-up of the many deserters, calling upon Ranuccio Farnese (Parma's son), and the republic of Genoa for support. He was confident that with their help many of the Spaniards would be caught and sent on.

The Catalans had an unexpected advantage when it came to desertion. Some stopped in Burgundy 'where they spend their time stealing', Don Pedro de Mendoza informed Philip II, 'as they can speak gascon (*sic*) they can cross the frontier through Cambray and France, and no one can stop them'.[21] He enlisted the Genoese authorities to help capture the fugitives. The king was adamant that severe measures must be taken to deal with the deserters. He recommended that they should be punished, especially those who had returned from the Netherlands. Terranova had appointed a special commissioner to go and seek out the wounded from October onwards, 'so that they will not die, and to bring them to the hospital in Alexandria because, once they are well, they can serve here' [in Milan]. But the king was so concerned that others might feign sickness, remain behind and later desert, that he ordered all sick and wounded to be sent north as soon as they could march.

The men who arrived at Thionville (Luxemburg) on 12 November were exhausted from the journey and the forced marches, and suffering from the severe weather conditions. Many were sick, others had died, and their commander commented on their lack of experience in dealing with these conditions. Although Parma had stored provisions for them at the river Meuse, he feared many more of the men would succumb from epidemics and the inclement weather. He was disappointed too that there were so few men; the companies were 'thin', that is, undermanned, as well as in very bad condition. Yet he was desperate for them, and he would not allow them to remain in Luxemburg to recover. On December 7 they halted near Ypres and were given clothing and weapons. On the 21st Parma noted that they had not yet reached the billets allocated near the coast; six days later a muster was taken and revealed there were 1,900 men in eighteen companies. The journey, despite the forced pace, had taken them sixty days, that is fifteen days more than the time averaged by the previous groups.

It was initially intended to use these men to reinforce the existing *tercios*, but perhaps because of the problems they had already caused, and their distinctive origin — 'they come from a region where men are not easily separated' — it was decided to create a separate *tercio* for the Catalans. Military wits dubbed them the 'Tercio of the Spanish Walloons' because they 'spoke broken Spanish', and the 'Tercio of the Parrots' because it was said that when a Catalan tried to speak Castilian he sounded like a chattering parrot.[22]

4. Ready to Sail

Once all the additional men had arrived from Italy and Spain, the Spanish infantry passed muster. In the spring of 1588 there were 8,718 Spaniards in eighty-two companies. From these Parma selected 6,000 men from four separate tercios for the invasion force, each containing a mixture of new and experienced troops.

As disease and death took their toll of the troops, the relative strength of each 'nation' altered somewhat. For a time, in March 1588, Parma feared he would only have 17,000 men for the invasion, but the levies of local and nearby troops successfully raised the total. By mid July the whole army for England was ready. The final musters gave a total of 26-27,000 men roughly divided as follows: the 6,000 Spaniards already mentioned, 8,000 Germans, 7,000 Walloons, 3,000 Italians, 1,000 Irish and Scots, 1,000 Burgundians, and the cavalry. Although it seems at first sight that he was still three thousand short of his total, it is not the case. Philip had agreed several months earlier, that the Armada would take an additional 6,000 men to him, so that the overall force to be commanded by Parma in England was in excess of his initial demand.

The invading forces were gradually brought close to the departure points. Parma set up headquarters in Bruges, near the coast, and spent the remaining time finalising preparations and going over the invasion plans: how they would maintain contact, how they would carry out the second wave of the invasion, where it was best to land, and so on. He had brought 173 vessels to the coast from the inland areas to supplement the coastal shipping from Nieuport and Dunkirk, but even then it did not suffice for the men and the necessary provisions. Those who did not fit in would have to wait for the return of the ships transporting this first wave. The vessels were mainly shallow, open boats, good cargo vessels which required a small crew, and might take up to two hundred men each with their equipment, as long as they were tightly packed in, both above and below deck. Expecting that Spain's galleons would have control of the sea, the flotilla would sail protected only by some twenty armed flyboats or small *bergantines*. It was thought that late evening would be the best time to set sail, so as to travel overnight and land at dawn.

Parma had chosen to land in the area between Dover and Margate, which, while it was close to the headquarters of the enemy, had considerable advantages: it was a wooded area, with hedges that would give an advantage to infantry, and reduce the possible impact of English cavalry which was much feared. Additionally, the enemy was left in suspense as to which side of the Thames Parma would eventually land his infantry, thus forcing the defenders to divide their troops. Once in England, Parma would establish a bridgehead and from this fortified position ensure that communications with Flanders were maintained. It would also guarantee the second wave of invasion a safe landing place. The main body of troops would march directly on London, hoping to capture Elizabeth I and so end all resistance quickly.[23] In the meanwhile, other ports and key positions might be taken, so that they would have bargaining counters when peace negotiations started. If all went very well, a contingent of Germans and Italians might be sent to Ireland to begin a rebellion and give support to the catholics. Parma also went over alternative strategies — taking the Isle of Wight, attacking Ireland — and considering other possibilities in which, jointly with Medina Sidonia, he might have to hastily devise another plan. As he did this, news of the progress of the Armada arrived: its departure from Lisbon, its dispersal and refit at La Coruña, its new departure, and then details of the fight in the Channel. There was no time to lose.

With the Armada less than seven leagues from the Flemish frontier, Parma rode to Nieuport where he supervised the embarkation of sixteen thousand men, including the German and Italian soldiers. At dawn he went to Dunkirk to do the same. Dunkirk had been selected for the embarkation of the Spanish infantry, and they had been billeted around the coast — Don Sancho de Leiva's *tercio* in Veurne, Winox-Bergues and Diksmuide; the *tercio* of Don Juan Manrique de Lara in Ypres; that of Don Francisco de Bobadilla in Bailleul and neighbouring villages, and the Catalans in the Warneton area, near the river Lys. When they heard that the Armada was at Calais, the troops were reunited in Woumen and then marched on to Dunkirk where they commenced embarkation.

They had not quite finished when news arrived that the Armada had been dispersed by fireships. The prince of Ascoli, Marolín de Juan and Sergeant Gallinato brought the alarming news of the hasty departure from Calais; the cutting of cables and anchors; and the belated attempt of the Armada to regroup and face the English fleet, just as a great storm threatened to overwhelm them. Without ports where they might seek refuge, Parma could not at first think where the matter would end. For a few days the army was kept near the coast, embarking and disembarking at the least rumour. They looked in vain for the sails that would announce the return of the fleet. Several ships were sent to establish contact, but the *gran Armada* had run northwards before the strong winds, and was unable to return to the Channel.

Parma's bitterness and disappointment are clearly expressed in his report to Don Juan de Idiáquez, the king's secretary; he spoke of 'my sadness that I was not able to do this noble deed for His Majesty, which, as is well known, would have earned me such honour and reputation; and to see so much money and effort spent by His Majesty without achieving the success he merits'.[24] The time spent waiting for the Armada had indeed been full of anguish; and the efforts to gather

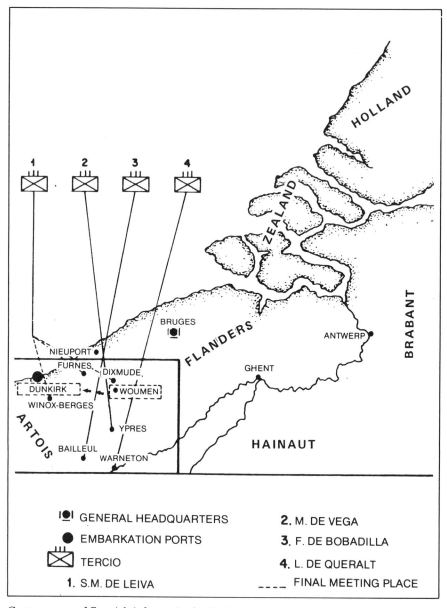

Cantonments of Spanish infantry in the Netherlands, October 1587 to August 1588.

sufficient troops had been exhausting. The forced marches of the troops, the campaigns before departure, the fearful epidemics had been harrowing; yet these men would have occasion to thank God that they did not suffer the fate of those who had embarked on the *Gran Armada*.

NOTES

1. Further details of these forces and the events in the Netherlands may be found in the following volumes from the *Gran Armada* series: H. J. O'Donnell y Duque de Estrada, *La fuerza de desembarco de la Gran Armada contra Inglaterra (1588). Su origen, organización y vicisitudes* (Madrid, 1989); G. Parente, H. O'Donnell, F. Fernández Segado, Mª-C Couceiro, Mª-A Armada, *Los sucesos de Flandes de 1588 en relación con la empresa de Inglaterra* (Madrid, 1988), F. Riaño Lozano, *Los medios navales de Alejandro Farnesio (1587–1588)* (Madrid, 1989).
2. AGS E 592 f. 98 to Philip II, 2 July 1587.
3. AGS E 590 f. 126.
4. E. Van Gelder, *Histoire des guerres civiles de Flandres* (Paris, 1620).
5. AGS E 590 f. 125 Parma to Philip, 5 April 1586.
6. A. Vázquez, *Sucesos de Flandes y Francia del tiempo de Alejandro Farnesio* in Codoin, LXXIII.
7. AGS E 596 f. 93.
8. A. Carnero, *Historia de las guerras civiles que ha habido en los estados de Flandes desde el año 1559 hasta el 1609 y las causas de la rebelion de dichos estados* (Brussels, 1625).
9. AGS E 1262 f. 26 the duke of Terranova, governor of Milan, to Philip II, 31 July 1587.
10. AGS E 592 f. 96.
11. AGS E 590 ff. 56–7.
12. AGS E 591 f. 46.
13. AGS E 104 Parma to the king, 30 Oct 1586.
14. See note 6.
15. AGS E 593 ff. 47–8.
16. AGS GA 196.
17. The *veedor* Pedro de Isunza to the king, 18 Aug 1587 AGS GA 200 f. 175.
18. AGS E 1262 f. 90.
19. AGS E 592 f. 141.
20. AGS E 1419 f. 156.
21. AGS E 592 f. 149.
22. A. Vazquez, note 6 above.
23. For further discussion of the strategy, see Adams, pp. 176–8 above.
24. AGS E 594 f. 146, 1 Jan 1589.

9

ENGLISH COMMERCE WITH SPAIN AND
THE ARMADA WAR, 1558–1603

Pauline Croft

It has usually been assumed that after Elizabeth's accession, trade between England and Spain slowly dwindled away, the decay of commercial contacts heralding the ultimate collapse of Anglo-Spanish political relations in 1585. This assumption is seriously misleading. Trade between England and Spain was already well established by 1300, and there was a rapid expansion in the later fifteenth and early sixteenth centuries. After 1540, a number of issues began to cause friction, not least religion, and a period of commercial stagnation ensued. Nevertheless after the problems of the mid-century, trade revived strongly. There were two stoppages caused by diplomatic difficulties, in 1563 and 1569, and occasional friction over increased customs dues and lading regulations, but such troubles were common to all branches of overseas commerce in the sixteenth century and should not be over-emphasised. Similarly unsettled circumstances had not prevented the expansion of the Spanish trade in the later middle ages. Likewise, although the Inquisition was a hazard unique to Spain, its pursuit of English merchants has been exaggerated, and in any case, the Muscovy and Levant trades had other difficulties at least as acute with their own host countries.[1] Hindsight has bedevilled the treatment of all aspects of Anglo-Spanish relations in the sixteenth century, and it is important to stress that in 1558, trade with Spain was in no way doomed. On the contrary, some twenty-five years of successful, even expanding commerce preceded the outbreak of privateering warfare in 1585.

On the accession of Elizabeth, English merchants trading to Spain were able to take advantage of the opportunities generated by the upsurge in the Indies trade, which inaugurated a forty-year boom. This newly-revived buoyancy followed the recession years of 1550–1559, when the temporary decline in the New World commerce of Seville had affected the Spanish economy as a whole.[2] Trade between England and Spain was still rooted in that complementarity of goods which had characterised it since the thirteenth century, but its value and significance were rising as the balance of trade was increasingly tilting in England's favour. However, the profits of merchants were already under scrutiny by both the English and Spanish monarchies as a possible source of government finance, and the upward revision of customs duties inaugurated by Lord Treasurer Winchester at the end of Mary's reign was paralleled by similar increases in Spain between 1559 and 1566. In addition, in 1561 Philip II attempted to strengthen his naval resources by reviving earlier legislation prohibiting the loading of goods in foreign vessels if Spanish ones were available.[3] More problems followed with English assistance to the Huguenots, and the growth of privateering in Biscayan and Channel waters after the outbreak of the first of the French wars of religion. English involvement in piracy was a cause of grave concern to the English mercantile communities in Spain, and as they had feared, Spain finally retaliated with an embargo on English shipping in December 1563. Over a thousand mariners and some thirty ships with their goods were affected.[4] The situation was made more serious by a subsequent breakdown of Anglo-Netherlands relations, which entailed a complete stoppage of English trade with the Low Countries, engineered by the regent Margaret of Parma on the advice of her minister Granvelle. Despite this web of inter-related problems, the situation in Spain was returning to normal by June 1564, with English ships once again loading in Seville, and between Easter and Michaelmas 1565, at least thirty-five ships sailed from London to Iberian ports.[5]

The idea of a regulated company to oversee the Spanish trade, reviving the Andalusia Company of 1530 which had fallen into disuse, was also mooted early in Elizabeth's reign. The merchants trading to southern ports suggested that by confining their commerce to San Lucar de Barrameda, at the mouth of the river Guadalquivir downstream from Seville, they could bring pressure to bear on Philip II to lower his new customs duties. Like so many towns in Spain, San Lucar did not belong to the Crown. Its lord was the duke of Medina Sidonia, who since the fifteenth century had granted special privileges to the English traders settled there. They already had a chapel, which served as their meeting-place, together with their own quayside and lodging facilities. Most important of all, the duke's customs were a mere 2½%, much lighter than those in royal ports.[6] Nothing came of the suggestions for a revived company, perhaps because after 1564 trade proceeded smoothly for some time and the need for organisation appeared less pressing.

However, in 1568 a breakdown occurred in Anglo-Portuguese relations, when King Sebastian banned English shipping in retaliation for repeated intrusions into Guinea and Barbary. As most ships sailing for southern Spain also traded en route in Portuguese ports, the dispute was an inconvenience, but Portuguese markets were still accessible from Spanish ports such as Vigo and Bayona in Galicia, and Ayamonte.[7] Unfortunately, at the end of 1568 the confiscation of the duke of Alba's payships brought Elizabeth and Philip II into direct conflict. Whatever the truth of this complex episode, it posed serious problems for merchants. Initially Philip balked at full-scale retaliation, imposing an embargo only in Seville and on the north coast. However, when it became clear that Elizabeth would neither return the money nor enter into negotiations, the embargo orders were made permanent and general. The whole of the Iberian coastline was now closed to English merchants.[8] Illicit trade at once grew up, and helped to lessen the impact of the stoppage, but the announcement of the official opening of Spanish ports in April 1573, the first move towards a settlement, was widely welcomed in London.

In the face of dissension within the privy council, Burghley had shown particular concern over commerce, seeing the restoration of the old Anglo-Burgundian alliance, which dated from the fifteenth century, as the most natural course for English diplomacy.[9] His efforts gradually bore fruit, and as legitimate trade revived so also did the proposal for a Spanish company. The merchants had collaborated on a number of occasions during the breach, selling off Spanish and Portuguese goods confiscated in England and distributing the proceeds in compensation for their own losses. With the aid of such notables as Burghley and Leicester, as well as the influential Londoner John Mershe of the Merchant Adventurers, a key organiser of the project, the company was eventually formed in 1577. It never succeeded in bringing all English merchants trading to Spain within its ranks, for the trade was always too diffuse for any effective monopoly, and opposition surfaced within London itself, where it was feared that the new organisation would cut across the extensive re-export trade between England, Spain and the Low Countries. There was also a degree of hostility in some of the outports against a London-based corporation. Nevertheless the Spanish Company served as a useful co-ordinator of mercantile efforts, mediating in commercial disputes between members, often at the request of the privy council. Its leaders administered the licensing scheme for outgoing vessels imposed in 1580 by the council, to ensure that large numbers of

English ships were not caught in the embargo expected around the time of the Spanish invasion of Portugal. The company battled for the merchants over the question of purveyance, especially the obligatory sale of Spanish wines to the royal household at artificially low prices, and opposed attempts to enforce the time-wasting system of restricted quays within the port of London.[10] Probably most important, the leaders of the company joined with the Spanish ambassador, Mendoza, after his arrival in May 1578 to protest repeatedly against the raiding of Spanish goods and territory by Drake on his Circumnavigation. The prospect of retaliation by Philip II on the great number of English ships and other valuable commercial property in Spain was a real one, and in their frequent appearances at court the merchants emphasised that, however great the windfall profits brought back by the *Golden Hind*, such gains had to be set against the regular, substantial customs revenues that would be lost if trade links were severed.[11] Here, there was a clash of economic interest at the heart of Elizabethan foreign policy, for there was a solid body of opinion in both the court and the city which disliked exploits as provocative as the Circumnavigation. Such feats appealed to adventurers and visionaries like Drake and Ralegh, who aspired to rival Spain in the New World, but on Drake's return Burghley and other courtiers refused his gifts, seeing them as the fruits of piracy. In mercantile circles the loss of lucrative and long-established trades weighed far more heavily than the dream of transatlantic expansion. The employment of many men, women and children in the manufacture of textiles for the peninsular market was another serious consideration. In July 1569, for example, during the earlier stoppage of trade, there had been widespread disturbances in Suffolk, which produced the most popular type of finished cloth sold in Iberian ports.[12]

1580 was a very tense year, with the Spanish takeover of Portugal and the landing of papal troops in Ireland after embarking from La Coruña with the permission of Philip II. Drake sailed home to a rapturous welcome and, later, a knighthood from Elizabeth. Yet despite the tensions there was no breach, thanks in no small part to the merchant lobby. They could claim some real successes, hindering the outfitting of the ships of the Portuguese pretender Dom António and bringing home to the queen and council the dangers of supporting him too openly.[13] Though he was once again trying to enforce the restrictions against loading on foreign vessels, Philip II like Burghley still yearned for the old Anglo-Burgundian alliance, and even the more aggressive

Mendoza conceded that an embargo on English ships in Spain was impossible during the crucial weeks of the vintage, when they were needed to take off the vast quantities of wine and perishable fruit exported from Andalucia.[14] For her part, Elizabeth cited the value of English mercantile property in Spain as a reason for restraint in England's dealings both with the rebel Dutch in 1577 and later with Henry III. She returned to the issue again in explaining why she could not afford to provoke Philip by joining the French Terceira project in support of Dom António. English commercial links with both the Iberian peninsula and the Atlantic islands remained a major consideration for the privy council. In 1584 Philip II for his part confirmed the privileges of English merchants trading to Portugal.[15] Yet as England ws inexorably drawn into the Low Countries conflict, both monarchs found themselves struggling with forces beyond there control. Meanwhile, the division was widening between those merchants who were still committed to peaceful trade and a working relationship with the empire of Philip II, and those who saw greater opportunities in a policy of hostilities. The merchants trading to Spain and Portugal were probably more aware than any other group of the riches that could be gained by direct contact with the New World and the East Indies. The majority of them still shunned confrontation, but the lure of both privateering and armed incursion into the Spanish overseas dominions was strong. Every merchant with a grievance against the Spanish authorities could turn to Dom António for a privateering licence, to recoup his losses by raiding Iberian shipping. By 1582 at least eleven English vessels were sailing under the pretender's flag.[16] The growing division in the ranks of the commercial community was making the efforts of the company lobby for peace less effective, especially after the gradual collapse of Mendoza's embassy in 1582. Nevertheless trade continued, and the merchants told the ambassador that they had never been so well received in Spain, nor ever made such great profits on goods and freight, as in the preceding eighteen months. The years between 1578 and 1585, and most particularly 1584–85, were a period of exceptional prosperity in the Indies trade of Seville, from which English merchants must have benefited; the buoyancy of the Andalucian market would have encouraged them to continue trading there despite the growing friction in Anglo-Spanish relations.[17]

In the autumn of 1584, as the privy council debated the possibility of an open alliance with the Dutch rebels after the assassination of William the Silent, a survey of the previous year's trade in the ports of

London, Bristol and Southampton was carried out for Burghley. It confirmed the large number of English ships sailing regularly to and from Iberian ports, and the great quantity and value of their cargoes. In addition to the usual exports, the spring of 1585 saw an increase in the number of ships sailing for Spain with cargoes of wheat, since Philip II had guaranteed their welcome after a poor harvest.[18] English ships were still coming into Spanish ports and the established English community of resident factors and agents was still continuing to trade, when late in May 1585 an embargo was ordered of all English, Dutch, German and Hanse shipping. This may in part reflect the particular irritation of Philip II against the first two groups, but the inclusion of the others indicates that the embargo was not part of any clearly articulated foreign policy measures undertaken with respect to the Low Countries.[19] Temporary embargoes were in any case a commonplace in Spanish ports, and this one was apparently intended to commandeer vessels for the squadron assembling in Lisbon under Santa Cruz to escort the New World fleet home. The French were excluded only on the grounds that their ships were too small. Although the international situation was fraught, there is no evidence whatsoever that Spain intended the stoppage as the first stage of hostilities with Elizabeth. In the summer of 1585 Philip had no thought of amassing his naval forces for an assault on England.[20] However, the impact of the embargo on English commercial opinion was devastating. Those merchants still arguing for the continuance of legitimate trade found the ground cut from under their feet, and it was those who had still been trusting in the good faith of Philip II who suffered the heaviest confiscations. In Seville alone the goods of English merchants rooted out in the year after the embargo amounted to £29,277–12s. 10d., three-quarters of the losses for all Spain in the earlier embargo of 1569 and eloquent testimony to the subsequent growth in trade.[21]

In July 1585 the privy council authorised the issue of letters of reprisal to those who could prove losses in Spain. All too soon, the Admiralty procedure deteriorated into the simple purchase of a permit to prey on Iberian shipping, regardless of personal injury. The legitimate merchants were themselves soon overwhelmed by a ragbag fleet of pirates, gentlemen voluntaries eager for action in the protestant cause, and those attracted by the idea of easy spoils. By the summer of 1585 England was waging an undeclared but effective sea war against Spain. The embargo of May had given a perfect cover to all those in England who wanted hostilities, for whatever reason. It precipitated English action at sea, at a time when Philip II had not intended any open conflict. Although other developments such as the treaty of Joinville were also alarming those on the English privy council who urged an alliance with the Dutch, the sequestration of English shipping in Spain silenced the last English voices for peace. It proved a crucial stage in urging the queen and her advisers down the road to war.[22] Since the evidence indicates that at the time Philip II had not attached any particular importance to his orders for an embargo, it must stand as one of the major misjudgements of international relations in the later sixteenth century. Even worse, the dramatic escape of the London vessel the *Primrose* from Portugalete, with the *teniente-corregidor* of Biscay on board, still carrying the royal orders for the confiscation of the ship, made it impossible for Philip to lift the embargo. He was enraged at English temerity, seen as a direct attack on the royal authority, and thereafter although the restraint was lifted for the Germans and the Hanse, it was applied with particular harshness to those English merchants still in Spain. Drake's assault on Vigo and Bayona widened the breach further. By December, preparations for a campaign began to get under way, though ironically many of the sequestered English vessels were left rotting in creeks rather than adding to Spain's naval strength.[23]

For the English merchants trading to Spain, the embargo was of course a disaster, and the following two years saw a major slump in the export trades, to which the loss of Iberian markets greatly contributed. By May 1586, the Spanish Company had virtually ceased to function. Many of its members switched their attention to privateering, and several made spectacular profits.[24] However, the decline of the company, and the cessation of official trade, did not mean the end of commercial contacts. Illicit and irregular trade sprang up as promptly as it had done after the previous stoppage of 1569, and over the war years it flourished, keeping alive those contacts that had been forged before 1585 and supplying both Spanish and English markets with each other's goods. Only three years after the Armada, there were demands in Seville for the return of unfettered trade with England.[25] By 1598, the prospect of re-entering the lucrative Spanish and Portuguese markets was one of the main considerations inclining the English privy council to peace. Customs revenues would increase, and the hope of much safer passage through the straits of Gibraltar attracted the merchants trading with Italy, Barbary and the Levant, all areas of commercial growth. As the war drew to a close with the accession of James I, open trade at once resumed without waiting for the formalities of the treaty of London. Commercial considerations formed a major part of the negotiations for the treaty, and although free access to the New World could not be prised out of Philip III, the conclusion of the peace in summer 1604 was regarded as highly satisfactory by its chief negotiator, Robert Cecil.[26] Restored to their old vigour, the Iberian trades were to lead the way in the English commercial resurgence which marked the early years of the seventeenth century, especially with the export of the new draperies. The economies of England and Spain were sufficiently complementary to generate a substantial volume of commerce. From a long-term mercantile point of view, the embargo of 1585 and even the Armada itself had proved little more than a temporary interruption in a vigorous commercial relationship that stretched back into the middle ages and was to rise to new heights· of prosperity in the later seventeenth and early eighteenth centuries.[27]

Any outline of the chronology of Anglo-Spanish trade must be filled in by an analysis of its structure. In the opening years of Elizabeth's reign, the export of woollen textiles was the dominant feature of English commerce. By far the greatest port of destination was Antwerp, which took 65% of London's cloth, and overall the dominions of Philip II absorbed an astonishing 79% of London's chief export. In return there came a great variety of goods, since Antwerp was the entrepot of northern Europe. There was also a lively trade between London and other Low Countries ports, such as Flushing and Amsterdam, and frequent contact with the Baltic cities of Hamburg and Danzig. Trade with France, especially the ports of Rouen and Bordeaux, was very substantial, with around two hundred cargoes a year coming into London worth around 22% of the capital's imports. Trade with Spain and Portugal was not quite so frequent, with around seventy cargoes annually, but the vessels themselves were larger and the cargoes often more valuable. A minimum of 11% of London's import trade came from Spain. Moreover the Iberian trade of the outports, especially Bristol, was notably vigorous.[28]

Trade with Spain shared the general characteristics of English trade as a whole, with exports composed very largely of various types of cloth. Iberian ports took just under 10% of London's direct cloth exports, and the figure would be larger if re-exports of English textiles to Spain and Portugal from Antwerp could be calculated. However, the textiles sold in Spain and Portugal had always been dyed and finished in England, unlike the unfinished cloths exported to Antwerp, and in consequence, the Spanish trade provided additional employment in the clothing counties. Smaller quantities of goods such as west-country tin and lead, and some re-exports such as Eastland wax, French canvas or German linens broadened the range of items sold by English merchants in Spanish ports. In return, there came largely agricultural products such as wine, oil, and fruit, together with raw materials like iron and fine wool. Within this overall pattern, however, there were two distinct areas of trade. On the one hand there was the north coast, its commerce centred on San Sebastian, Santander and Bilbao. Linked to these ports by coastal trade but forming a virtually separate market were the ports of Galicia, especially Bayona and Vigo which also had extensive contacts with northern Portugal. On the other hand, and more important, were the ports of Andalucia, above all San Lucar de Barrameda and Seville. Steadily increasing in significance were the ports of the western Mediterranean, headed by Malaga. Although most trading voyages concentrated on one coast or the other, north and south were not commercially isolated, for ships sailing to Andalucia frequently called in at Bilbao, San Sebastian or Lisbon, to take on fresh supplies and sell off the first part of their cargo. Similarly some vessels on their return journey up from the south would call again in Lisbon or on the north coast and bring back cargoes from most of their ports of call. It was presumably with such long coastal voyages in mind that the officials listing vessels taking on cargo in the port of London gave their destination simply as 'Hispania'.[29]

Evidence for the decade after 1558 shows that English cargoes to the north coast were made up of finished cloths, especially Suffolks, heavy broadcloths of coarse wool dyed in a range of blue tones which found their chief overseas markets in northern Spain and Portugal. Hampshire and northern kerseys (lighter fabrics dyed in various colours) were also popular. The coarse heavy cloths known as Bridgewaters had been sold in Spain since the middle ages, as had dozens, a white kersey usually made either in Devon or the north. Manchester and Welsh cottons, actually a light woollen cloth, were just beginning to penetrate the Iberian market, but were regarded as the bottom of the range, often used as wrappers for more valuable textiles. The most common re-export brought to the north coast of Spain on English vessels was wax from the Baltic.[30] The Cantabrian coastal strip, frequently short of foodstuffs, also received corn and victuals such as butter, herrings and pilchards, mostly from the English outports, a trade which hovered on the fringes of legality since exports of these commodities were in theory only allowed under licence, when prices at home were low. The main return cargoes were iron from Biscay, fine wool, and 'train oil'. Some of this oil was brought back by the whaling fleet from Iceland or Newfoundland, and some came from cod fished in north Atlantic waters, where the Basques still predominated. In addition, English merchants bought occasional quantities of pitch, resin, liquorice, and lamb budges — skins with the wool dressed outwards — together with consignments of felt hats made of Spanish wool. The Galician coast, lacking the commodities of San Sebastian and Bilbao, exported a few goods of slight value, chiefly Ribadavia wines and huge quantities of oranges and lemons, shipped to England in their thousands and presumably originating in the Algarve or Andalucia. These perhaps came up to Galicia as return cargoes in the Spanish coastal trade. 'Great onions twelve or thirteen inches in circumference', and walnut and chestnut boards, plentiful and cheap, were also loaded at Villaviciosa.[31]

Many features of this trading pattern were repeated on a more substantial scale in the south. A few Suffolks were shipped, though heavy cloths were less saleable in Andalucia. English kerseys were popular there, especially the finer kinds. In general the southern ports would only take quality textiles, and many high-grade kerseys were shipped on the Indies fleets to the New World.[32] Pipestaves for wine barrels, sometimes from Ireland, were sold by English merchants, and landowners such as the earl of Leicester had interests in the pipestave trade.[33] In exchange the south coast had far more to offer than the north. Seville was the centre of the richest area of Spain, producing enormous quantities of olive oil, both sweet oil for cooking and thick oil for milling cloth. Wine was extensively purchased, above all sack, and after the vintage, ships carrying nothing but tuns of sack were unloaded in London and Bristol. Bastards, a sweet wine, and other varieties such as cuit — wine boiled down to a syrupy consistency — were also in demand. Wine was the biggest single commodity coming into London at the beginning of Elizabeth's reign, worth over £68,400 or more than 10% of the total import bill, and although French wine was even more popular, the amount of sack and bastard shipped from Andalucia totalled over £23,000.[34] Fruit was also exported in quantity. Malaga was the centre of the raisin trade, and great raisins, 'raisins of the sun' (sun-dried), and raisins 'de lixa' (boiled in a preservative solution of lixivium of lee) filled whole ships. Figs, almonds, olives, capers and aniseed were also sent to England. Together with the thousands of oranges and lemons coming from the north coast, Spanish fruit made a notable contribution to the health of cities such as London and Bristol, or at least of their upper and middling classes. Other commodities shipped in smaller quantities included Spanish skins for fine quality leather, woven hand baskets, and cork. Spanish taffeta and satin, and coloured sewing silks, came from the silk weaving industry of Granada along with a few expensive items such as silk hose and garters. New World goods could also be found in the south — luxuries such as potatoes, sugar, and cochineal, and exotic rarities like parrots and turkeys. Far Eastern spices such as mace, cinnamon, cloves and pepper were also shipped to London, probably transshipped to Andalucia from Lisbon, but since as yet all these items were more easily available in Antwerp, the need to go south for them was less pressing.[35]

The evidence for the 1560s all indicates that despite periodic disturbances there was a vigorous and varied commerce between England and Spain. During the stoppage of 1569–73, only clandestine or indirect trade took place, but by 1576, the port-book evidence indicates not only that commerce had fully recovered, but that an increasing range of products was being exported. Bays begin to feature prominently in textile shipments to both the north and south coasts. These were types of cloths usually classed among the new draperies; lighter, dyed fabrics which were well suited to the Spanish market, which looked for a wide variety of colours. The export of Manchester and Welsh cottons had greatly increased, with 4,658 goads going mainly to Galicia. As Chester and Liverpool were also exporting Manchester cottons in substantial quantities to the north coast, it is clear that they had rapidly found their market. Hides and calfskins were also sent to both Biscay and Andalucia in large quantities, especially to Bilbao. Tar, lead, tarred ropes, cables and hawsers along with some pewter also went to the north, while Seville and San Lucar imported pewter, iron wire, nails, pins, coppeware, candlesticks and tin from England. The greater range of re-exported textiles on English ships is also notable, with white Normandy canvas, brown and white Holland cloth, moccadoes and chambletts, jeane fustians (originally from Genoa but subsequently made in the Low Countries), and Hondschoot says, another new drapery.[36]

The expansion in the range of goods exported continued over the next eight years, as can be seen from the surveys drawn up in autumn 1584. The new draperies were being shipped to Spain in increasing quantities.

Single and double bays and friezes were popular, while English-made says had joined those from the Low Countries. The rise of the new draperies by 1584 shows that the key development of the early seventeenth century, when the textiles created a boom in the Spanish trade, was well under way before the outbreak of war. Similarly, it is possible to trace the beginnings of the trade in knitted hosiery, another product later to be exported from England in greatly increasing quantities. Kersey stockings, the older style of cheap hose cut out of fabric on the bias rather than knitted, are listed in 1576, and kersey stockings continued to be sold in Spain after the market for them had all but disappeared elsewhere. Alongside these, however, can be found small shipments of knitted stockings, superior in fit and comfort; the more expensive new type of worsted stockings both long and short; and the most expensive, fine jersey stockings. The same pattern is visible in the export lists for 1584. Although as yet the quantities of hosiery were relatively insignificant, they indicate that, as with the new draperies, English exporters were already experimenting before 1585 with an item which after the war would prove very saleable in Iberian markets.[37]

There are also some remarkably varied cargoes, with small looking glasses, packthread, 'writing tables' (probably tablets), brushes, crewel lace, hooks and eyes, beeregar (vinegar), aqua vitae, Hallamshire knives, iron backs for chimneys, and reams of paper all listed. The knives signal the rise of the Sheffield cutlery trade, but in most cases there is no indication which goods are English products and which re-exports. Clearly the English share of the re-export trade was increasing. If some at least of the items were English-made, they are testimony to that diversification of manufactures which was steadily taking place. As for imports, it is noticeable by 1584 that with the collapse of Antwerp in the wake of the Dutch revolt, the direct trade in spices between Lisbon and London had greatly increased, with large quantities of pepper, mace, cloves and cinnamon coming in from the Portuguese empire. Where the imports are of the same commodities, most seem to have increased in quantity by the 1580s, as with fine Spanish wool.[38]

It has already been noted that the English textiles sold in Spain were already dyed and finished, unlike those exported to the Low Countries. Not only did the Spanish trade generate employment in the clothing counties, but also, a study of the imports from Spain from 1558 onwards reveals that many items were crucial in the development of the English textile industry. Spanish wool was increasingly important as shortages of high quality wool in England became more pronounced. It was mixed with coarser native varieties to improve the final product, and the manufacture of this so-called 'Spanish cloth' was to grow very rapidly in the early seventeenth century. The process was already beginning in Elizabeth's reign. There was a sharp increase in imports of Spanish wool in 1575, and the steadily rising import from the north coast is apparent by 1584.[39] Even more vital was olive oil, better and easier to use than butter or fat in preparing raw wool for carding. Although not the sole producer, Spain was by far the largest, as is evident from the early Tudor treatise 'concerning the Staple' which bemoaned England's crucial dependence on Spanish oil. Oil estimated at £38,020 was brought into London as early as 1559–60, the single most expensive commodity apart from wines and canvas, and although presumably not all of it was Spanish, and some was edible rather than industrial, the figure illustrates the major significance of oil in the import trade.[40]

Another vital group of imports included Spanish dyes and mordaunts, used to prepare the yarn or the woven cloth to take colour. Although cochineal reached Spain as early as 1526, its increasing importance in English dyeing was only apparent in the 1570s when large-scale import was taking place. Its growing popularity is evident from the quantities listed in 1583–4. With ten times the colouring power of kermes, the previously used dye for red cloth, it was much in demand and its high value and low bulk attracted the attention of the notorious Elizabethan monopolist William Typper, who had previously attempted to profit from Anglo-Spanish trade by obtaining a highly unpopular patent covering the accommodation of foreign merchants. Typper's scheme to take over the import of cochineal provoked an indignant counter-attack by the Spanish Company, which also made a firm statement of the value of cochineal to English cloth manufacture. The projected monopoly was thwarted.[41] Other dyes imported from the Iberian peninsula included Brazil wood, used as a mordaunt in such textiles as Lancashire cottons. Gall nuts and sumach, a fixative for blacks, came to England from Andalucia. Argol, a crude tartar formed in wine barrels and employed as a brightener in dyeing, came in both its red and black forms from the north coast. Green woad, another dye, came mainly from the Islands and was imported in quantity both at Bristol and London. At St. Michael's and Terceira, nothing could be sold for ready money and merchants were warned that 'you must truck your wares for green woad'.[42] Perhaps the most significant of these commodities is the one hardest to trace with any certainty. Alum, which was the most vital mordaunt used in the dyeing trade, had been mined in Murcia since the fifteenth century, but between 1560 and 1592 production at Mazarrón and elsewhere was organised in earnest. For this short period Spanish alum competed on the international market with that of Tolfa, although the production of the three main Andalucian mines never rose to more than two-thirds of the amount mined in the papal states. The quality too was generally regarded as inferior, and the absence of a suitable large port usually entailed its trans-shipment to Cadiz, which was also the entrepot for Tolfa alum. This unfortunately makes Spanish and Tolfa alum virtually indistinguishable in the port-books, and there is no description of the origin of the two shipments, each of four and a half hundredweight, brought into London from Spain in July 1568. Alum was also unloaded in Bristol, while other shipments arrived via Antwerp. Between 1566 and 1576 the Pallavicini firm acted as the monopoly contractor for both Spanish and Italian production, to be succeeded in 1581 by the customs farmer Thomas Smith. After the imposition of an extra tax on papal alum in 1581, sales of Spanish alum in England rose sharply until the boom ceased with the outbreak of war. The closure of English markets dealt a blow to Spanish alum production, and by 1592 alum mining in Castile was in decay. Thereafter England became increasingly self-sufficient, but it should not be forgotten that for a brief period, Spanish alum had found its chief market among English dyers.[43]

The imports of fine wool, oil, dyes and mordaunts all bear witness to the great value of the Spanish trade in providing commodities that in turn helped increase the value of English textiles, by permitting them to be finished at home before export. The dyeing trade is still obscure, but the imports of dyes from Spain, and the sales of coloured English cloth in Iberian markets, indicate that England derived a double economic benefit. Textile exports supported the return of commodities which facilitated the steadily increasing sophistication of cloth manufacture in England. In consequence the opportunities for skilled employment increased, as did the attractiveness, and hence the sale price, of the items exported.

The evidence for Anglo-Spanish trade most often concerns London, and there can be little doubt that the bulk of goods to and from the Iberian peninsula went via the capital, though sometimes in outport shipping. The great merchants of the trade were inevitably concentrated there, and the Spanish Company was viewed both in Elizabeth's reign and after 1603 as an instrument of metropolitan domination. However, the opposition to the Spanish Company is in itself evidence of the vital interest of the outports in the Spanish trade.[44] The surveys of autumn 1584 focussed on Bristol and Southampton, both ports having been involved in Iberian commerce since at least the thirteenth century. Many Bristol merchants had served part of their apprenticeship in Spain, mostly on the north coast, and the trade was crucial to the town's prosperity. Fifty-seven cargoes from Spain and Portugal were unloaded in Bristol between autumn 1583 and autumn 1584, while Southampton received eighteen. The list of imports in both cases shows a pattern very similar to London. Sack was the single most popular item, along with oil, figs and raisins from Andalucia. Train oil, iron, liquorice, oranges and lemons came from the north coast, with pepper and spices from Lisbon. Bristol conducted a thriving trade in Portuguese and Spanish salt, uncommon among London imports. Salt was essential for multifarious domestic uses including the preservation of meat through the winter. As civil disorder in France disrupted access to the salt of Bourgneuf, which had previously supplied the English market, the quantities imported from Iberian centres of production rose steadily, despite English efforts to increase home manufacture. Portuguese salt, which seems to have been the more popular variety, came from Setubal, while the chief outlet in Andalucia was Bonanza, a small anchorage within the bar of San Lucar. The combination cargo of sack, oil and salt was common on Bristol ships, and some of the vessels were large ones. The *Golden Lion*, which sank with her cargo of oil and salt in 1579, blocked the tidal channel at Bristol for over a year.[45]

Over the same period of 1583–84, sixty-seven cargoes went out from Bristol to Iberian ports. Textiles included Somerset coloured broadcloth, kerseys and graziers (cheap bays), along with cottons and dozens. Wheat, wax, lead from the mines of Mendip, and charcoal were also exported. Wheat was a particularly common cargo in 1583–84 with successive bad harvests in Spain. Bristol participated vigorously in Iberian trade, which appears to have been much more lucrative than the town's other main commerce, that with France. Inevitably Bristol was hard hit by the outbreak of war. As the Merchant Venturers later complained, before 1585 they had had 'a free and daily traffic with Spain, whereby ensured great riches and much employment of shipping', and they told the privy council early in the seventeenth century that whereas 'thirty tall barks' had been employed in the Spanish trade, now they had only 'eight or ten small ships'. Although illicit trade from Bristol and many other West-Country outports continued throughout the war years it could not employ the capital and tonnage of legitimate trade. Southampton and Exeter suffered too, while Liverpool which had just begun to expand rapidly, found its thriving trade in Manchester cottons totally cut off, since it had concentrated on the Spanish market.[46]

The great value of English trade to and from Spain before 1585 is beyond dispute. For merchants, profits must have increased between 1558 and 1585, since the burden of customs duties, at least in England, grew significantly lighter as inflation eroded the valuations in the book of rates. For the English crown, increasing trade brought in increasing customs dues, despite the impact of inflation. Moreover of all England's main markets in the 1560s, only Spain could be said with any confidence to offer favourable terms of trade.[47] The terms grew probably even more favourable over the next twenty years of increasing commerce. However, the precise nature and degree of its value calls for further discussion. One outstanding feature is that the trade was overwhelmingly conducted in English vessels by English merchants. All thirty-five ships carrying cloth exported by Englishmen from London between Easter and Michaelmas 1565 were registered in English ports, twenty-six of them in London. This was a boom period after the earlier stoppage and it is remarkable that even with such a large number of shipments, there was no use of alien vessels in the Spanish trade. Similarly all the goods imported direct from Spain and Portugal into London in 1567–68 came in English ships. In consequence the profits of freight charges went to English shipowners, and plentiful employment and training were available for English seamen. The evidence for 1567–68, an uninterrupted and well-documented year, indicates that English ships returning from Spain and Portugal amounted to nearly a quarter of the total English tonnage coming into the port of London.[48] In the 1580s, as both Cardinal Granvelle and the ambassador Mendoza acknowledged, goods transported between England and Spain were virtually all carried in English bottoms, with the exception of a handful of Low Countries ships. Mendoza informed Philip II that increasing exports to Spain were a major cause of the expansion of English shipping in the 1570s, and English dominance can be seen in the surveys of 1584. No Spanish ships were noted in either Bristol or Southampton, and only one, the *Santa Barbara* of Laredo, in London. The English maritime monopoly was to be vividly illustrated in 1588, when the lack of Spanish pilots with recent experience in Channel waters was a problem for the Armada.[49] The additional value of the Spanish trade can be seen by contrasting it with that between England and the Low Countries, in which vessels from Antwerp, Amsterdam, Dordrecht, Flushing and

Haarlem were all prominent, with a consequent drain abroad of freight charges and insurance costs, and less employment for Englishmen.[50]

There were other advantages. English vessels in the north sea trade were usually very small, unsuited to longer voyages or for naval purposes. This was not the case with ships sailing to Spain. The Andalucia trade in particular demanded larger, sturdier vessels, which further benefited native shipbuilding and increased England's maritime strength. Only four of the thirty-five ships sailing from London to Spain over the summer of 1565 were of fifty tons or less; the remainder averaged more than eighty tons. The same picture can be seen with imports. In 1567–8, the average size of English vessels entering the port of London was only 56 tons. Only sixteen English vessels coming into London in that year were above 90 tons, of which six were employed in the newly-opened Russia trade and five returned from southern Spain.[51] Between April and September 1576, twenty-five ships sailed to Spain from London, of which five, averaging 77 tons, were entered in the export port book for the north coast, and twenty for the south. Fourteen of the latter were over 90 tons, and the two largest, the *Emmanuel* of 200 tons and the *Trusty Burr* of 150 tons, were both loading for San Lucar.[52] The expansion of England's trading area to the Atlantic cod banks and the east coast of north America, and the opening of the Levant and east Indies trades — the great achievements tentatively begun in Elizabeth's reign and consolidated after 1603 — depended on the availability of larger ships, the expertise of English shipwrights in building them and the skill of English mariners in handling them. In all these areas the Spanish trade made a notable contribution, both in London and the outports. The size of Bristol's ships has already been indicated, while at Southampton, it was the participation of local merchants in the Spanish trade which prompted a remarkable increase in the average size of vessels built and used there in the 1570s.[53] Not merely English tonnage as a whole, but the most valuable sector of it, was stimulated by the flourishing Iberian trades of the years before 1585.

Just as English shipping predominated, so also English merchants enjoyed an effective monopoly of both imports and exports in the Spanish trade, and thereby also of its considerable profits. There were a handful of Spanish and Portuguese merchants resident in London as late as 1578, but the trade was overwhelmingly in the hands of denizens. Already by 1572 the London taxation lists show that of the top layer of eight exceptionally wealthy merchants, three (including Thomas Wilford the future president of the Spanish Company) were trading mainly to Spain, rather than to the markets of northern and central Europe.[54] However, the Iberian trades were unusual in the extent of the number of merchants involved. Although many of the greatest London merchants participated, they never succeeded in getting much more than half of the total trade into their hands. In 1565, ninety merchants are listed of whom only thirty-four could be regarded as leading men in the City. The rest sent small parcels of goods, and many of them cannot be regarded as full-time merchants at all, but rather as the retailers, winesellers and other shopkeepers of whom the Spanish Company regularly complained after 1577. Similarly in 1576, of seventy-one merchants exporting goods, only ten sent large cargoes; the overall pattern is very diffuse. In London in the early seventeenth century, the Spanish merchants were by far the most numerous and least concentrated of any commercial group; and in the outports, where inevitably large-scale merchants were far fewer than in the capital, the range of participation was even greater. Such widespread involvement by occasional small-scale traders goes far to explain why the Spanish Company, unlike other trading companies, never succeeded in such measures as the establishment of an effective consular system in the peninsula. The maintenance payments seemed too heavy, and the likelihood of ever needing consular services too remote, to most of the merchants involved. Commercial professionals such as the lord mayor and aldermen of London found the diffusion of the Spanish trade an irritant, and to the privy council it made regulation and oversight even more difficult in a key diplomatic area. However, the consequence was that prosperity was spread far more widely. The benefits of the Spanish trade were not confined to an exclusive metropolitan clique, such as that which still controlled the Merchant Adventurers. For the outports, the trade to Spain was the most valuable to which they had access, and not only merchants but also many small-scale manufacturers of provincial goods such as Manchester cottons, Tenby friezes and Somerset broadcloth benefited from local shipment, escaping the additional transport costs and inconvenience of trading through the capital.[55]

In assessing profitability there is also the question of re-exports. How much of the cargo sent from England came from elsewhere in Europe? The London port-books indicate that large quantities of goods were of non-English origin. Between Easter and Michaelmas 1576, some 45% of the trade to the north coast, in commodities other than broadcloth, was in re-exports, and some 42% of the trade to the south coast.[56] In November 1574, as plans were being made for the formation of a Spanish Company, there was strong opposition from a group headed by the leading aldermen Thomas Pullyson, Thomas Starkey and Anthony Gamage, whose commerce with Spain largely consisted of re-exports from Flanders, Hamburg and Emden, brought back to England to balance their trade as Merchant Adventurers. They were fearful that the terms of the proposed charter would restrict membership to those not already free of another trading company. If they were excluded, they told the privy council, the consequence would inevitably be that Flemish, Spanish and French merchants would take over the re-export trade, 'without bringing any of the same into this realm, to the great hindrance of the navigation . . . and the great diminishing of her majesty's customs'.[57] A compromise was finally worked out, whereby the merchants concerned were admitted into the Spanish Company while retaining their membership of the Merchant Adventurers, a concession which testifies to the influence of the re-export merchants. Further evidence comes from the papers of William Typper, who in arguing for a monopoly over cochineal asserted that the greater part of the Spanish trade was composed of re-exports. The argument must have had at least some plausibility, for Typper knew his way around the City of London. The importance of the re-export interest was underlined again in 1604. Asked to give an account of their trade before the war, the London merchants listed for the privy council the goods 'most vendible in Spain and needful for the West Indies', bought in exchange for English cloth sold in 'Russia, Eastland, Stade, Hamburgh and other parts of Germany, as also out of France'. These re-shipments to Spain included wax, tallow, hemp, cordage, copper, flax, linen cloth and canvas 'of all sorts and in great quantity', ironmongery from Germany, haberdashery, and battery for pans and kettles. In the last quarter of 1604 as legitimate trade rapidly got under way, these goods formed over half the total of non-broadcloth exports to Spain, in a pattern very similar to that of 1576, with wax and canvas the major items.[58]

In addition to re-exports through London, there was a sizeable volume of indirect trade which never entered English ports but which was nevertheless handled by Englishmen. Until the late 1570s, several major merchants continued to ship goods to Spain from Antwerp, a relic of the days only recently over when it had been the greatest European entrepot. Moreover the trade between England the Low Countries and Spain received a temporary fillip when the dangerous activities of the Sea-Beggars and other pirates led many catholic merchants to withdraw from Netherlands trade, leaving a vacuum which Londoners were briefly able to fill. Sir James Hawes, probably the leading merchant trading to Spain in the 1570s, had partners in Antwerp linked with agents in Seville, forming a network of factors and agents which covered most of the peninsula.[59] Hawes had been called on to mediate in the dispute over re-exports apparently settled in 1577, but in 1579 a further conflict broke out. This time it was within the Merchant Adventurers themselves, between those whose trade lay in shipping goods back to England and those who shipped Hamburg and Eastland goods direct to Iberian ports. It was alleged that the latter could afford to sell off their English exports to Germany at lower prices, since they drew an additional profit from their trade to Spain. Other men were undercut, and even worse, the servants of such merchants were 'made partakers of the secrets of the commodities and reckonings of our company, whilst they make their portable provisions for Spain and other countries'. The Merchant Adventurers' fear that their secrets would be revealed surely indicates a considerable degree of price-fixing. The situation was illuminated in 1580, when a temporary stay in traffic to Hamburg brought a group of London merchants before the privy council. Led by Alderman George Bond, later lord mayor, his son William, who was a major merchant in his own right, and their partner Simon Bourman, the group pleaded for some exemption from the stay. They explained that they had long been accustomed to buy wax and other goods in Lübeck, Luneberg and other north German towns. These items were shipped in English vessels from Hamburg direct to Spain and the Levant. The privy council agreed that they might send four English ships a year to continue the trade, provided that they deposited securities of a thousand pounds on each ship not to import Hamburg goods into England nor vice versa, which it was conceived would prejudice the Merchant Adventurers' trade to Emden.[60] The ambassador Mendoza, who hated the Bonds as arch-protestants and relatives of Sir Francis Walsingham, had earlier estimated that their trade in wax sent direct from Germany to Biscay was worth around three hundred thousand crowns per annum. He thought that several other Londoners, including Sir John Spencer, operated on the same scale. The regular trade in wax to the north coast, as revealed in the port books, may well have been only a fraction of the total trade handled by the English. In November 1586 it was reported that the value of English trade with the Eastland and Muscovy had shrunk greatly, since the goods imported from thence had formerly been sent on to Spain. Illicit commerce probably kept the trade alive over the war years, and with the advent of peace, the direct shipment of copper, wax, fustians and other goods, consigned by English merchants from Muscovy and the Baltic ports to English factors in San Sebastian and Pasajes, revived promptly. By 1606 it was once again flourishing.[61]

The existence of these indirect routes indicates that Anglo-Spanish commerce was not simply bilateral. Like the Dutch, the English benefited from their strategic geographical position half-way between the trading centres of the Baltic and the Mediterranean. The attractions of the Iberian market led to a proliferation of multilateral commercial contacts, which even in the heyday of the great chartered trading companies tended to spill out beyond the artificial confines imposed by those merchants anxious to preserve a simpler, older pattern of two-way trade. A similar multilateral arrangement can be seen with the beginnings of the triangular trade in Atlantic cod in the later sixteenth century. Here the English followed on the heels of the Biscayan ships which had sailed regularly to the Newfoundland banks since at least the mid-century. By 1578, however, an English observer noted that there were now two dominant groups, the Biscayners and the English, in the miscellaneous fishing fleets that crossed the north Atlantic. English vessels bringing cod were also extending their search for markets by sailing through the straits and into the western Mediterranean. The *Parnell* of London, having triumphed over the perils of the Atlantic crossing, sank through negligence while taking her ease in the harbour of Gibraltar in 1580. Well before 1585, English merchants knew that dried Newfoundland fish, pilchards and red herring were welcome in Leghorn, Mallorca, Minorca, Barcelona, Civita Vecchia and Venice. The triangular trade conducted by ships sailing from England to the Newfoundland banks and then on to Malaga and Italy was to be one of the most prosperous of the early seventeenth century.[62]

As has already been noted, the balance of trade usually ran in England's favour, despite the wide range of goods sent back from Spain. The problem dogged all overseas Spanish commerce, and in 1558 the Burgos controller of the artillery, Luis Ortiz, submitted a report to Philip II estimating that the value of Spanish imports was some eight or ten times larger than Spanish exports.[63] As a result, the only way that surplus profits could be removed from Spain was by the export of specie, which was strictly illegal except in repayment for victuals. The increasing export of wheat to the north coast and

Andalucia as Spanish harvests failed to provide an adequate supply probably helped many English merchants to obtain export permits for at least some specie. However, there is every indication that the amount of silver carried away illegally was very large. The lure of hidden silver on vessels coming up from Spain was a major cause of piracy in the bay of Biscay and the Channel. Despite the embargo then in effect, 'great sums of ready money' were loaded for Sir James Hawes at Bayona in 1571, together with eight or nine bags of ducats for another London merchant. The *Little Mary Martin* returning from Galicia in autumn 1584 was officially freighted with oranges, lemons and argol, but was also carrying over £1000 in cash, of more value than her whole cargo. Factors took considerable risks to get bags of coin rowed out to their ships. According to Mendoza in 1578, the profits of the exports of wax to the north coast shipped back by Alderman George Bond were almost entirely returned in money. Mendoza's letters are full of references to the 'vast sums of specie' which English merchants brought back regularly from Spain. He reported in July 1581 that Bond's ship the *Solomon* had loaded forty thousand ducats on board of which only six thousand were registered when she sailed from Fuenterrabía.[64] Even allowing for a degree of indignant exaggeration, the sums were obviously substantial, though it may be that there was a particular problem on the north coast, where return cargoes were both harder to find and lower in value than the goods sent out from England. Some of the profits were redeployed elsewhere. From Bilbao and San Sebastian, English merchants conveyed 'all our moneys, both silver and gold, for the lading of our ships in Bordeaux; for the which we run great and dangerous adventures'. Spanish silver thus facilitated the Gascon wine trade. Rich and varied return cargoes were much more easily available in Andalucia, and as it was permitted under licence to export Spanish money coastwise from one port to another, some English merchants perhaps moved their profits from the north coast down to Seville. Yet even there, by the early seventeenth century the Spanish authorities were unsurprised to intercept an English ship departing with over £20,000 in specie on board.[65] Although English merchants occasionally complained that silver could be hard to find in Spain, it seems incontrovertible that their own activities in exporting it contributed to the severe copper inflation from which Castile was suffering from the end of the sixteenth century. For England, however, the influx of Spanish silver was enormously useful in widening the range of commercial activity. Few English goods were saleable in the East Indies, and London merchants testified in

1611 that from its foundation the trade had always been dependent on the re-export of silver initially earned in the Iberian trades. Without Spanish specie the mighty East India Company could never have established itself.[66]

This survey of Anglo-Spanish commerce over the years leading up to the Armada war and beyond has argued for both its economic importance and its political significance. The contribution of the Iberian trades to the growth of the English economy was extensive and varied. English goods, above all textiles, were exported, employment encouraged, and skills such as dyeing fostered by the import of vital raw materials. Shipbuilding, navigation and the upkeep of a strong merchant marine all benefited from English trade with Spain, and other branches of commerce such as the Gascon wine trade relied on the earnings of Spanish bullion by English merchants. In politics, the merchants trading to Spain joined with the Spanish ambassador Mendoza to urge the continuation of the old Anglo-Burgundian alliance. It was a policy that appealed both to the queen and Lord Burghley, and weighed against the adventurism of Drake and Hawkins. The merchants' constant lobbying in the crucial years after 1577 reminded the privy council of the continuing importance of England's economic links with the Iberian peninsula. They helped keep the peace during difficult years in which trade continued to flourish despite diplomatic tensions. The embargo of May 1585 temporarily silenced the voice of the merchant community, but the network of illicit trade which operated during the war years kept alive the contacts and expertise that allowed the rapid re-opening of the trade in 1603. England and Spain, though divided in the later sixteenth century by religion and the Dutch revolt, had strong economic interests in common, which war could disrupt only temporarily. Men who had spent their lives in trade did not see the two countries as locked inexorably in an ideological struggle. Instead they spoke for a vision of mutually beneficial Anglo-Spanish co-operation which was to re-emerge as the foundation of the foreign policy of James I.

NOTES

1. W. R. Childs, *Anglo-Castilian Trade in the later Middle Ages* (Manchester, 1978). G. Connell-Smith, *Forerunners of Drake* (1954) pp. 189–99, for the alleged decline of trade after the Reneger incident of 1545. P. Croft,

'Englishmen and the Spanish Inquisition, 1558–1625', *English Historical Review*, LXXXVII (1972) pp. 249–68.

2. P. and H. Chaunu, *Séville et l'Atlantique* (8 vols, Paris, 1955–9) VIII (i) 'Structures' and VIII (ii–ii bis) 'Conjonctures'.

3. G. D. Ramsay, *The City of London in international politics at the accession of Elizabeth Tudor* (Manchester, 1975) pp. 150–3. PRO SP 70/26/155, 176. The best account of the complexities of the Spanish customs system is by M. Ulloa, *La Hacienda Real de Castilla en el Reinado de Felipe II* (2nd ed. Madrid, 1977). See also H. Lapeyre, *Une famille de marchands: les Ruiz* (Paris, 1956) pp. 381–4.

4. Ramsay, *City of London* pp. 138–9.

5. PRO SP 70/72/384, 419. Relations with the Netherlands were not restored until November 1564. Ramsay, *City of London*, pp. 283–3. PRO E 190/2/1 (Controller of petty customs, London, Easter–Michaelmas 1565).

6. P. Croft, *The Spanish Company* (1973) pp. vii–viii. PRO SP 12/255/26, 'A special direction for diverse trades', printed in R. H. Tawney and E. Power (edd.) *Tudor Economic Documents* (3 vols. 1924) III p. 202.

7. V. M. Shillington and A. B. W. Chapman, *The commercial relations of England and Portugal* (1907) pp. 139–40, 144–5. For the difficulty in distinguishing between Spanish and Portuguese trade, see below p. 244.

8. C. Read, 'Queen Elizabeth's seizure of the Duke of Alva's payships', *Journal of Modern History* V (1933), 443–64, and for a different interpretation, G. D. Ramsay, *The Queen's Merchants and the Revolt of the Netherlands* (Manchester, 1986) pp. 91–179.

9. *CSPSp* II pp. 377–8, 417–20, 423–4, 435–6. P. Croft, 'Trading with the enemy 1585–1604', *Historical Journal* XXXII (1989) II pp. 281–302.

10. Croft, *Spanish Company*, pp. x–xxix.

11. *CSPSp* III pp. 8, 47, 130, 208–9, 283–4, 385–6.

12. *CSPSp* II p. 179; III, p. 75. For Suffolk cloth, see below p. 244.

13. *CSPSp* III pp. 71, 129–30.

14. *Ibid.*, pp. 29, 40–1, 182, 208.

15. *CSPFor* XIV, p. 234; XVII, p. 213.

16. K. R. Andrews, *Elizabethan Privateering* (Cambridge, 1964) pp. 13–18.

17. *CSPSp* III p. 283, Chaunu, *Séville* I pp. 77–88, 97–121.

18. The results of the survey are in BL Lansdowne MS 41, arts. 37–43. For wheat cargoes, PRO HCA 13 (Examinations) 26 f. 395, 27 ff. 231, 246v. The king had looked to English merchants for grain supply on previous occasions, see *CSPSp* III pp. 102, 117.

19. As suggested by Martin and Parker, p. 100.

20. PRO SP 94/1/92–v. AGS GA 180 f. 81. For further evidence that Philip did not intend the embargo to lead to war in 1585, see Adams above, p. 56, and Rodríguez-Salgado above pp. 6–7.

21. PRO SP 12/191/34, 'A note of all such goods, debts and moneys as by the

king of Spain's order was discovered by Antonio de Guevara'.

22. R. B. Wernham, *Before the Armada* (1966) pp. 372–3. Andrews, *Privateering*, pp. 3–5. See also Adams above, p. 000.

23. PRO SP 94/2/78, 12/179/28–38. AGS GA 177 ff. 114, 116, 155; GA 180 f. 125. On 23 July Philip described the escape of the *Primrose* as 'aquel delito tan grave'. AGS EK 1448 f. 25.

24. J. D. Gould, 'The crisis in the export trade, 1586–87', *English Historical Review*, XXI (1956) pp. 212–22. Andrews, *Elizabethan Privateering*, pp. 101–18.

25. Croft, 'Trading with the enemy', pp. 285–94, and Gómez-Centurión, *Comercio*, pp. 187–99. *CSPVen* VIII, p. 528.

26. PRO SP 12/266/3, 275/55. HMC, *Eighth Report Part 1* (1881), appendix, p. 95.

27. The occasional complaints of merchants are over-emphasized by H. Taylor, 'Price revolution or price revision? the English and Spanish trade after 1604', *Renaissance and Modern Studies*, XII (1968), but the port-book evidence for strong commercial growth in the southbound trades is overwhelming. F. J. Fisher, 'London's export trade in the early 17th century', *Economic History Review* 2nd ser. III (1950) pp. 151–61. J. D. McLachlan, *Trade and Peace with Old Spain 1667–1750* (Cambridge, 1940).

28. B. Dietz, 'Antwerp and London: the structure and balance of trade in the 1560s', in E. W. Ives, R. J. Knecht and J. J. Scarisbrick (edd.), *Wealth and Power in Tudor England* (1978), p. 190. For the outports see below, p. 000.

29. PRO E 190/2/1, with further evidence from 190/4/2 (imports), edited by B. Dietz, *The Port and Trade of Elizabethan London* (1972), and Dietz, 'Antwerp and London', p. 190. Vessels are entered most commonly for 'Hispania', sometimes 'Andalozia' or occasionally for two ports, like the *Bark Ellyn* for 'Vigo and Maliga'. The usual practice of sailing along the coast of Portugal with calls at Porto, Lisbon and Faro makes it impossible to treat trade with Spain and Portugal as separate entities.

30. E. Kerridge, *Textile Manufacturers in Early Modern England* (Manchester, 1985). J. M. Vanes, 'The Overseas Trade of Bristol in the 16th Century' (London University, Unpub. PhD Thesis, 1975) pp. 318–19, 330. For wax exports, see below p. 000.

31. *Tudor Economic Documents* III, pp. 200–203.

32. PRO SP 12/15/67. Probably a substantial quantity of English goods sold in Seville crossed the Atlantic, but apart from occasional comments like this one by the Merchant Adventurers there is little information, since cargoes of the *flota de Indias* do not distinguish foreign-made goods. Chaunu, *Séville*, VIII (2.1) pp. 585–8.

33. BL Cottonian MS Vespasian CVII f. 371.

34. Dietz, *Port and trade of London* also prints (pp. 152–5) two important

lists of imports, PRO SP 12/8 ff. 63–9 (1559–60) and BL Lansdowne MS 8, ff. 75–6 (1565–66). The figures for wine are on p. 155.

35. *Ibid.*, e.g. cargo listed on p. 24. PRO E 190/6/3, and HCA 13/15 f. 21v.

36. PRO E 190/6/4 (1576, overseas exports, collector of tonnage and poundage). N. Lowe, *The Lancashire textile industry in the sixteenth century* (Manchester, 1972), pp. 65–6, 75–6.

37. BL Lansdowne MS 41, arts. 39–41, 42 (London), 43 (Bristol). P. Croft, 'The rise of the English stocking export trade', *Textile History*, XVIII (1987), pp. 3–16.

38. BL Lansdowne MS 41, art. 42, esp. entries for Sept 1584. J. Thirsk, *Economic Policy and Projects: the development of a consumer society in early modern England* (Oxford, 1978).

39. BL Lansdowne MS 41, art. 35 (Southampton), 36 (Bristol), 37–8 (London). G. D. Ramsay, *The English woollen industry 1500–1750* (1982) pp. 14, 20 and Kerridge, *Textile Manufactures*, pp. 36, 148. For some quantitative estimates of the export of wool, H. Lapeyre, 'Le commerce des laines en Espagne sous Philippe II', *Bulletin de la Société d'histoire moderne*, 11e ser., LIX (1955) pp. 5–8. BL Lansdowne MS 9 art. 63 and A. M. Millard, 'Analysis of Port Books . . . 1588–1640' (London University, Unpub. PhD thesis, 1956), tables 8 and 29.

40. 'A treatise concerning the Staple and the commodities of this realme', temp. 1519–35, printed in *Tudor Economic Documents*, III p. 99. Dietz, *Port and trade of London*, p. 154. Cf. Hakluyt, VIII, p. 155.

41. BL Lansdowne MSS 41, art. 37 and 122, art. 1, 'A discourse on cochineal', where the various 'answers' present Typper's case. R. L. Lee, 'American cochineal in European commerce 1526--1625'. *Journal of Modern History* XXIII (1951) follows the Lansdowne MSS Catalogue in dating the discourse after 1597, but the document itself indicates that the conflict followed immediately after the controversy on the hosting patent of 1578. J. R. Dasent (ed.), *Acts of the Privy Council* (32 vols, 1890–1907) X pp. 378–9.

42. Dietz, *Port and trade of London*. BL Lansdowne MS 41, art. 35–8. G. Scammell, 'The English in the Atlantic Islands, c. 1450–1650', *MM*, LXXII (1986) pp. 295–317. *Tudor Economic Documents* III, p. 203.

43. L. Stone, *An Elizabethan: Sir Horatio Palavicino* (Oxford, 1956) pp. 41–64. Dietz, *Port and trade of London*, pp. 109–10. Vanes, 'Overseas trade of Bristol', p. 343. H. Keniston, *Francisco de los Cobos* (Pittsburgh, 1960) pp. 216, 242–3, 317.

44. Croft, *Spanish Company*, pp. xvii–xx, and Croft, 'Free trade and the House of Commons, 1605–6', *Economic History Review*, 2nd ser. XXVIII (1975) pp. 17–27.

45. BL Lansdowne MS 41, arts. 35–6. Vanes, 'Overseas trade of Bristol', pp. 43–4, 315–65. For the salt trade to other provincial ports, N. J. Williams,

The maritime trade of the East Anglian ports 1550–1590 (Oxford, 1988) pp. 115–17.

46. BL Lansdowne MS 41 art. 43. Vanes, 'Overseas trade of Bristol', pp. 319, 322–4, 334–7, 360. Lowe, *Lancashire textile industry*, p. 77.

47. T. S. Willan, *A Tudor Book of Rates* (Manchester, 1962) p. xxxvi. Dietz, 'Antwerp and London', p. 201.

48. PRO E 190/2/1. My calculation, based on entries catalogued in Dietz, *Port and trade of London*, counts every cargo separately since several ships made repeated voyages.

49. *CSPSp* II pp. 590, 698; III pp. 11, 19, 67, 72, 148, 308. Mendoza thought the profits of English freight from Spain in 1579–80 were around 50,000 crowns. BL Lansdowne MS 41 art. 41 (26 April 1584). For pilots see Rodríguez-Salgado above, pp. 144–5.

50. Entries in Dietz, *Port and trade of London*.

51. For a complaint in 1564 of the Low Countries shipping, 'these two day voyages twice a year where every pedlar may practice, whereby there is scant either a good mariner or a good ship maintained', see HMC *Report on the Pepys Manuscripts at Magdalene College, Cambridge* (1911) p. 39. PRO E 190/2/1. Dietz, *Port and trade of London* and 'Antwerp and London', p. 202.

52. PRO E 190/6/4.

53. J. L. Wiggs, 'The seaborne trade of Southampton in the second half of the 16th Century' (Southampton University, Unpub. MA thesis, 1955) pp. 96–101, 168–81.

54. *Acts of the Privy Council*, X pp. 378–9. Guildhall Library (London) MS 2942.

55. My calculations are from PRO E 190/2/1 and 6/4. Croft, *Spanish Company*, pp. xiv–xx. Vanes, 'Trade of Bristol', p. 337.

56. My approximate figures are taken from PRO E 190/6/4.

57. Croft, *Spanish Company*, p. xii.

58. BL Lansdowne MS 122 art. 1 PRO SP 14/8/35, 11/17, 8/36. My approximate figures are from PRO E 190/12/3 (searcher, overseas outward).

59. PRO SP 12/99/9. AGS E 88 ff. 24–110.

60. Croft, *Spanish Company* pp. xv–xvi. *Acts of the Privy Council* XI pp. 439–43.

61. *CSPSp* II pp. 590–1; III, p. 652. PRO SP 94/12 f. 128.

62. H. A. Innes, 'The rise and fall of the Spanish fishery in Newfoundland', *Transactions of the Royal Society of Canada* XXV (1931) p. 54, PRO HCA 13/42 ff. 184v–5. *Tudor Economic Documents* III p. 3.

63. J. Lynch, *Spain under the Habsburgs* (2 vols., London, 1964), I, p. 144.

64. PRO HCA 13/19 f. 428v; 21 ff. 2–22; 25 ff. 162, 234, 242, 250. *CSPSp*

III, p. 152, Croft, 'English mariners trading to Spain and Portugal, 1558–1625', *MM* LXIX (1983) pp. 255–6.

65. *Tudor Economic Documents* III, p. 205. PRO SP 94/21 ff. 141, 194. For a general discussion, C. E. Challis, 'Spanish bullion and monetary inflation in England in the later 16th century', *Journal of European Economic History* IV (1975).

66. BL Harleian MS 7020, ff. 164–5.

10

THE NEW CRUSADE: IDEOLOGY AND RELIGION IN THE ANGLO-SPANISH CONFLICT

Carlos Gómez-Centurión Jiménez

My brother Bartolo
Is going to England
To capture Drake
and kill the Queen.
He will bring me
Back from the war
a little lutheran boy
with a chain
and a little lutheran girl
for our lady grandmother.[1]

Introduction

Although the invasion of England, the so-called *empresa de Inglaterra*, was primarily the result of economic and strategic conflicts — a point unanimously asserted by hispanic and anglo-saxon historiography — early modern Europe, that *divided Europe* described in Professor Elliott's magisterial study,[2] saw the war as a titanic ideological struggle, fought out against a clearly defined religious background. It was this image of two combatants locked in a purely religious battle that gave the duel a dramatic power which the Spaniards and the English experienced with particular intensity. These religious tensions not only affected relations between England and the Spanish Monarchy, but almost the whole of Europe; and they had become progressively worse in the final decades of the sixteenth century. The shock caused by the protestant reform movement had surprised the European states at a time of great weakness, just when they were in the process of consolidating and establishing their independent sovereign status. While religious unity had been no guarantee of peace, as different states at times proved incapable of mastering their mistrust or controlling their

264

secular rivalries, religious dissent soon turned into political dissent, active or passive, in every state, and the most solid international alliances were shaken or collapsed as a result of two states adopting opposing faiths.

Europe was submerged in a long process which profoundly transformed its political life, both on a national and an international level. Religious dissent played a key role in this process, acting as a catalyst to ideological change and conflict. Old ideals struggled to rejoin the lists: the primacy of the Roman Catholic Church was once again proclaimed as it tried to recover its lost prestige and authority; but it had to wait until the counter-reformation acted as a transformer and infused it with a new life before it recovered. Similarly, the Holy Roman Empire under Charles V declared itself the ultimate authority within the *Universitas Christiana*, a claim partly taken on by his son, Philip II. The European monarchies which tended towards absolutism considered religious divisions among their subjects as a threat to royal authority, but repression also provided them with a powerful means to assert themselves. As a result, these divisions inevitably gave rise to an asphyxiating drive for orthodoxy, equally evident in the catholicism of Spain, and the lutheran and calvinist churches of other states.[3] Protonationalist sentiments were submerged in the ensuing confusion. They could be fostered by opposition to external dangers, but they tended to be overwhelmed by the religious divisions at home which created dual loyalties that set English against English, Germans against Germans and French against French.[4] Europe was going through a period which, for better or worse, we have labelled the age of religious wars.[5] The fruit of these struggles was the extreme political and social conservatism of the following century; that conservative and regulated culture which was the essence of the Baroque.[6]

1. The Enterprise of England as a Crusade

One of the reasons why Philip II was eager to present the campaign against England as a crusade against heresy was his need to secure papal aid — not just financial support, but the pope's blessing for an attack that would undoubtedly appear to the rest of Europe as mere expansion of the Spanish Monarchy.[7] Although it was clear that the truce with the Ottomans would hold, a new ecclesiastical subsidy for 2.1 million ducats was successfully negotiated in May 1585, long before the last instalments of the previous ecclesiastical concessions had been paid. This money was to be spent on the *empresa de Inglaterra*.[8] Relations between the papacy and Philip II had become increasingly strained after the election of Sixtus V, however.[9] The pope's dislike of Philip and what he stood for — Spain's preponderance in the continent — are well known. Moreover, he had good reason to distrust the Catholic King's intentions towards England. True to his interests, Philip had always tried to maintain good relations with Elizabeth I, and had never given unconditional support to the attempts to establish Mary Stuart on the English throne, because he knew she would end up as a puppet of the Guise and a follower of France. To avoid this, Philip staunchly resisted the excommunication of Elizabeth, and when it happened in 1570, he refused to allow it to be published in all his lands. Moreover he hastened to inform the English queen of his profound disapproval of this papal initiative. In the following years he systematically ignored the demands of Gregory XIII for immediate action against England, and when he finally decided to act, he had the bad luck to be confronted by the reticent and sarcastic Sixtus V, who had himself followed a policy of handling the English sovereign with kid gloves.[10]

After Mary Stuart's execution, however, Sixtus had to face reality; he could no longer ignore Philip's plans, nor oppose them. In an atmosphere soured by disputes over titles, precedence, protocol, and jurisdiction, the negotiations between the Spanish ambassador and the pope finally led to a treaty in which the pope agreed to support the campaign and to contribute a million ducats which he would pay only after the expedition had landed. Even so, Sixtus V continued to behave with great suspicion towards the Spanish plan, bemoaning the delays, and contributing to the pessimism and distrust towards the campaign that pervaded Rome.[11]

Philip II defended himself repeatedly against papal accusations, as can be seen from the correspondence with his ambassador, the count of Olivares: 'I have no ambition to acquire more kingdoms and states, nor to win reputation, since our Lord has, by his mercy, granted me so much of both that I can rest content.'[12] His biographer, Luís Cabrera de Córdoba, later absolved him from such charges too, alleging that his primary motivation was to end and avenge the hostile actions of Elizabeth and the English against the true, catholic faith. 'This war against England, although offensive in the sense that Spain did attack, was in reality defensive and just, because it was waged against those who broke the peace although no injury or offence was given; against those who lied and destroyed the catholic church and our patrimony, and who seized Mary Stuart . . . and had her decapitated by the executioner'. Cabrera de Córdoba stressed Philip's duty towards the catholics, emphasising that 'this was his primary motive for the war against England'; all the other reasons were trifles by comparison.[13]

The propaganda which appeared in the months before the fleet's departure follows the same lines as Cabrera de Córdoba's arguments. Despite the bellicose tone of many of these texts, which extolled to unreal extremes the great power of the Catholic King,[14] all the official publications on the subject aimed to inform public opinion in Spain and abroad of the issues at stake in the war, both religious and secular. The *empresa de Inglaterra*, they insist, was not an offensive or expansionist act prompted by the ambitions of a greedy monarch, but a defensive operation, and as such, aimed to preserve the endangered privileges of English subjects, and to protect the catholic church. It was unquestionably a *just* war. Consequently, Philip II is presented in these texts as a lover of peace, whose main concern is the preservation of his extensive and vulnerable empire — just as he had been at the beginning of his reign.[15] The campaign was presented as necessary to protect the interests of the Indies merchants, since it was England 'who principally disturbs this commerce';[16] as well as the Low Countries — where English intervention was fast making the dangerous Dutch cancer, fed with the men and money of Castile, fatal.[17] Moreover, as later texts acknowledge, it was also intended to protect the peninsula, especially the worst affected coastal areas of Galicia and Andalucia. This confused mesh of religious, political and economic motives accurately reflects the stormy background against which we should set the Armada campaign, and subsequent Anglo-Spanish relations.

The desire — indeed the *need* — to turn the war against England into a crusade against heresy can only be partly explained by reference to the hostility of the papacy and the other European powers. In order to mount a campaign of such extraordinary magnitude, Philip would have to be fully supported by his own subjects who would need to make the most extreme sacrifices; and above all he must have the consent of Castile. The campaign against England involved the political and strategic interests of the Spanish Monarchy, but it also served important economic interests, particularly of the mercantile community and the shipbuilding industry within Iberia. This does not mean, however, that the Castilians responded unanimously; when they finally adhered to the royal plans they did not do so unconditionally or without question.[18]

Since the publication of Professor Jover's edition of the correspondence between Charles V and his wife Isabel twenty-five years ago, we have known that the wide-ranging concerns of the emperor had not received much support from the Castilian elites, who were as suspicious of his great imperial dreams in 1530 as they had been a decade earlier. They were not very interested in a crusade against the Turks in central Europe, nor in the internal divisions of the Holy Roman Empire. While he promoted a politico-religious programme embodying traditional imperial strategies, the Castilians focused their attention on the triangle Mahon-Gibraltar-Algiers, not because of the religious proclivities of the Barbary pirates and Turks operating in this region, but because of concern for the defence of the vulnerable levantine and southern coasts. 'It could be said', notes Jover, 'that "religious matters" and "the peace of Germany" only concerned Isabel and the Castilian elites in so far as they delayed and impeded the return of Charles V "to these realms".' At the same time they continued to demonstrate deep repugnance for wars between christian princes, which were regarded, in true Erasmian spirit, as civil wars.[19]

The mid-century crisis testifies to the strength of these attitudes in Castile. The period of transition from the emperor to his son is marked by a decline in the monarchy's prestige, and by dissent against the policies of the Spanish Habsburgs.[20] It was during these years that Felipe de la Torre promoted his vision of a kingdom of peace in his *Institución de un Rey Christiano.* Torre was conscious of the repercussions that the splintering of the Holy Roman Empire could have on Castilian society and its religious life. The hostility between catholics and protestants in Europe could accelerate the process of unifying and isolating Spanish catholicism, firmly protected by the monarch and the inquisition; as well as the marginalisation of the converso minority.[21] The hopes of an era of peace which crystallised in the treaty of Cateau-Cambrésis[22] were gradually dashed, first by the rebellion in the Netherlands and the outbreak of war in France, then by England's seaborne attacks, and lastly by the incorporation of Portugal, which opened new possibilities for Philip in Europe.

In a brilliant study Professors Jover and López-Cordón have recently demonstrated how the change in Philip II's political orientation towards the north was accompanied by a change in the ideological perceptions of Spanish foreign policy, which had hitherto focused on the Mediterranean and the conflict with North Africa and the Ottomans.[23] As the cause against the infidel — with whom it was possible to negotiate and make peace — weakened, the spirit of religious militancy embodied in the concept of a crusade — 'the only enterprise generally accepted and shared in the West'[24] — far from losing its strength, was transferred with all its inspiration and force to other political conflicts. Only now there was a different enemy — heresy — and the war was in a more distant setting — the north of Europe. The heretic and the schismatic became the new common enemy; his religious dissent spelt disloyalty towards the monarch — as in the case of the Netherlands rebels[25] — and he represented the constant threat of foreign aggression — as in the case of England. It was imperative to maintain a united and solid front against this dual danger; as a result, religious unity became the corner-stone of the political structure. In contrast to the internal calamities of Germany, England, France or the Netherlands, 'where a deep political crisis occurred when the catholic church was set aside, Spain enjoyed an internal peace that was a symbol of the unity of religion and state, of the Monarchy and the true faith'.[26] The constant repetition of this image in the works of theologians, political writers and propagandists, and even in royal speeches,[27] would eventually imprint a manichaean and dual image of the continent, where southern catholicism was irrevocably committed to a confrontation with northern heterodoxy.[28]

Few could match the jesuit Francisco Suárez's feat of advocating a dominant role for the Spanish Monarchy, service to the papacy, and the unity of Christendom without becoming hopelessly entangled in contradictions.[29] Anguished by the vision — so incomprehensible to many — of a fragmented Europe, Suárez argued that the reimposition of catholicism was the only way to restore peace and unity. Justice and religion were for him the foundations of the *political* order; thus the state could justify its actions with reference to a coherent combination of juridical, political, ethical and religious ideas. The sovereign's role in this theoretical exposition was as a paladin of the church and a spiritual subject of the pope, with an obligation to preserve, impose and extend the catholic faith. Suárez's vision of war as a necessary instrument to resolve the crisis in Europe led naturally to the corollary that only a powerful and large state could guarantee the triumph of catholicism over schism. Since the Holy Roman Empire had been weakened, the Spanish Monarchy had the duty to take up the mantle, inherit its destiny, and assume the role of universal defender of the faith. This was a new concept of *Imperium*, entirely devoted to the service of Christendom.

As far as England was concerned, religion was unquestionably the primary cause for the worsening relations with the Spanish Monarchy. The change of religion in England could not be viewed solely as an internal problem; due to its geographical proximity, it threatened the Netherlands. Fear of English intervention on behalf of the Dutch rebels, and conversely, of a Spanish invasion from the Netherlands, were the two favourite spectres raised by catholic and calvinist extremists. Their constant evocation soured relations and contributed far more to the widening breach than other political and economic considerations.[30] The failure of the relatively tolerant and friendly policy pursued by the Spanish Monarchy towards England during the 1570s,[31] unleashed a process of acute frustration which finally led not only to political rupture and open military conflict, but also to a radical and definitive rejection of English religious dissent, considered as the essential, *a priori* cause of an irreconcilable antagonism between the two states. The Englishman, who had been characterised in Spain as the *merchant*, now turned into the embodiment *par excellence* of the *pirate* and *heretic*.[32]

Placed within these historical coordinates, it would be anachronistic and sterile to reopen the debate of whether Philip II's foreign policy was primarily inspired by counter-reformation ideology,[33] or solely by religious sentiments — a notion dear to our national historiography[34] — or if on the contrary, he followed a genuinely machiavellian course, guided only by 'reason of state', as his enemies (including the clerical circles in Rome opposed to his policies) persistently claimed. Professor Maravall pointed out long ago that in the process of consolidating its power, the early-modern Spanish state had — along with, but somewhat earlier than, other European states — attained a substantial level of secularisation, without losing an ounce of its religious sentiments. 'We have to accept the existence of two sectors', Maravall explained, 'the one secular, the other belonging to a religious tradition, and until relatively recently the latter predominated.'[35] In fact, Philip II — appearances notwithstanding — acted with far greater prudence than his father, or than other European sovereigns (most notably his nephew, Sebastian of Portugal) when tackling international problems fused with religious matters. This does not mean that he did not mix religion and politics when it suited him, as all contemporary monarchs and princes did.[36] In this period, when machiavellian *virtù* was practiced in all fields, catholics and protestants used religion and morality as tools to help them achieve political domination. Maravall insists that 'this practice in some ways turned religion and morality into matters that could be useful in a well-defined context; and even those who pretended to adhere to the most rigorous religious beliefs — on both sides — habitually used religion as an *instrumentum regni*, which was tantamount to nurturing within it strong secular tendencies'.[37]

Perhaps the most important reason why our perception of this reality has been distorted for so long, is the heavy utopian baggage of sixteenth-century Spanish thought, which hid or obscured the existence of a deeply rooted empirical and realistic current that can be directly traced to Machiavelli's influence in more than one instance.[38] Yet at the same point in Philip II's reign when the ecumenical utopia crystallised, and his international policy turned northwards, anti-machiavellian thought reached its apogee. With its ethical strain, and its profound preoccupation with the fusion of morality and politics, anti-machiavellian literature (in an intellectual exercise hampered by internal contradictions that often defied solution) would on occasion — for example in Ribadeneyra's works — serve as a spur to the counter-reformist activities of Philip II in Europe.[39] After 1580 Philip II and his associates were caught on the horns of a dilemma: on the one hand they made use of machiavellian political principles that were indispensable if satisfactory political results were to be achieved; and on the other, they became more and more enmeshed in an ideology with a mystical and idealised vision of the world that openly conflicted with the needs of pure, naked reason of state.[40] The resulting tension would give rise to one of the most fruitful currents of Spanish political thought in the Baroque era, tacitism (*el tacitismo*).[41]

The fact that Philip II frequently used religion in order to promote reason of state does not mean that his profound religiosity had diminished, or his fervent catholicism had cooled. At this stage of his life he was deeply concerned with death, as Pierson has noted. It seems probable therefore that he eventually became convinced that the *empresa de Inglaterra* was pleasing to God, who had commended it to him as the most powerful monarch in Christendom, so that he would bring it to a successful conclusion.[42] Ubaldini claimed that Philip's decision to invade was influenced by the exhortations of devout men.[43] Divine favour was certainly expected to smooth out all difficulties and put into the hands of his Catholic Majesty the means required to send his fleet sailing happily into northern waters — 'these are open and dangerous waters, but with the crucified Christ everything is possible', reads a note in one of the maps drawn at the time showing the route that the Spanish fleet should follow.[44]

Time and again in the months before the *Gran Armada* sailed the same arguments about the religious inspiration and motivation of the enterprise were heard. All official correspondence alludes to it whenever the campaign against England is mentioned, in order to arouse a sense of duty and urgency in all officials so that they would work to ensure the fleet was ready to sail on time. Philip II used the same language when addressing his nephew, the Archduke Albert, urging him to give his utmost attention to the Armada then gathered in Lisbon:

> The injuries committed by the English against Our Lord and their persecution of his church and flock forces His Majesty, who has a duty to defend them, to seek a remedy. This zeal and obligation, and his desire to see England — that great and ancient kingdom — once again within the catholic fold and subject to the obedience of the Church of Rome, are his principal motives. The other particular reasons for acting now are of far lesser importance.[45]

With the same care — in effect a mixture of duty and distrust — which he customarily lavished on the tiniest bureaucratic details, Philip II set to work on the Armada, giving particular attention to organising the religious rituals necessary in an expedition of this sort. On 9 February 1588 when he believed the Armada was ready to sail, the king wrote to Cardinal Quiroga asking him to organise public prayers and services:

> to beseech our Lord most earnestly for the success of the said Armada, for His greater glory and well-being, and the increase of His church. It would be very efficacious to take out the Holy Sacrament in procession, beginning with your own cathedral, then sending out the order to the whole diocese. Once the people have been moved by all this, they too will entreat Our Lord with even greater devotion and fervour to give His help and favour in our present great predicament; for the cause is His.

The jesuit Jerónimo Román de la Higuera, who cites this letter in his *Historia de la Ciudad de Toledo* tells us that Cardinal Quiroga 'ordered that this matter should be commended to God, and organised many public prayers, processions, rogations and flagellations for this expedition'.[46] All dioceses received the same instructions, with the same results, judging by the correspondence of the papal nuncio and the

Venetian ambassador. This liturgical frenzy continued during the spring and summer of 1588, renewed each two months on the orders of the ecclesiastical authorities owing to the delays in the departure of the fleet.[47] Even the Castilian *cortes* which had gathered in Madrid about this time, and had shown great reluctance towards all corporative participation in these public demonstrations of piety, finally agreed to offer a silver lamp to Our Lady of Atocha:

> costing 250 ducats inclusive of workmanship, and no more. It should be put at the front of the chapel, and should bear the arms of this realm, and a label stating that the kingdom, as represented in these *cortes*, has given this gift, and why it was given, which is to ensure the success of this fleet.[48]

A few days after writing to the archbishop of Toledo, Philip II addressed the duke of Medina Sidonia in similar terms, urging him to watch over the morals of the soldiers and sailors waiting to depart, taking care that they should behave as befitted their exalted status of soldier-crusader, called to carry out this elevated task, and to make sure that the expedition was not endangered as a result of their sins: 'Let the men on the fleet live in a christian manner; let them avoid swearing and blasphemy, and other vices which so offend God, Our Lord, that He sometimes prevents endeavours from reaching the desired end, even when they are done in His service.'[49]

As time passed, the spiritual aspects of the invasion of England became more accentuated. It was no longer merely a question of using religious arguments to justify it to the pope and the curia (who should therefore support and bless the enterprise), nor to the rest of Europe (who should therefore remain inactive and not intervene), nor even for the benefit of the Castilians (who were being asked to fill up the royal coffers). The appeal to God now had, in equal measure, elements of magical invocation and divine blackmail. It was precisely the notion of crusade which now characterised the invasion — added to the strong economic interests at stake — that ensured the Armada campaign eventually took a firm hold in the Spanish imagination and turned it into a collective enterprise. It obtained more widespread support than the conflict in the Low Countries, or the intervention in France. The publications inspired by the campaign are redolent of religious and patriotic passion, and this must have made it easier for the people to tolerate the extraordinary fiscal burden and other sacrifices demanded of them by royal officials who, week after week, seized and embargoed their goods and did not fear to stoop to bribery and corruption on occasion.

Notwithstanding the seemingly inexhaustible economic potential of Castile, there were limits and they were close to reaching them. Consequently, the impression of Spanish arrogance which emanates from the *empresa de Inglaterra* should be attributed not so much to the blindness of the Spanish government, but to their need to promote the *Gran Armada* as a truly *invincible* force and infallible expedition, in order to inspire security and confidence in their own subjects, and fear abroad. *Treme Auris Batava* was the motto in a medal minted in the Netherlands depicting a Spaniard pulling a Dutchman by the ear; the reverse showed the arms of Spain and Portugal between the pillars of Hercules, and above them a single crown with the inscription *Inmensi Tremor Oceani 1587.*[50] While the official propaganda boastfully reiterated the supposed weakness of England, the government was far from confident; they were aware of the risks they were taking, but it was a useful argument to reinforce Spain's military vocation.[51] For this reason they multiplied the parades and public statements assuring victory. Although it seems that the term *The Invincible Armada* was invented by the English after the event to enhance their success,[52] we should realise that Spanish propaganda loudly proclaimed its absolute confidence in the power of the Spanish Monarchy and its forces. As Cervantes put it at the time: 'Tell them we are so certain of triumph and glory/that Spain is already claiming victory.'[53] The vast preparations for the enterprise of England were described in manuscript and print, in prose and verse. There were lists of ships, soldiers and sailors, light and heavy artillery, victuals and all the *matériel* aboard the fleet, which had been so patiently assembled in Andalucia and Portugal to terrorise the enemy and surprise the whole of Europe.[54] Perhaps the clearest manifestation of the popular image of the Invincible Armada are the *Romances* of Juan de Mesa. These poems illustrate far better than those from more illustrious pens the vision of the Armada as a collective campaign of all the estates, cities, realms and lordships of the Monarchy for their common interests and religion, and destined for certain victory.[55]

It is likely that the *Historia eclesiástica del cisma de Inglaterra* would have sunk in the mire of mass-produced catholic anti-Elizabethan propaganda but for the enduring interest in its author, the jesuit Pedro de Ribadeneyra, and for the undeniable political and ideological opportunism that inspired this work. Published at the beginning of

1588, few works illustrate so clearly the political and religious tensions inherent in Philip II's policy towards England, and quite specifically in the episode of the Invincible Armada.[56]

Ribadeneyra informs us in the introduction how his book was inspired by the work of Nicolas Sanders.[57] Sanders' Latin manuscript had been adapted and published on two occasions already, in 1585 and 1586 by the English priests Rishton and Persons,[58] and within a few years it became one of the best known catholic works on the English reformation, with French, Italian, Portuguese, Castilian and German editions.[59] In Spain there were two separate adaptations of this work within a few months of each other, Ribadeneyra's book and Antonio de Herrera y Todesillas' *Historia de lo sucedido en Escocia e Inglaterra en cuarenta años que vivió María Estuardo, Reyna de Escocia* which appeared in 1589.[60] Neither is a straight translation; they are more like a re-working of the original, and they form part of a vast body of work, sometimes semi-clandestine, which was published around the time of the *Gran Armada*, fanned by the ardour of English catholic exiles in Spain, both in courtly circles and in the colleges and seminaries which were almost always under the protection of the jesuits.[61] They were all produced to the same immediate end — to alert Spanish public opinion to the persecution suffered by catholics in England — 'the great sufferings past and present of the christians who adhere to our holy, catholic faith' — and to contribute to the formation of a favourable climate of opinion for armed intervention against Elizabeth.[62]

Ribadeneyra justified the publication of his work by reference to the general interest and curiosity awakened by the English reformation and the persecution of catholics, but he also put particular stress on two other factors: 'first, I am a Spaniard; second, I am a member of the Society of Jesus'. It is precisely his ardent promotion of the affinity of interests of the catholic Church, the Spanish Monarchy, and the Society of Jesus, which makes Ribadeneyra's *Historia eclesiástica* far more interests of the Catholic Church, the Spanish Monarchy, and the Society desirable, cooperation between Sixtus V, Philip II and the jesuits was far from real. But for Ribadeneyra the restoration of catholicism in England was so important it could overcome the internal problems of the Society of Jesus and even the disputes between Philip II and Sixtus V. His letter to Cardinal Quiroga in 1587 shows he was fully conscious of the importance of the moment, and of the key role of the Jesuits in the battle against English protestantism: 'the queen of England fears, hates and persecutes the Jesuits above all others'.[63] It is not surprising therefore that in his eagerness to contribute to the *empresa de Inglaterra* he should have produced his adaptation of Sanders's book so quickly.[64]

Ribadeneyra begins with the premise that Islam, the traditional enemy, has been replaced by another much more powerful and daring enemy acting from within christendom. In his work, England has been transmuted into the origin of all present evils: it is the bastion of infernal heresy and the base from which attacks are launched against the Spanish Monarchy and other catholic powers. 'If she is wicked towards God, to whom will she be merciful? If she can show such tyranny towards the saints in heaven, who can be sure of her on earth?'[65] Faced with such a threat there was only one solution: to act decisively, to crush the serpent, destroy the temple of heresy and free the world from the evil unleashed by this satanic beast. This task, according to Ribadeneyra, rightly belonged to Spain and her monarch, because 'it will be no less honour for Spain to throw the devil out of England, than it was to cast him out of the Indies, where he was worshipped and adored before the Word was preached there.'[66] It was imperative, however, that this godly mission should be carried out for purely religious ends, and not out of political and economic interests. The war with England must be above all a *crusade*: 'not only to ensure our defence, and to prevent English corsairs from infesting our seas and robbing our fleets — although these are just but less important aims — but to glorify God and to advance His holy church.'[67] Ribadeneyra was aware of the contradictory motives for sending that Most Happy Fleet now ready to sail from Lisbon. His desire was to restore the primacy of divine over human motives and this is brought out most clearly in the final sentence of his book, which touches upon the distinction between the concepts of *true* and *false* reason of state — further developed in his later works. He was not alone in having scruples about the reasons for sending the Armada; nor was he the only one who tried to focus the campaign away from a 'material' motivation towards more elevated aims. Fray Antonio de la Concepción, a benedictine from Lisbon, begged the king about that time not to undertake the *empresa de Inglaterra* 'to avenge the offences committed by the English against His Majesty, nor to increase his lands; but only for the greater glory and honour of Our Lord, and to bring these heretics who have left His Church back into the fold.'[68]

Most of the arguments aired in the *Historia del Cisma* were reiterated in a much more energetic work, the *Exhortación para los soldados y capitanes que van a esta jornada de Inglaterra.*[69] Although Ribadeneyra claimed he had written this as an epilogue to the *Historia del Cisma*, it appears to be a quite separate treatise, self-contained and aimed at a wider audience. Arguments and whole paragraphs from the book are used again in the *Exhortación*, but the tone is completely different. The historical, moral and theological reflections in the book have been transformed into an ardent, aggressive spirit that is the purest expression of jesuit and counter-reformation teaching. The *Exhortacíon*, even more than the book, is the fruit of Ribadeneyra's desire to make the Armada a holy enterprise; to force the catholic church — led by the jesuits — to close ranks with the Spanish Monarchy, and to make the subjects of Philip II support their king.[70] Ribadeneyra stressed the crusading character of this 'just and holy war' against England. He declared it a defensive war: 'you must not think that you are attacking that realm, but defending your own', but he insisted that while there were political and economic motives, the mission that God had entrusted to Spain must be executed for purely religious reasons.

Ribadeneyra favoured an active policy of conquest rather than a passive policy limited to warding off danger:[71]

> It would bring great glory to our nation if we not only succeeded in preserving the purity and vigour of the catholic church within these realms, but were also instrumental in restoring it to others; if we not only had an Inquisition to punish the heretics who might come from outside to infect Spain, but sent armies and soldiers from Spain to burn the heretics in other provinces and kingdoms.[72]

As an advocate of armed intervention against heresy, Ribadeneyra tried to make Philip II the champion of the counter-reformation he never became. It is paradoxical, as Maravall pointed out, that it was precisely the anti-machiavellian writers such as Ribadeneyra, with their stress on morality, who 'expunged all general ethical principles that might lead them to condemn war as Vives and Erasmus had done . . . extolling the military valour of christendom in crudely pragmatic terms'.[73] The *Exhortación* exudes military fervour, enthusiasm for the fight, and desire for a conflict considered decisive as well as inevitable.[74] For Ribadeneyra only the invincible Spanish army, sent by heaven, can save English catholicism. The men leaving Lisbon were the soldiers of the Lord;[75] the English catholic martyrs were the Lord's captains — 'so valiant and strong that . . . every day they are persecuted, suffering exile, imprisonment, lies, false testimonies, abuse, torments; some even dismembered in violent executions'[76] — and the Society of Jesus — itself a symbol of the re-militarization of catholicism — formed an integral part of this army.[77]

Although for Ribadeneyra the true honour and glory of Spain depended on the defence of the catholic religion, he could not deny that there were other motives for war with England, such as the reputation of the Spanish Monarchy and the preservation and defence of the state; but all these were linked and subordinate to the fundamental cause of the conflict, which was religion.[78] 'Everything was monolineal and coherent: the shameful progression of the English dynasty from heresy to civil discord and the support of rebels . . .'[79] From these premises Ribadeneyra concluded that the war could only end in a rapid and easy victory. Along with other writers, he dwells on England's military weakness, but for him this was due to ethical and religious causes. He assured readers that in all previous confrontations between catholics and protestants — in Germany, Switzerland, France and the Netherlands — the catholics have always won. The English, he states with some contempt, are as valiant in war as they are loyal in peace — 'there has hardly been a hostile nation whose attack has failed to win and subject them'. He concludes therefore:

> We have embarked on an easy campaign, because God, Our Lord, whose cause and most holy faith we are defending, will be in the vanguard. With such a captain we have nothing to fear.
>
> The saints in heaven will be with us, especially the patron saints of Spain. The patron saints of England who are persecuted by English heretics, and wish and beg God for vengeance, will receive and favour us on the way; as well as other blessed saints who with their lives and heavenly doctrine planted our holy faith there and watered the seed with their blood — they too will be waiting for us . . . God will prove stronger than the devil; truth stronger than lies; the catholic faith stronger than heresy; the saints and angels in heaven stronger than the powers of hell, and the invincible spirit and sturdy arm of the Spaniard will be stronger than the cold bodies and weak, drooping spirits of the heretics.[80]

2. Sins and Tribulations

When news of the disaster of the *Gran Armada* was confirmed in the summer of 1588, English, Dutch and Huguenots, along with the protestants of the Holy Roman Empire and Scandinavia, were naturally delighted with a victory that guaranteed, for the time being at least, the triumph and relative security of the protestant cause in Europe against the Spanish Monarchy. In the following years England would assume a role akin to leadership of the protestant cause, and not only head the military and naval response to Philip II — for which it was only very partially qualified — but also the ideological reaction, orchestrating an anti-Spanish propaganda campaign similar to that of the rebels in the Netherlands earlier. As Maltby has demonstrated, the Armada campaign represented, without a doubt, the apogee of English anti-hispanism, not only in the sheer volume of pamphlets, songs and other printed material from the pens of the English publicists of the time, but also in the tenor and gravity of the accusations against Spain.[81]

It is not easy to assess the influence these waves of anti-Spanish criticism had within the Spanish Monarchy. It has been said that one of the most significant elements in the gradual evolution of Spain's identity during the early modern period was the image created of the Spaniards in the rest of Europe.[82] It is possible to trace with some precision the development of a *Black Legend* within Spain itself during the eighteenth- and nineteenth-centuries, but its origins and evolution during the previous two centuries is limited to a few known documents; the very scarcity of the material making it impossible to judge precisely how representative it was. Philip II's reign is full of such disconcerting and suspicious 'silences' as Teofánes Egido has noted.[83] In the last decade of his life and after his death there were a number of attacks against him and other manifestations of discontent, due largely to the disastrous orientation of his foreign policy. The problems created by the need to finance these wars finally provoked a hostile response, particularly in the worst-affected area, Castile. It does not seem to us too far fetched to suggest that this reaction may have been linked to the defeat of the Invincible Armada, with all the material and symbolic weight this must have carried.

It is also very difficult to establish the immediate Spanish reaction to the events of 1588, precisely because of the confusion. The piecemeal fashion by which the news spread in the peninsula may have gradually prepared public opinion until certainty dispelled any lingering doubts. During August news of a favourable outcome of the campaign reached Spain and was rapidly disseminated by manuscript and print, in fly-sheets and ballads, some of which were translated and circulated through half of Europe.[84] But the confusion on the continent was gradually dissipated, and at the same time the optimism of the Spanish monarch and his officials vanished. Although the king had refused to believe some of the bad rumours at one stage, noting 'I trust in God that He has not permitted such an evil end as some fear, because it was all done in His service'.[85] he finally accepted it as God's will, as proved by his letter to the Spanish bishops on 13 October ordering the end of prayers for the Armada — virtually his only known public statement on the failure of the Invincible.[86]

The providentialist interpretation of the event by the protestants, who claimed that God was on their side, as well as the shock of the catholics at the disastrous end to the campaign seem to have moved that passionate advocate of the war, the jesuit Pedro de Ribadeneyra, to take up his pen again during the autumn of 1588. Two works resulted from his propagandistic labours after the Armada, the *Tratado de la Tribulación* and the *Memorial al Rey* in which he tried, within his ideological parameters, to reflect upon what had happened, and offer the public an explanation for the defeat. In it he includes harsh recriminations against society in general as well as against the highest levels of command within the Spanish Monarchy.

The *Tratado* is partly a work of consolation, conceived within the framework of a providentialism more or less impregnated with senecan stoicism. Still deeply influenced by the image of the inevitable struggle against heresy, he argued that the battle had only just started. Conscious of the negative impression created by the disaster, he set out to find a coherent explanation to the sequence of events from within catholic ideology. Since he could not accept the protestant claim that *they* were God's chosen people, nor, as some had suggested, that the wrecks of the Most Happy Fleet had been like the sunken chariots of Pharaoh's army, it was necessary to offer a different interpretation that would eliminate all shadow of a doubt in catholic consciences; that would be an effective response to the protestants; and finally, that would also provide the necessary arguments to ensure that the Spanish Monarchy, far from conceding defeat, should begin anew the offensive against England in the name of God and His church.

For these reasons, Ribadeneyra defended the theory that the storms sent by God had caused the disaster. God had wanted to punish the Spaniards not with defeat, but with a serious setback. He reiterated that the heretics had always been defeated in battle by the catholics. Now they had suffered no harm simply because there had been no battle — 'there was no fight, because God wanted to punish us, not by their hand, but by His, so that we would grow humble and they would not be able to grow proud as a result of our punishment.'[87] The disaster could not therefore be blamed on Medina Sidonia's lack of experience, nor on the indiscipline of the soldiers, nor on the lack of munitions, victuals, nor even on the climatic conditions of the journey, but only the will of God. The reason for his punishment was simple: sin. Among the sins committed during the campaign, Ribadeneyra isolated the pride and presumption of the Spaniards and the mixing of good and bad motives for the war. While it had been prompted by two just causes — the cause of God and of Spain — he argued that it was not always the divine which had predominated in men's minds. The conclusion he reached in both works was that if God had allowed 'the infidel and heretic to flourish, and the faithful and catholic to suffer' it was because the time had not yet come to punish the former. The Spanish catholics had no choice therefore but to abandon their lukewarm attitude, to reform, and to launch another campaign.

Although there are many versions of how Philip reacted to the news of the defeat — most of them very far-fetched — we hardly know what the king felt at the loss of his fleet.[88] He certainly accepted it as God's will, but in silence, as the curt note on the margin of a letter from Parma demonstrates: 'there is no question of losing or gaining reputation; whatever God has done should be accepted without discussion'.[89] But an overpowering sense of sin appears to have overwhelmed the old king. Marañón believes that Philip II's decision to end the murky affair of Pérez and Escovedo after the Armada is proof of his uneasy conscience.[90] Until recently we lacked the sort of private correspondence that Philip's grandson, Philip IV, exchanged with Sor María de Agreda, which revealed the king's conviction that God was punishing him and his subjects for the king's own sins. Recently, however, an important document from Philip II to his chaplain and secretary, Mateo Vázquez, has been discovered which comes close. The tone is of abject despair:

I promise you that unless some remedy is found . . . very soon we shall find ourselves in such a state that we shall wish that we had never been born . . . And if God does not send us a miracle (which is what I hope from Him), I hope to die and go to Him before all this happens — which is what I pray for, so as not to see so much ill fortune and disgrace. All this is for your eyes alone. Please God, let me be mistaken: but I do not think it is so. Rather we shall have to witness, quicker than anyone thinks, what we so much fear, if God does not return to fight for His cause. We have already seen all this in what has happened, which would not have been permitted, except to punish us for our sins.[91]

This moving royal confession is not the only testimony we possess. After 1589 there are increasingly frequent statements to the effect that the ills and disasters that had befallen the peninsula — it was, after all, a decade of acute crisis[92] — were a divine punishment, and consequently, a result of Spain's sins. There was also growing interest in all sorts of natural catastrophes — storms, deluges, earth-quakes — throughout the peninsula, which might be interpreted as signs of divine displeasure. That their impact was profound is proved by the fact that fifty years later the same arguments were still in use. In order to determine the intensity and duration of such emotions, however, as well as the influence they might have had on the world of ideas and the process of decision-making, it is important to dig even deeper into the historical consciousness of the Spanish Baroque.

The two famous inquisitorial trials initiated in the Spanish Monarchy as a result of the Armada campaign — that of Sor María de la Visitación, the so-called 'monja de Lisboa', and of Miguel de Piedrola and his followers — are illuminating in this respect.[93] Both took place in that extraordinary, impassioned atmosphere so redolent with political unrest and general uneasiness which surrounded the disaster of the Invincible Armada. Like that defeat, these trials were affected by the wall of silence Philip II constructed around him and his subjects after the event. There is no doubt that the trials involved two quite extraordinary individuals, whose peculiar personal experiences could not be held up as a true reflection of the popular response to the disaster of 1588; but the king's determination to silence them does indicate that, at the very least, their voices were listened to. Philip's reaction is proof that he knew by then that his popularity had been largely eclipsed and that his subjects might fall into the temptation of blaming him personally for the failure of a campaign that — as had been repeatedly claimed — was God's work. Despair, fear and horror must have taken hold of many Iberians in 1588, and it is likely that voices were heard reviling the king and blaspheming against God.[94]

While it was certainly not the only cause, the failure of the Invincible Armada coincided chronologically with the beginning of a new and acute period of political unrest in the peninsula, which inevitably recalls the restless atmosphere at the beginning of Philip II's reign. The unrest in Castile was closely linked to the frustration felt after the defeat, but above all to the increasing fiscal burden made necessary by the monarch's foreign commitments and the economic damage caused by inadequate defence of the Atlantic coast and waters. In this way contemporaries came to see a direct causal relationship between the northern wars, the fiscal burden, and the end of Castilian prosperity; and they used this more than any other argument to reject the foreign policy of the Catholic Monarch.

The stupor caused by the unexpected loss of the Armada, and the fear that there would be a repeat of attacks such as Drake's assault on Cadiz in 1587 ensured that the deputies of the *cortes* of Castile, which were in session in Madrid throughout 1588, did not reject in principle the crown's request for new sacrifices and subsidies. Nevertheless, afraid that the cities might oppose him, the king used the usual means to make certain of their cooperation. He instructed the *corregidores* to make sure that the cities gave their representatives the necessary powers to grant what he requested. He insisted that the votes of the *regidores* should be individually registered in writing, and that communication between the city councils should be prevented. At the same time, the king instructed the archbishop of Toledo 'to make sure that by means of the preachers, confessors and other grave persons, you communicate to those who have a vote on the city council, that they have a duty to serve us in the present crisis . . . without it being known . . . that I have written to you on this matter'.[95]

As a result of either personal conviction or of bribery, the attitude of some of the delegates in the *cortes* was extremely favourable to the crown's request for a new tax. One of the deputies from Granada got so carried away at one stage he even declared that if the monarch, due to lack of the necessary funds, decided to abandon the war against England, the whole kingdom 'on their knees would beg him to continue' so as to avenge this latest affront, and in order to silence 'the murmurs in foreign courts'.[96] Yet the primary concern of the deputies was not really the redressing of the honour of the monarchy, but security. During the two years or so that the *cortes* remained in session, defence and defence-related issues were repeatedly debated, especially the fortification of the Iberian frontiers and the inescapable and urgent necessity of defending the sea routes.

The concession of a new tax, the *millones*, should therefore be seen essentially in terms of the defensive needs of the Iberian coast and waters. The quantity they offered — eight million ducats — further suggests a defensive rather than offensive intent. Philip II had repeatedly refused to give a figure for the new tax, skilfully limiting his intervention to reminding the *cortes* that the *Gran Armada* had cost over ten million ducats, and that now it was necessary to repair the losses as well as to fund the new preparations.[97] When an agreement was finally reached in February of 1589, there were some deputies — such as the one from Leon — who proposed much lower concessions. He suggested a subsidy of four rather than eight million ducats, which would be earmarked to 'fortify the kingdom and its frontiers, and to organise a strong defensive fleet made up of galleons and other ships for the preservation and protection of these kingdoms and the Indies routes'. He also wanted the *cortes* to beg 'His Royal Majesty to be merciful and to seek aid and support from the other kingdoms subject to his crown and royal service in order to pay for his other needs'.[98] Even those who were more generous with their offers insisted that 'this subsidy granted by the realm is a special concession not to be repeated, and intended to cover just and general needs as well as the defence of these realms'.[99] What made the grant of the *millones* possible in 1589 were the complementary needs of the crown and the Castilian cities: the monarch was anxious to reconstruct his fleet, and the Castilian oligarchies were concerned to ensure the defence of the realm.[100]

Despite the fact that Philip II's memoranda to the *cortes* during 1588–1589 and the exhortations of the president, the count of Barajas, all dwelt on the dangers assailing Iberia, and the threat to the Monarchy's lines of communication after the failure of the Armada; and notwithstanding the very specific objective of the new subsidy which was openly declared to be the refitting of the Spanish fleet and the launch of a second campaign against England, the money that was collected from the *millones* was spent on very different things. It was used to pay off the loans raised for the military forces in the Netherlands and to subsidise the French Catholic League; 'naval matters', as Ulloa pointed out, 'did not get preferential treatment when it came to assigning the money from the *millones*.'[101]

Castilian resentment against the escalation of military commitments in Europe during the following years spread to most levels of society, and was manifested in the highly unusual debates that ensued between the crown and the *cortes* over the issue of taxation. As the 1590s progressed, weariness with the seemingly endless increase of taxation from the later 1560s onwards grew and became more perceptible, just as the Monarchy's commitments abroad expanded. Thompson has demonstrated that in little over two decades these northern and Atlantic conflicts led to a three-fold increase in the Monarchy's ordinary expenditure. Making allowances for the increase in the quantities of precious metals sent from America, which helped to save the situation, and gave Philip II room for political and military manoeuvre he had hitherto lacked, there is no doubt that it was the Castilian taxpayer who bore the brunt of the war now, as he had always done.[102]

The resistance of the *cortes* to further increases in taxation which were necessary to fund the monarch's foreign policy, and their disapproval of his commitments abroad, were made clear in the spring of 1593 and came to a climax in the memorable session of the 19 May. The arguments put forward in the king's speech — the religious unity of Christendom, the internal peace of Castile contrasted to the internal discord of surrounding monarchies, the wretched state of royal finances, and the vital need to cover multiple military commitments, including, of course, funding the army sent to pacify Aragon — left the representatives unmoved, and unwilling to alter their resistance to all new taxes. The most determined opponents of the crown's policy were the cities of Burgos and Seville. Their economies had suffered more than the others as a result of the wars in northern Europe and the Atlantic. The speeches made by their representatives have come down to us in the form of reports from the *Actas de Cortes*; beneath the traditional expressions of moderation and respect the message is clear — they would not continue to shoulder the fiscal burden of the monarch's foreign policy. The procurator for Burgos, Jerónimo de Salamanca, argued that as they still had four years left before finishing payments for the *millones*, and since 'within the body of this realm there is no part that is healthy', adding new taxation was not therefore doing true service to His Majesty. On the contrary, it would inflict 'notable damage to this realm, and we would be greatly to blame if we offered to do something so damaging'. Burgos and Seville, soon joined by Madrid, insisted that as the excessive costs of the wars in the Netherlands, England and France were draining the royal finances, and had led to intolerable increases in taxation, the *cortes* must beg the king 'in the most appropriate terms' to 'suspend the said wars for now, leaving them as best he might'.

The rejection of the wars and their intolerable burdens inevitably led to a rejection of the arguments put forward to justify these European conflicts as just and unavoidable, indeed necessary, to preserve catholicism and maintain the unity of the Spanish Monarchy. The majority of the deputies argued in favour of protecting the Mediterranean and the Straits of Gibraltar, as well as the Iberian coasts and the Indies, and they insisted that whatever concessions they made should be used to fund these specific needs; but they refused to accept the argument that, in order to do this, it was necessary to intensify and extend the wars being waged by the king. They were critical of the proposition that they should intervene in foreign realms in order to defend religion even if this entailed endangering their own state. The messianic providential-ism that projected the Spanish Monarchy as the right arm of the Lord was little in evidence in these *cortes*; instead they evinced another form of providentialism — more cynical and moderate, with a propensity to leave in God's hand the punishment of heresy, as can be seen in the speech of the Seville representative:

> It is very clear that the whole world acknowledges that His Majesty intervenes in these just wars with the most saintly zeal, and as the only defender and protector of the faith; but it is also evident that our enemies are so numerous and so obstinately attached to their errors and infidelity, that it has not been possible in all these years to reduce them. God, Our Lord has seen how His Majesty has made the utmost effort to do so, and therefore he is under no obligation to do any more, especially as continuing these wars will bring the risks and dangers before mentioned. Since this is His cause, [God] will fight for it, destroying His enemies with His powerful hand, or by inflicting upon them civil wars such as they are engaged in at the moment, or by other means; and He will ensure that France gets a catholic king, since that kingdom needs one so badly'.

The deputy for Madrid, Francisco de Monzón, put it more starkly: if the heretics remain obdurate, Castile should no longer interfere; 'if they wish to be damned, let them be damned'.[103]

This same disdainful indifference towards the religious struggles in northern Europe pervades the *Discurso relativo al tributo de la harina* of the *licenciado* Gonzalo de Valcárcel, which is perhaps the most violent Spanish attack on Philip II's foreign policy to be issued in his lifetime.[104] The *Discurso* encapsulates the war-weariness and anguish caused by the incessant burdens of these foreign and distant conflicts which nevertheless drained the countryside and cities of an exhausted Castile. Valcárcel argues that it is no longer reasonable to expect a positive result from conflicts that have lasted so long without a successful outcome. He parades his secular principles by firmly espousing a division between political and religious conflicts. The restoration of catholicism, he argues, must not be confused with the war; nor the need to evangelise with military expenditure:

I ask you, what is the connection between our paying a tax on flour here, and ending heresy there? Will the Netherlands and England be better off when Spain is poorer? Nineveh's sin was not to increase the contribution of Palestine in order to conquer them, but to send someone over there to convert them. God alone knows what sins He is punishing when He allows kingdoms and princes to leave the flock and fall into error'.

Valcárcel defended toleration against aggressive and intransigent ideals. Instead of accepting the argument that it is necessary to go out and conquer heretical lands, he proposed a defensive response which was sensitive to the enemy's movements. Heresy, he argued, was a product of divine will, imposed 'because of the blindness and obstinacy of people who allow grave sins when they arise to take root among them'. It is therefore irrational to blame its survival on the inactivity of the Catholic Monarch, who does not have sufficient economic and military power to crush the enemies of the faith. Moreover, the eradication of heresy is a collective enterprise and responsibility for it belongs to the whole of the Spanish Monarchy, indeed to the rest of catholic Europe: 'the burden of this policy should not fall entirely on Castile; the other kingdoms, princes and republics should participate, especially in view of the fact that the subjects of this realm are exhausted and oppressed with so many taxes already'. The king therefore must carefully weigh up his forces and those of his adversaries; he must not begin wars where victory is a chimera, and he must definitely not continue interminable conflicts which only serve his particular interests: 'let every one measure and balance his desires with his revenues; and if the king or prince cannot support the wars he is involved in, he should only fight those he can afford'.

From this purely Castilian perspective, even the war in the Netherlands becomes in the final instance a dynastic matter — a problem for the whole Spanish Monarchy which should be resolved by using the whole royal patrimony, not merely Castilian funds. Only a determined defence of Castile's strategic interests and the fiscal relief which would result from peace could begin to palliate the worst effects of the war, such as the decline of the countryside, the fall of wool production, the collapse of commerce and manufacturing, and to change the attitudes that war had fostered. Valcárcel confirmed the worst predictions of Luis Ortiz by asserting that a society addicted to the pursuit of the mirage of rich spoils in war had been created. For these reasons he does not restrict himself to opposing the new fiscal demands of the crown, but launches a bitter attack against the monarch, who is accused of being deaf to the laments of his subjects, and responsible for their ruin:

> the imposition of the extraordinary tax of eight million ducats payable over a six year period has caused the depopulation of towns. Peasants have fled to the mountains leaving the land untilled, reviling their homes, their region and the kingdom . . . How can it be said that adding another regular tax, so heavy and wide-ranging, will alleviate the realm? This is incomprehensible language, an argument I cannot understand, a miracle I cannot believe. Pardon my crudeness if I make a plain comparison, but I cannot think of a muleteer who is so inexperienced or so cruel with his animals that perceiving their exhaustion and seeing them fall at each step with their heavy burden, believes that doubling their load is a good way to relieve them.

The call for a retreat from the European conflicts and passionate defence of peace so evident in the preceding testimonies emerged in Castile during the later sixteenth century as a direct response to the providential manichaeism of those who considered a global confrontation between the Spanish Monarchy and protestantism unavoidable. At the same time it is possible to trace what professors Jover and López-Cordón have termed 'the acceptance of plurality', an expression of 'a double consciousness: that they lived in a disunited monarchy whose problems and antagonisms were too powerful to resolve harmoniously; and that they belonged to a diverse world, not one split into two, nor even solely a European world, which they could not dominate but where they must fit in.'[105] These sentiments were not really new. They can be traced to the traditional opposition of some groups within Castile to the imperial and continental policies they had been forced to pursue because of the dynastic concerns of the Spanish Habsburgs. They reveal a capacity for religious and ideological toleration as vibrant and deeply rooted in the spirit of some Spaniards as the unbounded messianic fervour of some of their fellows. These sentiments were unquestionably the result of a different vision of common defence, far more modest than any notion of universal monarchy, but far more realistic economically and socially for a Castilian kingdom which saw itself thrust towards the Mediterranean and the Atlantic; and which could see benefits from remaining neutral in the conflicts shaking its neighbours.

But neither the opposition in the *cortes* to new subsidies, nor the voices of protest now heard, nor even the grave situation in the Atlantic sufficed to change the course of Philip II's foreign policy. From 1595 he had to face a triple alliance of the United Provinces, France and England, which his diminished revenues could scarcely cope with. Neither the conquest of Calais in 1596, nor the reconstruction of the fleet sufficed to give Spain a firm position in the North Sea — let alone carry out the much-desired *empresa de Inglaterra* with success. On the contrary, in 1596 Philip II had to declare a new bankruptcy, in itself a symptom of the inadequacy of the royal rents, which (even with their irregular infusion of Indies bullion) could not cover the multiple costs.

It would be absurd, however, to think that the monarch was alone in his advocacy of this active foreign policy. Providentialist theories were still as avidly defended then as in 1588. Even in the famous *cortes* of 1593 there were dissonant voices unconditionally supporting the foreign policy of Philip II. The deputy for Murcia, Don Ginés de Rocamora, delivered an impassioned speech defending intervention in France as the sacred duty of the Catholic Monarch who was the only powerful 'protector of Christendom'. For him there was no doubt of the necessity for a major campaign irrespective of the material difficulties they faced: 'If this is done to defend God's cause, as indeed it is, there is no reason to leave it because it appears impossible. He will give us what we need; He will discover new Indies and mines of Potosí and Guadalcanal, as He discovered for the Catholic Monarchs'.[106] It was the duty of Castilians to spend the wealth God had given them to support catholics in the neighbouring realm before heresy triumphed. If greed or weakness prevented them from launching this campaign, they would have to face a future with a heretical, and therefore hostile, France. For these reasons, Rocamora maintained that 'the war His Majesty is waging in France cannot be called offensive; it is defensive', it was destined to safeguard the true faith as much as the security of the Monarchy. Both causes appeared inseparable. Along with the king and some of his advisers, Rocamora saw the French campaigns as the first step towards the containment of England and the pacification of the rebellion in the Netherlands — the first step even to the imposition of unity in Europe. In this vision of Europe the common creed of catholicism could overcome its diversity and mutual antagonisms and bring unity. And the House of Austria had the very important task of saving and preserving the purity of the catholic church.

That same year the indefatigable Ribadeneyra published an expanded version of his *Historia del Cisma de Inglaterra*, in which he narrated Elizabeth's recent persecutions in England in gory detail. He also took the opportunity to advocate a new invasion of England and to encourage the new crusade in France.[107] In 1595 he also published the *Tratado de la religión y virtudes que debe tener un príncipe cristiano*. It encapsulated much of his political thought, but the fundamental objective of this work, according to its author, was to refute the doctrines of Machiavelli and his followers, the *politicos* as he called them, for promoting a *false reason of state* in their teachings on how to maintain the integrity of the state, and as such, for leading it to destruction, rather than contributing to its preservation. His most vehement arguments were used to refute the machiavellian thesis that religion should be used by the prince in order to achieve secular goals. He believed that the *politicos* — the heirs of Machiavelli and followers of Bodin and of heretical doctrines nurtured during the French Wars of Religion — aspired through the manipulation of religion to neutralise the ethical controls religion imposed on the daily practices of government. The *Tratado de un príncipe cristiano*, dedicated to the then Prince Philip [Philip III], attacked these doctrines because he feared they might influence and divert the Spanish Monarchy from the course he approved. He also hoped to provide certainty and full support for the catholic Church in the future. But all this was done from the rather oblique perspective given by recent events, and amidst the confusion and disorder that these had provoked in the consciences of the Europeans.

There was perhaps no better exposition of the universalist and ecumenical mission of the Catholic Monarch at the close of the sixteenth century than the one provided by the Calabrian Tommaso Campanella in 1593: 'Since the creation of the world there has been no greater empire, nor one more worthy of admiration than the Spanish empire of today. I find that the Spanish empire, more than any other, is founded on God's hidden providence, and not in human providence or strength . . . For this reason, it is evident that the Spanish Monarchy, which embraces all of the world's states, is God's own monarchy'.[108] Not many decades later the political thinkers of the Spanish baroque advanced another view, far less optimistic, of the future of that empire — that just as with humans, monarchies have a cyclical nature: they are born, they grow, and then they die'.[109]

NOTES

1. Anon. This little song is found in the *Entremés de los romances* which was attributed for a time to Cervantes, given the similarity of its plot to the *Quijote* — its main protagonist also goes mad from reading too many romances. V. J. Huerta Calvo (ed.) *Teatro breve de los siglos XVI y XVII* (Madrid, 1985).

2. J. H. Elliott, *La Europe dividida 1,559–1,598* (London, 1968; Spanish edn., Madrid, 1973).

3. *Ibid.*, pp. 396–406.

4. G. Parker, *Felipe II* (London, 1979; Spanish edn., Madrid, 1984) pp. 249–50.

5. K. Repgen, 'What is a "Religious War"?', in E. I. Kouri and T. Scott (edd.), *Politics and Society in Reformation Europe. Essays for Sir G. Elton on his sixty-fifth birthday* (London, 1987) pp. 311–328.

6. J. A. Maravall, *La cultura del Barroco* (Barcelona, 1975).

7. Henry III's opinion is highly significant in this respect. He publicly expressed doubt as to whether Philip intended to invade England to place James VI on the throne, on the grounds that the Spaniards, unlike monks, could not be made to leave merely by papal command. The papal nuncio in Madrid similarly expressed fears that at the end of the day, the conquest of England would be another step on the ladder to universal monarchy. Whether justified or not, these accusations demonstrate the general opinion prevalent in Europe on the eve of the *Gran Armada*. Even Bernardino de Mendoza, Philip's ambassador in Paris, could hardly repress his optimism when writing to the king after the death of Mary Stuart, considering her death as divine encouragement for Philip's invasion. See also H. G. Koenigsberger, 'El arte de gobierno de Felipe II' *Revista de Occidente*, 107 (1972) pp. 127–159, Engl. versn. 'The statecraft of Philip II' *European Studies Review*, I (1971) pp. 1–21, rprtd. in his *Politicians and Virtuosi* (London, 1986); and Rodríguez-Salgado above pp. 10–11, 16.

8. M. Ulloa, *La Hacienda Real de Castilla en el reinado de Felipe II* (Madrid, 1977) p. 615.

9. J. Lynch, 'Philip II and the papacy', *Transactions of the Royal Historical Society*, 5th ser., II (1961) pp. 23–42. A shorter version of this can be found in his *España bajo los Austrias* (2 vols, Oxford, 1964; 3rd Spanish edn., Barcelona, 1973) pp. 335–352; The classic work of L. Pastor, *Historia de los Papas* vol. XXII (Spanish edn., Barcelona, 1941) is still very useful in providing details of Sixtus' papacy.

10. Many contemporary records survive of Sixtus V's praise for Elizabeth I, see Pastor XXII pp. 29–30.

11. Lynch, *España bajo los Austrias*, pp. 347–8.

12. Cit by Parker, *Felipe II*, p. 182.
13. L. Cabrera de Córdoba, *Felipe Segundo, Rey de España* (3 vols., Madrid, 1877) III pp. 220-1.
14. BNM Mss 1750, ff. 217r–227v, 'Discurso hecho en el año de 1588'.
15. J. Mª Jover Zamora and Mª V. López-Cordón, 'La imagen de Europa y el pensamiento político-internacional', in R. Menéndez Pidal and J. Mª Jover Zamora (edd.) *Historia de España* XXVI (*El siglo del Quijote (1580–1680)*) (Madrid, 1986) p. 363.
16. BNM Mss 1750 ff. 418r–423r 'Discurso del caballero Spanoquio'.
17. BNM Mss 5,785 f. 79v 'Discurso de Inglaterra'.
18. During 1586 and 1587 the *cortes* clearly demonstrated their reluctance to provide the vast funds required for the war in the Netherlands and the struggle against England. They complained of the heavy fiscal pressure and the heavy losses incurred as a result 'of the decline and loss of trade and commerce between these realms and the Netherlands and England, and the resulting disdain for tillage and breeding cattle.' Attitudes changed after Drake's attack on Cadiz. The representatives accepted after this 'how necessary it is for Your Majesty to settle this matter with England, otherwise we will not see an end to the war in Flanders. This long war is consuming your Majesty's royal patrimony and our forces too. Let the money that could be spent over a long period be used in the next few years to finish this once and for all'. *ACC* VIII p. 468.
19. J. Mª Jover Zamora, *Carlos V y los españoles* (Madrid, 1963) p. 59.
20. F. Braudel, *El Mediterráneo y el mundo mediterráneo en la época de Felipe II* (2 vols, Paris 1966, 2nd Spanish edn. 2 vols., Mexico, 1976) II pp. 411–14. E. Belenguer Cebriá, 'La problemática del cambio político en la España de Felipe II. Puntualizaciones sobre su cronología', *Hispania* XL (1980) pp. 541–542. The most detailed analysis of the crisis of the 1550s can be found in M. J. Rodríguez-Salgado, *The changing face of empire: Charles V, Philip II and Habsburg authority, 1551-9* (Cambridge, 1988) esp. pp. 278–96, 339–47.
21. J. I. Gutierrez Nieto, 'La discriminación de los conversos y la tibetización de Castilla por Felipe II', *Revista de la Universidad Complutense*, 87 (1973) pp. 99–129; J. A. Maravall, 'La oposición político-religiosa a mediados del siglo XVI: el erasmismo tardío de Felipe de la Torre', in his *La oposición bajo los Austrias* (Barcelona, 1972) pp. 53–92.
22. M. Fernández Alvarez, 'La paz de Cateau-Cambresis', *Hispania*, CLXXVII (1959) pp. 530–544.
23. Jover & López-Cordón, 'La imagen de Europa' esp. chapters I and II.
24. *Ibid.*, p. 370.
25. The crusading and religious aspects of the war in the Netherlands have been dealt with by L. Van der Essen, 'Croisade contre les herétiques ou guerre contre les rebelles?', *Revue d'Histoire Ecclésiastique* (1956) pp. 42–78.

26. Jover and López-Cordón, 'La imagen de Europa' p. 372.

27. As we shall see, this argument was used more than any other by the crown in the *cortes* in order to justify the demand for new subsidies to fund its foreign policy.

28. Jover and López-Cordón, 'La imagen de Europa' pp. 372–3.

29. *Ibid.*, pp. 414–15; L. Pereña, *Teoria de la guerra en Francisco Suárez* (Madrid, 1954) pp. 115–125.

30. The permanent contacts between England and the Low Countries due not only to their geographical proximity but to their intense commercial exchanges, had worried the Spanish authorities for some time. In 1564, on the eve of the rebellion, Cardinal Granvelle blamed Queen Elizabeth for the spread of heresy in the Netherlands, and the English merchants as the principal and most dangerous disseminators of protestant ideas in the area. M. Van Durme, *El Cardenal Granvela (1517–1586)* (Barcelona, 1957) pp. 274–6.

31. C. Gómez-Centurión Jiménez, 'Pragmatismo económico y tolerancia religiosa: Los acuerdos Cobham-Alba de 1576', *Cuadernos de Historia Moderna y Contemporánea*, VIII (1987) pp. 57–81.

32. M. Herrero, *Ideas de los españoles en el siglo XVII* (2 edn., Madrid, 1966) pp. 444–486.

33. This is the argument of two well-known and classic books despite the fact that their authors espoused opposing ideologies: F. de los Rios, *Religión y estado en la España del siglo XVI* (2 edn., Mexico, 1957); R. Schneider, *Felipe II, o religión y poder* (Sp. trans, Madrid 1943).

34. As late as 1949 V. Palacio Atard re-stated the traditional view: 'All the power he possessed was channelled to the primary aim of defending the cause of the catholic church'. *Derrota, agotamiento y decadencia en la España del siglo XVII* (Madrid, 1949) pp. 29–30.

35. He goes on to say: 'This coincidental and complementary relationship between the forces in favour, and those against, secularization can be found everywhere in the social life of sixteenth-century Europe'. J. A. Maravall, 'Consideraciones sobre el proceso de secularización en los primeros siglos modernos', *La Oposición política* pp. 156–157. In his contribution to the on-going polemic over the emergence of 'the state' in the early-modern period, P. Fernández Albadalejo pointed out that 'it was precisely its acceptance of the church's sacred status — with all that this implied — that prevented the Spanish Monarchy from evolving into a *genuine* state', 'Iglesia y configuración del poder en la Monarquía Católica (siglos XV–XVIII). Algunas consideraciones.' in J. Ph. Genet and B. Vincent (edd.), *Etat et Eglise dans la genese de l'etat moderne* (Madrid, 1986) pp. 209–216.

36. E. I. Kouri has analysed the issue from an English perspective in: 'For true faith or national interest? Queen Elizabeth and the protestant powers', in *Politics and society in Reformation Europe*, pp. 411–436.

37. Maravall, 'Consideraciones sobre el proceso de secularización', p. 190.

38. J. A. Maravall, 'Maquiavelo y maquiavelismo en España' in his *Estudios de historia del pensamiento español. Siglo XVII* (Madrid, 1973) pp. 39–76.

39. *Ibid.* See also J. A. Fernández Santamaria, *Razón de estado y política en el pensamiento Español del Barroc o (1595–1640)* (Madrid, 1986).

40. J. A. García Vilar, 'El maquiavelismo en las relaciones internacionales (La anexión de Portugal a España en 1580)', *Revista de Estudios Internacionales*, II/3 (1981) pp. 599–644.

41. J. A. Maravall, 'La corriente doctrinal del tacitismo político en España', in *Estudios de Historia del pensamiento Español* pp. 77–105; E. Tierno Galván, 'El tacitismo en las doctrinas políticas del siglo de oro español', *Anales de la Universidad de Murcia* curso 1947–8, cuarto trim., pp. 895–988, reprtd. in his *Escritos políticos, 1950–1960* (Madrid, 1971).

42. P. Pierson, *Felipe II de España* (London, 1975; Spanish edn., Mexico, 1975) pp. 251–264.

43. D. W. Waters, *The Elizabethan Navy and the Armada of Spain* (National Maritime Museum Monograph series XVII; London, 1975) includes an English version of one of Petruccio Ubaldini's *Comentari*.

44. BNM mss 5,785 f. 168.

45. Herrera Oria, *Armada*, pp. 33–4.

46. BNM mss 1239 f. 263v. After the defeat, Fray José de Siguenza commented on this atmosphere of religious exaltation: 'In the midst of such loss there was also great interest and gain of souls, because in these realms they held the most extraordinary public prayers and devotions I have ever seen; so much so that foreigners mocked us saying in their pasquinades that with so many prayers, the Spanish Armada had been raised to heaven . . . In Madrid so many people went to church and took the sacraments during the feast days of St John the Baptist, St Peter and St Paul, that it appeared more like Holy Week than the eve of St John'. *La fundación del monasterio de El Escorial* (Madrid, 1986) p. 120.

47. Pastor XXII pp. 47–8; N. Alonso Cortés 'Valladolid y la Armada Invencible', *Miscelanea Vallisoletana* 3a ser. (Valladolid, s.a.) p. 26.

48. *ACC* X pp. 60, 143–5.

49. FD I pp. 426–8 February 28, 1588. In July Medina Sidonia assured Philip from La Coruña that he had followed these instructions, and that the clergy in the fleet had confessed and given the sacraments to more than 800 men.

50. FD I p. 162.

51. BNM mss 1750 ff. 228r–232v 'Aviso de las fuerzas y puertos de Inglatera y Escocia, con declaración o relación de todos los aparatos de guerra que la Reina tiene hechos en tierra y en la mar, temiendo la Armada del Rey Católico.'

52. Martin and Parker, p. 266.

53. *Poesía* ed. A. Lewis de Galanes (Zaragoza, 1972) p. 57.

54. The best known account is the pamphlet *Relación verdadera del Armada que el Rey Don Felipe nuestro señor mandó juntar en el puerto dela ciudad de Lisboa en el Reyno de Portugal en año de 1588*, BNM Ca/V 224 n. 15, which was widely disseminated in Europe and translated into various languages.

55. Mesa's 'Obra nuevamente compuesta donde por maravillosa orden se cuentan los grandes y bravos bastimientos, géneros y cantidad de carnes y pescados de diversas suertes y maneras que van en la brava y poderosa armada que el Rey nuestro señor ha mandado juntar en Lisboa', in FD II pp. 85–97; better known are the works of Luis de Góngora, 'Canción heroica a la Gran Armada del Rey Don Felipe', ed. A. De Castro, *Biblioteca de Autores Españoles* XXXII (Madrid, 1966) p. 449, and Lope de Vega, 'Famosa Armada' etc. FD I p. 239.

56. My comments on Ribadeneyra are partly based on the brilliant analysis by Jover and López Cordón, 'La imagen de Europa' pp. 373–380.

57. Ribadeneyra, E. Ruiz (ed.), *Historia eclesiástic a del cisma de Inglaterra.* in *Historias de la Contrarreforma, Biblioteca de Autores Españoles* (Madrid, 1945) p. 895.

58. *Ibid.*, introduction by Eusebio Ruíz pp. 855–888.

59. T. McNevin Veech, *Dr Nicholas Sanders and the English Reformation* (Louvain, 1935); P. Milward, *Religious controversies of the Elizabethan Age* (London, 1977) pp. 71ff. Milward points out that besides historical and doctrinal texts, these years saw the publication of collections of engravings, such as those by J. B. Cavaleriis and Richard Verstegan which depicted graphically the cruelty and persecution against the catholics in England, and caused a profound impression in Europe. Verstegan's *Theatrum Crudelitatum* went through four consecutive editions in 1587 on the eve of the Invincible Armada's campaign. A similar reaction was provoked in England and the other protestant states by the publication of books and prints describing the tortures used by the Inquisition against heretics, and the atrocities of the Spaniards against the native American peoples. W. S. Maltby, *La leyenda negra en Inglaterra. Desarollo del sentimiento antihispánico, 1558–1660* (Durham, N.C., 1971; Spanish edn., Mexico, 1982) pp. 19–58. We have no study as yet of the impact these graphic images had on the art of the counter-reformation and the production of religious 'kitsch' so popular in this period, and so typical a manifestation of baroque culture. See J. A. Maravall, *La cultura del Barroco* pp. 174–223; and V. Romano 'Poder, culto y kitsch. Relaciones sociopolíticas desde el punto de vista de la comunicación', *Revista Internacional de Sociología* XLIV (1986) pp. 135–144.

60. R. Cueto, 'Propaganda Fidei: la propaganda española y el mundo celta de

1588 hasta 1700', *Cuadernos de Investigación Histórica* X (1986) pp. 5–29.

61. English catholic emigration to Spain has been dealt with by A. J. Loomie, *The Spanish Elizabethans* (London, 1963); the seminaries by M. E. Williams, *St. Alban's college, Valladolid: 400 years of English catholic presence in Spain* (London and New York, 1986).

62. Some of these publications have been collected by M. Agulló, 'Relaciones de sucesos I: Años 1477–1619', *Cuadernos Bibliográficos* XX (Madrid, 1966); and J. Simón Díaz, 'Algunas relaciones de sucesos de los años 1540–1650', separata of the *Revista Bibliotheca Hispana* XV (1957) pp. 506–523.

63. Ribadeneyra's correspondence is in *Monumenta Ribadeneirae, Monumenta Historica Societatis Iesu* LVIII–LIX (Madrid, 1920–1923); his letter to Quiroga, LIX p. 341.

64. It was finished soon after Drake's attack on Cadiz. Accounts of the reformation in England became popular in Spain after 1585. In 1587 one Alvaro Picardo published an account of Drake's attack on Cadiz which included several chapters on the main episodes of the English reformation, described as 'the principal cause for the conflict and war between Spain and England.' See Maura, p. 164.

65. Ribadeneyra, *Historias de la contrarreforma*, p. 1197.

66. *Ibid.*, p. 1198.

67. *Ibid.*, p. 1199.

68. Maura, p. 271.

69. Ribadeneyra explained that he was moved to write this after hearing of the Duke of Medina Sidonia's piety: 'they write to us from Lisbon of his severity in punishing offences against Our Lord, and public sins, and this is the only true way to secure victory and to become a loyal minister of God'. (*Historias de la contrarreforma*, pp. 1131–1132.)

70. Ribadeneyra might have been inspired to do this because of the earlier lack of enthusiasm in Castile towards the war in Portugal in 1580–3. His bleak analysis of the situation in Castile at the time of the Portuguese expedition, and the unpopularity of the king is well known: 'I perceive that this realm is gravely afflicted and little inclined to see his Majesty expand, especially in that kingdom, since it appears to them either very dangerous, or worth very little. To speak clearly, as I should, I perceive that their hearts have turned from that love and affection they once had, and from that desire for the glory and honour of their king that was so deeply embedded, they longed for the life and health of his Majesty more than for their own. This is no longer true of any of the estates; the towns because of the *alcabalas*; the grandees because they believe they have lost influence; the nobles because the favours they receive are so few and small; the clergy because of the *subsidio, escusado* and other dues they

have to pay; the prelates for the same reason and because of the sale of vassals from church lands; even the monks, who resent the reforms which have been imposed in some of the orders are bitter and upset, and stirred up against his Majesty. In other words, while he is a powerful king, obeyed and respected, he is not as loved as he once was, nor does he have such power over the wills and hearts of his subjects; and these are the ones who form his armies, and who must fight for him. They will do this badly if their hearts are cool and their love of the king weakened.' Cit. in A. Castro's *España en su historia. Cristianos, moros y judíos.* (2nd edn, Barcelona, 1983) pp. 613–14.

71. Jover and López-Cordón, 'La imagen de Europa' p. 375.
72. Ribadeneyra, *Historias de la contrarreforma*, p. 1137.
73. 'Maquiavelo y maquiavelismo' p. 54; also J. A. Fernández Santamaría, *El estado, la guerra y la paz* (Madrid, 1988).
74. In the letter to doña Ana Félix de Guzmán included in the *Exhortación*, Ribadeneyra bemoans the fact that his health will not permit him to sail in the Armada, along with twenty-three other jesuits: 'I would consider it a great favour from Our Lord if he allowed me to die in the attempt'. *Historias de la contrarreforma*, pp. 1331–1332.
75. See R. Puddu, *El Soldado Gentilhombre, autorretrato de una sociedad guerrera en el siglo XVI* (Barcelona, 1984) for a definition of the religious ideals in the military at the end of the sixteenth century, especially ch. 4 pp. 237ff.; Gutierrez Nieto commented in his 'La discriminación de los conversos' p. 109: 'It is probable that the political principle so frequently repeated during the sixteenth century, that heresy was an inseparable companion to social and political subversion, prompted a belief in the need for a controllable bourgeoisie. On the other hand, as if sensing the need for a society that would consider 'poner una pica en Flandes', that is committing themselves fully to a difficult struggle; a society in conclusion, that would serve to uphold the hegemony of the House of Austria in Europe, it was necessary to galvanise it by stimulating military, and quite definitely, anti-bourgeois elements'.
76. Ribadeneyra, *Historias de la contrarreforma*, p. 899.
77. J. Caro Baroja, *Las formas complejas de la vida religiosa (siglos XVI y XVII)* (Madrid, 1985) pp. 434–6.
78. Ribadeneyra, *Historias de la contrarreforma* pp. 1345–1346.
79. Jover and López-Cordón, 'La imagen de Europa' p. 376.
80. Ribadeneyra, *Historias de la contrarreforma*, p. 1348.
81. Maltby, *La Leyenda Negra en Inglaterra*, pp. 97–111.
82. M. Tuñón de Lara (ed.) *Historia de España*, V (*La frustración de un imperio (1476–1714)*) (Barcelona, 1982) pp. 287–294.
83. See his edition of *Sátiras políticas de la España moderna* (Madrid, 1973) pp. 18–22.

84. FD II pp. 175–200.
85. Cit. Parker, *Felipe II* pp. 189–90.
86. FD II pp. 314–15.
87. Ribadeneyra, *Obras escogidas*, V. de la Fuente (ed.), *Biblioteca de Autores Españoles* LX (Madrid, 1952) p. 424.
88. A great deal of ink has been spilt on this theme. A compendium of laudatory anecdotes was collected by L. Fernández y Fernández de Retama, *España en tiempo de Felipe II*, R. Menéndez Pidal and J. Mª Jover Zamora, *Historia de España* XXII pt. ii pp. 467–469.
89. *Ibid.*, p. 468.
90. G. Marañón, *Antonio Pérez* (2 vols., 9th edn, Madrid, 1977) I p. 462.
91. Martin and Parker, cit. p. 258. See also Rodríguez-Salgado above note 83 p. 49.
92. P. Clark (ed.) *The European crisis of the 1590s. Essays in comparative History* (London, 1985).
93. A. Huerga, 'La vida seudomística y el proceso inquisitorial de sor María de la Visitación (La monja de Lisboa)', *Hispania Sacra* XII (1959) pp. 35–130; J. Blázquez Miguel (ed.), *Sueños y procesos de Lucrecia León* (Madrid, 1988).
94. Until Richard Kagan's eagerly awaited book on Lucrecia León and prophecy in Spain during the sixteenth century appears, some of his findings can be read in *El Escorial: Arte, poder y cultura en la corte de Felipe II* (Universidad Complutense de Madrid, 1989) pp. 63–79.
95. Ulloa, *La Hacienda Real* p. 507.
96. *ACC* X p. 357.
97. *ACC* X p. 258.
98. *ACC* X pp. 400–401.
99. *ACC* X p. 405.
100. Work on the first concession of the *millones*, its economic implications, and its importance for the evolution of crown-city relations in Castile has increased in recent years: A. W. Lovett, 'The vote of the Millones (1590)', *Historical Journal* n. 30 (1987) pp. 1–20; C. Jago 'Habsburg absolutism and the cortes of Castile', *American Historical Review* n. 86 (1981) pp. 307–326; I. A. A. Thompson, 'Crown and cortes in Castile, 1590–1665', *Parliaments, Estates and Representation* (1982) pp. 29–45; P. Fernández Albadalejo, 'Monarquía, cortes y cuestión constitucional en Castilla durante la edad moderna', separata of the *Revista de las Cortes Generales* I (1984) pp. 11–33.
101. *La Hacienda de Castilla*, pp. 527–530.
102. I. A. A. Thompson, *Guerra y decadencia* (London, 1976; Spanish edn, Barcelona, 1981) pp. 85–93.
103. *ACC* XII pp. 444–474.
104. BNM mss. 18,731–9.

105. Jover and López-Cordón, 'La imagen de Europa' p. 384.
106. *ACC* XII pp. 458–9.
107. Ribadeneyra, *Historia de la contrarreforma*, pp. 1205–1326.
108. Cit. by Luís Díez del Corral, *La Monarquía Hispánica en el pensamiento político europeo. De Montesquieu a Humboldt* (Madrid, 1975) pp. 320–1.
109. J. Mª Jover, 'Sobre la conciencia histórica del Barroco Español', *Arbor*, 39 (1949) pp. 355–374.

INDEX